W9-CQJ-985

High-resolution Computer Graphics Using Pascal

High-resolution Computer Graphics Using Pascal

Ian O. Angell and Gareth Griffith

Department of Information Systems
London School of Economics
University of London
Houghton Street, London WC2A 2AE

A HALSTED PRESS BOOK

JOHN WILEY & SONS
New York

First published 1988 by

MACMILLAN EDUCATION LTD
London and Basingstoke

Published in the United States by
Halsted Press, a division of
John Wiley & Sons, Inc., New York

Printed in China

ISBN 0–470–21164–4

Library of Congress Cataloging-in-Publication Data
Angell, Ian O.
   High-resolution computer graphics using Pascal.

   "A Halsted Press book."
   Bibliography: p.
   Includes index.
   1. Computer graphics. 2. Pascal (Computer program
language) I. Griffith, Gareth. II. Title.
T385.A5214   1988   006.6'6   88–17135
ISBN 0–470–21164–4

Contents

model. Implementation of shading models: random sampling, pixel patterns and RGB colour shading using constant shading. Gouraud intensity interpolation and Phong normal interpolation. Methods of colour definition

Preface

Until recently, all but the most trivial computer graphics was the province of specialised research groups. Now with the introduction of inexpensive micro-computers and 'graphics-boards', the subject will reach many more users and its full potential can be realised. Computer-generated pictures involving smooth shading, shadows and transparent surfaces, for example, have made a major impact in television advertising. The 'mysterious' techniques for producing such pictures have gained a (false) reputation of complexity for computer graphics.

This book gives a practical description of these ideas and, after studying the contents and implementing the examples and exercises, the reader will be ready to attempt most tasks in graphics.

It is assumed that the reader has an elementary knowledge of the Pascal programming language, and of Cartesian co-ordinate geometry. For those who wish to read good texts on these subjects we recommend books by Wilson and Addyman (1982) and Cohn (1961). This knowledge will be used to produce simple diagrams, and to create the basic programming tools and routines for the more advanced colour pictures. Then, hopefully, the reader will be inspired to seek a greater understanding of geometry and also to read the more advanced journals (such as *SIGGRAPH* and *ACM Transactions*) describing recent research developments in computer graphics. We give a number of relevant references throughout the text, but for a more comprehensive bibliography readers are advised to refer to Newman and Sproull (1973) and Foley and Van Dam (1981).

The only way to understand any branch of applied computing is to study and write a large number of programs; this is why the format of this book is that of understanding through program listings and worked examples. The chapters are centred around numerous examples and the ideas that lead from them. Many students readily understand the theory behind graphics, but they have great difficulty in implementing the ideas. Hence great emphasis is placed on the program listings; well over a hundred routines are given — some quite substantial. Total understanding of the theory given in this book will be achieved only by running these programs and experimenting with them. The programs can be thought of as an embryonic graphics package, but most importantly they are a means of describing the algorithms required in the solution of the given problems. They are readily translatable into other computer languages such as Basic, C and FORTRAN. The routines given all relate to a small number of graphics primitives, which are necessarily device or package dependent. Examples of these primitives are given for the Tektronix 4100 range, for the G.K.S. standard, and the GINO and sample microfilm packages in an appendix.

On occasions, efficiency has been sacrificed in favour of clarity in the description of algorithms. The programs are written in a modular form, which makes the interchanging of program functions relatively straightforward. A unique name is given to any routine that solves a given problem, but we will give more than one example of such a routine if different, perhaps more general, solutions are required. For example, routine **facetfill** can be used to draw a polygon in a fixed colour, but other manifestations may include smooth shading of that polygon and even various textures.

The main purpose of this book, which is essentially a third year undergraduate and M.Sc. course at the University of London, is to set the groundwork of computer graphics. Some of the figures given in this book were produced by past students of the course. Figure 5.1 was produced by Hilary Green, figure 9.11 by Colin Ching, figure 12.5 by Andrew Pullen and figure 18.3 by Paul Mclean Thorne. All of the figures can be produced by using the listings in this book (with some extensions). We would also like to thank Digital Arts Production Ltd for the use of their computing facilities. The programs given are NOT the only way of solving the problems of computer graphics: they reflect the teaching and research interests of the authors. They do, however, provide a general strategy for gaining a thorough understanding of computer graphics and should lead the reader to research level in the subject. With this advanced groundwork done, readers can reorganise the approach with their own specific interests in mind. The listings are in a limited form of Pascal in order to make the programs applicable to many of the Pascal subsets now available on microcomputers.

The package developed in this book is for teaching purposes only. Although the authors place no copyright restrictions on the use of the listings in a lecture course, no commercial exploitation is permitted without prior agreement with the authors.

Computer graphics is fun! We hope that readers will make this discovery and spend many enjoyable and productive hours in front of their graphics console.

Ian O. Angell and Gareth Griffith

1 Familiarisation with Programs, Graphics Devices and Primitives

Computer graphics devices come in all shapes and sizes: storage tubes, raster devices, vector refresh displays, flat-bed plotters etc., which is why in recent years so much effort has been put into graphics software standards (such as G.K.S. (Hopgood *et al.*, 1983)) as well as into the portability of graphics packages (GINO, CalComp etc.). This book will concentrate on the techniques of *modelling* and *rendering* (that is, drawing, colouring, shading etc.) two-dimensional and three-dimensional objects, which surprisingly require only a small part of the above systems. Rather than restrict ourselves to one software system, and in order to make this book relevant to as many different graphics devices as possible, we will identify a general model for a graphics device together with a few (nine) elementary routines (*primitives*) for manipulating that model. *From the outset it must be realised that we are using the word 'primitive' in the literal sense of describing the basic level at which the programs in this book communicate with graphics devices*; the word has different meanings in other graphics environments, such as G.K.S. The Pascal programs that follow will use only these primitives for drawing on this basic model (apart from a few very exceptional cases). Since even the most complex programs given in this book interface with the model device through relatively few primitive routines, the graphics package we create is readily portable. All that is needed is for users to write their own device-specific primitives, which relate to their particular graphics device or package! Later in this chapter we give ideas of how such primitives may be written, and in the appendix there are example listings of primitives suitable for some of the more popular graphics devices and standards.

The Structure of PROGRAMs in this Book

The programs in this book are meant to be used with as many computers and graphics devices as possible and with many versions of Pascal. Because of this, we cannot claim that they are well structured — far from it! For example, the vast majority of variables and arrays are globally declared in the outermost block and organised to fit into a 64K block of memory. The programs too were

1

designed to fit into a separate 64K block of memory; the stack and heap also fit into a similar sized memory block. In this way the programs will run not only on large main frames but also, more importantly, on small personal computers.

As you progress through this book you will find that many programs are extensions of earlier programs, and the list of CONSTant, TYPE, VARiable and PROCEDURE declarations needed to run these programs becomes larger and larger. Because of this and because of the peculiar infrastructure of the Pascal programming language, we present the program listings in this book in a consistent way. A schematic description of all the graphics programs (that is, all programs except those dealing with data structures in chapter 2) is given in listing 1.1. This outline identifies the required primitive procedures, mentioned above, that drive a particular graphics device, as well as indicating the position of CONSTants, TYPEs, VARiables, FUNCTION and PROCEDURE declarations together with the need for a main PROGRAM block, in particular those given in listing 1.3 which define a co-ordinate system for your graphics terminal. You will be expected to write your own version of these primitives for your particular graphics device, using as guidelines the examples given in the appendix.

The remaining listings in this book (except chapter 2) consist of (possible) declarations of CONSTants, TYPEs, VARiables, FUNCTIONs and PROCE-DUREs, and main PROGRAM block which must be merged into the schema of listing 1.1 (and listing 1.3) at the separate positions indicated. This seemingly contrived and limited structure will allow us to make major expansions and extensions to the programs required in this book, while still fitting in with the memory restrictions mentioned in the last but one paragraph. Care must be taken when adding new FUNCTIONs and PROCEDUREs to ensure that scope requirements are correct (that is, if routine A is called by routine B, make sure that routine A appears before B in the combined listings). Global CONSTant, TYPE and VARiable declarations will not cause scope problems because they are all declared in the outer main PROGRAM. As you delve deeper into this book, culminating with the display of complex three-dimensional scenes, you will find that most required routines have been given to you; you need only write the primitive routines and a few routines for modelling three dimensional space. But more of this later.

The Model Graphics Device

We assume that the display of the graphics device contains a *viewport* (or *frame*) made up from a rectangular array of points (or *pixels*). This matrix is nxpix pixels horizontally by nypix pixels vertically. The variables nxpix and nypix are declared in listing 1.1 and initiated in procedure prepit along with CONSTants sizeofpixelarray and epsilon, TYPEs pixelvector and pixelarray, integer VARiable currcol and text VARiables indata and outdata used for input and output — but more of these later.

Listing 1.1

```
{ Structure of programs given in this book }

PROGRAM main(input,output,indata,outdata) ;

CONST
    sizeofpixelarray = 32 ;
{ other global CONSTANTs from the text added here }

TYPE
    pixelvector = RECORD x,y : integer END ;
    pixelarray  = ARRAY[1..sizeofpixelarray] of pixelvector ;
{ other global TYPEs from the text added here }

VAR
    currcol,nxpix,nypix : integer ;
    indata,outdata : text ;
{ other global VARiables from the text added here }

{ include here any PROCEDUREs or FUNCTIONs (if any) that may be needed by }
{ your implementation of the Device Dependent primitives routines below }

PROCEDURE finish ;
PROCEDURE setcol(col : integer) ;
PROCEDURE erase ;
PROCEDURE setpix(pixel : pixelvector) ;
PROCEDURE movepix(pixel : pixelvector) ;
PROCEDURE linepix(pixel : pixelvector) ;
PROCEDURE polypix(n : integer ; poly : pixelarray ) ;
PROCEDURE rgblog(i : integer ; red,green,blue : real ) ;
PROCEDURE prepit ;

{ followed by required Device Independent PROCEDUREs and FUNCTIONs }

{ Concluding with body of the 'main' PROGRAM }
```

An individual pixel in the viewport can be accessed by referring to its *pixel co-ordinates*, a pair of integers stored as RECORD TYPE pixelvector, which give the position of the pixel relative to the *bottom left-hand corner* of the viewport. The pixelvector position, pixel (say), is the co-ordinate pair (pixel.x, pixel.y) which is pixel.x pixels horizontally and pixel.y pixels vertically from the bottom left-hand corner (which naturally has pixel co-ordinates (0, 0)). Note that for all pixels, $0 \leqslant$ pixel.x $<$ nxpix and $0 \leqslant$ pixel.y $<$ nypix, and the top right corner is (nxpix $- 1$, nypix $- 1$). See figure 1.1. There are a few commercial graphics systems which use top left as (0, 0) and bottom right as (nxpix $- 1$, nypix -1), but this can be compensated for in the primitives we construct and will not require a major rewrite of the larger programs.

Colour television and *RGB colour monitors* work on the principle of a colour being a mixture of red, green and blue components. Each pixel is made up of three tiny dots, one each of red, green and blue, and different colours are produced by varying the relative brightness of the dots. Red is given by a bright red dot with no green or blue; yellow is produced by bright red and green dots with no blue, and so on (see chapter 15 for a more detailed description). For this reason most graphics devices define colours in terms of red, green and blue components. We assume that our graphics device has a *colour look-up table* which contains the definitions in this form of numcol colours, each accessed by an integer value between 0 and numcol − 1. Such an integer value is called a *logical colour* while the entries in the look-up table are referred to as *actual colours*. The entries in the look-up table may be redefined by the user, but initially we assume the entries take *default values*. We assume that the display on the model graphics device is based upon a *bit-map*: associated with every pixel there is an integer value (representing a logical colour) and the pixel is displayed in the corresponding actual colour.

We imagine a cursor that moves about the viewport; the pixel co-ordinate of this cursor at any time is called its *current position*. Objects are drawn by moving the cursor around the viewport and resetting the value in the bit-map at the current position to the required logical colour.

The Nine Primitives

The viewport may need some preparatory work done before it can be used for graphical display. We assume that this is achieved by the primitive call

    prepit;

After pictures have been drawn some 'housekeeping' may be needed to finish the frame (see the section on the command code method later in this chapter for an explanation of buffers), and this is done by the primitive call

    finish;

Only one logical colour can be used at a time, so to change the *current colour* currcol to logical colour col, $0 \leqslant col < numcol$, we use the call

    setcol (col);

We can erase all the pixels in the viewport with the current colour by

    erase;

If we are using microfilm then erase may also be used to move onto the next frame of the film.

We can colour the current pixel pixel, of TYPE pixelvector, in the current colour by

    setpix (pixel);

The graphics cursor can be moved about the viewport to its current position pixel without changing the colour by the primitive call

    movepix (pixel);

Or we can draw a line in the current colour from the current position to a new position pixel

    linepix (pixel);

pixel then becomes the current position.

We can fill in a polygon whose vertices are defined by n pixel vectors poly[i], $i = 1, \ldots, n$ taken in order, by the call

    polypix (n, poly);

Finally, we need a primitive which defines the actual colours in the colour look-up table. There are several methods for dealing with such definitions (Ostwald, 1931; Smith, 1978; Foley and Van Dam, 1981), but we assume that the table entry referred to by logical colour i is made up of red (r), green (g) and blue (b) components which may be set by

    rgblog (i, r, g, b);

The intensity of each component is a value between zero and one: zero means no component of that colour is present, one means the full colour intensity. For example, black has RGB components 0, 0, 0, white has 1, 1, 1, red has 1, 0, 0, while cyan is 0, 1, 1. These colours can be 'darkened' by reducing the intensities from one to a fractional value. Initially we shall use just eight default actual colours, comprising black (logical 0), red (1), green (2), yellow (3), blue (4), magenta (5), cyan (6) and white (7). Note the three bits of the binary representation of the numbers 0 to 7 give the presence (1) or absence (0) of the three component colours. The default background and foreground logical colours may be set by the user, we assume 0 and 7 respectively, although for the purpose of diagrams in this book we use black foreground and white background for obvious reasons.

These primitives are by no means the last word. Users of special-purpose graphics devices should extend the list of primitives in order to make full use of the potential of their particular device. For example, many raster devices have different styles of line drawing; thus a line need not simply be drawn in a given (numerical) colour, each pixel along the line may be coloured by a bit-wise boolean binary operation (such as exclusive OR) on the value of the present colour of that pixel and the current drawing colour. A line could be dashed! We shall introduce a new (tenth) primitive in chapter 5 for introducing different *line styles*. Another possible primitive would be the window manager referred to below. In this book we concentrate on geometric modelling; we do not consider the whole area of computer graphics relating to the construction and manipulation of two-dimensional objects which are defined as groups of pixels (*user-*

defined characters (Angell, 1985), *icons* and *sprites*). You could introduce your own primitives for manipulating these objects should your particular graphics application need them.

Implementing the Primitives

We consider two different ways of writing the primitive routines. The first is applicable to users who have access to a two-dimensional graphics package (either in software or hardware), in which case all communication between the primitives and the graphics display will be made via that package. The second is for users of a device for which all manipulation of the display is done by sending a sequence of graphics commands, each command being an *escape character*, followed by a *command code*, possibly followed by a list of integers referring to pixels and/or colours.

The graphics package method

Many graphics packages will have their own routines similar to our nine primitives of listing 1.1 and the appendix. Do *not* go through the program listings given in this book, replacing all references to our nine primitives with the names of the equivalent package routines. It is far more efficient to write individual PRO-CEDUREs for our nine primitives, each of which simply calls the corresponding package routine. You must, however, be aware of any peculiarities or restrictions of your package, in order to ensure that your use of the package corresponds exactly to the definition of the nine primitives above.

Note that graphics commands for microcomputers, such as the IBM PC, also fall into this category. You should further note that some graphics systems (such as microfilm: see the appendix) use the concept of addressable points as opposed to pixels. If a dot is drawn at such an addressable point, then the area centred at that dot will contain a number (certainly tens, perhaps hundreds) of other addressable points. To use our system you will have to identify squares of addressable points with individual pixels.

A graphics package could give you a number of different ways of obtaining the effect of one primitive. The most obvious example is that of filling a polygonal area. Some devices give you a normal area fill (or perhaps a triangle fill), whereby the polygon defined by the pixel co-ordinates of its vertices is filled in the current colour; a *flood fill* which uses the current colour to fill in all pixels in the viewport connected to and of the same colour as an initially specified pixel (seed point); a *boundary fill* which starts at a given pixel, and colours all connected pixels out to a given boundary colour. Some give *pie fills* — that is, filling segments of circles. Others allow *pattern filling*, where areas are filled not in single colours but with combinations of different coloured pixels. All of these can be included in your own specialised primitives should you have a need for them.

If you are working with a single-colour line-drawing package or one which does not give you an area fill, then you have to write your own area-fill primitive using sequences of parallel lines (see chapter 5).

Example primitives for the Graphical Kernel System (G.K.S.) and GINO, and sample Microfilm packages are given in the appendix.

The command code method

Many high-resolution raster display terminals fall into this category. They are normally connected to a host computer, with communication achieved via character string transfer along a pre-defined input/output channel. Graphical information is distinguished from ordinary text by preceding the string of graphics information with a special escape symbol, the strings being sent to the terminal by the usual Pascal write statement. Since this character transfer process can be slow, many systems accept *buffered and/or encoded information* for increased efficiency where a section of memory is used to hold a number of commands, and only when the buffer is full is the information transferred to the display device. *Flushing* of a partially filled buffer on the completion of a drawing may be included in the finish primitive. Examples of primitives for the Tektronix 4100 series are also given in the appendix.

Listing 1.2

```
{ a simple demonstration of use of primitives }

{ insert VARiables at position indicated in LISTING 1.1 }
VAR
    pt1,pt2,pt3,pt4,centre : pixelvector ;
    polygon : pixelarray ;

{ 'main' PROGRAM block : insert at end of LISTING 1.1 }
BEGIN
{ Prepare graphics viewport }
    prepit ;
{ Define logical colour 8 to be grey and current colour }
    rgblog(8,0.5,0.5,0.5) ; setcol(8) ;
{ Define the vertices of a triangle }
    polygon[1].x := 0 ; polygon[1].y := 0 ;
    polygon[2].x := nxpix-1 ; polygon[2].y := 0 ;
    polygon[3].x := 0 ; polygon[3].y := nypix-1 ;
{ Fill in this triangle in current colour }
    polypix(3,polygon) ;
{ Define the vertices of a square centred in the viewport }
{ First the bottom left-hand corner }
    pt1.x := round(nxpix*0.25) ; pt1.y := round(nypix*0.25) ;
{ Then the top right-hand corner }
    pt3.x := round(nxpix*0.75) ; pt3.y := round(nypix*0.75) ;
{ Then the other two corners. }
    pt2.x := pt1.x ; pt2.y := pt3.y ;
    pt4.x := pt3.x ; pt4.y := pt1.y ;
{ Set current colour to white }
```

```
    setcol(7) ;
{ Draw the outline of the square }
    movepix(pt1) ;
    linepix(pt2) ; linepix(pt3) ;
    linepix(pt4) ; linepix(pt1) ;
{ Draw white dot in the centre of the viewport }
    centre.x := round(nxpix*0.5) ; centre.y := round(nypix*0.5) ;
    setpix(centre) ;
{ Call the end of frame procedure }
    finish
END. { of main PROGRAM }
```

Example 1.1
In listing 1.2 we give further variables and a main program block to complete
a contrived program which draws a pattern of dots, lines and areas. It uses all
nine primitives – erase is implicit in prepit. This listing must be merged correctly with your version of listing 1.1 to complete the program.

Exercise 1.1
Many packages allow the construction of more than one viewport on the display
whereas our routines refer to just one viewport, *the current viewport*.
    Introduce your own routines which allow for multiple viewports. Assume
that your display will hold numvpt ($\geq$ 1) viewports. Replace the declarations of
nxpix and nypix in listing 1.1 with declarations of two integer variables numvpt
and nowvpt, two integer arrays nxpix and nypix, and a pixelarray base. The ith
viewport is a rectangle of nxpix[i] pixels by nypix[i] pixels, with the bottom
left-hand corner of that viewport being a display pixel with co-ordinates base[i].
Only one viewport is active at any given time, and the index of the current viewport is denoted by nowvpt. You will have to change some of the above primitives accordingly.

**Starting a Graphics Library: Routines that Map Continuous Space onto the
Viewport**

The use of pixel vectors for drawing (in particular) three-dimensional pictures is
very limiting. The definition of objects using such discrete pairs of integers has
very few real applications. We need to consider plotting views on the graphics
display, where the objects drawn are defined in terms of real units, whether they
be millimetres or miles. Since our primitives draw using pixels, we have to consider a library of CONSTants, TYPEs, VARiables and routines which relate *real
space* with the pixels of our viewport. Before attempting this step we must first
discuss ways of representing two-dimensional space by means of Cartesian co-
ordinate geometry.
    We may imagine two-dimensional space as the plane of this page, but extend-
ing to infinity in all directions. In order to specify the position of points on this
plane uniquely, we have to impose a Cartesian co-ordinate system on the plane.

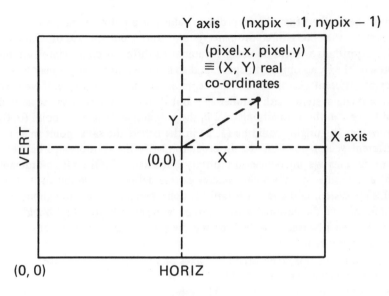

Figure 1.1

We start by arbitrarily choosing a fixed point in this space, which is called the *co-ordinate origin*, or origin for short. A line, that extends to infinity in both directions, is drawn through the origin – this is the *x-axis*. The normal convention, which we follow, is to imagine that we are looking at the page so that the *x*-axis appears from left to right on the page (the horizontal). Another two-way infinite axis, the *y-axis*, is drawn through the origin perpendicular to the *x*-axis; hence conventionally this is placed from the top to the bottom of the page (the vertical). We now draw a scale along each axis; unit distances need not be the same on both axes or even linearly distributed along the axes, but this is normally the case. We assume that values on the *x*-axis are positive to the right of the origin and negative to the left: values on the *y*-axis are positive above the origin and negative below.

We can now uniquely fix the position of point *p* in space with reference to this co-ordinate system by specifying its *co-ordinates* (figure 1.1). The *x co-ordinate*, X say, is that distance along the *x*-axis (positive on the right-hand half-axis, and negative on the left) at which the line perpendicular to the *x*-axis, that passes through *p*, cuts the axis. The *y co-ordinate*, Y say, is correspondingly defined by using the *y*-axis. These two values, called a *co-ordinate pair* or *two-dimensional point vector*, are normally written in brackets thus: (X, Y), the *x* co-ordinate coming before the *y* co-ordinate. We shall usually refer to the pair as a vector – the dimension (in this case dimension two) will be understood from the context in which we use the term. A vector, as well as defining a point (X, Y) in two-dimensional space, may also be used to specify a direction, namely the direction that is parallel to the line that joins the origin to the point (X, Y) – but more of this (and other objects such as lines, curves and polygons) in chapter 3.

It must be realised that the co-ordinate values of a point in space are totally dependent on the choice of co-ordinate system. During our analysis of computer graphics algorithms we will be using a number of different co-ordinate systems to represent the same objects in space, and so a single point in space may have a number of different vector co-ordinate representations. For example, if we have two co-ordinate systems with parallel axes but different origins — say separated by a distance 1 in the x direction and 2 in the y direction — then the point $(0, 0)$ in one system (its origin) could be $(1, 2)$ in the other: the same point in space but different vector co-ordinates. In order to clarify the relationships between different systems we introduce an arbitrary but fixed **ABSOLUTE** co-ordinate system, and ensure that all other systems can be defined in relation to it. This **ABSOLUTE** system, although arbitrarily chosen, remains fixed throughout our discussion of two-dimensional space. (Some authors call this the *World Co-ordinate System*.) Normally we will define the position and shape of objects in relation to this system.

Having imposed this fixed origin and axes on two-dimensional space, we now isolate a rectangular area (or *window*) of size horiz by vert units, which is also defined relative to the **ABSOLUTE** system. This window is to be identified with the viewport so that we can draw views of two-dimensional scenes on the model graphics device. We may wish to move the window about two-dimensional space taking different views of the same objects. To do this we create a new co-ordinate system, the WINDOW system, whose origin is the centre of the window, and whose axes are parallel to the edges of the window, are scaled equally in both x and y directions, and extend to infinity outside the window. Since we will be defining objects such as lines, polygons etc. in terms of the **ABSOLUTE** system, we have to know the relationship between the **ABSOLUTE** and WINDOW systems — that is, the relative positions of the origins and orientations of the respective axes. Having this information, we can relate the **ABSOLUTE** co-ordinates of points with their WINDOW co-ordinates and thence represent them as pixels in the viewport.

We begin our graphics package by assuming that the ABSOLUTE and WINDOW systems are identical, so that objects defined in the ABSOLUTE system have the same co-ordinates in the WINDOW system: in chapter 4 we will consider the more general case of the window moving around and about the ABSOLUTE system. We give routines that operate on points given as real co-ordinates in the WINDOW system, convert them to the equivalent pixels in the viewport, and finally operate on these pixels with the graphics primitives mentioned earlier. Naturally these routines will then be *machine-independent*, and to transport the package between different computers and graphics displays all that is needed is a Pascal compiler and the small number of *display specific* primitives. Programs dealing with the display of two- (and three-) dimensional scenes should rarely directly call the primitives: all communication to these primitives should be done indirectly using the routines below, which treat objects in terms of their real (rather than pixel) co-ordinates (listing 1.3).

We assume that the window is horiz units horizontally, hence the vertical side of the window (vert) is horiz * nypix/nxpix units, and we define the WINDOW co-ordinate origin to be at the centre of the window (figure 1.1). In order to identify the viewport with this window we must be able to find the pixel co-ordinates corresponding to any point within the window. The horizontal (and vertical) scaling factor relating window to viewport is xyscale = (nxpix − 1)/horiz and since the window origin is in the middle of the window we note that any point in space with WINDOW co-ordinates (x, y) will be mapped into a pixel in the viewport with horizontal component trunc (x * xyscale + nxpix * 0.5 − 0.5) and vertical component trunc (y * xyscale + nypix * 0.5 − 0.5). Here trunc is the Pascal function that *rounds down* − hence the final 0.5 for rounding to the nearest integer. These two components are programmed as two functions fx and fy included in the library of routines in listing 1.3. All CONSTant, TYPE and VARiable information needed about the dimensions of the window is declared in this listing. Record TYPE vector2 is declared here to hold the real x, y co-ordinates of two-dimensional vectors, along with an array TYPE of such vectors, vector2array. TYPEs of arrays integerarray and realarray, all of constant size vectorarraysize, are also declared together with pi (π) and epsilon the smallest acceptable positive real.

Note if we do not assume that ABSOLUTE and WINDOW systems are identical and we have an object defined in ABSOLUTE system co-ordinates, then each point in the object must be transformed to its WINDOW co-ordinates before it can be drawn in the viewport − but more of this in chapter 4.

Listing 1.3

```
{ Library of CONSTants, TYPEs, VARiables and PROCEDUREs and 'main' PROGRAM }
{ block needed for Graphics on the Two-Dimensional Plane measured in real }
{ units. Add at positions indicated in listing 1.1 }

CONST
     vectorarraysize = 32 ; pi = 3.1415926535 ; epsilon = 0.000001 ;

TYPE
     vector2 = RECORD x,y : real END ;
     vector2array = ARRAY[1..vectorarraysize] OF vector2 ;
     realarray = ARRAY[1..vectorarraysize] OF real ;
     integerarray = ARRAY[1..vectorarraysize] OF integer ;

VAR
     horiz,vert,xyscale : real ;

PROCEDURE start(horiz : real) ;
BEGIN
{ Set up viewport }
     prepit ;
{ Set up window dimensions }
```

```
        vert := horiz*nypix/nxpix ; xyscale := (nxpix-1)/horiz
END ; { of start }

FUNCTION fx(x : real) : integer ;
BEGIN
        fx := trunc(x*xyscale+nxpix*0.5-0.5)
END ; { of fx }

FUNCTION fy(y : real) : integer ;
BEGIN
        fy := trunc(y*xyscale+nypix*0.5-0.5)
END ; { of fy }

PROCEDURE moveto(pt : vector2 ) ;
VAR pixel : pixelvector ;
BEGIN
        pixel.x := fx(pt.x) ; pixel.y := fy(pt.y) ;
        movepix(pixel)
END ; { of moveto }

PROCEDURE lineto(pt : vector2 ) ;
VAR pixel : pixelvector ;
BEGIN
        pixel.x := fx(pt.x) ; pixel.y := fy(pt.y) ;
        linepix(pixel)
END ;  { of lineto }

PROCEDURE polyfill(n : integer ; polygon : vector2array) ;
VAR i : integer ;
        pixelpolygon : pixelarray ;
BEGIN
        FOR i := 1 to n
        DO BEGIN
                pixelpolygon[i].x := fx(polygon[i].x) ;
                pixelpolygon[i].y := fy(polygon[i].y)
              END ;
        polypix(n,pixelpolygon)
END ; { of polyfill }

FUNCTION angle ; { from listing 3.3 }

{ other routines including 'draw_a_picture' }

BEGIN   { main PROGRAM block }
{ Prepare graphics device }
        writeln(' Type in horizontal size of window') ;
        readln(horiz) ; start(horiz) ;
{ Draw a picture using a PROCEDURE 'draw_a_picture' }
        draw_a_picture ;
        finish
END. { of 'main' PROGRAM }
```

Listing 1.3 also includes routine start which defines a window using the horizontal side length (horiz) given as a parameter. The cleared viewport is identified with the window, and the value xyscale is calculated. We assume that in start (via prepit), the viewport is cleared in black (logical colour 0) and the current colour is set to white (logical 7). These default colours can, of course, be changed at the beginning in prepit or at any time using setcol and/or erase.

In our primitives we have routines which move between pixels or join them in pairs with a line (movepix or linepix) and we naturally require routines which do the same for points defined in our real WINDOW co-ordinate system. Routines moveto and lineto (listing 1.3) do this by changing a real co-ordinate pair to its equivalent pixel and then calling either movepix or linepix. You may find that with each operation the current cursor position, say pixel cursor, has to be stored. This will usually be done in the device hardware and hence you need not worry about it, but if it is not on your machine, simply declare pixelvector cursor in listing 1.1. We also have polyfill, the real equivalent of polypix: also see chapter 5 for an alternative polyfill. The main program block of listing 1.3 reads in the value for horiz and prepares the screen before calling a procedure draw_a_picture and finishing. **All programs in the remainder of this book will use listings 1.1 and 1.3 via draw_a_picture!**

Example 1.2

To demonstrate this we create a window of horizontal size 4 units, and draw a square of side 2 units inside. (See draw_a_picture of listing 1.4 and figure 1.2a.) Note that the order in which the lines are drawn is critical: if the two marked lines in the listing had been interchanged, then the incorrect figure 1.2b would be produced.

Listing 1.4

```
PROCEDURE draw_a_picture ;      {  PROCEDURE to draw a simple SQUARE }
VAR pt1,pt2,pt3,pt4 : vector2 ;
BEGIN
    pt1.x := -1.0 ; pt1.y := -1.0 ;
    pt2.x :=  1.0 ; pt2.y := -1.0 ;
    pt3.x :=  1.0 ; pt3.y :=  1.0 ;
    pt4.x := -1.0 ; pt4.y :=  1.0 ;
    moveto(pt1) ;
    lineto(pt2) ;                   {  **   interchange   **   }
    lineto(pt3) ;                   {  ** these two lines **   }
    lineto(pt4) ;
    lineto(pt1)
END ;  { of draw_a_picture }
```

Exercise 1.2

Alter these routines so that they work with the primitives defined by exercise 1.1 for a multi-viewport/window system. This will allow you to have different window views of the same two-dimensional scene on the graphics device at the same time. In such systems the viewports do not fill the device display area. Naturally we do not want lines and polygons extending beyond the window

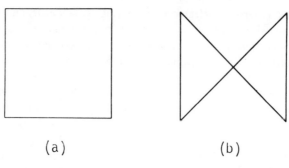

(a)   (b)

Figure 1.2

boundaries. You will have to read the section on *clipping* in chapter 5 to solve this problem.

Exercise 1.3
Draw separate line pictures of a triangle, a pentagon and a hexagon; use only moveto and lineto in a program similar to that above. Also draw a picture with all of these figures in the same window, but with the polygons drawn in different colours (if possible), and at different centres and orientations. Also draw solid (or filled) polygons using polyfill.

All the co-ordinate points constructed in listing 1.4 are given explicitly in the program. This is a relatively rare event; usually the points are implicitly calculated as the program progresses, as in the next example.

Example 1.3
Draw a circle, centred in the window, whose radius value is read by the program. Do not assume the availability of a machine-dependent circle routine, use only moveto and lineto. If your device does include a circle-drawing routine then also write an alternative circle-drawing procedure that makes use of this utility.

In our programs input from the keyboard is by the read routine, text-screen output with the write routine. These routines can also be used for input from and output to file by using text variables indata and outdata respectively.

As for the circle, obviously it is impossible to draw a true curve with the currently defined moveto and lineto routines; we can only draw approximate straight lines! We are, however, rescued from this dilemma by the inadequacy of the human optical equipment — the failure of our eyes to resolve very small lines. If a continuous sequence of short lines is drawn, and this approximates to the curve, then provided that the lines are small enough, our eyes convince our brain that a true curve has been drawn. Obviously this process can only produce a picture up to the quality of the resolution of the graphics device you are using. Low-resolution and medium-resolution devices will display circles (and lines) with jagged edges — the *jaggies* or more formally *aliasing*. Some devices have hardware *anti-aliasing* to minimise this problem (see chapter 5).

So the problem of drawing a circle reduces to one of specifying which lines approximate to that circle. An arbitrary point on a circle of radius r and centre (0.0, 0.0) may be represented by a vector ($r \cos \theta$, $r \sin \theta$), where θ is the angle that the radius through the point makes with the *positive x-axis*. Hence by incre-menting θ between 0 and 2π radians in n equal steps of $2\pi/n$ radians, n + 1 points are produced (the first and last are identical), and these, if joined in the order that they are calculated, define an equilateral polygon with n sides (an *n-gon*). If n is large enough then the *n*-gon approximates to a circle. Listing 1.5 (which incidentally is almost the solution to exercise 1.3) when merged with listings 1.1 and 1.3 draws a circle (a 100-gon) of radius r, centred in the window.

Listing 1.5

```
PROCEDURE draw_a_picture ;     { Drawing a circle }
VAR r : real ;

    PROCEDURE circle(r : real) ;
    VAR theta,thinc : real ;
        i : integer ;
        pt : vector2 ;
    BEGIN
        theta := 0.0 ; thinc := 2*pi/100.0 ;
    { Move to first point }
        pt.x := r ; pt.y := 0.0 ; moveto(pt) ;
    { Draw edges of 100-gon }
        FOR i := 1 TO 100
        DO BEGIN
                theta := theta+thinc ;
                pt.x := r*cos(theta) ; pt.y := r*sin(theta) ;
                lineto(pt)
            END
    END ;   { of circle }

BEGIN
{ Read in radius and draw circle }
    writeln(' Please type in radius') ;
    readln(r) ; circle(r)
END ; { of draw_a_picture }
```

The display produced by this program is shown in figure 1.3a and, as previously stated, the 100 points are not stored but calculated, used and then discarded as the program progresses. This listing may also be used to demonstrate that in a Pascal program it is essential to give all angles in radians and *not* degrees. If angles had been given in degrees — that is thinc = 3.6 (= 360/100) — then the disastrous figure 1.3b is drawn.

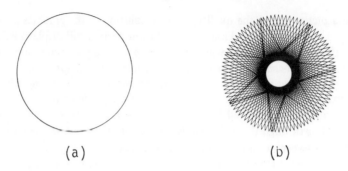

(a)   (b)

Figure 1.3

Exercise 1.4
Draw an ellipse with a major axis of 6 units and a minor axis of 4 units centred on the window. Choose the horiz value so that the ellipse fits inside the window.

Note that a typical point on this ellipse may be represented as a vector (6 cos θ, 4 sin θ), where $0 \leqslant \theta \leqslant 2\pi$, but it must be remembered that this angle θ is *not* the angle made by the radius through that point with the positive x-axis; it is simply a descriptive parameter.

Exercise 1.5
Draw a diagram similar to figure 1.4. Note the optical illusion of two diagonal 'white' lines.

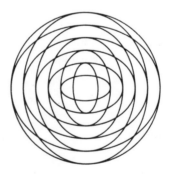

Figure 1.4

Exercise 1.6
Draw examples of Piet Hein's super-ellipses (Gardner, 1978). These figures are given by the general point (a cos^r θ, b sin^r θ) where r is a fixed real number. If $r = 3$ we get an *astroid*, and when $r = 0.8$ we get a peculiar oval popular among architects.

Example 1.4
Draw a spiral centred on the origin with six turns, and which has an outer radius of six units (see draw_a_picture, listing 1.6).

Note that a typical point on a spiral of n turns centred on the origin is again of the form $(r \cos \theta, r \sin \theta)$, where now $0 \leqslant \theta \leqslant 2n\pi$ and the radius depends on θ; $r = \theta/2\pi$ in example 1.4. Since there are likely to be a number of occasions when we need to draw a spiral, we give a general routine which centres the spiral of outer radius radius and n turns at vector2 point centre. Furthermore the value of θ (theta) varies between ang and ang + 2nπ.

In order to complete this example the following procedure call is needed

    spiral (centre, 6.0, 0.0, 6);

where

    centre.x = 0.0 and centre.y = 0.0

whence figure 1.5a is drawn.

Listing 1.6

```
PROCEDURE draw_a_picture ;   { drawing a SPIRAL }
VAR centre : vector2 ;

    PROCEDURE spiral(centre : vector2 ; radius,ang : real ; n : integer) ;
    VAR theta,thinc,r : real ;
        i,ptnumber : integer ;
        pt : vector2 ;
    BEGIN theta := ang ; thinc := 2*pi/100.0 ;
{ Move to first point }
        moveto(centre) ;
{ Draw spiral of 'n' turns ('ptnumber=n*100' points) }
        ptnumber := 100*n ;
        FOR i := 1 TO ptnumber
        DO BEGIN
                theta := theta+thinc ; r := radius*i/ptnumber ;
                pt.x := r*cos(theta)+centre.x ;
                pt.y := r*sin(theta)+centre.y ;
                lineto(pt)
            END
    END ; { of spiral }

BEGIN
    centre.x := 0.0 ; centre.y := 0.0 ;
    spiral(centre,6.0,0.0,6)
END ; { of draw_a_picture }
```

Exercise 1.7
Using procedure spiral of listing 1.6, produce another procedure

    twist (centre : vector2 ; r, ang : real);

which will draw diagrams similar to figure 1.5b. Again centre is the centre of the

(a) (b)

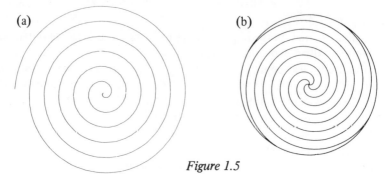

Figure 1.5

figure relative to the WINDOW origin, r is the radius of the circle containing the four spirals, and **ang** is the initial angular value of one of the spirals.

It is now time to consider some more attractive examples to illustrate how, even with only a beginner's knowledge of computer graphics, it is still possible to draw aesthetically pleasing patterns. Furthermore, you must familiarise yourself with your graphics device before going on to the more complex three-dimensional displays, and drawing patterns is an ideal way to start.

Example 1.5
Produce a general program that places n points ($n \leqslant 100$), equally spaced on the circumference of a unit circle, and then joins each point to every other.

Figure 1.6 shows the pattern produced by listing 1.7 with $n = 30$. The n points are required over and over again, and so it is sensible to calculate them once only, store them in an array and recall them when necessary. The points are

$$\mathrm{pt}[i] = (X_i, Y_i) = (\cos(2\pi i/n), \sin(2\pi i/n)) \quad i = 1, 2, \ldots, n$$

Also note that if $i \geqslant j$ then the ith point is not joined to the jth point at this stage, since the line will already have been drawn in the opposite direction. See chapter 2 for a more detailed explanation of arrays.

Listing 1.7

```
PROCEDURE draw_a_picture ;  { Simple point to point plot }
VAR pt : ARRAY[1..100] OF vector2 ;
    i,j,n : integer ;
    theta,thinc : real ;
BEGIN
{ Read in 'n', the number of points }
    writeln('Type in number of points') ; readln(n) ;
{ Calculate 'n' points on a unit circle }
    theta := 0.0 ; thinc := 2*pi/n ;
    FOR i := 1 TO n
    DO BEGIN
            pt[i].x := cos(theta) ; pt[i].y := sin(theta) ;
```

```
                theta := theta+thinc
            END ;
{ Join point 'i' to point 'j' for all '1 <= i < j <= n' }
    FOR i := 1 TO n-1
    DO FOR j := i+1 TO n
        DO BEGIN
                moveto(pt[i]) ; lineto(pt[j])
            END
END ; { of draw_a_picture }
```

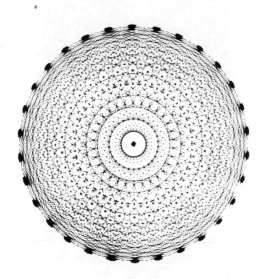

Figure 1.6

Exercise 1.8
If you are using a pen plotter then listing 1.7 is not a very efficient way of draw-ing the pattern; the pen goes to and fro across the page and yet half the time no line is drawn since the pen is just returning to the start point of a new line. Write a program that draws the same diagrams, but is more efficient than this listing.

Exercise 1.9
Draw a diagram similar to figure 1.7.

This diagram (another 'pin and cotton' picture – so called after the child's toy) is drawn by first reading in a value for *n*. The program then calculates the co-ordinates of $4n$ points $\{p[i] \mid i = 1, 2, \ldots, 4n\}$ around the edges of a unit square. There is one point at each corner and the points are placed so that the distance between consecutive points is $1/n$. Then pairs of points are joined according to the following rule: $p[i]$ is joined to $p[j]$, for all positive i, j not greater than $4n$, such that $j - i$ is a Fibonacci number less than $4n$, the subtrac-

Figure 1.7

Figure 1.8

tion being carried out modulo 4*n*. (Note that the sequence of Fibonacci numbers is the set of positive integers 1, 2, 3, 5, 8, 13, 21, 34, . . . , where each element is the sum of the previous two elements in the sequence.) Because the indices of our arrays start at 1, we define modulo 4*n* as referring to the residue classes 1, 2, . . . , 4*n*, and not the usual 0, 1, . . . , 4*n* − 1. For example, if *n* = 10 then the point p[32] would be joined to p[33], p[34], p[35], p[37], p[40], p[5], p[13] and p[26]. The outer unit square must be drawn as part of the diagram and thus, for efficiency, there is no need to join points which lie on the same side of the square.

Example 1.6

We use colour in the draw_a_picture procedure of listing 1.8 to draw diagrams similar to figure 1.8. *m* sets of *n* points on regular *n*-gons, and one set of *n* coincident points, are given by the following formulae

The ith point in the jth set, $1 \leqslant i \leqslant n$ and $0 \leqslant j \leqslant m$, is $(r \cos \theta, r \sin \theta)$ where *r* and θ are given by

$$r = (m - j)/m \quad \text{and} \quad \theta = 2\pi i/n + \alpha$$

where $\alpha = 0$ if i mod 2 is zero, and π/n otherwise.

Triangles are then formed by joining every pair of neighbouring points on all but the inner *n*-gon to the nearest point inside them. These triangles are then filled in with logical colour 1 (red) and a logical colour 7 (white) edge drawn around the outside.

Listing 1.8

```
PROCEDURE draw_a_picture ;   { drawing a simple ROSE pattern }
VAR inner,outer : ARRAY[1..100] OF vector2 ;
      triangle : vector2array ;
      i,j,m,n : integer ;
      r,theta,thinc : real ;
BEGIN
{ Read in 'n' and 'm' }
      writeln('Type n and m') ; readln(n,m) ;
      thinc := 2*pi/n ;
{ Initial inner circle is degenerate }
      FOR i := 1 TO n
      DO BEGIN
             inner[i].x := 0.0 ; inner[i].y := 0.0
             END ;
{ Loop through the 'm' levels }
      FOR j := 1 TO m
      DO BEGIN
             theta := -j*pi/n ; r := j/m ;
{ Calculate 'n' points on outer circle }
             FOR i := 1 TO n
             DO BEGIN
                    theta := theta+thinc ;
                    outer[i].x := r*cos(theta) ;
                    outer[i].y := r*sin(theta)
                    END ;
{ Construct/draw triangles with vertices on inner and outer circles }
             FOR i :=  1 TO n
             DO BEGIN
                    triangle[1] := outer[i] ;
                    triangle[2] := outer[(i MOD n)+1] ;
                    triangle[3] := inner[i] ;
{ Fill 'triangle' in red }
```

```
                 setcol(1) ; polyfill(3,triangle) ;
{ Outline 'triangle' in white }
                 setcol(7) ; moveto(triangle[1]) ;
                 lineto(triangle[2]) ;
                 lineto(triangle[3]) ;
                 lineto(triangle[1])
             END ;
{ Copy points on outer circle to inner arrays }
        FOR i := 1 TO n
        DO inner[i] := outer[i]
        END
END ; { of draw_a_picture }
```

Exercise 1.10
Use the methods of examples 1.3 and 1.6 to draw a solid circle (a disc): figure
1.9 (green with a red edge). Approximate to the disc with a sequence of triangles
whose vertices consist of the centre of the circle and two neighbouring points on
the circumference. If your device has a hardware circle-fill (or pie-fill), then incorporate this in an alternative routine to solve this exercise.

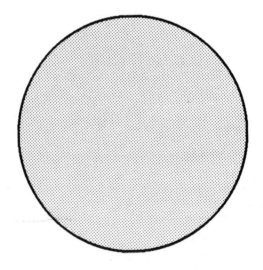

Figure 1.9

Example 1.7
Emulate a Spirograph ®, in order to produce diagrams similar to figure 1.10.
   A Spirograph consists of a cogged disc inside a cogged circle, which is placed
on a piece of paper. Let the outer circle have integer radius *a* and the disc
integer radius *b*. The disc is always in contact with the circle. There is a small

hole in the disc at a distance *d* (also an integer) from the centre of the disc, through which is placed a sharp pencil point. The disc is moved around the circle in an anti-clockwise manner, but it must always touch the outer circle; the cogs

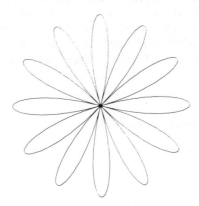

Figure 1.10

ensure there is no slipping. The pencil traces out a pattern, which is complete when the pencil returns to its original position.

We assume that, initially, the centres of the disc and circle and also the hole all lie on the positive *x*-axis, the centre of the circle being the WINDOW origin. In order to emulate the movement of the Spirograph it is essential to specify a general point on the track of the pencil point. We let θ be the angle made with the positive *x*-axis by the line joining the origin to the point where the circle and disc touch. The point of contact is thus $(a \cos \theta, a \sin \theta)$ and the centre of the disc is $((a - b) \cos \theta, (a - b) \sin \theta)$. If we let $-\phi$ be the angle that the line joining the hole to the centre of the disc makes with the *x* direction (note the angle ϕ has opposite orientation to θ, hence the minus sign), then the co-ordinates of the hole are

$$((a - b) \cos \theta + d \cos \phi, (a - b) \sin \theta - d \sin \phi)$$

The point of contact between the disc and circle will have moved through a distance $a\theta$ around the circle, and a distance $b(\theta + \phi)$ around the disc. Since there is no slipping these distances must be equal and hence we have the equation $\phi = ((a - b)/b)\theta$. The pencile returns to its original position when both θ and ϕ are integer multiples of 2π. When $\theta = 2n\pi$ then $\phi = 2\pi n (a - b)/b$; hence the pencil point returns to the original position for the first time when $n (a - b)/b$ becomes an integer for the first time, that is, when *n* is *b* divided by the highest common factor of *b* and *a*. The function **hcf** given in listing 1.9 uses Euclid's

Algorithm to calculate the h.c.f. of two positive integers (see Davenport, 1952). The listing also includes a procedure spirograph which calculates the value n, and then varies θ (theta) between 0 and $2n\pi$ in steps of $\pi/100$; for each θ, the value of ϕ (phi) is calculated and thence the general track is drawn. Obviously the size of the window must be chosen so that the shape defined by values of a, b and d actually fits into the window: the radius of such a shape is $a + d - b$. Figure 1.10 is drawn by the call spirograph (12, 7, 5) from within draw_a_picture, which is merged into listings 1.1 and 1.3 as previously indicated.

Listing 1.9

```
PROCEDURE draw_a_picture ;   { Spirograph }

   FUNCTION hcf(i,j : integer ) : integer ;
{ Returns the H.C.F. of two positive integers 'i' and 'j' }
{ 'i' is initially greater than 'j' }
   VAR remain : integer ;
   BEGIN
      REPEAT remain := i MOD j ;
             i := j ; j := remain
      UNTIL   remain = 0 ;
      hcf := i
   END ; { of hcf }

   PROCEDURE spirograph(a,b,d : integer ) ;
   VAR i,n,ptnumber : integer ;
       phi,theta,thinc : real ;
       pt : vector2 ;
   BEGIN
      theta := 0.0 ; thinc := pi*0.02 ;
      n := b DIV hcf(a,b) ; ptnumber := n*100 ;
      pt.x := a-b+d ; pt.y := 0.0 ; moveto(pt) ;
      FOR i := 1 TO ptnumber
      DO BEGIN
             theta := theta+thinc ; phi := theta*(a-b)/b ;
             pt.x := (a-b)*cos(theta)+d*cos(phi) ;
             pt.y := (a-b)*sin(theta)-d*sin(phi) ;
             lineto(pt)
         END
   END ; { of spirograph }

BEGIN
   spirograph(12,7,5)
END ; { of draw_a_picture }
```

Exercise 1.11

Use this routine in a program which draws a field of 'flowers', each flower consisting of a thin rectangular (green) stem with multicoloured Spirograph petals.

2 Data Structures

In the previous chapter we saw examples of subscripted variables or arrays. Now we are going to discuss the general use in computer graphics of this and other *abstract data structures*, and in particular the implementation in Pascal of those structures that are necessary for the more complex algorithms given in this book. Those readers who do not wish to delve too deeply into data structures at this stage may skip this chapter and return to it later in order to understand the complex algorithms. We will limit our discussion to those data structures that will be of value in this book; for those who wish to find out more we recommend books by Aho, Hopcroft and Ullman (1983), Horowitz and Sahni (1976) and Knuth (1973).

Arrays and Subscripted Variables

We assume that readers will be aware of the concept of *subscripts*. That is the grouping together of data of the same type under one name (or *identifier*) and accessing individuals within that grouping (or *array*) by use of subscripts. For example, the first five prime numbers can be given the name p — that is, p represents ALL the numbers $2, 3, 5, 7, 11$. An individual from within the grouping is indicated by a subscript — that is, p_4 indicates the fourth member of the array (the prime number 7). Often the subscript is given by a *variable name*; therefore p_i is the ith element of the array, where i must be in the range of the possible subscripts. It is possible for an array to have multiple subscripts; for example, in an m by n *matrix* (a double subscripted array) identified with the name a, the individual element in the ith *row* and j^{th} *column* ($1 \leqslant i \leqslant m$ and $1 \leqslant j \leqslant n$) is indicated by a_{ij}. In Pascal all statements will appear on an output line, not above or below that line (we cannot have subscripts or superscripts). Therefore, to implement subscripted variables in Pascal we always declare an array using ARRAY in a TYPE or VAR statement, as we saw in chapter 1. One or more subscripts (now called an *index* or *indices*) are placed inside (square) brackets and separated by commas — for example, p[4] and a[i, j]. In the text that follows a pair of dots (. .) will be used to specify a *range* or *subrange* of subscript values; for example, a[i, 3 . . k] means the array values a[i, 3], a[i, 4], . . , a[i, k].

We shall see the importance and power of arrays when we deal with the concept of vertex co-ordinates, lines and facets in the chapters on two-dimensional and three-dimensional space. (A *facet* is a closed convex polygon which is normally defined by the co-planar vertices that form the corners of the polygon.) For example, a set of three-dimensional vertices can be grouped together and the x, y and z co-ordinates can be stored as an array of RECORDs, v (say), where the ith vertex is v[i]. Hence the ith vertex from the set will have Cartesian co-ordinates (v[i].x, v[i].y, v[i].z).

Pointers

The use of arrays has drawbacks in certain situations, as in the case where the grouping of data in a double subscripted array is *sparse*. For example, we could have m static *sets* of integer data, where the largest set contains n values, but on average the sets contain n/4 values (say). If we stored the sets in an m by n matrix, then only a quarter of the array locations (m * n/4) would be used. One solution to this problem is the use of *pointers*. Many programming languages (including Pascal) have pointers built into the language. It is also possible, however, to implement these ideas in Pascal using arrays, which in some cases may prove more efficient. A large array is used to store data values, and an integer index, sometimes called a *cursor* (that is, a pointer), is used to indicate an element or group of elements in that array. Our set example above can be solved in this way. Suppose each set is indicated by an integer value between 1 and numberofsets and the elements from all sets are placed in array listofsets, the values of set i coming immediately after those of set i − 1 in the array, where $2 \leqslant i \leqslant$ numberofsets. In order to access an individual set stored in this way we need to know the start location of that set in listofsets as well as the number of elements. We let the ith set have size[i] elements stored in locations

listofsets[firstofset[i] + 1], . . . , listofsets[firstofset[i] + size[i]]

We give a rather artificial program in listing 2.1 to demonstrate this technique. Note that in our implementation the start location of set i is not firstofset[i] but firstofset[i] + 1. We store values this way to ensure that the ith element of the ith set is stored at location listofsets[firstofset[i] + n]. Also we introduce a variable last which points to the last used location in the array.

In the study of data structures it is often useful to draw diagrams to represent them. One-dimensional arrays are normally represented as a row (or column) of boxes holding the array values; if necessary array indices are placed outside the relevant boxes. If an integer value is used as a pointer then it is sometimes drawn in the diagram as an arrow; one end indicates where the integer is stored and the other which location is being pointed at. A pointer which points nowhere (?), the *null pointer* (see figure 2.4), is usually represented by a diagonal line: since we are using arrays then the integer value corresponding to the null pointer will be zero. See figure 2.1 as an example of a data structure diagram for listing 2.1.

Listing 2.1

```
PROGRAM sets(input,output) ;
{ Program to demonstrate sets and cursors }
VAR firstofset,size : ARRAY[1..10] OF integer ;
    listofsets : ARRAY[1..100] OF integer ;
    i,j,last,numberofsets,whichset : integer ;
BEGIN
{ Create sets and place in array 'listofsets' }
    last := 0 ;
    REPEAT
        writeln(' How many sets?') ;
        readln(numberofsets) ;
    UNTIL (numberofsets > 0) AND (numberofsets < 11) ;
    FOR i := 1 TO numberofsets
    DO BEGIN
            firstofset[i] := last ;
            writeln(' How many elements in set',i:3) ;
            readln(size[i]) ;
            IF size[i] < > 0
            THEN BEGIN
                    last := firstofset[i] + size[i] ;
                    writeln(' Type in',size[i]:4,' integers, one per line') ;
                    FOR j := 1 TO size[i]
                    DO readln(listofsets[firstofset[i] +j])
                END
        END ;
{ Output any set }
    REPEAT
        write(' Which set do you wish output ') ;
        readln(whichset) ;
        IF (whichset > 0) AND (whichset < = numberofsets)
        THEN IF size[whichset] = 0
                THEN writeln(' Empty Set')
                ELSE BEGIN
                        FOR j := 1 TO size[whichset]
                        DO write(listofsets[firstofset[whichset] +j]:5) ;
                        writeln
                    END
    UNTIL (whichset = 0)
END. { of PROGRAM sets }
```

Listing 2.1a

```
PROGRAM sets_alternative(input,output) ;
{ Program to demonstrate sets and cursors }
TYPE setptr = ^setnode ;
     setnode = RECORD value : integer ; ptr : setptr END ;
VAR listofsets : ARRAY[1..10] OF setptr ;
    p : setptr ;
    i,j,numberofsets,size,whichset : integer ;
BEGIN
{ Create sets and place in array 'listofsets' }
    REPEAT
```

```
        writeln(' How many sets?') ;
        readln(numberofsets) ;
UNTIL (numberofsets > 0) AND (numberofsets < 11) ;
FOR i := 1 TO numberofsets
DO BEGIN
        listofsets[i] := NIL ;
        writeln(' How many elements in set',i:3) ;
        readln(size) ;
        IF size < > 0
        THEN BEGIN
                writeln(' Type in',size:4,' integers, one per line') ;
                FOR j := 1 TO size
                DO BEGIN
                        new(p) ; readln(p^.value) ;
                        p^.ptr := listofsets[i] ;
                        listofsets[i] := p
                        END
                END
        END ;
{ Output any set }
    REPEAT
        write(' Which set do you wish output ') ;
        readln(whichset) ;
        IF (whichset > 0) AND (whichset < = numberofsets)
        THEN IF listofsets[whichset] = NIL
                THEN writeln(' Empty Set')
                ELSE BEGIN
                        p := listofsets[whichset] ;
                        WHILE p < > NIL
                        DO BEGIN
                                write(p^.value:5) ;
                                p := p^.ptr
                                END ;
                        writeln
                        END
    UNTIL (whichset = 0)
END. { of PROGRAM sets_alternative }
```

This technique is used for storing information about polygonal facets in two-dimensional and three-dimensional space. For example, in a given scene we could have both triangles and dodecagons (say), nof in total, each polygon defined by a list of the vertices on its perimeter, taken in order. Hence the vertices for a given polygon in the scene fall into the category of the set type described above, and so the method of listing 2.1 will prove very efficient in storing such polygonal information. It is obviously inefficient to use an nof by 12 array to store the vertices in the scene if most of the polygons are triangles.

Exercise 2.1
There is strictly no need to include the size array in listing 2.1, after all size[i] = firstofset[i+1] — firstofset[i]. We use the size array explicitly to aid our explanation in the text. You can change our programs to avoid using the size locations

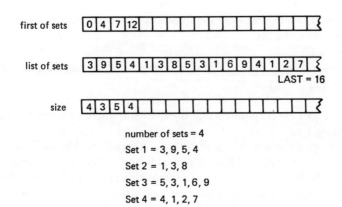

Figure 2.1

if you wish; try with listing 2.1 — note you must now have a value for firstofset[numberofsets + 1]. You can even change the meaning of firstofset[i] so that it actually points at the first element of the ith set.

Linked Lists

Not all information is static. There are so-called *dynamic* data structures where information can be added and/or discarded from the grouping. When using arrays to represent such structures, we have to allow space for the maximum size of the grouping, and furthermore discarded information will leave holes in the array, which often requires resequencing of the array values — a very time-consuming process. One such dynamic data structure which avoids this problem and which is used throughout this book is the *linked list* or *linear list*.

Like an array, a linked list is a means of grouping together elements of the same type, but, unlike an array, the information in such a structure is not accessed by an index but by a movable pointer. A linked list is made up of separate links and each link consists of two parts: the *information part* which contains a value of the type being grouped together, and the *pointer part* which indicates the next link in the chain. This implies the existence of

(a) a pointer to the front of the list
(b) a *null pointer* which indicates an empty list or the end of a list, and
(c) a facility whereby a variable pointer will enable us to move along the list, accessing individual links in the list.

The manipulation of such a structure can be quite complex. We could have routines to

(1) add new links to the front, back or at a specified position within a list

(2) read/print/delete links from the front, back or specified position in a list
(3) make copies of a list
(4) reverse a list
(5) add new values to a list so that an *ordering* is imposed on the values stored
in the list.

Listing 2.1a uses Pascal pointers and linear lists to give a program equivalent to
that of listing 2.1.

There are many, many more possibilities and variations. The list data structure
is a very powerful tool, and has wide ranging applications in computer science.
For our needs, however, we will concentrate on a restricted form of a list called
a *stack of integers*. The information part of elements in the list is limited to
integers, and these can only be added to and deleted from the front of the list:
respectively the so-called *push* and *pop* routines.

One method of implementing a stack is to have an array stack (say) holding integer information values for each link in the list and a variable top, initially
the null pointer zero, which points to an element in the array: the top of the
stack. The inter-link pointers are understood to be the indices of the array stack.
A push routine for such a stack implementation increases the value of top by
one and puts the value to be stored into location stack[top]. The pop routine
simply finds the value of stack[top] then decrements top by one. See listing 2.2
and figure 2.2.

Listing 2.2

```
PROGRAM stackexample(input,output) ;
{ To demonstate 'push' and 'pop' routines using integer cursor }
VAR stack : ARRAY[1..100] OF integer ;
    i,value,top : integer ;

    PROCEDURE push(stackvalue : integer) ;
{ Routine to 'push' the integer 'stackvalue' onto the 'stack' array }
    BEGIN
        IF top = 100
        THEN writeln(' Stack size exceeded')
        ELSE BEGIN
                top := top+1 ; stack[top] := stackvalue
             END
{ Move up 'top' of 'stack', and store 'stackvalue' there }
    END ; { of push }

    PROCEDURE pop(VAR stackvalue : integer) ;
{ Routine to 'pop' the 'stackvalue' from the array 'stack' }
    BEGIN
        IF top = 0
        THEN writeln('Stack is empty')
        ELSE BEGIN
                stackvalue := stack[top] ; top := top-1
             END
    END ; { of pop }
```

```
BEGIN
    top := 0 ;  { Initialise stack pointer }
{ Some sample 'push'es } ;
    push(5) ; push(7) ;
{ A sample 'pop' }
    pop(value) ; writeln(' popping',value:2,' from stack') ;
{ Another 'push' }
    push(2) ;
{ write out 'top' and first five locations of 'stack' array }
    writeln(' top of the stack is',top:2) ;
    FOR i := 1 TO 5
    DO writeln('index=',i:2,' stack value=',stack[i]:3)
END.  { of PROGRAM stackexample }
```

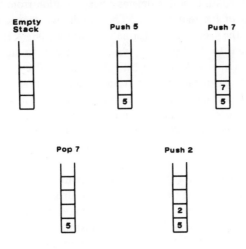

Figure 2.2

Of course the above method requires one array to be declared for each stack. This can prove a costly store requirement, so we introduce another method to implement a stack which uses a *heap* implemented as a VARiable array heap, each element being of RECORD TYPE, heapcell, with two fields info and pointer referring to the information and pointer parts of links in the lists respectively. The pointer value will be the index of another location in the heap array. The size of this array (maxheap) must be chosen large enough to deal with our applications, and may be set by a CONSTant declaration. Initially

heap[i] .pointer: = i + 1 for i = 1, . . . , maxheap − 1 and
heap[maxheap] .pointer: = 0

An integer variable free (a pointer) is set to 1. Hence using free we can locate index 1 of array heap. heap[1] .pointer sends us to index 2 and so on along the maxheap elements of the heap until the zero null pointer is found. Lists (we may have more than one!) will be stored on this heap. free points to the so-called list of free locations in the heap; such a list is necessary because we do not want to overwrite heap locations that have been used for the construction of other lists! Initially the whole heap is free, hence the above values for heap[1 . . maxheap −1].pointer and free. The end of a list is indicated by the zero null pointer: see heap[maxheap] .pointer. Note that at this stage no values have been stored in the info fields — we are only organising the pointer system between links.

If we wish to place a list on the heap, we first have to give it an identifier (stack1 say) and set it to an empty list (stack1 = 0), and then create it link by link. stack1 will denote the heap index of the link at the front of the list. It is extended by a push routine, which deletes a heap location from the free list and adds it to the front of the required list. This implies we change the stack1 and free values, store the necessary information in heap[stack1] .info, and set heap[stack1].pointer to the previous value of stack1 to maintain the link pointers in stack1. Other links in the list can be accessed by moving along the sequence of pointers starting at location heap[stack1] .pointer.

Should we pop (read and delete) an element from the list, we must not only change stack1 to heap[stack1] .pointer, but also replace the vacated heap location in the free list (*garbage collection*). Listing 2.3 holds the heap initialisation, push and pop routines, together with a contrived program, which manipulates two lists (stack1 and stack2): two diagrams of the resulting heap are given in figures 2.3 and 2.4. These data structure diagrams are typical examples of those found in most textbooks. Figure 2.3 is an array diagram of the final stage of listing 2.3, and shows a named vertical set of boxes which contain the array values: indices are placed alongside the boxes. Listing 2.3a gives a Pascal pointer version of listing 2.3. Figure 2.4 is a *box and pointer* diagram·of the final stage of listing 2.3a, where boxes show the links in a linear list and the arrows indicate connections between them.

Listing 2.3

```
PROGRAM stacktest(input,output) ;
{ Program to demonstrate 'push' and 'pop' routines, for manipulating }
{ various stacks stored using a 'heap' array }
CONST maxheap = 10 ;
TYPE heapcell = RECORD info,pointer : integer END ;
VAR  heap : ARRAY[1..maxheap] OF heapcell ;
     free,stack1,stack2,stackvalue : integer ;

   PROCEDURE push(VAR stackname : integer ; value : integer) ;
{ Routine to 'push' the integer 'value' onto the stack-type }
{ linear list 'stackname' which is stored on a 'heap' }
     VAR location : integer ;
     BEGIN
{ create new node for stackname }
```

```
       IF free=0
       THEN BEGIN
                 writeln(' Heap size exceeeded') ;
                 EXIT
                 END
       ELSE BEGIN
{ Obtain 'location' from 'heap', and delete it from 'free' list }
                 location := free ; free := heap[free].pointer ;
{ Add 'location' to front of 'stackname', store 'value' there }
                 heap[location].info := value ;
                 heap[location].pointer := stackname ;
                 stackname := location
                 END
   END ; { of push }


   PROCEDURE pop(VAR stackname,value : integer) ;
{ Routine to 'pop' the first 'value' from the linear list 'stackname' }
   VAR location : integer ;
   BEGIN
{ 'value' is stored at the front of list 'stackname' }
       IF stackname = 0
       THEN BEGIN
                 writeln(' Stack is empty') ; value := -9999
                 END
       ELSE BEGIN
                 location := stackname ; value := heap[stackname].info ;
{ Delete front element of stackname, and dispose }
                 stackname := heap[stackname].pointer ;
                 heap[location].pointer := free ;
                 free := location
                 END
   END ; { of pop }


   PROCEDURE printstack(stackname : integer) ;
   VAR location : integer ;
   BEGIN
       location := stackname ;
       WHILE location < > 0
       DO BEGIN
                 writeln(heap[location].info:5) ;
                 location := heap[location].pointer
              END ;
           writeln
   END ; { of printstack }

   PROCEDURE heapstart ;
{ Initialise the 'heap'. At first no 'info'rmation is stored }
{ Only 'pointer', which points to next cell in the 'heap' }
   VAR i : integer ;
   BEGIN
       free := 1 ;
       FOR i := 1 TO maxheap-1
       DO heap[i].pointer := i+1 ;
       heap[maxheap].pointer := 0
   END ; { of heapstart }
```

```
BEGIN
{ Prepare the 'heap' }
   heapstart ;
{ Create two stacks : 'stack1' and 'stack2' }
   stack1 := 0 ; stack2 := 0 ;
{ Some sample 'push'es }
   push(stack2,5) ; push(stack1,7) ;
   push(stack2,8) ; push(stack1,3) ;
{ A sample 'pop' }
   pop(stack2,stackvalue) ;
   writeln(' popping',stackvalue:3,' from stack2') ;
{ Another 'push' }
   push(stack1,2) ;
{ write out the two stacks }
   writeln('stack1 ') ; printstack(stack1) ;
   writeln('stack2 ') ; printstack(stack2)
END. { of PROGRAM stacktest }
```

Listing 2.3a

```
PROGRAM stacktest_alternative(input,output) ;
{ Program to demonstrate 'push' and 'pop' routines, for manipulating }
{ various stacks stored using pointers }
TYPE stackptr = ^stacknode ;
     stacknode = RECORD info : integer ; ptr : stackptr END ;
VAR  stack1,stack2 : stackptr ;
     stackvalue : integer ;

   PROCEDURE push(VAR stackname : stackptr ; stackvalue : integer) ;
{ Routine to 'push' the integer 'stackvalue' onto the stack-type }
{ linear list 'stackname' which is stored using pointers }
   VAR p : stackptr ;
   BEGIN
{ create new node for 'stackname' }
       new(p) ; p^.info := stackvalue ;
       p^.ptr := stackname ; stackname := p
   END ; { of push }

   PROCEDURE pop(VAR stackname : stackptr ; VAR stackvalue : integer) ;
{ Routine to 'pop' the 'stackvalue' from the linear list 'stackname' }
   VAR p : stackptr ;
   BEGIN
{ 'stackvalue' is stored at the front of list 'stackname' }
       IF stackname = NIL
       THEN writeln(' Stack is empty')
       ELSE BEGIN
               p := stackname ; stackvalue := stackname^.info ;
{ Delete front element of 'stackname', and dispose }
               stackname := stackname^.ptr ; dispose(p)
            END
   END ; { of pop }

   PROCEDURE printstack(stack : stackptr) ;
```

```
    VAR p : stackptr ;
    BEGIN
        p := stack ;
        WHILE p < > NIL
        DO BEGIN
                write(p^.info:5) ; p := p^.ptr
            END ;
        writeln
    END ; { of printstack }

BEGIN
{ Create two stacks : 'stack1' and 'stack2' }
    stack1 := NIL ; stack2 := NIL ;
{ Some sample 'push'es }
    push(stack2,5) ; push(stack1,7) ;
    push(stack2,8) ; push(stack1,3) ;
{ A sample 'pop' }
    pop(stack2,stackvalue) ;
    writeln(' popping',stackvalue:3,' from stack2') ;
{ Another 'push' }
    push(stack1,2) ;
{ write out the two stacks }
    writeln('stack1') ; printstack(stack1) ;
    writeln('stack2') ; printstack(stack2)
END. { of PROGRAM stacktest_alternative }
```

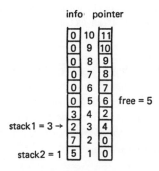

Figure 2.3

Both the array stack and heap methods will be used throughout the book and in particular in the quad-tree algorithm we give in chapter 17.

Graphs and Networks

Another very important data structure in computer graphics is the *graph*, or more specifically the restricted form of graph called a *network*. A graph is a set

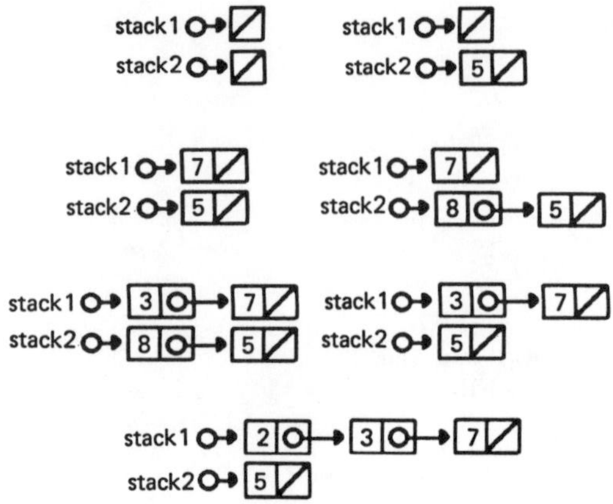

Figure 2.4

of *nodes* and *directed edges*: see figure 2.5. For simplicity we label the n nodes of a graph with the first n integers. A directed edge, say from node i to node j, is denoted by $\{i, j\}$. A path in a graph is a consecutive sequence of edges — for example, the path $\{i, j, k, l\}$ consists of the three edges $\{i, j\}$, $\{j, k\}$, $\{k, l\}$. A network is a graph that does not contain a *cycle* or *loop* — that is, there is no path, other than the trivial path $\{i, i\}$, starting and ending at the same node. Figure 2.5 is therefore a network: if an extra edge $\{5, 2\}$ (say) had been added then there would be cycles, such as $\{2, 5, 2\}$ and $\{2, 4, 5, 2\}$, and the graph would no longer be a network.

We implement a graph by defining an array **netlist** of pointers. **netlist**[i] will be a pointer to a list stored on the heap; the list will be a stack of all nodes j, such that there is an edge $\{i, j\}$ in the graph. See figure 2.6. If such a graph is a network, then we say that the n nodes are *partially ordered*, and that it is possible to print out the node labels in a *topological order*. A topological order of a network is a permutation of the first n integers

$$[I_1, I_2, \ldots, I_n]$$

such that there are no i and j, $1 \leqslant i < j \leqslant n$, where there is a path in the network leading from node I_j back in the order to node I_i. Note a topological order for a network need not be unique. For example, in figure 2.5 both $[1, 2, 3, 4, 5, 6, 7]$ and $[1, 3, 2, 4, 6, 5, 7]$ are topological orders.

A program of the process of finding a topological order for a given network is in listing 2.4. The method is to keep another stack which holds a list of all nodes with no edges entering them. Each time the stack is popped, we delete that node and any edges leaving that node, from the network. If this process throws up further nodes with no edges entering them, then these are also pushed on the stack. After n pops, we have a topological ordering: if the stack becomes empty before this point then the graph has a cycle, and is therefore not a network.

This method is fundamental to the hidden surface algorithm of chapter 13, where the nodes represent polygonal facets, and the edges denote overlapping relationships between facets. For example, if, on viewing, facet I is behind facet J, then there will be an edge from node I to node J in the network representing the scene. If the facets do not overlap then there is no edge between them in the network. The topological ordering of such a network gives a (non-unique) order of facets in the scene, starting from the back and moving forward, and hence furnishes us with a straightforward hidden surface algorithm.

Listing 2.4

```
PROGRAM networkexample ;
{ To demonstrate a simple network and topological sort. The }
{ network is represented by a 'net'list of up to 'maxnet' stacks }
{ The 'netlist[i]' stack holds the indices of all nodes 'j', such }
{ that there is an edge from 'i' to 'j'. 'edgein[j]' holds the }
{ number of edges entering node 'j' }
CONST maxnet = 200 ;
TYPE stackptr = ^stacknode ;
     stacknode = RECORD info : integer ;
                        ptr : stackptr
              END ;
VAR entrystack : stackptr ;
    netlist : ARRAY[1..maxnet] OF stackptr ;
    edgein : ARRAY[1..maxnet] OF integer ;
    i,j,numnodes : integer ;

{ PROCEDURE push(VAR stackname : stackptr ; stackvalue : integer) ;    }
{ PROCEDURE pop(VAR stackname : stackptr ; VAR stackvalue : integer) ; }
{ From previous listing }

PROCEDURE denode(fromnode : integer) ;
{ Routine to delete the 'fromnode' from network. It must scan }
{ the linear list of nodes joined by an edge 'fromnode' 'tonode' }
{ and decrement their 'edgein' value by 1. }
VAR tonode : integer ;
BEGIN
   WHILE netlist[fromnode] < > NIL
   DO BEGIN
        pop(netlist[fromnode],tonode) ;
        edgein[tonode] := edgein[tonode]-1 ;
{ If this 'tonode' now has no edges entering it then it can }
{ be pushed onto the stack ready for writing. }
        IF edgein[tonode] = 0
        THEN push(entrystack,tonode)
      END
END ; { of denode }

PROCEDURE topologicalsort ;
{ Routine to calculate the topological order of a'network' of 'numnode'}
{ nodes. The 'i'th node has edges entering other nodes and these are }
{ stored in a list named 'netlist[i]'. }
```

```
{ 'edgein[j]' holds the number of edges entering node 'j' }
VAR i,node : integer ;
BEGIN
{ Any node with no edge entering it is 'stack'ed }
{ Initially 'stack' is empty. }
   entrystack := NIL ;
   FOR i := 1 TO numnodes
   DO IF edgein[i] = 0 THEN push(entrystack,i) ;
{ Deal with node stored on top of 'entrystack'. }
{ Loop through process to consider every node. }
   FOR i := 1 TO numnodes
   DO BEGIN
{ Remove 'node' on the top of 'entrystack' }
         IF entrystack = NIL
{ If stack is empty then there is an error }
         THEN BEGIN
                  write(' Error : loop in the network') ;
                  EXIT
               END
         ELSE BEGIN
{ write out 'nodevalue' }
                  pop(entrystack,node) ;
                  writeln(' Unstacking node:',node) ;
{ Call 'denode' to delete 'node' from the network. }
                  denode(node)
               END
      END
END ; { of topologicalsort }

BEGIN
{ Set up the network data structure }
   writeln(' type in number of nodes') ; readln(numnodes) ;
   FOR i := 1 TO numnodes
   DO BEGIN
         edgein[i] := 0 ; netlist[i] := NIL
      END ;
{ Read in edge information : node 'i' to node 'j' }
{ Process ends when 'i=j' }
   writeln(' type in edges') ; readln(i,j) ;
   WHILE (i < > j)
   DO BEGIN
         edgein[j] := edgein[j] + 1 ; push(netlist[i],j) ;
         readln(i,j) ;
      END ;
   writeln(' Topological order of network is') ;
   topologicalsort
END. { of PROGRAM networkexample }
```

Trees

The last structure we consider in this chapter is a tree of integers, or more specifically a *binary tree*. A binary tree is a special form of network in which there is a unique node called the *root* with no edges entering it. All other nodes

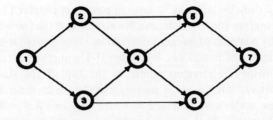

Figure 2.5

Node number	edgein	netlist
7	2	
6	2	
5	2	
4	2	
3	1	
2	1	
1	0	

Figure 2.6

have just one edge entering, and at most two edges leaving. A node may be considered to hold an integer information part, with two pointers (perhaps null) referring to two *subtrees*, one to the left, and one to the right of the node. The values stored on the nodes can be used to introduce a *left-right ordering* on each node value, by insisting that all the node values in the left subtree are less than the value on the node, and all values in the right subtree are greater than that on the node. See figure 2.7.

There are a number of different ways of implementing tree in Pascal. Which you choose really depends on the complexity of the tree manipulation you require. See Knuth (1973). You can

(i) add a node to a tree
(ii) delete a node
(iii) copy a tree
(iv) *balance* it
(v) print out the tree in various orders

     preorder, inorder, postorder

and many more operations.

Since we will only be referring to trees in passing in chapter 17, we include a simple implementation for completeness. We assume that the tree will be ordered, and is created by a stream of integer information. Once created it is used only as a storage structure and it will not be changed! The method is to use an array stack **treelist** listing 2.5. **treetop** points to the top of the stack. Trees are inherently recursive, but we use a non-recursive stack in order to implement these ideas. New nodes can be added to a tree only as a *leaf* – that is, a node with no edges leaving it. Each time a new node is created its required position is found using the left-right ordering. A variable pointer **nodeindex** will move left or right through the edges of the tree until it finds a null pointer: this null pointer is replaced by a pointer to the new node. To create a new node, three locations are taken from the top of the stack: one for the integer information and two for the (initially null) edge pointers. Figure 2.7 shows the data structure diagram of the tree created by listing 2.5, and figure 2.8 shows the equivalent array diagram. For a Pascal implementation of trees see Wilson and Addyman (1982).

Listing 2.5

```
PROGRAM tree_example(input,output,indata) ;
{ An example to demonstrate a binary tree using arrays }
VAR treelist : ARRAY[1..100] OF integer ;
    treetop,i,value : integer ;
    indata : text ;

    PROCEDURE leaf(leafvalue,nodeindex : integer ) ;
{ add a new leaf at the top of the 'treelist' array   point at these }
{ three new locations with 'treelist[nodeindex]' }
    BEGIN
        IF treetop < >0 THEN treelist[nodeindex] := treetop+1 ;
        treelist[treetop+1] := leafvalue ;
        treelist[treetop+2] := 0 ;
        treelist[treetop+3] := 0 ;
        treetop := treetop+3
    END ; { of leaf }

    PROCEDURE extend(leafvalue : integer ) ;
{ extend tree with 'leafvalue', maintaining left/right order }
    VAR nodeindex : integer ;
    BEGIN
{ Add new root to an empty tree }
        IF treetop=0
        THEN leaf(leafvalue,1)
        ELSE BEGIN
{ tree is not empty }
                nodeindex := 1 ;
                REPEAT
                    IF i < treelist[nodeindex]
{ If 'leafvalue' is less than value on node with given index then }
{ extend subtree to the left. If subtree is empty then add new leaf }
```

```
                    THEN BEGIN
                              IF treelist[nodeindex+1] = 0
                              THEN BEGIN
                                        leaf(leafvalue,nodeindex+1) ;
                                        nodeindex := 0
                              END
                              ELSE nodeindex := treelist[nodeindex+1]
                    END
{ If 'leafvalue' is less than value on node with given index then }
{ extend subtree to the left. If subtree is empty then add new leaf }
                    ELSE BEGIN
                              IF treelist[nodeindex+2] = 0
                              THEN BEGIN
                                        leaf(leafvalue,nodeindex+2) ;
                                        nodeindex := 0
                              END
                              ELSE nodeindex := treelist[nodeindex+2]
                    END
              UNTIL nodeindex=0
         END
   END ; { of extend }
BEGIN
{ Prepare the array which will hold the binary tree }
   FOR i := 1 TO 100
   DO treelist[i] := 0 ;
   assign(indata,'treedata.dat') ; reset(indata) ;
{ File 'treedata.dat' contains : 6  1  8  3  7  2  4  5  9 }
{ Binary tree is originally empty, extend with these 9 values }
   treetop := 0 ;
   FOR i := 1 TO 9
   DO BEGIN
         read(indata,value) ; extend(value)
      END ;
{ Write out first thirty elements of the array }
   FOR i := 1 TO 30
   DO writeln(' index:',i:3,'  array value:',treelist[i]:2 )
END. { of PROGRAM tree_example }
```

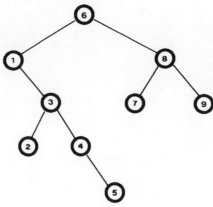

Figure 2.7

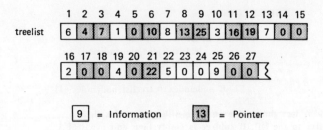

Figure 2.8

Exercise 2.2

Implement various output procedures for a tree constructed in the above manner.

3 An Introduction to Two-dimensional Co-ordinate Geometry

The underlying mathematical theory is important in any branch of computer programming but particularly so in graphics. The majority of techniques presented in this book rely entirely upon a solid background of co-ordinate and vector geometry and it is imperative that the reader gains some grounding in the methods involved before progressing to the later applications.

We work with the x–y rectangular Cartesian co-ordinate system introduced in chapter 1; the positive x-axis is horizontal and to the right of the co-ordinate origin, and the positive y-axis is vertical and above the origin. A typical point in this system is represented by the *co-ordinate pair* (x, y). The two values x and y are the perpendicular projections of the points on the respective axes. This is also sometimes called a *vector pair*, or *point vector*, and may be given in vector notation $p \equiv (x, y)$. Note that $\equiv$ means 'equivalent to'.

We start with straight lines. Of course a line or, more specifically, a general point (x, y) on a line, may be represented in the familiar form of a linear equation

$$y = mx + c$$

which is better expressed as

$$ay = bx + c$$

where b/a is the tangent of the angle that the line makes with the positive x-axis (called the *gradient*, or *slope*, of the line), and c/a (if finite) is the intercept of the line with the y-axis (see figure 3.1). If c/a is infinite (that is, if $a = 0$) then the line is parallel to the y-axis and so has infinite slope.

Before introducing a second way of representing a line (which, as we shall see, is more useful in computer graphics) two operations on vectors, scalar multiple and addition, must be defined along with the magnitude or modulus of a vector. Suppose we have two vectors $p_1 \equiv (x_1, y_1)$ and $p_2 \equiv (x_2, y_2)$, multiplying the individual components of the vector p_1 by a scalar real value k gives the *scalar multiple*

$$kp_1 \equiv (k \times x_1, k \times y_1)$$

while adding the x components together and the y components together gives the vector

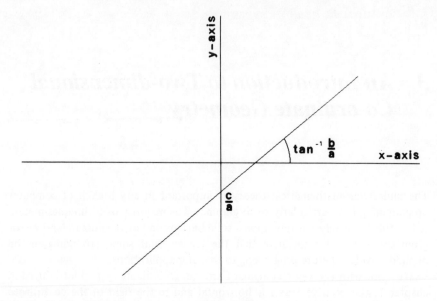

Figure 3.1

$$p_1 + p_2 \equiv (x_1 + x_2, y_1 + y_2)$$

by *vector addition*.

The *modulus* of a vector p_1 is defined as the distance of the point (x_1, y_1) from the origin, denoted $|p_1|$

$$|p_1| \equiv \sqrt{(x_1{}^2 + y_1{}^2)}$$

To define a line we choose any two fixed points on the line which we again call $p_1 \equiv (x_1, y_1)$ and $p_2 \equiv (x_2, y_2)$. The general point $p(\mu) \equiv (x, y)$ on the line is given by the vector combination

$$(1 - \mu)p_1 + \mu p_2$$

for some real μ. This is the vector pair

$$((1 - \mu)x_1 + \mu x_2, (1 - \mu)y_1 + \mu y_2)$$

We place the μ in brackets after p to show the dependence of the vector on the value of μ. Later, when the relationship is more fully understood, the (μ) will be omitted. If $0 \leqslant \mu \leqslant 1$ then $p(\mu)$ lies on the line somewhere between p_1 and p_2. For any specified point $p(\mu)$, the value of μ is given by the ratio

$$\mu = \frac{\text{distance of } p(\mu) \text{ from } p_1}{\text{distance of } p_2 \text{ from } p_1}$$

where the measure of distance is positive if $p(\mu)$ is on the same side of p_1 as p_2, and negative if on the other side.

The (positive) distance between any two vector points p_1 and p_2 is given by (Pythagoras)

$$|p_2 - p_1| \equiv \sqrt{\{(x_1 - x_2)^2 + (y_1 - y_2)^2\}}$$

Figure 3.2 shows a line segment between points $(-3, -1) = p(0)$ and $(3, 2) = p(1)$: the point $(1, 1)$ lies on the line as $p(2/3)$. Note that $(3, 2)$ is at a distance $3\sqrt{5}$ away from $(-3, -1)$ whereas $(1, 1)$ is $2\sqrt{5}$ away. From now the (μ) is omitted from the point vector representation.

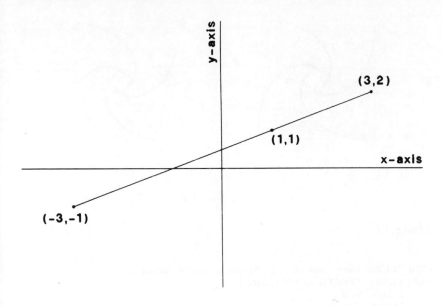

Figure 3.2

Example 3.1
This idea is further illustrated by drawing the pattern shown in figure 3.3a. At first sight it looks complicated, but on closer inspection it is seen to be simply a square, outside a square, outside a square etc. The squares are getting successively smaller and they are rotating through a constant angle. In order to draw the diagram, a technique is needed which, when given a general square, draws a smaller internal square rotated through this fixed angle. Suppose the general square has corners $\{(x_i, y_i) | i = 1, 2, 3, 4\}$ and the ith side of the square is the line joining (x_i, y_i) to (x_{i+1}, y_{i+1}) — assuming additions of subscripts are modulo 4 — that is, $4 + 1 \equiv 1$. A general point on this side of the square, (x_i', y_i'), is given by

$$((1 - \mu) \times x_i + \mu \times x_{i+1}, (1 - \mu) \times y_i + \mu \times y_{i+1}) \text{ where } 0 \leqslant \mu \leqslant 1$$

In fact $\mu : 1 - \mu$ is the ratio in which the side is cut by this point. If μ is fixed and the four points $\{(x_i', y_i') | i = 1, 2, 3, 4\}$ are calculated in the above manner, then the sides of the new square make an angle

$$\alpha = \tan^{-1} [\mu/(1 - \mu)]$$

with the corresponding side of the outer square. So by keeping μ fixed for each new square, the angle between consecutive squares remains constant at α. In figure 3.3a, generated by routine **draw_a_picture** given in listing 3.1 merged with listings 1.1 and 1.3, there are 21 squares and $\mu = 0.1$.

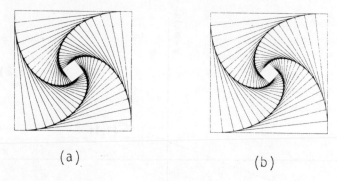

(a)   (b)

Figure 3.3

Listing 3.1

```
PROCEDURE draw_a_picture ;   {  Square in Square pattern }
VAR   pt,ptd : ARRAY[1..4] OF vector2 ;
      mu,um : real ;
      i,j,nextj : integer ;
BEGIN
{ Initialise the first square }
   pt[1].x :=  1.0 ; pt[1].y :=  1.0 ;
   pt[2].x :=  1.0 ; pt[2].y := -1.0 ;
   pt[3].x := -1.0 ; pt[3].y := -1.0 ;
   pt[4].x := -1.0 ; pt[4].y :=  1.0 ;
{ Set up window }
   start(4.0) ;
{ Set 'mu' value and produce 20 squares }
   mu := 0.1 ; um := 1.0-mu ;
   FOR i := 1 TO 21
   DO BEGIN
         moveto(pt[4]) ;
{ Draw the square and calculate the co-ordinates of the next square }
         FOR j := 1 TO 4
         DO BEGIN
               lineto(pt[j]) ;
               nextj := (j MOD 4)+1 ;
               ptd[j].x := um*pt[j].x+mu*pt[nextj].x ;
               ptd[j].y := um*pt[j].y+mu*pt[nextj].y
```

```
        END ;
{ Reset square co-ordinates }
        FOR j := 1 TO 4
        DO pt[j] := ptd[j]
        END
END ;  { of draw_a_picture }
```

There is an unsatisfactory feature of the pattern in figure 3.3a: the inside of the pattern is 'untidy', the sides of the innermost square being neither parallel to nor at $\pi/4$ radians to the corresponding side of the outermost square. This is corrected simply by changing the value of μ so as to produce the required relationship between the innermost and outermost squares. As was previously noted, with the calculation of each new inner square, the corresponding sides are rotated through an angle of $\tan^{-1}[\mu/(1 - \mu)]$ radians. After $n + 1$ squares are drawn, the inner square is rotated by $n \times \tan^{-1}[\mu/(1 - \mu)]$ radians relative to the outer square. For a satisfactory diagram this angle must be an integer multiple of $\pi/4$. That is, $n \times \tan^{-1}[\mu/(1 - \mu)] = t(\pi/4)$ for some integer t, and hence

$$\mu = \frac{\tan[t(\pi/4n)]}{\tan[t(\pi/4n)] + 1}$$

To produce figure 3.3b, $n = 20$ and $t = 3$ are chosen, making μ approximately 0.08.

It is useful to note that the vector combination form of a line can be reorganised

$$p_1 + \mu(p_2 - p_1)$$

When given in this new representation the vector p_1 may be called a *base vector*, and $(p_2 - p_1)$ called the *direction vector*. In fact any point on the line can stand as a base vector, it simply acts as a point to anchor a line which is parallel to the direction vector. This concept of a vector acting as a direction needs some further explanation. It has already been noted that a vector pair, (x, y) say, may represent a point; a line joining the co-ordinate origin to this point may be thought of as specifying a direction — any line in space which is parallel to this line is defined to have the same direction vector. A line that goes from the origin O towards (x, y) has the so-called *positive sense*; a line from (x, y) towards the origin has *negative sense*.

The linear equation and vector forms of a line are, of course, related. It was mentioned earlier that the line $ay = bx + c$ had slope b/a. This means, in fact, that the line has direction vector (a, b). Thus given any point on the line, (x_1, y_1) say, we may derive its vector representation

$$(x_1, y_1) + \mu(a, b)$$

Conversely, if a line has vector form $b + \mu d$ (where $b \equiv (b_x, b_y)$ and $d \equiv (d_x, d_y)$) then it has slope d_y/d_x and hence analytic (or functional) form

$$d_x \times y = d_y \times x + c' \text{ for some } c'$$

The value of c' can be determined by inserting the co-ordinates of any point on the line into the above equation; in particular we may use (b_x, b_y)

$$d_x \times b_y = d_y \times b_x + c'$$

so

$$c' = d_x \times b_y - d_y \times b_x$$

and this gives the equation

$$d_x \times y = d_y \times x + d_x \times b_y - d_y \times b_x$$

This method can be used to obtain the equation of a line joining two given points $p_1 \equiv (x_1, y_1)$ and $p_2 \equiv (x_2, y_2)$. We know that the line has direction vector $(p_2 - p_1) \equiv (x_2 - x_1, y_2 - y_1)$ and that it passes through p_1 so we may substitute these values into the above equation

$$(x_2 - x_1) \times y = (y_2 - y_1) \times x + (x_2 - x_1) \times y_1 - (y_2 - y_1) \times x_1$$

which gives

$$(x_2 - x_1) \times (y - y_1) - (y_2 - y_1) \times (x - x_1) = 0$$

The Intersection of Two Lines

This base and direction representation is also very useful for calculating the point of intersection of two lines, a problem that frequently crops up in two-dimensional graphics. Suppose there are two lines $p + \mu q$ and $r + \lambda s$, where $p = (x_1, y_1)$, $q = (x_2, y_2)$, $r = (x_3, y_3)$ and $s = (x_4, y_4)$ for $-\infty < \mu, \lambda < \infty$. These lines will intersect either at no point (if they are parallel and non-identical), an infinity of points (if they are identical) or at a unique point. Should such a unique point exist, it is defined by values of μ and λ satisfying the vector equation

$$p + \mu q = r + \lambda s$$

that is, a point which is common to both lines. This vector equation can be written as two separate equations

$$x_1 + \mu \times x_2 = x_3 + \lambda \times x_4 \tag{3.1}$$
$$y_1 + \mu \times y_2 = y_3 + \lambda \times y_4 \tag{3.2}$$

Rewriting these equations

$$\mu \times x_2 - \lambda \times x_4 = x_3 - x_1 \tag{3.3}$$
$$\mu \times y_2 - \lambda \times y_4 = y_3 - y_1 \tag{3.4}$$

Multiplying (3.3) by y_4, (3.4) by x_4 and subtracting

$$\mu \times (x_2 \times y_4 - y_2 \times x_4) = (x_3 - x_1) \times y_4 - (y_3 - y_1) \times x_4$$

If $(x_2 \times y_4 - y_2 \times x_4) = 0$ then the lines are parallel and there is no point of intersection (μ does not exist), otherwise

$$\mu = \frac{(x_3 - x_1) \times y_4 - (y_3 - y_1) \times x_4}{(x_2 \times y_4 - y_2 \times x_4)} \tag{3.5}$$

and similarly

$$\lambda = \frac{(x_3 - x_1) \times y_2 - (y_3 - y_1) \times x_2}{(x_2 \times y_4 - y_2 \times x_4)} \tag{3.6}$$

The solution becomes even simpler if one of the lines is parallel to a co-ordinate axis. Suppose this line is $x = d$, then $r = (d, 0)$ and $s = (0, 1)$, which when substituted in equation (3.5) gives

$$\mu = (d - x_1)/x_2$$

and similarly if the line is $y = d$

$$\mu = (d - y_1)/y_2$$

Substituting the value of μ (or λ) thus found into $p + \mu q$ (or $r + \lambda s$) yields the point of intersection.

Example 3.2
Find the point of intersection of the two infinite lines (a) joining $(1, -1)$ to $(-1, -3)$ and (b) joining $(1, 2)$ to $(3, -2)$.

The lines may be written:

$$(1 - \mu)(1, -1) + \mu(-1, -3) \quad -\infty < \mu < \infty \tag{3.7}$$
$$(1 - \lambda)(1, 2) + \lambda(3, -2) \quad -\infty < \lambda < \infty \tag{3.8}$$

or when placed in the base/direction vector form

$$(1, -1) + \mu(-2, -2) \tag{3.9}$$
$$(1, 2) + \lambda(2, -4) \tag{3.10}$$

Substituting these values in equation (3.5) gives

$$\mu = \frac{(1 - 1) \times -4 - (2 + 1) \times 2}{(-2 \times -4 - (-2) \times 2)} = -0.5$$

whence the point of intersection is

$$(1, -1) - 0.5(-2, -2) = (2, 0)$$

The general case is solved by the procedure ill2 shown in listing 3.2.

Listing 3.2

```
PROCEDURE ill2(v1,v2,v3,v4:vector2 ; VAR v:vector2 ; VAR flag:boolean ) ;
VAR mu,delta : real ;
BEGIN
{ Finds the point vector of intersection, 'v', of two lines. }
{ 'v1 + mu.v2' and 'v3 + lambda.v4' }
{ flag is returned as true if an intersection exists, else false }
     delta := v2.x*v4.y-v2.y*v4.x ;
{ If 'delta' is zero then the lines are parallel : no intersection }
     IF abs(delta) < epsilon
     THEN flag := false
     ELSE BEGIN
               flag := true ;
{ Find 'mu' value for (v.x,v.y) on first line }
             mu := ((v3.x-v1.x)*v4.y-(v3.y-v1.y)*v4.x)/delta ;
{ Calculate x and y co-ordinates of 'v' }
             v.x := v1.x+mu*v2.x ; v.y := v1.y+mu*v2.y
          END
END ; { of ill2 }
```

You can experiment by creating your own exercises.

Direction Vectors

Returning to the use of a vector ($d \equiv (x, y) \neq (0, 0)$, say) representing a direction. (Note that any positive scalar multiple kd, for $k > 0$, represents the same direction and sense as d, and if k is negative then the direction has its sense inverted.) In particular, setting $k = 1/|d|$ produces a vector ($x/\sqrt{(x^2 + y^2)}$, $y/\sqrt{(x^2 + y^2)}$)) with unit modulus.

A general point on a line, $p + \mu d$, is a distance $|\mu d|$ from the base point p, and if $|d| = 1$ (d is a *unit vector*) then the point is a distance $|\mu|$ from p.

Now consider the angles made by direction vectors with various fixed directions. Suppose that θ is the angle between the line joining O (the origin) to $d = (x, y)$, and the positive x-axis measured anti-clockwise from the positive x-axis. Then $x = |d| \times \cos \theta$ and $y = |d| \times \sin \theta$ − see figure 3.4.

If d is a unit vector (that is, if $|d| = 1$) then $d = (\cos \theta, \sin \theta)$. Note that $\sin \theta = \cos (\theta - \pi/2)$ for all values of θ. Thus d may be rewritten as $(\cos \theta, \cos(\theta - \pi/2))$. But $\theta - \pi/2$ is the angle that the vector makes with the positive y-axis. Hence the co-ordinates of a unit direction vector are called its *direction cosines*, since they are the cosines of the angle that the vector makes with the corresponding positive axes.

Before continuing, let us take a brief look at the trigonometric functions available in Pascal. The two functions sin and cos return the sine and cosine

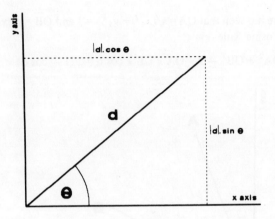

Figure 3.4

respectively of an angle (in radians) provided as a parameter. The values of sin and cos lie, of course, between -1 and 1. Pascal also includes the inverse of the tangent function, arctan, which returns an angle whose tangent is equal to the given real parameter. The angle returned lies within a principal range between $-\pi/2$ and $\pi/2$.

A necessity often arises, however, to find the angle that a general direction $d = (x, y)$ makes with the positive x-axis, and this angle must not be restricted to a principal range but must be able to take any value between 0 and 2π. This problem is solved by the function angle (listing 3.3) which will be used extensively in the chapters dealing with three dimensions and should be located as indicated in listing 1.3.

Listing 3.3

```
FUNCTION angle(x,y : real) : real ;
{ Returns the 'angle' whose tangent is 'y/x' }
{ All anomalies such as 'x=0' are also checked }
BEGIN
   IF abs(x) < epsilon
   THEN IF abs(y) < epsilon
            THEN angle := 0.0
            ELSE IF y > 0.0
                     THEN angle := pi*0.5
                     ELSE angle := pi*1.5
   ELSE IF x < 0.0
            THEN angle := arctan(y/x) + pi
            ELSE angle := arctan(y/x)
END ; { of angle }
```

Now suppose there are two direction vectors $A \equiv (x_1, y_1)$ and $B \equiv (x_2, y_2)$ – for simplicity both are assumed to be unit vectors and to pass through the origin (see figure 3.5). The acute angle, α, between these lines is required.

From the figure it is seen that $OA = \sqrt{(x_1{}^2 + y_1{}^2)} = 1$ and $OB = \sqrt{(x_2{}^2 + y_2{}^2)} = 1$. So by the Cosine Rule

$$AB^2 = OA^2 + OB^2 - 2 \times OA \times OB \times \cos \alpha = 2(1 - \cos \alpha)$$

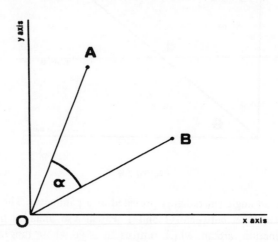

Figure 3.5

But also, by Pythagoras

$$
\begin{aligned}
AB^2 &= (x_1 - x_2)^2 + (y_1 - y_2)^2 \\
&= (x_1{}^2 + y_1{}^2) + (x_2{}^2 + y_2{}^2) - 2(x_1 \times x_2 + y_1 \times y_2) \\
&= 2 - 2(x_1 \times x_2 + y_1 \times y_2)
\end{aligned}
$$

Thus $(x_1 \times x_2 + y_1 \times y_2) = \cos \alpha$. It is possible that $x_1 \times x_2 + y_1 \times y_2$ is negative, in which case $\cos^{-1}(x_1 \times x_2 + y_1 \times y_2)$ is obtuse and the required acute angle is $\pi - \alpha$. Since $\cos(\pi - \alpha) = -\cos \alpha$, the acute angle is given immediately by $\cos^{-1}(|x_1 \times x_2 + y_1 \times y_2|)$. For example, given the two lines with direction cosines $(\sqrt{3}/2, 1/2)$ and $(-1/2, -\sqrt{3}/2)$, then $x_1 \times x_2 + y_1 \times y_2 = -\sqrt{3}/2$ and thus $\alpha = \cos^{-1}(\sqrt{3}/2) = \pi/6$. This simple example was given in order to introduce the *scalar product* (or *dot product*, denoted by $\cdot$) of two vectors: $(a, b) \cdot (c, d) = a \times c + b \times d$. Scalar product is extendable into higher-dimensional space (see chapter 6 for a three-dimensional example) and it always has the property that it gives the cosine of the angle between any pair of lines with directions defined by the two (unit) vectors.

Now suppose that we have a direction vector $d \equiv (d_x, d_y)$. We know that any line parallel to d can be described by direction vector λd for some $\lambda \neq 0$, but we may also determine the direction vector of any line perpendicular to d.

Using the scalar product defined above, we know that any vector $s \equiv (s_x, s_y)$, perpendicular to d, must satisfy $s \cdot d = 0$, since the cosine of the angle between the two vectors is zero. That is

$$(s_x, s_y) \cdot (d_x, d_y) = 0$$

so

$$s_x \times d_x + s_y \times d_y = 0$$

which gives

$$s_x/d_y = -s_y/d_x = \mu \text{ say.}$$

Thus

$$s_x = -\mu d_y \quad \text{and} \quad s_y = \mu d_x$$

so

$$s \equiv \mu(-d_y, d_x)$$

But since μs is parallel to s for all $\mu \neq 0$ we may take $s \equiv (-d_y, d_x)$ to be the direction vector of any line perpendicular to d. If (d_x, d_y) is a unit vector then the perpendicular $(-d_y, d_x)$ is also a unit vector.

This method may also be used to find a perpendicular to a line given in linear equation form. Since $ay = bx + c$ has direction vector (a, b), a perpendicular line has direction vector $(-b, a)$ which has equation

$$-by = ax + c' \quad \text{for some } c'$$

The value of c' does not affect the direction of the line so every value of c' gives a line perpendicular to $ay = bx + c$.

Curves: Analytic (Functional) Representation and Parametric Forms

A curve in two-dimensional space can be considered as a relationship between x and y co-ordinate values, the *analytic form*, or, alternatively the co-ordinates can be individually specified in terms of other variables or parameters, the *parametric form*. We use the term 'analytic', as opposed to the equivalent word 'functional', to avoid any possible confusion with Functional Programming.

It has already been seen that a line may be expressed as $ay = bx + c$. If the equation is rearranged so that one side is zero — that is, $ay - bx - c = 0$, then the algebraic expression on the left-hand side of the equation which relates the x and y values is called a *analytic representation* of the line and is written as a function definition

$$f(x, y) \equiv ay - bx - c$$

All, and only, those points with the property $f(x, y) = 0$ lie on the straight line (which is a special form of curve). This representation divides all the points in two-dimensional space into three sets: the *zero set*, with $f(x, y) = 0$; the *positive set*, with $f(x, y) > 0$ and the *negative set* with $f(x, y) < 0$. This is true for all curves with given analytic representation $f(x, y)$. If the function divides space into the curve and two other *connected areas* only (that is, any two points in a connected area may be joined by a finite curvilinear line which does not cross the curve), then these areas may be identified with the positive and negative sets defined by f. However, be wary, there are many elementary functions (such as $g(x, y) \equiv \cos(y) - \sin(x)$) which define not one but a series of curves and hence divide space into possibly an infinite number of connected areas (note $g(x, y) = g(x + 2m\pi, y + 2n\pi)$ for all integers m and n), so it is possible that two disconnected areas can both belong to the positive (or negative) set.

Note that the analytic representation need not be unique. For example, a line can be put in an equivalent form

$$f'(x, y) \equiv bx + c - ay$$

for which the positive set corresponds to the negative set of the original, and vice versa.

The case where the curve does divide space into two connected areas is very useful in computer graphics, as will be seen in the study of two-dimensional and (especially) three-dimensional graphics algorithms. Take the straight line for example

$$f(x, y) \equiv ay - bx - c$$

A point (x_1, y_1) is on the same side of the line as (x_2, y_2) if and only if $f(x_1, y_1)$ has the same non-zero sign as $f(x_2, y_2)$. The analytic representation tells more about a point (x_1, y_1) than just on which side of a line it lies — it also enables the distance of the point from the line to be calculated.

Consider the line defined above. Its direction vector is (a, b). A line perpendicular to this will have direction vector $(-b, a)$ so the point q on the line closest to the point $p = (x_1, y_1)$ is of the form

$$q = (x_1, y_1) + \mu(-b, a)$$

that is, a new line joining p to q is perpendicular to the original line. Since q lies on this original line

$$f(q) = f((x_1, y_1) + \mu(-b, a)) = 0$$

that is

$$f(x_1 - \mu b, y_1 + \mu a) = a \times (y_1 + \mu a) - b \times (x_1 - \mu b) - c$$
$$= f(x_1, y_1) + \mu(a^2 + b^2) = 0$$

Hence $\mu = -f(x_1, y_1)/(a^2 + b^2)$.

The point q is a distance $|\mu(-b, a)| = |\mu|\sqrt{(a^2 + b^2)}$ from (x_1, y_1) which naturally means that the distance of (x_1, y_1) from the line is given by $|-f(x_1, y_1)/\sqrt{(a^2 + b^2)}|$. The sign of the value of $-f(x_1, y_1)$ denotes the side of the line on which the point lies. If $a^2 + b^2 = 1$ then $|f(x_1, y_1)|$ gives the distance of the point (x_1, y_1) from the line.

We may use these ideas in the consideration of *convex* areas (an area is convex if it totally contains a straight line segment joining any two points lying inside it). More specifically, we consider only convex *polygons*, but any convex area may be approximated by a polygon, provided that the polygon has enough sides.

Consider the convex polygon with n vertices $\{p_i \equiv (x_i, y_i) | i = 1, 2, \ldots, n$ taken in order around the polygon (either clockwise or anti-clockwise). Such description of a convex polygon is called an *oriented convex set of vertices*. The problem of finding whether such a set is clockwise or anti-clockwise is considered in chapter 5. The n boundary edges of the polygon are segments of the lines

$$f_i(x, y) \equiv (x_{i+1} - x_i) \times (y - y_i) - (y_{i+1} - y_i) \times (x - x_i)$$

where $i = 1, \ldots, n$, and the addition in the subscripts is modulo n (that is $n + j \equiv j$ for $1 \leqslant j \leqslant n$).

The analytic representation of a given line segment, say the one joining p_i to p_{i+1} for some i, is calculated in the above way in order to take advantage of an interesting property of this formulation. If you imagine yourself astride the line looking from p_i towards p_{i+1} then the positive side of the line is to the left and the negative side to the right.

If the vertices of a convex polygon are oriented anti-clockwise, then the inside of the polygon is classified by the set

$$\{(x, y) | f_i(x, y) > 0 \text{ for all } i, \quad 1 \leqslant i \leqslant n\}$$

A point on the boundary is given by

$$\{(x, y) | f_i(x, y) \geqslant 0 \text{ for all } i, \quad 1 \leqslant i \leqslant n$$
$$\text{and there is at least one } i \text{ such that } f_i(x, y) = 0\}$$

The outside of the polygon is defined by

$$\{(x, y) | f_i(x, y) < 0 \text{ for at least one } i, \quad 1 \leqslant i \leqslant n\}$$

This technique of 'inside and outside' is fundamental to the calculation of the intersection of two polygons in chapter 5 and the hidden surface algorithms of later chapters.

Example 3.3

Consider the convex polygon with vertices $(1, 0)$, $(5, 2)$, $(4, 4)$ and $(-2, 1)$: see figure 3.6. In this order the vertices obviously have an anti-clockwise orientation. Are the points $(3, 2)$, $(1, 4)$, $(3, 1)$ inside, outside or on the boundary of the polygon? What is the distance of $(4, 4)$ from the first line?

$$f_1(x, y) \equiv (5 - 1) \times (y - 0) - (2 - 0) \times (x - 1) \equiv 4y - 2x + 2$$
$$f_2(x, y) \equiv (4 - 5) \times (y - 2) - (4 - 2) \times (x - 5) \equiv -y - 2x + 12$$
$$f_2(x, y) \equiv (-2 - 4) \times (y - 4) - (1 - 4) \times (x - 4) \equiv -6y + 3x + 12$$
$$f_4(x, y) \equiv (1 + 2) \times (y - 1) - (0 - 1) \times (x + 2) \equiv 3y + x - 1$$

Hence point $(3, 2)$ is inside the body because $f_1(3, 2) = 4, f_2(3, 2) = 4, f_3(3, 2) = 9$ and $f_4(3, 2) = 8$: all have positive signs.

Point $(1, 4)$ is outside the body because $f_3(1, 4) = -9$ (negative).

Point $(3, 1)$ is on the boundary because $f_1(3, 1) = 0$, and the values $f_2(3, 1) = 5$, $f_3(3, 1) = 15$ and $f_4(3, 1) = 5$ are all positive.

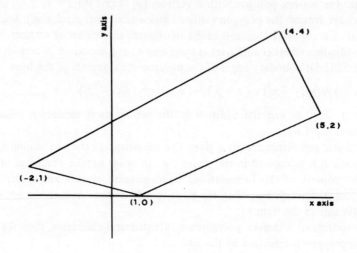

Figure 3.6

$(4, 4)$ is at a distance $f_1(4, 4)/\sqrt{(4^2 + 2^2)}$ $(= 10/\sqrt{20} = \sqrt{5})$ from the first line.

Having dealt with the analytic representation of a line, what about the parametric form? It was noted above that this form is one where the x and y coordinates of a general point on the curve are given in terms of parameter(s) (which could be the x or y values themselves), together with a range for the parameter. A parametric form of a line has already been considered, it is simply the base and direction representation

$$b + \mu d \equiv (x_1, y_1) + \mu(x_2, y_2)$$
$$\equiv (x_1 + \mu \times x_2, y_1 + \mu \times y_2) \text{ where } -\infty < \mu < \infty$$

μ is the parameter, and $x_1 + \mu \times x_2$ and $y_1 + \mu \times y_2$ are the respective x and y values which depend only on variable μ.

Analytic representations and parametric forms can be produced for most well-behaved curves. For example, a sine curve is given by $f(x, y) \equiv y - \sin(x)$ in analytic representation, and by $(x, \sin(x))$ with $-\infty < x < \infty$ in its parametric form. The general conic section (ellipse, parabola and hyperbola) is represented by the general function

$$f(x, y) \equiv a \times x^2 + b \times y^2 + h \times x \times y + f \times x + g \times y + c$$

Coefficients a, b, c, f, g, h uniquely identify a curve. A circle centred at the origin of radius r has $a = b = -1, f = g = h = 0$ and $c = r^2$, whence $f(x,y) \equiv r^2 - x^2 - y^2$. All the points (x, y) on the circle are such that $f(x, y) = 0$, the inside of the circle has $f(x, y) > 0$, and the outside of the circle $f(x,y) < 0$. The parametric form of this circle is $(r \cos \alpha, r \sin \alpha)$ where $0 \leqslant \alpha < 2\pi$. (The parametric forms of a circle, ellipse and spiral were met in chapter 1.)

These concepts are very useful in the study of graphics and experimenting with them now will prove to be of great value later. There will be many occasions when such ideas must be used in the solution of problems including, of course, the generation of co-ordinate data for diagrams and model scenes.

Example 3.4
Draw figure 3.7. A circular ball (radius r) disappears down an elliptical hole (major axis a, minor axis b). Parts of both the ellipse and circle may be obscured.

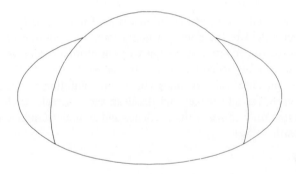

Figure 3.7

Let the ellipse be centred on the origin with the major axis horizontal, and the centre of the circle a distance d vertically above the origin. The ellipse has analytic representation

$$f_e(x, y) \equiv x^2/a^2 + y^2/b^2 - 1$$

and in parametric form $(a \times \cos \alpha, b \times \sin \alpha)$ with $0 \leqslant \alpha < 2\pi$. For the circle

$$f_c(x, y) \equiv x^2 + (y - d)^2 - r^2 \text{ and in parametric form}$$
$$(r \times \cos \beta, d + r \times \sin \beta) \text{ where } 0 \leqslant \beta < 2\pi.$$

In order to generate the picture, the points (x, y) common to the circle and ellipse (if any) must be calculated. As a useful demonstration the representations are mixed in the search for a solution, using the analytic representation for the circle and the parametric form of the ellipse. The problem is to find points $(x, y) = (a \times \cos \alpha, b \times \sin \alpha)$ on the ellipse, which also satisfy $f_c(x, y) = 0$. That is

$$a^2 \times \cos^2\alpha + (b \times \sin \alpha - d)^2 - r^2 = 0$$

or, expanding the expression

$$a^2 \times \cos^2\alpha + b^2 \times \sin^2\alpha - 2 \times b \times d \times \sin \alpha + d^2 - r^2 = 0$$

and since $\cos^2 \alpha = 1 - \sin^2\alpha$

$$(b^2 - a^2) \times \sin^2 \alpha - 2 \times b \times d \times \sin \alpha + a^2 + d^2 - r^2 = 0$$

This is a simple quadratic equation in the unknown $\sin \alpha$, which is easily solved: the quadratic equation $Ax^2 + Bx + C = 0$ has two roots

$$\frac{-B \pm \sqrt{(B^2 - 4 \times A \times C)}}{2 \times A}$$

For each value of $\sin \alpha$ it is possible to find values for α with $0 \leqslant \alpha < 2\pi$ (if they exist) and then calculate the points of intersection $(a \times \cos \alpha, b \times \sin \alpha)$. Naturally, if a root of the equation is complex or has absolute value greater than 1, then no intersection occurs corresponding to that root.

There is no universal rule regarding which representation to use in any given situation — each has advantages and disadvantages. A feel for the method is required and that only comes with experience and an understanding of Euclidean geometry (Heath, 1956).

Exercise 3.1
Write a program that will draw figure 3.7.

4 Matrix Representation of Transformations in Two-dimensional Space

In all pictures drawn so far the co-ordinate origin, axes and scale of the window have been identified with the ABSOLUTE axes defined for two-dimensional space. This is not the general case. Usually we want the window to move around in space, not necessarily being anchored to this arbitrary but fixed co-ordinate system. We must, therefore, consider what happens to the definition of an object, be it a point, line or curve, when the co-ordinate system is changed. As we have seen in previous chapters, the drawing of any object in computer graphics may ultimately be considered in terms of specifying and joining groups of points, and so all that is necessary is to discover what happens to the co-ordinate representation of a point with a change of co-ordinate system.

For the purposes of representing two-dimensional or three-dimensional space there need only be three fundamental forms of co-ordinate system change. These are translation of origin, change of scale and rotation of axes; all other changes can be formulated as combinations of these three types. These changes are examples of *affine transformation*. On some devices these operations are available in hardware. We shall not assume this to be the case, however, and a full description of the techniques involved is given. The contents of this chapter may seem somewhat excessive for dealing with two-dimensional space, but the methods we introduce here in the conceptually simpler dimension will prove indispensable when dealing with three-dimensional space.

It will often be necessary to transform large numbers of points, and to do this efficiently the transformations are represented by matrices. Before looking at these transformations and their matrix representations, a brief reminder of the properties of matrices and column vectors is warranted. In fact only square matrices are required: so our attention may be restricted to 3×3 matrices (said 3 by 3) for the study of two-dimensional space (we will declare a TYPE matrix3x3 in listing 4.1 to hold such values), and later 4×4 matrices for considering three-dimensional space (TYPE matrix4x4). In the programs given in this book a matrix identifier is always given in upper-case characters. Such a 3×3 matrix (A say) is simply a group of real numbers placed in a block of 3 rows by 3 columns while a column vector (D say) is a group of numbers placed in a column of 3 rows thus

$$\begin{pmatrix} A_{11} & A_{12} & A_{13} \\ A_{21} & A_{22} & A_{23} \\ A_{31} & A_{32} & A_{33} \end{pmatrix} \text{ and } \begin{pmatrix} D_1 \\ D_2 \\ D_3 \end{pmatrix}$$

A general entry in the matrix is usually written A_{ij}, the first subscript denotes the ith row, and the second subscript the jth column (for example, A_{23} represents the value in the second row, third column). The entry in the column vector, D_i, denotes the value in the ith row. All these named entries will be explicitly replaced by numerical values. It is essential to realise that not only are the values of individual entries in a matrix or column vector significant, but also their positions within the structure are important. Naturally Pascal programs are written along a line (no subscripts or superscripts) and hence matrices and vectors are implemented as arrays and the subscript values appear inside round brackets following the array identifier. We declare all TYPEs and PROCEDUREs necessary for manipulating these matrices in listing 4.1. It should be merged into our program listing following function angle — see listing 1.3.

Matrices can be added. Matrix $C = A + B$, the sum of two matrices A and B, is defined by the general entry C_{ij} thus

$$C_{ij} = A_{ij} + B_{ij} \quad 1 \leqslant i, j \leqslant 3$$

Matrix A can be multiplied by a scalar k to form a new matrix B

$$B_{ij} = k \times A_{ij} \quad 1 \leqslant i, j \leqslant 3$$

Matrix A can be multiplied by a column vector D to produce another column vector E thus

$$E_i = A_{i1} \times D_1 + A_{i2} \times D_2 + A_{i3} \times D_3 = \Sigma A_{ik} \times D_k \quad \text{where } 1 \leqslant i \leqslant 3$$

The ith row element of the new column vector is the sum of the products of the corresponding elements of the ith row of the matrix with those in the column vector. Furthermore, the product (matrix) $C = A \times B$ of two matrices A and B may be calculated

$$C_{ij} = A_{i1} \times B_{1j} + A_{i2} \times B_{2j} + A_{i3} \times B_{3j} = \Sigma A_{ik} \times B_{kj} \quad \text{where } 1 \leqslant i, j \leqslant 3$$

The $(i, j)^{th}$ element of the product matrix is the sum of each element in the ith row of the first matrix multiplied by the corresponding element in the jth column of the second. The product of matrices is not necessarily *commutative* — that is, $A \times B$ need not be the same as $B \times A$. For example

$$\begin{pmatrix} 0 & 1 & 0 \\ 0 & 0 & 1 \\ 1 & 0 & 0 \end{pmatrix} \times \begin{pmatrix} 0 & 0 & 1 \\ 0 & 1 & 0 \\ 1 & 0 & 0 \end{pmatrix} = \begin{pmatrix} 0 & 1 & 0 \\ 1 & 0 & 0 \\ 0 & 0 & 1 \end{pmatrix}$$

but

$$\begin{pmatrix} 0 & 0 & 1 \\ 0 & 1 & 0 \\ 1 & 0 & 0 \end{pmatrix} \times \begin{pmatrix} 0 & 1 & 0 \\ 0 & 0 & 1 \\ 1 & 0 & 0 \end{pmatrix} = \begin{pmatrix} 1 & 0 & 0 \\ 0 & 0 & 1 \\ 0 & 1 & 0 \end{pmatrix}$$

Experiment with these ideas until you have enough confidence to use them in the theory that follows. For those who want more details about the theory of matrices, books by Finkbeiner (1978), and by Stroud (1982) are recommended.

There is a special matrix called the *identity matrix I* (sometimes called the *unit matrix*)

$$I = \begin{pmatrix} 1 & 0 & 0 \\ 0 & 1 & 0 \\ 0 & 0 & 1 \end{pmatrix}$$

Every square matrix A has a determinant $\det(A)$

$$\det(A) = A_{11} \times (A_{22} \times A_{33} - A_{23} \times A_{32}) + A_{12} \times (A_{23} \times A_{31} - A_{21} \times A_{33}) + A_{13} \times (A_{21} \times A_{32} - A_{22} \times A_{31})$$

Any matrix whose determinant is non-zero is called *non-singular*, and those with zero determinant are called *singular*. All non-singular matrices A have an *inverse* A^{-1}, which has the property that $A \times A^{-1} = I$ and $A^{-1} \times A = I$. For methods of calculating an inverse of a matrix see Finkbeiner (1978): a listing is given in chapter 6 (listing 6.8) which uses the Adjoint method.

Now consider the effects of a transformation of axes. Suppose a point **p** has co-ordinates (x, y) relative to an existing axis system and (x', y') relative to a set of axes obtained by a transformation of this system. The transformation is totally described if equations are given which relate the new co-ordinate values x' and y' to the values of x and y. An affine transformation is one which defines the new co-ordinate values in terms of linear combinations of the old — that is, the equations contain only multiples of x and y and additional real values: it includes neither non-unit powers, products or other functions of x and y, or other variables. Such equations may be written

$$x' = A_{11} \times x + A_{12} \times y + A_{13}$$
$$y' = A_{21} \times x + A_{22} \times y + A_{23}$$

The A values are called the coefficients of the equations. The result of the transformation is a combination of multiples of x values, y values and unity. Another equation may be added

$$1 = A_{31} \times x + A_{32} \times y + A_{33}$$

For this to be true for all values of x and y, it follows that $A_{31} = A_{32} = 0$ and $A_{33} = 1$. This may seem a rather contrived exercise, but it ensures that A is a square matrix and this will prove very useful. If each point vector (x, y) (alternatively called a *row vector* for obvious reasons) is set in the form of a three-rowed column vector

$$\begin{pmatrix} x \\ y \\ 1 \end{pmatrix}$$

then the above three equations can be written in the form of a matrix *pre-multiplying* a column vector

$$\begin{pmatrix} x' \\ y' \\ 1 \end{pmatrix} = \begin{pmatrix} A_{11} & A_{12} & A_{13} \\ A_{21} & A_{22} & A_{23} \\ A_{31} & A_{32} & A_{33} \end{pmatrix} \times \begin{pmatrix} x \\ y \\ 1 \end{pmatrix}$$

So, if the axes transformation is stored as a matrix, the new co-ordinates of any point can be calculated by considering it as a column vector and pre-multiplying it by the matrix.

Many writers on computer graphics do not use column vectors. They prefer to extend the row vector – for example, (x, y) to $(x, y, 1)$ – and post-multiply the row vector by the transformation matrix so that the above equations in matrix form become

$$(x', y', 1) = (x, y, 1) \times \begin{pmatrix} A_{11} & A_{21} & A_{31} \\ A_{12} & A_{22} & A_{32} \\ A_{13} & A_{23} & A_{33} \end{pmatrix}$$

Note that this matrix is the *transpose* of the matrix of coefficients in the equations. This causes a great deal of confusion among those who are not confident in the use of matrices. It is for this reason that this book keeps to the column vector notation. It really does not matter which method you finally use as long as you are consistent. (Note that the transpose B of a matrix A is given by $B_{ij} = A_{ji}$, where $1 \leqslant i, j \leqslant 3$).

We can now turn our attention to the transformations themselves. Throughout the following sections, bear in mind that the point itself is not being moved – its co-ordinates are simply specified with respect to a new set of axes.

Translation of Origin

In this case the co-ordinate axes of the old and new systems are in the same direction and are of the same scale; however, the new origin is a point $t \equiv (t_x, t_y)$ relative to the old axes. Hence in the new system the old origin has co-ordinates $(-t_x, -t_y)$ and the general point (x, y) of the old system is represented in the new by (x', y') where

$$x' = 1 \times x + 0 \times y - t_x$$
$$y' = 0 \times x + 1 \times y - t_y$$

so the matrix describing this transformation is:

$$\begin{pmatrix} 1 & 0 & -t_x \\ 0 & 1 & -t_y \\ 0 & 0 & 1 \end{pmatrix}$$

A routine for generating such a matrix A, tran2, given the values tx and ty (corresponding to t_x and t_y) is given in listing 4.1.

Listing 4.1

```
{ PROCEDUREs for matrix manipulation for two-dimensional modelling }
TYPE
   matrix3x3 = ARRAY[1..3,1..3] OF real ;

PROCEDURE tran2(tx,ty : real ; VAR A : matrix3x3 ) ;
{ Calculate 2-D axes translation matrix 'A' }
{ Origin translated by vector '(tx,ty)' }
VAR i,j : integer ;
BEGIN
   FOR i := 1 TO 3
   DO BEGIN
          FOR j := 1 TO 3
          DO A[i,j] := 0.0 ;
          A[i,i] := 1.0
        END ;
   A[1,3] := -tx ; A[2,3] := -ty
END ;  { of tran2 }

PROCEDURE scale2(sx,sy : real ; VAR A : matrix3x3 ) ;
{ Calculate 2-D scaling matrix 'A' given scaling vector '(sx,sy)' }
{ One unit on the x axis becomes 'sx' units }
{ and one unit on the y axis becomes 'sy' units }
VAR i,j : integer ;
BEGIN
   FOR i := 1 TO 3
   DO FOR j := 1 TO 3
        DO A[i,j] := 0.0 ;
   A[1,1] := sx ; A[2,2] := sy ; A[3,3] := 1.0
END ; { of scale2 }

PROCEDURE rot2(theta :real ; VAR A : matrix3x3 ) ;
{ Calculate 2-D axes rotation matrix 'A'. The axes are }
{ rotated anti-clockwise through an angle 'theta' radians }
VAR i : integer ;
    c,s : real ;
BEGIN
   FOR i := 1 TO 2
   DO BEGIN
          A[i,3] := 0.0 ; A[3,i] := 0.0
        END ;
   A[3,3] := 1.0 ;
   c := cos(theta) ; s := sin(theta) ;
   A[1,1] := c ; A[2,2] :=  c ;
   A[1,2] := s ; A[2,1] := -s
END ; { of rot2 }

PROCEDURE mult2(A,B : matrix3x3 ; VAR C : matrix3x3 ) ;
{ Calculate the matrix product 'C' of two matrices 'A' and 'B' }
VAR i,j,k : integer ;
    ab : real ;
BEGIN
   FOR i := 1 TO 3
   DO FOR j := 1 TO 3
        DO BEGIN
```

```
            ab := 0 ;
            FOR k := 1 TO 3
            DO ab := ab+A[i,k]*B[k,j] ;
            C[i,j] := ab
         END
END ; { of mult2 }
```

Change of Scale

Now the origin and direction of axes are the same in both systems, but the scale of the axes is different; for example, 1 unit on the old x-axis could become 3 units on the new x-axis, while the scale of the y-axis remains the same. Suppose a unit distance on the original x-axis becomes Sx on the new x-axis, and a unit distance on the old y-axis becomes Sy on the new. Then a point (x, y) in the old system has co-ordinates (x', y') relative to the new where

$$x' = Sx \times x + 0 \times y + 0$$
$$y' = 0 \times x + Sy \times y + 0$$

giving the matrix

$$\begin{pmatrix} Sx & 0 & 0 \\ 0 & Sy & 0 \\ 0 & 0 & 1 \end{pmatrix}$$

The **scale2** routine in listing 4.1 produces such a scaling matrix A, given the values Sx and Sy.

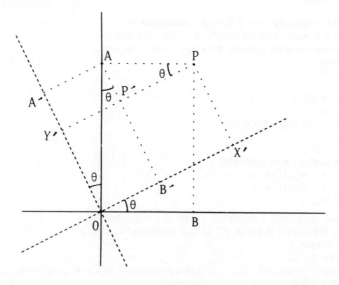

Figure 4.1

Rotation of Axes

The original system is shown in figure 4.1 with solid lines, and the new system with equi-spaced dashed lines; the systems have common origin and scale. The new axes are derived by rotating the old ones through an angle θ radians anti-clockwise about the origin. (This is the usual mathematical way of measuring angles). If the point P in figure 4.1 has co-ordinates (x, y) relative to the old system and (x', y') relative to the new then we have the relationships

$$x' = OX' = OB' + B'X' = AA' + P'P$$
$$= OA \times \sin \theta + AP \times \cos \theta$$
$$= OB \times \cos \theta + OA \times \sin \theta$$
$$= \cos \theta \times x + \sin \theta \times y + 0$$

$$y' = OY' = A'O - A'Y' = -AP' + AB'$$
$$= -AP \times \sin \theta + OA \times \cos \theta$$
$$= -OB \times \sin \theta + OA \times \cos \theta$$
$$= -\sin \theta \times x + \cos \theta \times y + 0$$

and the matrix is

$$\begin{pmatrix} \cos \theta & \sin \theta & 0 \\ -\sin \theta & \cos \theta & 0 \\ 0 & 0 & 1 \end{pmatrix}$$

The rot2 routine to produce a rotation matrix A for an angle θ is given in listing 4.1.

Exercise 4.1: other transformations
Obviously these three types of transformation do not exhaust all the possible choices of matrix A. There are other types of transformation – *shear*, for example, giving matrices of the types

$$\begin{pmatrix} 1 & a & 0 \\ 0 & 1 & 0 \\ 0 & 0 & 1 \end{pmatrix} \text{ or } \begin{pmatrix} 1 & 0 & 0 \\ b & 1 & 0 \\ 0 & 0 & 1 \end{pmatrix}$$

which cause distortions in space and axes; however, for our purposes we will restrict ourselves to translation, scaling and rotation. Write routines to construct such alternative transformation matrices.

Combination of Transformations

A very useful property of this matrix representation of transformations is that the combination of two transformations, say transformation (or matrix) A followed by transformation B, is represented by their product $C = B \times A$. Note the order of multiplication – the matrix representing the first transformation is pre-multiplied by the second. This is because the final matrix will be used to pre-multiply a column vector representing a point, and so the first transformation must appear on the right of the product and the last on the left. For the mathematically minded, the matrices may be considered as prefix operators on the column vectors. (If the row vector method is used then the matrices act as post-fix operators, and the product would appear in the natural(?) order from left to right – this is the price paid for identifying the transformation matrix with the coefficients of the equations.)

We include a routine mult2 (listing 4.1) which multiplies two 3 × 3 matrices A and B to return a third 3 × 3 matrix C.

We will concentrate on the natural transformations of axes which may be reduced to a combination of the three basic forms of affine transformation: translation, change of scale and rotation of axes. It should also be noted that all valid applications of these transformations return *non-singular matrices*, that is those which have an inverse.

Inverse Transformations

For every transformation there is an inverse transformation which will restore the co-ordinates of a point to their original value. If a transformation is represented by a matrix A, then the inverse transformation is represented by the inverse matrix A^{-1}. There is no need to calculate this inverse using listing 6.8, it can be found directly by using the routines in listing 4.1, with parameters derived from the parameters of the original transformation

(1) A translation of origin to the point (t_x, t_y) is inverted by another translation to the point $(-t_x, -t_y)$.

(2) A change of scale by Sx and Sy is inverted by changing the scale again by $1/Sx$ and $1/Sy$. Naturally both Sx and Sy are non-zero, for otherwise the two-dimensional space would degenerate into a line or a point.

(3) A rotation of axes by an angle θ is inverted by another rotation by an angle $-\theta$.

(4) If the transformation matrix is a product of a number of translation, scaling and rotation matrices $A \times B \times C \times \ldots \times L \times M \times N$ (say), then the inverse transformation matrix is

$$N^{-1} \times M^{-1} \times L^{-1} \times \ldots \times B^{-1} \times A^{-1}$$

Note the order of multiplication!

The Placing of an Object

Objects may be drawn in various positions within the viewport and at arbitrary orientations. While it may be quite simple to calculate the co-ordinates of the vertices of an object in a simply defined position, about the origin for instance, it may be difficult to do so for some peculiar orientation. If, furthermore the same object was to be drawn at several different positions, then it would be very inefficient to calculate by hand the vertices for every position. It is preferable to define the object as simply as possible and then to move it to its required position and orientation. This process involves transforming the positions of the vertices themselves rather than transforming the co-ordinate axes. The same three basic transformations — translation, change of scale and rotation — still suffice, however, and with a small alteration to the parameters, the routines already written for the transformation of axes may again be used:

Translation
An object is to be moved by a vector $t \equiv (t_x, t_y)$; thus a vertex (x, y) is moved to $(x + t_x, y + t_y)$. This is exactly equivalent to keeping the object fixed and translating the origin of the axes to $(-t_x, -t_y)$. Thus the matrix representing this transformation may be calculated by

```
tran2(−tx, −ty, A);
```

Change of scale and reflection
The origin is fixed and a general point (x, y) is moved to $(Sx \times x, Sy \times y)$. This transformation is equivalent to changing the scale of the co-ordinate axes so that 1 unit on the x-axis becomes Sx units and 1 unit on the y-axis becomes Sy units. The transformation matrix may thus be calculated by

```
scale2(sx, sy, A);
```

Furthermore, if one of the co-ordinates is multiplied by a negative factor Sx or Sy, this corresponds to a reflection in the other axis; for example, $Sx = -1$, $Sy = 1$ gives a reflection in the y-axis.

Rotating an object about the origin
Rotating an object about the origin anti-clockwise by an angle θ is equivalent to keeping the object fixed and rotating the axes by an angle θ clockwise, or, alternatively, by an angle $-\theta$ anti-clockwise. The rotation matrix is therefore returned by

```
rot2(−theta, A);
```

SETUP and ACTUAL Positions

In order to define a scene consisting of an object in some position and orientation in two-dimensional space, we define an arbitrary but fixed co-ordinate system for two-dimensional space, which we call the *ABSOLUTE system*.

Next the co-ordinates of the vertices of the object are defined in some simple way, usually about the origin. This we call the *SETUP position*. Lines and polygonal facets within the object are defined by specifying the vertices forming their end-points or corners.

Each vertex of the object is moved from its SETUP position to the desired position in space by pre-multiplying the column vector holding its co-ordinates by the matrix representing the required transformation. (Naturally, each vertex undergoes the same transformation.) This new position is called the *ACTUAL position*. Co-ordinates are still specified with respect to the ABSOLUTE system. The line and facet relationships are preserved with the transformed vertices. The matrix which relates the SETUP to ACTUAL position will be called P throughout this book (it sometimes has a letter subscript to identify it uniquely from other such matrices) and may be calculated using one of, or a combination of, the transformations described above.

We must reiterate that the co-ordinates of all vertices in both the SETUP and ACTUAL positions are defined with respect to the same set of axes – those of the ABSOLUTE system.

Storing Information about Scenes

At this stage we must draw attention to the various different methods of creating and storing information about a scene. It will be gathered from chapter 1 that this data always consists of number of vertices identified by their co-ordinates relative to an arbitrary co-ordinate system which we call the ABSOLUTE system: a set of lines, each joining one vertex to another, and polygonal facets which are identified by the vertices at its corners. Most of the pictures created so far have been drawn by specific routines which both create the data and draw the scene, subject to some implicit transformations of the vertex co-ordinates. In much of the work that follows, however, the data representing objects undergoes various manipulations between its creation and the eventual drawing of the scene and so may need to be stored in an easily accessible form in a database. The construction of a section of the database relevant to one occurrence of one particular object will be achieved by a call to a *Construction Routine* for that object.

When required, we use global arrays declared in listing 4.2 to store this information. The scene is assumed to contain **nov** vertices, **nol** lines and **nof** facets. The ACTUAL x and y co-ordinates of the **nov** vertices are stored in an array act[1..maxv] with elements of RECORD TYPE **vector2** (that is, TYPE **vertex2array**), where **maxv** is not less than **nov**. A vertex with co-ordinates (act[j].x,act[j].y) is said to have index j. Information about nol lines is stored in an array line[1..maxl] with elements of RECORD TYPE linepair. The value of maxl must not be less than nol, and values line[i].front and line[i].back indicate respectively the indices of the front and back vertices of the ith line. The description of facets may vary far more than that of either lines or vertices: a vertex always has an *x* co-ordinate and a *y* co-ordinate, a line always has two end-points taken from the list of vertices, but a facet may have any number of sides and hence any number of vertices around its boundary. The most efficient method of representing a facet without imposing unreasonable limits upon the number of vertices around the boundary involves the use of a linear list implemented using three arrays as described in chapter 2. A large array of integers, faclist[1..maxlist], contains a list of indices of vertices in the ACTUAL array and each of nof facets is indicated by two integer arrays facfront[1..maxf] and size[..maxf] ;maxf is not less than nof. facfront[i] points to the element of the faclist array preceding that which holds the index of the first vertex of the ith facet; thus facfront[1] = 0. The value size[i] contains the number of vertices on the boundary of the ith facet, and these in turn are stored in the faclist array as faclist[facfront[i] + 1], faclist[facfront[i] + 2], ..., faclist[facfront[i] + size[i]]. The only constraint thus placed upon the number of vertices on the boundary of a facet is that the total number on all facets must not exceed the dimension maxlist of the faclist array. To aid calculations a special integer variable last points to the last entry of the nof facet in the faclist array. Again it must be stated that the use of these structures is somewhat excessive for the two-dimensional case, but we introduce them in this form so that the methods can be fully understood before we consider similar structures for the more complex three-dimensional situation.

We also introduce the idea of attributes associated with facets and lines. Initially this will involve only the colour in which they are to be drawn, but several more attributes will be introduced when more complex pictures of three-dimensional objects are considered. These attributes will also be stored in arrays relating to the facets. The colour of facet i will be stored in the array colour[1..maxf] as colour[i].

Previously many of the construction routines drew lines and facets immediately after calculating their position. In what follows these routines will be used mostly to update the initially empty database of facets, lines and vertices in their ACTUAL positions; the placement of an observer and the drawing of objects will be left to other routines including transform, findQ, look2 and observe of listing 4.2 together with a special version of routine draw_a_picture which initialises the database before calling a routine scene which will control the construction of the complete scene and the way it is displayed. Procedure **draw_a_picture** links the modelling and display routines that follow to the primitive routines of listing 1.1 and the graphics library of listing 1.3. In order for you to construct and draw two-dimensional scenes, you need only write a scene routine, and to help you in this task a number of example scene routines will follow. Note that listing 4.2

includes a procedure **transform** for transforming a vector **v** by a matrix A into a vector **w**.

Listing 4.2

```
{ data base for two dimensional models }

CONST
    maxv=400 ; maxl=400 ; maxf=400 ; maxlist=2000 ;

TYPE
    linepair = RECORD front,back : integer END ;
    vertex2array = ARRAY[1..maxv] OF vector2 ;

VAR
    nov,nol,nof,last : integer ;
    act,obs,setup : vertex2array ;
    line : ARRAY[1..maxl] OF linepair ;
    colour,size,facfront : ARRAY[1..maxf] OF integer ;
    faclist : ARRAY[1..maxlist] OF integer ;
                            { variables needed to position observer }
    alpha : real ; eye : vector2 ; Q : matrix3x3 ;

PROCEDURE transform(v : vector2 ; A : matrix3x3 ; VAR w : vector2) ;
{ transform column vector 'v' using matrix 'A' into column vector 'w' }
BEGIN
    w.x := A[1,1]*v.x + A[1,2]*v.y + A[1,3] ;
    w.y := A[2,1]*v.x + A[2,2]*v.y + A[2,3]
END ; { of transform }

PROCEDURE findQ ;
{ Calculates the observation matrix 'Q' for an observer }
{ given the vector 'eye' with head inclined 'alpha' radians }
VAR A,B : matrix3x3 ;
BEGIN
{ Calculate translation matrix 'A' }
    tran2(eye.x,eye.y,A) ;
{ Calculate rotation matrix 'B' }
    rot2(alpha,B) ;
{ Combine the transformations to find 'Q' }
    mult2(B,A,Q)
END ; { of findQ }

PROCEDURE look2 ;
{ Reads in position of 'eye' and inclination of head }
{ and then calculates the observation matrix 'Q' }
BEGIN
{ Read in observation data }
    writeln ;
    writeln(' Type in eye vector and tilt of head alpha') ;
    read(eye.x,eye.y,alpha) ; findQ
END ; { of look2 }
```

```
PROCEDURE observe ;
VAR i : integer ;
BEGIN
   FOR i := 1 TO nov
   DO transform(act[i],Q,obs[i])
END ; { of observe }
```

{ Further PROCEDUREs and FUNCTIONs including 'scene', indicated in text }

```
PROCEDURE draw_a_picture ;
BEGIN
{ Initialise vertex, line and facet counts }
   nov := 0 ; nol := 0 ; nof := 0 ; last := 0 ;
{ Construct and draw scene }
   scene
END ; { of draw_a_picture }
```

The CONST declaration is used to define the upper indices maxv, maxl, maxf and maxlist:

CONST maxv = 400; maxl = 400; maxf = 400; maxlist = 2000;

These values are arbitrarily chosen, and for very complex models they may be greatly increased. The counts of vertices, lines and facets for a particular scene or model are also declared here

{VAR} nov,nol,nof,last : integer;

and the ACTUAL co-ordinate vertices of the scene, act, are declared along with other interpretations of these co-ordinates, setup and obs (see later) thus:

{VAR} act,obs,setup : vertex2array;

where {TYPE} vertex2array = ARRAY [1..maxv] OF vector2;

The lines are declared thus:

{TYPE} linepair = RECORD front,back : integer END;
{VAR} line = ARRAY [1..maxl] OF linepair;

Should these lines require peculiar properties — for example, drawn in a particular colour or in an unusual line type (see chapter 5), then other arrays must be declared in this global database to hold these attributes in a manner similar to that used to store the description and attributes of the facets:

{VAR} colour,size,facfront : ARRAY [1..maxf] OF integer;
{VAR} faclist : ARRAY [1..maxlist] OF integer;

If they are required, the SETUP x and y co-ordinates of the vertices and the line and facet information of any particular object type are stored in the special arrays, specific to that object in a manner similar to those declared above, with values either read from file or perhaps implied by the program listing as in examples 4.1 and 4.2. Note we have already declared space for SETUP vertices, setup[1..maxv] above.

Observing a Scene

We now introduce the concept of an observer. Our eventual aim is to represent, in the graphics viewport, a scene as viewed by a person looking at a position specified relative to the ABSOLUTE system for two-dimensional space. Imagine standing in front of a large wall, representing the Cartesian plane, which contains the two-dimensional scene to be drawn. When observing such a scene, the eye is assumed to be looking directly at vector2 point (eye.x, eye.y) of the ABSOLUTE system and the head is tilted anti-clockwise through an angle α (alpha). This defines a new co-ordinate system called the *OBSERVER system*, which has vector2 origin eye relative to the ABSOLUTE system, and is rotated by an angle α. In order to determine the position at which a point is seen, its co-ordinates relative to this OBSERVER system must be calculated. These are called the *OBSERVED co-ordinates* of the point and they are calculated by transforming the ACTUAL co-ordinates of the point using the transformation which relates the ABSOLUTE axes to the OBSERVER axes (that is, a translation of the origin to eye followed by a rotation of the axes anti-clockwise through an angle α). The matrix which executes this transformation from ACTUAL to OBSERVED co-ordinates will be called Q throughout this book and is calculated by the routines findQ and look2 (again note the order of matrix multiplication). Q, eye and alpha are declared in listing 4.2:

{VAR}alpha:real; eye:vector2; Q:matrix3x3

The OBSERVED co-ordinates of vertices will, in general, be stored in the vector2array, obs, already declared.

The co-ordinates (obs[i].x, obs[i].y) correspond to the OBSERVED co-ordinates of the vertex with ACTUAL co-ordinates (act[i].x, act[i].y) (relative to ABSOLUTE axes) for all i. This transformation from ABSOLUTE to OBSERVER systems is achieved with routine observe (also listing 4.2).

Drawing a Scene

We now come to the drawing of the scene on the graphics viewport, which is initiated from within routine scene. We wish to represent in the viewport the scene as viewed by the observer. Recall that in chapter 1 we identified the viewport with a rectangular window in two-dimensional space. We can define such a window with axes co-incident with those of the OBSERVER system defined above, so the WINDOW co-ordinates of each vertex are identical to the OBSERVED co-ordinates. The viewport equivalent of each vertex may then be calculated using precisely the method devised in chapter 1. It is important to note that the order in which lines and facets are drawn may be critical; on raster devices, earlier lines and facets can be obscured by later over-drawing. Views of two-dimensional scenes will be drawn in the viewport by a routine called **drawit**.

The Structure of the scene Construction

All these ideas must now be put together in a Pascal program for modelling and drawing a two-dimensional scene. We can assume that the previously defined routines are properly declared and that **draw_a_picture** calls the **scene** routine after the scale of the graphics WINDOW has been created (in the body of the main program, listing 1.3) and the database has been cleared (in the body of the **draw_a_picture**, listing 4.2). Procedure **scene** must then model (via construction routines), observe (via **findQ**, **look2** and **observe**) and display (via **drawit**, see later examples) the object in the two-dimensional scene, before **finish** finally 'flushes the buffers'. In general this takes place in three stages.

(1) The SETUP stage introduces information about vertices, lines and facets of given object-types in their SETUP position. This information is usually presented to construction routines as input from file in a routine we will call **datain**, in a form consistent with the database, or it can be calculated by a small program segment, perhaps reading data from file, but not in the database format.

(2) The main body of **scene** constructs the ACTUAL position of vertices, lines and facets for the complete two-dimensional scene. This is normally achieved with a sequence of calls to construction routines, which places each object within the scene in the required ACTUAL position. You can of course input from disk the ACTUAL positions directly without the use of construction routines. If this latter method is required, use the routine **datain** to replace the data initialisation and construction routines.

(3) The third stage involves placing the observer, and using routines **findQ**, **look2** and **observe**, as well as a (yet to be defined) routine **drawit** to construct a view of the whole scene.

The individual parts of a stage need not be executed together, the routines are grouped above simply to differentiate between major tasks. For example, we may call **look2** before the ACTUAL scene is constructed. We have organised our approach to graphics in this modular way, so that users have a clear view of the routines they must write, and it also minimises the need to write *one-off* programs. For their specific purposes, readers must write the **scene** routine and perhaps if required **datain** and **drawit** and construction routines. Note that your **datain** routine may read in vertex information in SETUP and/or ACTUAL position, and your **drawit** routines will reflect the order in which you wish the lines and facets drawn. These will be in a form similar to the examples we give, so this should not prove too difficult.

This process is only a guideline. You may find that there are some simple situations where there is no need to store the data about a given scene, it may be drawn directly by the construction routines instead. In this case no **drawit** routine is needed, as in example 4.3. There will be situations when the SETUP information can be included directly into the construction routines (example 4.1) and there will be no need to have an explicit **datain** routine. What is important is that the reader recognises the various stages in construction and drawing.

Example 4.1
In listing 4.3 we create a database consisting of information relating to the flag shown in figure 4.2. It consists of two triangles (one red, the other green), with the edges and sinister diagonal coloured blue, and was SETUP as arrays **setup**, **storefacet** and **storecolour** in the construction routine **flag**; the line colour is implied in the **drawit** routine. (You can write your own **drawit** routine which displays the same data in a different manner.) A **scene** routine initialises the ACTUAL database and by calculating the SETUP to ACTUAL matrix P and calling **flag** (with parameter P), it adds one occurrence of the flag to the database. In our example, the flag is left in its SETUP position so that matrix P is the identity matrix. Then the observation data is read in, so that **look2** and **observe** and put the object in OBSERVED position. Finally **drawit** is called, to draw figure 4.2. This may seem a wasteful duplication of effort just to draw a flag in its original position, but we shall see that this flexible structured process can be used in the general case and will pay dividends in the long run — as with the next example.

Listing 4.3

```
PROCEDURE drawit ;
{ Drawing a 'scene': 'nof' facets drawn before 'nol' lines }
VAR i,j,vertex : integer ;
    polygon : vector2array ;
BEGIN
{ Draw the facets }
  FOR i := 1 TO nof
  DO BEGIN
        FOR j := 1 TO 3
        DO BEGIN
              vertex := faclist[facfront[i] +j] ;
              polygon[j].x := obs[vertex].x ;
              polygon[j].y := obs[vertex].y
           END ;
        setcol(colour[i]) ; polyfill(3,polygon)
     END ;
```

```
{ Draw the lines in colour 0 }
  setcol(0) ;
  FOR i := 1 TO nol
  DO BEGIN
          moveto(obs[line[i].front]) ;
          lineto(obs[line[i].back])
        END
END ; { of drawit }


PROCEDURE flag(P : matrix3x3) ;
{ Construction routine for a simple 'flag' }
VAR storefacet : ARRAY[1..2,1..3] OF integer ;
    storecolour : ARRAY[1..2] OF integer ;
    i,j : integer ;
BEGIN
{ 'P' IS SETUP to ACTUAL matrix. setup is the array of SETUP vertices }
{ 'storeflag' are SETUP facets and 'storecolour' SETUP colours for facets }
    setup[1].x := 1 ; setup[2].x := -1 ; setup[3].x := -1 ; setup[4].x := 1 ;
    setup[1].y := 1 ; setup[2].y := 1 ; setup[3].y := -1 ; setup[4].y := -1 ;
    storefacet[1,1] := 1 ; storefacet[1,2] := 2 ; storefacet[1,3] := 4 ;
    storefacet[2,1] := 4 ; storefacet[2,2] := 3 ; storefacet[2,3] := 2 ;
    storecolour[1] := 1 ; storecolour[2] := 2 ;
{ Add facets to data base. Note 'nov' value must be added to }
{ facet and line data, since values append data base }
    FOR i := 1 TO 2
    DO BEGIN
            FOR j := 1 TO 3
            DO faclist[last+j] := storefacet[i,j]+nov ;
            nof := nof+1 ;
            facfront[nof] := last ; size[nof] := 3 ;
            last := last+size[nof] ; colour[nof] := storecolour[i]
          END ;
{ Add SINISTER line to data base }
    nol := nol+1 ;
    line[nol].front := 2+nov ; line[nol].back := 4+nov ;
{ Add vertex data in ACTUAL position }
    FOR i := 1 TO 4
    DO BEGIN
            nov := nov+1 ; transform(setup[i],P,act[nov])
          END
END ; { of flag }

PROCEDURE scene ;
{ Creating a 'scene' with simple 'flag' in SETUP position }
VAR P : matrix3x3 ;
BEGIN
{ SETUP to ACTUAL matrix is identity matrix }
    tran2(0,0,P) ; flag(P) ;
{ create ACTUAL to OBSERVED matrix }
    look2 ;
{ Put vertices in OBSERVED position and draw scene }
    observe ; drawit
END ; { of scene }
```

Figure 4.2

Complicated Pictures – the 'Building Block' Method

Pictures containing a number of similar objects can be drawn with a minimum of extra effort. A scene such as figure 4.3 containing four flags, for example, may be constructed by calling the **flag** routine several times within the **scene** routine (which was called from **draw_a_picture** etc.), on each occasion with a different matrix *P*. This is called the *building block* method. Each call to a construction routine creates a block of data relating to one occurrence of that object type, and this is included in the database which models the scene.

Listing 4.4

```
{ PROCEDURES 'flag' and 'drawit' from previous listing }

PROCEDURE scene ;
{ Creating a scene of 4 simple flags }
VAR A,B,C,D,E,F,G,H,DM,EM,P : matrix3x3 ;
    i : integer ;
BEGIN
{ Flag a }
    tran2(0,0,P) ; flag(P) ;
{ Flag b }
    scale2(4,2,A) ; rot2(-pi/6,B) ; tran2(-6,-3,C) ;
    mult2(B,A,G)  ; mult2(C,G,P)  ; flag(P) ;
{ Flag d }
    tran2(0,-3,D) ; tran2(0,3,DM) ;
    rot2(arctan(-0.75),E) ; rot2(arctan(0.75),EM) ;
    scale2(1,-1,F) ;
    mult2(D,P,G)  ; mult2(E,G,H)  ; mult2(F,H,G) ;
    mult2(EM,G,H) ; mult2(DM,H,P) ; flag(P) ;
{ Flag c }
    mult2(B,C,G) ; mult2(A,G,P) ; flag(P) ;
{ Draw 4 views of the same scene }
    FOR i := 1 TO 4
    DO BEGIN
{ create ACTUAL to OBSERVED matrix }
            look2 ; erase ;
{ Place vertices and draw scene }
            observe ; drawit ;
        END
END ; { of scene }
```

Example 4.2

We can draw many views of the same scene, including the one in figure 4.3, using listing 4.4. There are four flags labelled (a), (b), (c) and (d) on a frame with

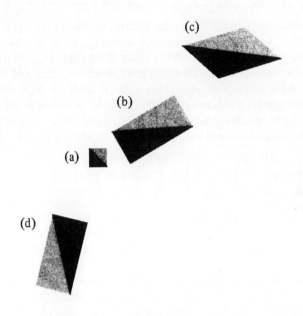

Figure 4.3

horiz = 120. Flag (a) is placed in the SETUP position, that is $P_a = I$ (the subscript a means the matrix relates to flag (a)). Flag (b) is moved from SETUP to ACTUAL position by the following transformations

(1) Scale flag with $Sx = 4$ and $Sy = 2$, producing matrix A.
(2) Rotate figure through $\pi/6$ radians, matrix B.
(3) Translate flag by $t_x = 9$ and $t_y = 6$, matrix C.

Note that these transformations are of the object itself, and not of the co-ordinate axes.

$$A = \begin{pmatrix} 4 & 0 & 0 \\ 0 & 2 & 0 \\ 0 & 0 & 1 \end{pmatrix} \quad B = \begin{pmatrix} \sqrt{3}/2 & -1/2 & 0 \\ 1/2 & \sqrt{3}/2 & 0 \\ 0 & 0 & 1 \end{pmatrix} \quad C = \begin{pmatrix} 1 & 0 & 9 \\ 0 & 1 & 6 \\ 0 & 0 & 1 \end{pmatrix}$$

The complete transformation is given by $R_b = Q \times P_b = Q \times C \times B \times A$ (note the order of the matrix multiplication). For simplicity, in this example we will assume that the observer is already looking at the origin with head upright — that is, Q is the identity matrix.

If the order $A \times B \times C = P_c$ had been used instead, then

$$P_b = \begin{pmatrix} 2\sqrt{3} & -1 & 9 \\ 2 & \sqrt{3} & 6 \\ 0 & 0 & 1 \end{pmatrix} \quad P_c = \begin{pmatrix} 2\sqrt{3} & -2 & 18\sqrt{3} - 12 \\ 1 & \sqrt{3} & 6\sqrt{3} + 9 \\ 0 & 0 & 1 \end{pmatrix}$$

which are obviously two different transformations. Matrix $R_c = Q \times P_c$ produces flag (c). Note how this flag has become distorted, no longer having mutually perpendicular adjacent sides, as do the other three flags; be careful with the use of scaling — remember that scaling is defined about the origin and this can cause distortions in the shape of an object that is moved away from the origin!

To further illustrate this example, the ACTUAL positions of the four corners of flag (b) in the window are calculated. The co-ordinates of the corners are put into column vector form and pre-multiplied by matrix $R_b = I \times P_b$. For example

$$\begin{pmatrix} 2\sqrt{3} & -1 & 9 \\ 2 & \sqrt{3} & 6 \\ 0 & 0 & 1 \end{pmatrix} \times \begin{pmatrix} 1 \\ 1 \\ 1 \end{pmatrix} = \begin{pmatrix} 2\sqrt{3} + 8 \\ \sqrt{3} + 8 \\ 1 \end{pmatrix}$$

When returned to the usual two-dimensional vector form, the four vertices $(1, 1)$, $(-1, 1)$, $(-1, -1)$ and $(1, -1)$ have been transformed to $(2\sqrt{3} + 8, \sqrt{3} + 8)$, $(-2\sqrt{3} + 8, \sqrt{3} + 4)$, $(-2\sqrt{3} + 10, -\sqrt{3} + 4)$ and $(2\sqrt{3} + 10, -\sqrt{3} + 8)$ respectively.

Flag (d) is flag (b) reflected in the line $3y = -4x - 9$. This line cuts the y-axis at $(0, -3)$ and makes an angle $\alpha = \cos^{-1}(-3/5) = \sin^{-1}(4/5) = \tan^{-1}(-4/3)$ with the positive x-axis. If the origin is moved by a vector $(0, -3)$, matrix D say, this line will go through the new origin. Furthermore, rotating axes by angle α, matrix E say, means the line is now identical with the x-axis. Matrix F can reflect the flag in the x-axis, E^{-1} puts the line back parallel to its original direction, and D^{-1} returns the line to its original position. Matrix $G = D^{-1} \times E^{-1} \times F \times E \times D$ will therefore reflect the ACTUAL vertices of the flag (b) about the line $3y = -4x - 9$, and $R_d = Q \times P_d = Q \times G \times P_b$ can therefore be used to draw flag (d). That is matrix P_b is used to move the SETUP flag into position (b), and then matrix G to place it in position (d).

$$D = \begin{pmatrix} 1 & 0 & 0 \\ 0 & 1 & 3 \\ 0 & 0 & 1 \end{pmatrix} \quad E = \begin{pmatrix} -3/5 & 4/5 & 0 \\ -4/5 & -3/5 & 0 \\ 0 & 0 & 1 \end{pmatrix} \quad F = \begin{pmatrix} 1 & 0 & 0 \\ 0 & -1 & 0 \\ 0 & 0 & 1 \end{pmatrix}$$

and

$$P_d = 1/25 \begin{pmatrix} -14\sqrt{3} - 48 & -24\sqrt{3} + 7 & -279 \\ -48\sqrt{3} + 14 & 7\sqrt{3} + 24 & -228 \\ 0 & 0 & 25 \end{pmatrix}$$

Figure 4.3 is drawn using the **scene** routine given in listing 4.4. Note the **flag** and **drawit** routines (and of course findQ, look2, observe etc.) are the same as those of example 4.1. This modular approach of solving the problem of defining and drawing a picture may not be the most efficient, and is perhaps rather excessive in simple two-dimensional scenes. It does, however, greatly clarify the situation for beginners, enabling them to ask the right questions about constructing a required scene. Also when dealing with multiple views (for example, in animation), this approach will minimise problems in scenes where not only are the objects moving relative to one another, but also the observer itself is moving.

Exercise 4.2
Once the scene for figure 4.2 is constructed in its ACTUAL position, instead of drawing the figure, store the information on disk with a routine called **dataout** (that is, before you enter the observation information). Then write a new program which replaces the construction routine calls in **scene** by a call to a routine of your own, **datain**, which will read the data back off disk, before placing the observer and calling **findQ**, **look2**, **observe** and **drawit**.

The most important reason for this modular approach will be seen when it comes to drawing pictures of three-dimensional objects. These three-dimensional constructions will be described as an extension of the ideas above, and full understanding of two-dimensional transformations is essential before going on to higher dimensions.

In summary, the process from defining vertices to drawing the scene is as follows

(1) Define the co-ordinates of each vertex as simply as possible relative to the ABSOLUTE co-ordinate system — their SETUP position. If the scene is to be stored in a database then define also the relationships between the vertices (that is, the lines and facets), otherwise these will be generated immediately before drawing.

(2) Move the vertices to their ACTUAL position in space, the co-ordinates still being specified in relation to the ABSOLUTE system. The matrix executing this transformation is called P.

(3) Calculate the co-ordinates of each vertex relative to the OBSERVER co-ordinate system using matrix Q. Note that in this case the vertices themselves are not actually being moved — their co-ordinates are simply being specified in relation to a different system of axes. The OBSERVED co-ordinates of each vertex can be calculated directly from the SETUP co-ordinates by pre-multiplication by the matrix $R = Q \times P$.

(4) The object is finally drawn in the graphics viewport by identifying a WINDOW system with the OBSERVER system and calculating the viewport equivalent of each vertex using the window to viewport transformation discussed in chapter one. The lines and facets connecting the vertices may then be plotted on the viewport. All relationships of lines and facets with vertices are maintained throughout all transformations. In general, parts (1) and (2) of this process are achieved by **scene** using construction routines, while part (3) is achieved with **findQ**, **look2** and **observe** controlled by **scene**, and finally part (4) is programmed in **drawit**.

On some graphics devices the transformation routines may be incorporated into the hardware. It is, nevertheless, very important that the reader becomes familiar with the idea of axis transformation since it plays a fundamental part in the understanding of many of the more complex techniques covered in this book. Also it should be noted that the polygonal facet approach for the construction of data which we are advancing here is not the only way of tackling the problem. The alternative analytic method, which is discussed in chapter 17, defines a scene in terms of logical combinations of primitive shapes which are defined by the analytic representations of their surfaces. This method also uses the techniques of transformations using matrices which we have discussed in this chapter.

Exercise 4.3
Construct a dynamic scene. With each new view, the objects will move relative to one another in some well-defined manner. The observer also should move in some simple way; for example, the eye can start looking at the origin, and twenty views later it is looking at the point (100, 100), and with each view the head is tilted a further 0.1 radians. The values of **eye** and **alpha** are no longer read in but should, instead, be calculated in **scene**. See the animation section of chapter 5.

Exercise 4.4
Construct a scene which is a diagrammatic view of a room in your house — with schematic two-dimensional drawings of tables, chairs etc. placed in the room. Each different type of object has its own construction routine, and **scene** should read in data for placing objects around the room in their ACTUAL position. Once the scene is set, produce a variety of views looking from various points **eye** and orientations (**alpha**).

Or you can set up a line-drawing picture of a map, and again view it from various orientations. The number of possible choices of scene is enormous! Also see the *menu* method of chapter 5 for ideas on how to move objects into ACTUAL position interactively.

Example 4.3
As we mentioned earlier, there may be situations where it is inefficient to store the vertex, line and facet data. For example, in the **scene** routine in listing 4.5 the program draws figure 4.4 which is a series of *super-ellipses* (Gardner, 1978) at a variety of orientations and scales. There is no need to store the ACTUAL positions, we can go directly from SETUP to OBSERVED position, by pre-multiplying the SETUP vertices by $R = Q \times P$. No lines are stored, vertices are joined by lines as soon as they have been evaluated, and then the values discarded. The drawing is achieved inside the construction routine **superellipse**, which takes the SETUP to OBSERVED matrix R as a parameter together with the exponent of the super-ellipse, and transforms the vertices into OBSERVED position before joining them by lines in the correct order. Note that **superellipse** actually constructs the vertices of a *super-circle*, but scaling matrix A included in matrix P distorts it into a super-ellipse.

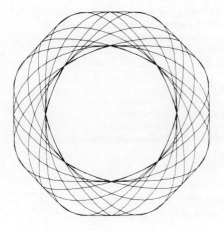

Figure 4.4

Listing 4.5

```
PROCEDURE scene ;
{ 'scene' routine to draw a set of super-ellipses }
VAR P,R,A,B : matrix3x3 ;
    index : ARRAY[1..3] OF real ;
    phi,phinc : real ;
    i,j : integer ;

    PROCEDURE superellipse(R : matrix3x3 ; index : real ) ;
{ Construction routine for super-ellipse. SETUP to OBSERVER matrix }
{ will distort super-circle into super-ellipse of given 'index' }
    VAR ellsetup,observed : vector2 ;
        theta,thinc,c,s : real ;
        i : integer ;

        FUNCTION signedpower(r,index : real) : real ;
        VAR power : real ;
        BEGIN
            power := exp(ln(abs(r))*index) ;
            IF r<0
            THEN signedpower := -power
            ELSE signedpower := power
        END ; { of signedpower }


    BEGIN
{ Move to first OBSERVED vector point on super-ellipse }
```

```
      ellsetup.x := 1 ; ellsetup.y := 0 ;
      transform(ellsetup,R,observed) ; moveto(observed) ;
{ Draw lines to 200 successive observed points }
      theta := 0 ; thinc := pi*0.01 ;
      FOR i := 1 TO 200
      DO BEGIN
              theta := theta+thinc ;
              c := cos(theta) ; s := sin(theta) ;
              ellsetup.x := signedpower(c,index) ;
              ellsetup.y := signedpower(s,index) ;
              transform(ellsetup,R,observed) ; lineto(observed)
           END
   END ; { of superellipse }

BEGIN
   index[1] := 0.5 ; index[2] := 1 ; index[3] := 1.5 ;
{ calculate ACTUAL to OBSERVED matrix 'Q' }
   look2 ;
{ Matrix 'A' changes super-circle into super-ellipse }
   scale2(3,2,A) ;
{ Draw four such objects symmetrically placed around the }
{ origin for three choices of 'index' }
   phi := 0 ; phinc := pi*0.25 ;
   FOR i := 1 TO 4
   DO BEGIN
           rot2(phi,B) ;
{ 'P' is SETUP to ACTUAL matrix and 'R' SETUP to OBSERVED matrix }
           mult2(B,A,P) ; mult2(Q,P,R) ;
           FOR j := 1 TO 3
           DO superellipse(R,index[j]) ;
           phi := phi+phinc
        END
END ; { of scene }
```

5 Techniques for Manipulating Two-dimensional Objects

The methods introduced so far enable us to create and draw a simple representation of any two-dimensional scene consisting of a set of vertices, lines and polygonal facets. In this chapter we shall consider a number of techniques which may be used for more complex pictures of two-dimensional scenes along with some which we will need when developing algorithms to deal with three-dimensional solid models. Naturally these routines must be merged into the complete program at positions that ensure a valid scope.

Line Clipping in Two Dimensions

In chapter 4 the drawing of an object was achieved by identifying the viewport with a rectangular window centred on the origin of the OBSERVER system. The OBSERVER system consists of a pair of axes representing the entire Cartesian plane and is consequently of infinite size. The viewport, unfortunately, is not. Of course we do not wish to draw the entire Cartesian plane, only that section containing the vertices of the scene. No problem arises provided that the window, which is identified with the viewport, contains all of the vertices (and hence all of the lines and facets). If, however, part of the object lies outside the window then we must be able to identify those parts which should be drawn. For the moment we shall restrict our attention to dealing with lines. The problem of polygons lying wholly, or partly, outside the window area is considered later in this chapter. The plotting of single points provides no problem, of course, since a point can be plotted if it lies inside the window and cannot be plotted if it lies outside.

In many devices the external line segments are dealt with in hardware or system software but on some (in particular microfilm plotters) these lines are reflected back into view causing great, but artistic, confusion. This effect may be deliberately used to produce some unusual designs such as that shown in figure 5.1 which is formed by stacking 16 copies of figure 3.3b in a 4 by 4 grid and choosing too small a window.

Many microcomputers have very peculiar algorithms for dealing with such situations and on some of the older flat-bed plotters an attempt to draw outside the graphics area can actually damage the equipment!

Figure 5.1

Usually these external line segments should be suppressed or *clipped*. For example, clipping the line segments external to the outer rectangle in figure 5.2a ought to give figure 5.2b.

In practice each line will be clipped just before it is to be drawn, so the problem reduces to calculating which part (if any) of a line segment joining point (x_1, y_1) to point (x_2, y_2) lies within the window. The following algorithm, due to Cohen and Sutherland, achieves this. The window is considered to be a rectangular area with the co-ordinate origin at its centre. The rectangle is of length 2 x clippedx and depth x ± clippedy so that it has vertices (± clippedx, ± clippedy). These values are declared globally. It will be seen that this algorithm may be used to clip lines outside any rectangle centred on the origin and not just the window which is identified with the viewport, but care should be taken to ensure that any other *clipping rectangle* used lies entirely within this window, otherwise the problem of external line segments will remain (unless your system includes hardware clipping). All references to the clipping rectangle in the description of this algorithm should be understood to apply equally to the entire viewport/window or to a smaller rectangle within.

The sides of the rectangle are extended, thus dividing space into nine sectors, see figure 5.3, in which a number of different line segments have been drawn to aid the explanation of the algorithm. Each point in space may now be classified by two parameters ix and iy where

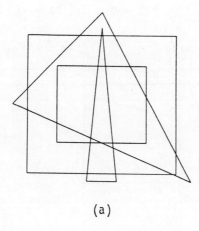

(a)

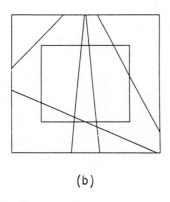

(b)

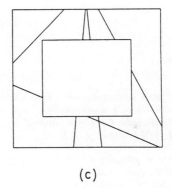

(c)

Figure 5.2

(1) $ix = -1$, 0 or $+1$, depending on whether the x-coordinate value of the point lies to the left, within the x bounds or to the right of the clipping rectangle.
(2) $iy = -1$, 0 or $+1$, depending on whether the y-coordinate value of the point lies below, within the y bounds or above the clipping rectangle.

These values are calculated, when needed, inside the clipping program using the function **mode** (listing 5.1): a point on the boundary of the window is considered to be *inside* the window.

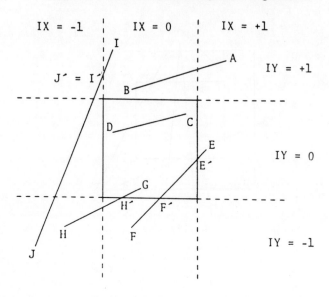

Figure 5.3

Listing 5.1

```
FUNCTION mode(z,clippedz : real) : integer ;
{ Returns -1 if 'z < -clippedz', }
{ 0 if '-clippedz < = z < = clippedz' }
{ and 1 if 'clippedz < z' }
BEGIN
   IF z < -clippedz
   THEN mode := -1
   ELSE IF clippedz < z
        THEN mode := 1
        ELSE mode := 0
END ; { of mode }
```

If the two points at the end of the line segment — that is, **vector2** points **p1** and **p2** — have parameters ix1 and iy1, and ix2 and iy2 respectively, then there are a number of possibilities to consider.

(i) If ix1 = ix2 ≠ 0 or iy1 = iy2 ≠ 0, then the whole line segment is outside the rectangle and hence may be safely ignored — for example, line AB in figure 5.3.

(ii) If ix1 = iy1 = ix2 = iy2 =0, then the whole line segment lies in the rectangle and so the complete line must be drawn − for example, line CD.

(iii) The remaining case must be considered in detail. If $ix1 \neq 0$ and/or $iy1 \neq 0$ then the **vector2** point $\mathbf{p1} \equiv (x_1, y_1)$ lies outside the rectangle and so new value for x_1 and y_1 must be found − to avoid confusion these are called x'_1 and y'_1. $\mathbf{p1d} \equiv (x'_1, y'_1)$ is the **vector2** point on the line segment nearer to **p1** where the line cuts the rectangle. The formula for this calculation was considered in chapter 3 − that is, the intersection of a line with another line parallel to a co-ordinate axis. If the line misses the rectangle, then **p1d** is defined to be that point where the line cuts one of the extended vertical edges. If ix1 = iy1 = 0 then **p1d** = **p1**. The **vector2** point $\mathbf{p2} \equiv (x'_2, y'_2)$ is calculated in a similar manner. This algorithm is implemented in listing 5.2. The required clipped line segment is that joining **p1d** to **p2d**. If the original line misses the rectangle, then the algorithm ensures that **p1d** = **p2d** and the new line segment degenerates to a point and is ignored. In figure 5.3, for example, EF is clipped to E'F', GH is clipped to GH' (G = G') and IJ degenerates to a point I' = J'.

Thus the routine **clip** takes the two end-points of the line, **p1** and **p2**, and discovers which of the above three possibilities is relevant, dealing with it thus

(i) exit the routine immediately, or

(ii) join the two points with a line segment, or

(iii) calculate the 'dashed' points and join them with a line segment.

Listing 5.2

```
VAR
    clippedx,clippedy : real ;

PROCEDURE clip(p1,p2 : vector2 ) ;
{ Routine to find that segment of the line from vector 'p1' }
{ to vector 'p2' which lies within the clipping rectangle }
{ The required segment will be between vectors 'p1d' and 'p2d' }
VAR p1d,p2d : vector2 ;
    ix1,iy1,ix2,iy2 : integer ;
    xx,yy : real ;
BEGIN
{ Initially identify 'p1d' with 'p1' and 'p2d' with 'p2' }
    p1d.x := p1.x ; p1d.y := p1.y ; p2d.x := p2.x ; p2d.y := p2.y ;
{ Find frame 'mode's of 'p1d' and 'p2d' }
    ix1 := mode(p1d.x,clippedx) ; iy1 := mode(p1d.y,clippedy) ;
    ix2 := mode(p2d.x,clippedx) ; iy2 := mode(p2d.y,clippedy) ;
```

```
{ ignore points that are in same sector outside clipping rectangle }
  IF (ix1*ix2 <> 1) AND (iy1*iy2 <> 1)
  THEN BEGIN
      IF iy1 <> 0
{ If point 1 is outside the y bounds of the clipping rectangle }
{ then move it to the nearest y edge }
      THEN BEGIN
              yy := clippedy*iy1 ;
              p1d.x := p1d.x+(p2d.x-p1d.x)*(yy-p1d.y)/(p2d.y-p1d.y) ;
              p1d.y := yy ; ix1 := mode(p1d.x,clippedx)
          END ;
      IF ix1 <> 0
{ If point 1 is outside the x bounds of the clipping rectangle }
{ then move it to the nearest x edge }
      THEN BEGIN
              xx := clippedx*ix1 ;
              p1d.y := p1d.y+(p2d.y-p1d.y)*(xx-p1d.x)/(p2d.x-p1d.x) ;
              p1d.x := xx ;
          END ;
      IF iy2 <> 0
{ If point 2 is outside the y bounds of the clipping rectangle }
{ then move it to the nearest y edge }
      THEN BEGIN
              yy := clippedy*iy2 ;
              p2d.x := p1d.x+(p2d.x-p1d.x)*(yy-p1d.y)/(p2d.y-p1d.y) ;
              p2d.y := yy ; ix2 := mode(p2d.x,clippedx)
          END ;

      IF ix2 <> 0
{ If point 2 is outside the x bounds of the clipping rectangle }
{ then move it to the nearest x edge }
      THEN BEGIN
              xx := clippedx*ix2 ;
              p2d.y := p1d.y+(p2d.y-p1d.y)*(xx-p1d.x)/(p2d.x-p1d.x) ;
              p2d.x := xx ;
          END ;
{ Plot line between new points if they are not coincident }
{ If part of the figure is to be blanked (see later) then the calls }
{ to 'moveto' and 'lineto' should be replaced by a single call: }
{      ' blank(p1d,p2d) '     }
      IF (abs(p1d.x-p2d.x) > epsilon) OR (abs(p1d.y-p2d.y) > epsilon)
      THEN BEGIN
              moveto(p1d) ; lineto(p2d)
          END
      END
END ; { of clip }
```

If line clipping is required in a program, then each pair of calls to the line-drawing routines moveto and lineto should be replaced by a call to clip which may subsequently call them to draw the internal segment. Naturally the declaration of clip (and later blank) should follow moveto and lineto in the program listing. This algorithm solves the simplified case of clipping around a rectangular area centred on the origin, which of course is sufficient to ensure that no drawing is attempted outside the viewport. Situations arise, however, where one might want to clip the lines outside a rectangle in a peculiar position and orientation. In order to solve this general problem, where one pair of the rectangle's sides makes an angle α with the x-axis and it has centre with WINDOW co-ordinates (x_c, x_c), we use the transformation techniques of chapter 4. We reiterate that, unless your system includes hardware clipping, the transformed clipping rectangle must lie entirely within the window, or the clipping routine must be called twice — the first time to clip the line to the window, the second to clip to the rectangle.

Suppose the clipping rectangle defines a new pair of axes with origin at (x_c, y_c) and axes parallel to its sides (that is, the x-axis makes an angle α with the existing x-axis). If the co-ordinates of the line to be clipped are specified with relation to these new axes, then the clipping problem reduces to the simple case. The matrix R used to transform the co-ordinates of the end-points may be found by calculating the matrix A which translates the origin to (x_c, y_c) and matrix B which rotates the axes through an angle α, and setting $R = B \times A$. The co-ordinates of each point must be pre-multiplied by R and the clipping algorithm may proceed as above. However, the end-points of the line to be drawn on the viewport must have co-ordinates specified relative to the WINDOW co-ordinate system so, before plotting, the co-ordinates must be transformed back to this form by pre-multiplication with the matrix $R^{-1} = A^{-1} \times B^{-1}$. There is, of course, no need to calculate the inverses of the matrices A and B directly, since B^{-1} represents an axes rotation through $-\alpha$ and A^{-1} is the matrix for the transformation of the origin to $(-x_c, -y_c)$. The end-points of the line to be plotted may be the original end-points or new 'dashed' points. Either way, care must be taken not to corrupt the information in the database during transformation or clipping — copies must be made of all co-ordinate variables and these copies should be altered, not the originals.

Exercise 5.1
Clip figure 1.6 inside a diamond of side $\sqrt{2}$. (The diamond is a square of side $\sqrt{2}$ rotated through $\pi/4$ radians.)

Blanking an Area of the Window

The problem of *blanking* (or *covering*) an area of the window, which may arise when part of the viewport is to be reserved for text for instance, is the exact opposite of clipping. Again we have a rectangle (2 x blankedx by 2 x blankedy), but in this case all line segments inside the rectangle are deleted. The values of blankedx and blankedy are declared globally. Figure 5.2c shows the result of blanking the inner rectangle of figure 5.2b.

If a colour raster scan display is being used, then blanking an area of the viewport is a trivial exercise. The entire picture is drawn as if no blanking is required and then the area to be blanked is simply blotted out using the polygon-filling routine **polyfill**. The following algorithm need only be used, therefore, on non-raster scan devices.

As with clipping, the problem is simplified by assuming that the blanking rectangle has four corners (±**blankedx**, ±**blankedy**), and the transformations of chapter 4 may be used to manipulate the general case into this simple form.

Again, two-dimensional space is divided into nine sectors by extending the edges of the rectangle. Each point is given two parameters **ix** and **iy** using the same function **mode** (listing 5.1), and blanking a line segment that joins the **vector2** points **p1** and **p2** is achieved by

blank (p1, p2);

which calls the routine shown in listing 5.3.

Listing 5.3

```
VAR
    blankedx,blankedy : real ;

PROCEDURE blank(p1,p2 : vector2 ) ;
{ Routine to blank out that segment of the line from 'p1' to 'p2' }
{ which lies within the blanking rectangle }
VAR p1d,p2d : vector2 ;
    ix1,iy1,ix2,iy2 : integer ;
BEGIN
{ Find frame 'mode's of 'p1' and 'p2' }
    ix1 := mode(p1.x,blankedx) ; iy1 := mode(p1.y,blankedy) ;
    ix2 := mode(p2.x,blankedx) ; iy2 := mode(p2.y,blankedy) ;
{ If points are on the same side of one of the extended edges of the }
{ blanking rectangle then draw the whole line segment }
    IF (ix1*ix2 = 1) OR (iy1*iy2 = 1)
    THEN BEGIN
            moveto(p1) ; lineto(p2)
         END
    ELSE BEGIN
{ The blanked segment will be from 'p1d' to 'p2d' }
{ Calculate the first point 'p1d', corresponding to 'p1'. If 'p1' is }
{ outside the x bounds of the blanking rectangle then put point 'p1d'}
{ on the nearest x edge, else 'p1d=p1' for the moment }
            IF ix1 < > 0
            THEN BEGIN
                    p1d.x := blankedx*ix1 ;
                    p1d.y := p1.y+(p2.y-p1.y)*(p1d.x-p1.x)/(p2.x-p1.x) ;
                    iy1 := mode(p1d.y,blankedy)
                 END
            ELSE BEGIN
                    p1d.x := p1.x ; p1d.y := p1.y
                 END ;
{ If 'p1d' is outside the y bounds of the blanking rectangle then }
{ move it to the nearest y edge }
            IF iy1 < > 0
```

```
            THEN BEGIN
                    p1d.y := blankedy*iy1 ;
                    p1d.x := p1.x+(p2.x-p1.x)*(p1d.y-p1.y)/(p2.y-p1.y)
                    END ;
{ Join 'p1' to 'p1d' unless they are almost coincident }
            IF (abs(p1d.x-p1.x) > epsilon) OR (abs(p1d.y-p1.y) > epsilon)
            THEN BEGIN
                    moveto(p1) ; lineto(p1d)
                    END ;
{ Repeat the above process with 'p2' and 'p2d' }
            IF ix2 < > 0
            THEN BEGIN
                    p2d.x := blankedx*ix2 ;
                    p2d.y := p1.y+(p2.y-p1.y)*(p2d.x-p1.x)/(p2.x-p1.x) ;
                    iy2 := mode(p2d.y,blankedy)
                    END
            ELSE BEGIN
                    p2d.x := p2.x ; p2d.y := p2.y
                    END ;
            IF iy2 < > 0
            THEN BEGIN
                    p2d.y := blankedy*iy2 ;
                    p2d.x := p1.x+(p2.x-p1.x)*(p2d.y-p1.y)/(p2.y-p1.y)
                    END ;
{ Join 'p2' to 'p2d' unless they are almost coincident }
            IF (abs(p2d.x-p2.x) > epsilon) OR (abs(p2d.y-p2.y) > epsilon)
            THEN BEGIN
                    moveto(p2) ; lineto(p2d)
                    END
        END
END ; { of blank }
```

The algorithm is again explained with reference to figure 5.3. If both of the points defining the line segment lie on the same side of one pair of rectangle edges (that is, $ix1 * ix2 = 1$ or $iy1 * iy2 = 1$) then the line lies completely outside the rectangle and must be drawn in total (or alternatively sent to the clipping routine) — for example, AB. When both points are inside the rectangle ($ix1 = ix2 = 0$ and $iy1 = iy2 = 0$) then nothing is drawn — for example, CD. When neither of these is the case, we calculate (as required) the points **p1d** corresponding to **p1** and **p2d** corresponding to **p2**. If **p1** lies inside the rectangle, then **p1d** = **p1**; if it is outside then **p1d** is produced in the same way as in the clipping routine. **p2d** is found in a similar way. The routine joins **p1** to **p1d** if the points are not coincident, and similarly **p2** to **p2d**. For example, CD is not drawn because both C and D lie inside the rectangle; EE′ and FF′ are drawn, HH′ is drawn from GH, and since I′ = J′ lines II′ and JJ′ combine to give the complete line IJ.

If blanking is required in a program, then each call to the line-drawing routines **moveto** and **lineto** should be replaced by a call to **blank**. If both clipping and blanking are required, then the **moveto** and **lineto** calls in one of the routines, **clip** or **blank**, should be replaced by a call to the other and this decision dictates the order for declaring **clip** and **blank**. The choice of which routine should be changed depends upon which process you want executed first. Efficiency will dictate which one you choose.

Exercise 5.2
Draw figures 5.2a, b and c.

Exercise 5.3
Draw figure 5.4, which is figure 1.6 clipped by a square with side $\sqrt{2}$ and covered by a square with side $\frac{1}{3}$. Both squares are centred at the origin — the centre of a circle of 30 points.

Exercise 5.4
Create a routine which clips a line segment to a circular window and a similar routine which blanks a circular part of a picture.

These methods for clipping and blanking apply only to line drawings, as we mentioned above. Some consideration will be given later to the clipping and covering of polygonal areas, but let us first look at methods of representing lines and polygonal areas on a line-drawing device.

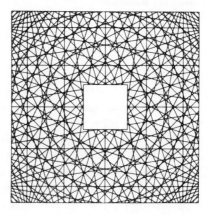

Figure 5.4

Line Types

Before considering what we mean by line types, it is important to realise how a line in space is represented on our pixel-based viewport model. The line is obviously constructed as a discrete set of pixels joining the pixel equivalents of the end-points of the real line. A number of algorithms for deciding which pixels go into this set are available (Newman and Sproull, 1973): we assume that this is achieved by the hardware. In general, these algorithms assume that the line in space has no thickness and, when transformed to the viewport, all pixels intersected by this line are given a logical colour which is calculated from the line colour. The vector graphics device methods of line drawing are not considered here.

In the text thus far we have assumed just one line type − that is, a *solid line* of pixels in the given fixed line colour and intensity that obliterates the original colour of every pixel it covers. In reality the variety of graphics devices or packages allows the user many different line types.

Exercise 5.5

If you do not have built-in dashed lines available, write a routine **dash (n:integer; p1, p2:vector2)** which draws a line of n dashes between the **vector2** points **p1** and **p2** in the window: note the dashes must start and end on these points, so if the distance between the two end-points is d and the size of dashes equal the gap size between them, then the size of the dash is $d/(2n - 1)$. What if the dashes are twice the size of the gaps? What if you wish to make the dash a given size, and the gaps approximately the same size as each other?

The solid line type mentioned above takes no account of the original colour of the pixels that define the line. It is possible to have line types where the colour of each component pixel depends not only on the logical colour of the line but also on the original logical colour of that pixel. Boolean operators AND, OR, XOR (exclusive OR) can operate *bit-wise* on the binary value of these two logical colours. Suppose that we have a line of logical colour 6 (binary 110) running through pixels coloured 0 through 7 (binary 000 through 111). The following table shows the resulting 3-bit pixel colours for the above three operators.

Original colour	0	1	2	3	4	5	6	7
Binary bits	000	001	010	011	100	101	110	111
OR with 6 (110)	110	111	110	111	110	111	110	111
AND with 6	000	000	010	010	100	100	110	110
XOR with 6	110	111	100	101	010	011	000	001

If you have such a facility on your machine, then add an extra primitive **setype(op:integer)** to our earlier list, which enables normal plotting (REPLACE), OR, AND or XOR corresponding to **op** values 0, 1, 2 or 3 respectively. (You may also have to adjust the **linepix** routine in your primitives to allow for Boolean plotting.)

These routines are often used in conjunction with a peripheral device called a *mouse* that is held in the hand and moved over a rectangular *graphics tablet* or *digitising tablet*. The position of the mouse on this tablet corresponds to the position of the *cursor* in the viewport. They may also be used with an equivalent input configuration such as a *light pen*. In order to access pixel information indicated by such a device, another primitive routine must be added to the library: mouse (p;pixelvector, status:integer). This routine returns the pixel coordinates p corresponding to the present mouse/light-pen position together with a status value status which is set to 1 when a special button is pressed (or the pen is pressed down), and 0 otherwise.

It is important to note that when two identical XOR lines are drawn one over the other, then the pixel components of the line will return to the colours they had before the lines were drawn. This type of Boolean plotting is available on many microcomputers for drawing blocks of pixels (sprites), and is the basis of many video games. Great care must be taken when using XOR in complicated scenes; it is very easy to change, inadvertently, parts of objects other than those you intend.

Example 5.1
We use this option to achieve a very useful operation known as *rubber-banding*. To illustrate we give a very simple example in which we draw a line from a fixed pixel point pixelvector p1 on the viewport to another, but we are not sure where that pixel p is to be positioned. The idea is that a mouse moves around the tablet, and with each new position the corresponding cursor indicates a pixel, and hence a new line. Naturally the old line has to be deleted and a new line drawn for each new pixel position; the process is programmed in listing 5.4 as routine rubber. Note how XOR is used repeatedly inside a loop to achieve this. This routine terminates if the status value is reset to 0 (by releasing the button on the mouse) and the final value of p is used.

Listing 5.4

```
PROCEDURE rubber(p1 : pixelvector ; VAR p2 : pixelvector ) ;
{ Routine using rubber banding to define a line from fixed }
{ pixel point 'p1' to a moveable pixel point 'p2' }
VAR p : pixelvector ;
      status : integer ;
BEGIN
{ Move mouse to initial end of line 'p2' and press button }
    REPEAT mouse(p2,status)
    UNTIL status < > 0 ;
{ Draw the first line }
    setype(0) ; movepix(p1) ; linepix(p2) ;
{ Hold button down while moving mouse, release button when }
{ required end of line achieved }
{ Store old end of line and use mouse for new 'p2' }
    REPEAT p := p2 ; mouse(p2,status) ;
{ XOR away the old line }
            setype(3) ; movepix(p1), linepix(p) ;
```

```
{ REPLACE it with new line from 'p1' to 'p2' }
        setype(0) ; movepix(p1) ; linepix(p2)
    UNTIL status=1
{ exit procedure when button is released }
END ; { of rubber }
```

Exercise 5.6
Use rubber-banding in a program that modifies a polygon on the viewport. A mouse is used first to indicate a vertex of the polygon, and then it must indicate movement of the chosen vertex about the viewport (the two polygon edges that enter that vertex must also move). Note that if XOR plotting is not available, then you have to clear the viewport and totally redraw every edge of the polygon for each new position of the mouse, and not just the two relevant edges. It is very difficult to point at a particular pixel using a mouse, you are lucky to keep your hand steady within one or two pixels of the target. In this exercise the nearest vertex to the mouse pixel must be found in order to be sure of which vertex is to be edited.

One very useful process in computer graphics is the development of a *menu*: a displayed list of possible options (as text or perhaps *icons*: idealised symbols, stored as blocks of pixels, representing a concept) are drawn on the viewport and the mouse is used to indicate which you require. We have not explicitly mentioned how to mix text with graphics. This is usually a trivial exercise, and we leave it to readers to write their own text primitives. Having written menu options on the viewport, we now have to ensure that the correct text or icon is indicated, so we imagine a discrete *rectangular grid* of pixels over the viewport and, when the mouse indicates a pixel, it is a simple matter to work out which grid point is nearest that pixel. A list of grid points nearest to each displayed option is stored or calculated, and it is easy to decide which option is indicated.

Exercise 5.7
Include all these ideas in a *draw, drag, delete* program. You will have a series of routines that can draw two-dimensional objects (such as plan views of chairs, tables etc.) at mouse-specified positions in the viewport. The whole scene (for example, furniture in a room) must then be edited interactively using a mouse. The grid/menu method is used to indicate whether you wish to draw a new occurrence of an object, to drag an indicated object around the viewport using XOR plotting, or to delete an object all together.

The last line type we consider is an *anti-aliased* line (see Foley and Van Dam, 1981). Lines of fixed colour and intensity drawn on raster devices tend to look jagged (aliased), since they are simply groups of squares (the pixels) that approximate to the line and so naturally they display this staircase effect. Some graphics devices have hardware anti-aliasing, to minimise the effect. Now lines are considered to have a thickness, and the pixels that are intersected by this line are not given a fixed colour; instead they are given a mix of the background colour and line colour proportional to just how much of the pixel is covered by the thick line. The same ideas are used to construct solid text characters so that they do not display the irritating jagged edge effect. If you have hardware anti-aliasing then incorporate it in new line-drawing primitives.

Hatching Polygons

One of the most useful routines in any line-graphics package is one which hatches a polygonal area using equi-spaced parallel lines (see figure 5.5). This facility is built into many graphics systems such as G.K.S. but for the benefit of readers not having access to these systems, and also for a useful demonstration of an application of the geometry introduced so far, we will discuss the theory behind such a routine. The polygon is assumed to have n vertices $\{p_i \equiv (x_i, y_i) | i = 1 \ldots n\}$ in order and implemented as the **vector2array p**. It may be convex or concave and its boundary may even cross itself.

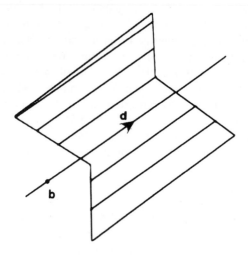

Figure 5.5

Without loss of generality it may be assumed that there is only one set of parallel hatching lines. For combinations of sets of hatching lines, the following theory is repeated for each set in turn.

Suppose the direction of the parallel lines is given by **vector2d** $\equiv$ (d.x, d.y) and the distance between neighbouring hatching lines is defined to be **dist**. This still leaves an infinite number of possible sets of parallel lines! To define one set uniquely, it is still necessary to specify a base point, $b \equiv$ (b.x, b.y), on any one of the lines from the set.

Note that a line with direction d which passes through b has the general vector form in the base/direction vector notation

$$b + \mu d \quad \text{where} \quad -\infty < \mu < \infty$$

As we have seen, a straight line may also be defined in the form

$$a \times y = b \times x + c$$

which has analytic representation

$$f(x, y) \equiv a \times y - b \times x - c$$

whence a general point $q \equiv (x, y)$ on the line is given by the equation $f(q) = 0$.

Since a hatching line has direction vector d, a may be taken as d.x and b as d.y, and so a line is given by

$$d.x \times y = d.y \times x + c$$

Each hatching line is defined by a unique 'c-value'. The line which passes through b has the 'c-value' cmid given by:

$$cmid = d.x \times b.y - d.y \times b.x$$

It is possible to calculate all the 'c-values' for the n lines with direction d (not necessarily in the set of hatching lines) which pass through each of the n vertices of the polygon, and then find the extreme values cmax and cmin thus

$$cmax = \max_{1 \leqslant i \leqslant n} \{d.x \times y_i - d.y \times x_i\}$$

and

$$cmin = \min_{1 \leqslant i \leqslant n} \{d.x \times y_i - d.y \times x_i\}$$

This means that the polygon lies totally between the two lines

$$d.x \times y = d.y \times x + cmin \quad \text{and} \quad d.x \times y = d.y \times x + cmax$$

In order to hatch the given polygon with lines parallel to d, then naturally only lines with 'c-values' between these extremes need be considered from the set. It should be noted that even though vector b is used to 'anchor' the set of parallel lines with inter-line distance dist, there is no need for the line which passes through b to intersect the polygons.

For ease of calculation it is sensible to resort to the vector notation for lines. Note that the hatching lines are all in the form

$$q + \mu d \quad \text{where} \quad -\infty < \mu < \infty$$

Here q represents a base point on a general hatching line. So it is necessary to find a vector q for each of the hatching lines that cuts the polygon. The q values are defined to be the points of intersection of this set of hatching lines with the line through b with direction d' (which is perpendicular to d — that is, to the hatching lines). Note that d' may be represented by the vector $(-d.y, d.x)$.

Hence the base points q are all of the form

$$q = b + \lambda d' \quad \text{where} \quad -\infty < \lambda < \infty$$

This formulation naturally represents every point on the new line perpendicular to the hatching lines, but only its points of intersection with the hatching lines are required. Note that any non-zero scalar multiple of d' may also represent the direction of the new line, and choose $s = (\text{dist}/|d'|) \times d'$ which means that vector s has length (or modulus) dist. Now note that q can be considered

$$q = b + ns = b + n \times (\text{dist}/|d'|) d' \text{ for some } n$$

If n is an integer, this vector combination gives all, but only, the points of intersection of the new line with a set of parallel lines of direction d in which neighbouring lines are a distance dist apart. Since b is one of these intersections ($n = 0$), then this formulation contains the base vectors for the required set of hatching lines. However, lines still have to be restricted to those with 'c-values' that lie between cmin and cmax. This is achieved by insisting that the 'n-values' of the base points of the hatching lines lie between nmin and nmax, where

$$\text{nmin} = \lceil (\text{cmin} - \text{cmid})/(\text{dist} \times |d'|) \rceil \text{ and}$$
$$\text{nmax} = \lfloor (\text{cmax} - \text{cmid})/(\text{dist} \times |d'|) \rfloor$$

Here $\lceil r \rceil$ gives the smallest integer not less than r, and $\lfloor r \rfloor$ gives the largest integer not greater than r. Note that 0, the 'n-value' corresponding to b, need not lie in this range.

Given any integer n, the corresponding vector q which then identifies one hatching line can be calculated. Intersect this line with the edges of the polygon defined by vertices $p_1, \ldots, p_n$. Suppose there is an intersection between points p_i and p_{i+1}, then note that the intersection on this edge may be given in the form

$$p_i + \alpha(p_{i+1} - p_i) \quad \text{where} \quad 0 \leqslant \alpha \leqslant 1,$$

as well as by $q + \mu d$ on the hatching line. The hatching line only cuts the polygon at this edge if the α value lies between 0 and 1. The μ value for each valid intersection must be stored.

As i varies through all the edges of the polygon (when $i = n$ then p_{n+1} is identified with p_1), all the μ values of proper intersections are calculated and then placed in increasing numerical order. Care must be taken with rounding errors and coincident points! There are always an even number of these μ values. The points on the hatching line corresponding to the μ values are found and the first joined to the second, third to the fourth etc., and this gives the correct hatching on one line. Varying n between nmin and nmax gives the complete hatching for the polygon. The process is programmed as procedure **hatch** in listing 5.5, which should be declared after **moveto** and **lineto**.

Listing 5.5

```
PROCEDURE hatch(n : integer ; p: vector2array ; b,d : vector2 ; dist : real) ;
{ Hatches an 'n-GON' with vertices 'p[1],...,p[n]' using equi-spaced }
{ parallel lines. The distance between neighbouring lines is 'dist' and each }
{ line has direction vector 'd'. One hatching line passes through 'b'. }
{ We impose the 'vectorarraysize' limit of 32 on the facet size. }
VAR np : integerarray ;
    mu : realarray ;
    e,inter,p1,p2,q,s : vector2 ;
    alpha,c,cmin,cmid,cmax,dmod,mu1,mu2 : real ;
    i,ii,isec,j,jj,ni,nint,nmin,nmax : integer ;
BEGIN
{ Find 'cmid', 'cmin' and 'cmax' }
    cmid := d.x*b.y-d.y*b.x ;
    cmin := d.x*p[1].y-d.y*p[1].x ; cmax := cmin ;
    FOR i := 2 TO n
    DO BEGIN
        c := d.x*p[i].y-d.y*p[i].x ;
        IF c < cmin
        THEN cmin := c
        ELSE IF c > cmax
             THEN cmax := c
    END ;
{ Construct vector 's' }
    dmod := sqrt(d.x*d.x+d.y*d.y) ;
    s.x := -dist/dmod*d.y : s.y := dist/dmod*d.x ;
{ Calculate 'nmin' and 'nmax' }
    nmin := trunc((cmin-cmid)/(dist*dmod)+0.9999) ;
    nmax := trunc((cmax-cmid)/(dist*dmod)) ;
{ Hatch the polygon }
    FOR j := nmin TO nmax
    DO BEGIN
{ Find 'q' the base vector of the hatching line }
        q.x := b.x+j*s.x ; q.y := b.y+j*s.y ;
{ Find the intersections of hatching line with edges of polygon }
        nint := 0 ; ni := n ;
        FOR i := 1 TO n
        DO BEGIN
            e.x := p[i].x-p[ni].x ;
            e.y := p[i].y-p[ni].y ;
            ill2(p[ni],e,q,d,inter,isec) ;
            IF isec = 1
            THEN BEGIN
                alpha := (inter.x-p[ni].x)/e.x ;
                IF (alpha >= 0) AND (alpha <= 1)
                THEN BEGIN
                    nint := nint+1 ;
                    np[nint] := nint ;
                    mu[nint] := (inter.x-q.x)/d.x
                END
            END ;
            ni := i
        END ;
```

```
{ Sort 'mu' values into order }
        FOR ii := 1 TO nint-1
        DO FOR jj := ii+1,nint
                DO IF mu[np[ii]] < mu[np[jj]]
                   THEN BEGIN
                                nnp := np[ii] ;
                                np[ii] := np[jj] ;
                                np[jj] := nnp
                        END ;
{ Join corresponding pairs of intersections }
        ni := 1 ;
        WHILE ni < nint
        DO BEGIN
                mu1 := mu[np[ni]] ; mu2 := mu[np[ni+1]] ;
                p1 := q.x+mu1*d.x ; p1.y := q.y+mu1*d.y ;
                p2 := q.x+mu2*d.x ; p2.y := q.y+mu2*d.y ;
                moveto(p1) ; lineto(p2) ;
                ni := ni+2
           END
      END
END ; { of hatch }
```

Exercise 5.8

If the polygon is composed of a large number of vertices then there is no need to waste time calculating all the intersections, only to find that most of the α values do not lie between 0 and 1 and so are irrelevant. A trick to save time is to put the hatching line in analytic form

$$f(v) \equiv f(x, y) \equiv a \times y - b \times x - c$$

Now if consecutive vectors p_i and p_{i+1} are such that $f(p_i)$ and $f(p_{i+1})$ have the same sign — that is, they are both positive or both negative — then there cannot be a useful point of intersection between them. Incorporate this into the routine above.

Convex Polygonal Area Filling

A routine which fills in a convex polygon with a given colour is a simple example of the general hatching problem, where the hatching lines are horizontal and correspond to neighbouring lines of pixels. The algorithm is to find the minimum and the maximum row of pixels $0 \leqslant \text{ymin} \leqslant \text{ymax} < \text{nypix}$ that lie on the edge or inside the polygon. For each *scan line* (row of pixels) in this range, find the pixel columns where it cuts the polygon; there will be two intersections which are joined by a line of the required colour. This is programmed in listing 5.6 and should be declared globally as **polyfill** if your graphics device does not have hardware area-fill.

Listing 5.6

```
PROCEDURE polypix(n : integer ; q : pixelarray ) ;
VAR i,iv,iy,xmin,ymin,xmax,ymax,nv : integer ;
      factor : real ;
BEGIN
   ymax := q[1].y ; ymin := ymax ;
   FOR i := 2 TO n
   DO BEGIN
            IF q[i].y > ymax THEN ymax := q[i].y ;
            IF q[i].y < ymin THEN ymin := q[i].y
         END ;
   IF ymax >= nypix THEN ymax=nypix-1 ;
   IF ymin <0 THEN ymin := 0 ;
   FOR iy := ymin TO ymax
   DO BEGIN
            xmin := nxpix ; xmax := -1 ; iv := n
            FOR nv := 1 TO n
            DO BEGIN
                  IF ((q[iv].y >= iy) OR (q[nv].y >= iy)) AND
                     ((q[iv].y <= iy) OR (q[nv].y <= iy)) AND
                     (q[iv].y <> q[nv].y)
                  THEN BEGIN
                           factor := (q[nv].x-q[iv].x)/(q[nv].y-q[iv].y) ;
                           ixi := q[iv].x+round((iy-q[iv].y)*factor) ;
                           IF ixi < xmin THEN xmin := ixi ;
                           IF ixi > xmax THEN xmax := ixi
                        END ;
                  iv := nv
               END ;
            IF xmax >= nxpix THEN xmax := nxpix-1 ;
            IF xmin <0 THEN xmin := 0 ;
            IF xmin <= xmax
            THEN BEGIN
                     pix1.x := xmin ; pix1.y := iy ;
                     pix2.x := xmax ; pix2.y := iy ;
                     movpix(pix1) ; linpix(pix2)
                  END
         END
END ; { of polypix }


PROCEDURE polyfill(n : integer ; p : vector2array) ;
{ Maximum facet size is '32=vectorarraysize' }
VAR q : pixelarray ;
BEGIN
   FOR i := 1 TO n
   DO BEGIN
            q.x := fx(p[i].x) ; q.y := fy(p[i].y)
         END ;
   polypix(n,q)
END ; { of polyfill }
```

Exercise 5.9

Write a routine which hatches a polygon using both vertical and horizontal hatching lines. Again this is an easier problem than the general case. Incorporate this routine in a program which produces histograms or bar-charts.

Exercise 5.10

Write a routine which hatches a segment of a circle for use in pie-charts. This problem is more involved as checks must also be made for intersections with the circular arc.

The Orientation of a Convex Polygon

In chapter 3 we defined a convex polygon with n sides in terms of an ordered list of its vertices $\{p_i \equiv (x_i, y_i) | i = 1 \ldots n\}$. These vertices were ordered either as they occur in a clockwise direction around the boundary of the polygon or in an anti-clockwise direction. As we discovered then, it is very important that we know in what orientation the polygon is defined, clockwise or anti-clockwise. We shall now consider how to determine this information from the list of vertices.

Since the polygon is convex, given the relative orientation of any two consecutive sides we may deduce the orientation of the whole. Thus we need consider only the first three vertices and the two lines joining them. Consider the line from p_1 to p_2. The analytic representation of this line may be written

$$f_1(x, y) \equiv ay - bx - c$$

where $a = (x_2 - x_1)$, $b = (y_2 - y_1)$ and $c = a \times y_2 - b \times x_2$.

In chapter 3 it was shown that looking from p_1 to p_2 a point (x, y) with $f_1(x, y) > 0$ lies to the left of the line p_1 to p_2, and if $f_1(x, y) < 0$ then (x, y) lies to the right.

From figure 5.6 it may be seen that for the polygon to be in anti-clockwise orientation p_3 should lie to the left of the line from p_1 to p_2, and for clockwise orientation it should lie to the right. Therefore, in order to determine the orientation of a polygon defined in the above form, we need simply calculate $f_1(x_3, y_3)$

$$
\begin{aligned}
f_1(x_3, y_3) &\equiv a \times y_3 - b \times x_3 - c \\
&= (x_2 - x_1) \times y_3 - (y_2 - y_1) \times x_3 - (x_2 - x_1) \times y_2 \\
&\quad + (y_2 - y_1) \times x_2 \\
&= (x_2 - x_1) \times (y_3 - y_2) - (y_2 - y_1) \times (x_3 - x_2)
\end{aligned}
$$

If this is positive then the polygon is oriented anti-clockwise, and if negative then the orientation is clockwise. If $f_1(x_3, y_3)$ is zero then the three vertices p_1, p_2 and p_3 are collinear and the orientation of the polygon cannot be thus determined. The inclusion of three consecutive collinear vertices in the boundary

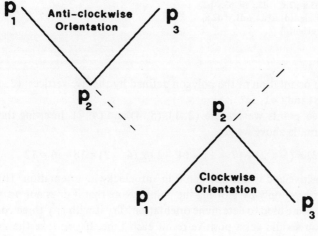

Figure 5.6

of a polygon is never necessary and, since it may cause problems, should be avoided. The integer function orient (listing 5.7) determines the orientation of a polygon. The value 1 is returned if the polygon is in anti-clockwise orientation, and −1 if it is clockwise. If the polygon is degenerate (that is, if the three points are collinear or even coincident) then the value 0 is returned. The routine calls a function sign (also given in listing 5.7) which returns the sign (+1, 0 or −1) of a real number. sign will be used many times in the three-dimensional routines that follow.

Listing 5.7

```
FUNCTION sign(r : real) : integer ;
{ Returns    1 if r>0,  0 if r=0    or    -1 if r<0 }
BEGIN
    IF r > epsilon
    THEN sign := 1
    ELSE IF r < -epsilon
            THEN sign := -1
            ELSE sign := 0
END ; { of sign }

FUNCTION orient(p1,p2,p3 : vector2) : integer ;  ·
{ Returns the orientation of the polygon with consecutive }
{ vertices p1, p2 and p3 /  -1 : clockwise orientation }
{                          +1 : anti-clockwise orientation }
{                           0 : degenerate - line or point }
VAR d1,d2 : vector2 ;
BEGIN
    d1.x := p2.x-p1.x ; d1.y := p2.y-p1.y ;
```

```
    d2.x := p3.x-p2.x ;  d2.y := p3.y-p2.y ;
    orient := sign(d1.x*d2.y-d1.y*d2.x)
END ; { of orient }
```

Example 5.2
What is the orientation of the polygon defined by the five vertices: $(2, 1), (5, 4)$, $(4, 7), (1, 8)$ and $(-1, 5)$?

The three points we use are $(2, 1), (5, 4)$ and $(4, 7)$. Inserting these values into the formula above we get

$$f_1(4, 2) = (5 - 2) \times (7 - 1) - (4 - 1) \times (4 - 2) = 18 - 6 = 12$$

which is positive and so the polygon is in anti-clockwise orientation. This may be checked easily, simply by plotting the points. Note that it does not matter which three vertices are used to determine orientation. Try it with any three consecutive vertices. You should get a positive result each time. If you take the same three vertices in the opposite order, then naturally you get a negative value.

The Intersection of Two Convex Polygons

Imagine two convex polygons A and B. Their area of intersection is either null or another convex polygon. The following method for finding the polygon of intersection of two convex polygons has far-reaching applications in the three-dimensional work later in this book and should consequently be carefully studied. Because the 'inside and outside' method of chapter 3 will be used, it is necessary that both polygons are given in the same orientation – we assume anti-clockwise. This may be checked using the method given above.

Suppose polygon A has numa vertices and polygon B has numb vertices, the co-ordinates of which are stored in the array apoly[1..numa] and bpoly[1..numb]. The area of intersection is that part of polygon A which is also part of polygon B. The method employed to find this area is to take each of the boundary lines of polygon B in turn and repeatedly 'slice off' the area of polygon A which lies on the negative side of the extended line.

In order to describe the process in more detail, we introduce the term *feasible polygon* to mean the polygon which contains precisely the points which have not been proved to lie outside either A or B, the vector2 array f[1..2, 1..n] and the variables I1, initially of value 1, and I2, initially 2.

As we have mentioned previously, the array structure is not very flexible. The value n must be specified precisely, so a value greater than the maximum possible index must be chosen. See chapter 2 for a description of the use of arrays.

Initially, of course, the whole of polygon A may lie within polygon B, so the feasible polygon is A and the co-ordinates of the vertices of A, apoly[1..numa], should be copied into array f[I1, 1..numa]. At each stage of the slicing process we begin with a feasible polygon C, the numc vertices of which will be stored in array f[l1, 1..numc], and the parts of this area lying on the negative side of the slicing line will be discarded leaving a new feasible polygon C', having numcdash vertices, which is entered in array f[l2, 1..numcdash]. The values of l1 and l2 are then swapped and the process repeated with the next line on the boundary of polygon B, replacing numc with numcdash. If, at any stage during the slicing, the feasible polygon has fewer than 3 vertices then it may be considered empty (since a triangle is the polygon with fewest vertices)and so the process may stop, as no further slicing could revive it. After each of the numb boundary lines of B has been used to slice the feasible polygon, the vertices of the true polygon of intersection are left in the array f[l2, 1..numc]. These may be copied into new array cpoly[1..numc] for return. If the area of intersection is empty then the routine overlap (listing 5.8), which implements this algorithm, returns numc as zero.

The only question remaining is how to execute the slicing. This is where we use the 'inside and outside' technique. We must discard the part of the area of possible intersection which lies to the negative side of the slicing line, bpoly[i] to bpoly[j].

The analytic representation of this line is

$$f_i \equiv a \times y - b \times x - c$$

where a = bpoly[j].x − bpoly[i].x ; b = bpoly[j].y − bpoly[i].y
c = a × bpoly[i].y − b × bpoly[i].x;

It can be determined easily whether vertices of the feasible polygon lie on the negative side of the line by finding the value of $f_i(x, y)$ for each vertex (x, y). The problem is to find the co-ordinates of the points where the slicing line actually cuts the boundary of the feasible polygon. We do this by considering this boundary one line segment at a time. Consider line segment from $v_k \equiv$ f[l1, k] to $v_l \equiv$ f[l1, l]. If $f_i(v_k) \geqslant 0$ then v_k is copied to the array containing the new feasible polygon. If the points v_k and v_l lie on strictly opposite sides of the slicing line, then find the point of intersection of the line v_k to v_l with the slicing line and store this.

This process will, in fact, suffice. k varies from 1 to numc (with $l = k + 1$ modulo numc) for each value of i varying from 1 to numb (with $j = i + 1$ modulo numb). The process may be understood more easily through study of figure 5.7.

Listing 5.8

```
PROCEDURE overlap(numa,numb : integer ; apoly,bpoly : vector2array ;
                  VAR numc : integer ; VAR cpoly : vector2array ;
                  VAR intersection,orientation : integer) ;
{ Finds the area of intersection between the two polygons 'apoly' and }
{ 'bpoly' with given 'orientation's (1 means anti-clockwise,-1 clockwise }
{ The area of intersection is returned with 'numc' vertices stored in }
{ the 'cpoly' array. If no intersection exists then 0 'intersection' else 1 }
```

```
VAR i,j,index1,index2,l1,l2,numcdash : integer ;
    f : ARRAY[1..2,1..32] OF vector2 ;
    end1,end2,v1,v2 : vector2 ;
    ca,cb,cc,fv1,fv2,absfv1,absfv2,delta : real ;
BEGIN
{ Copy the details of polygon 'apoly' into the first 'f' store }
    l1 := 1 ; numc := numa ;
    FOR i := 1 TO numc
    DO f[l1,i] := apoly[i] ;
{ Slice feasible polygon (in arrays 'f[1,1..numc]' with each edge of }
{ 'bpoly'. The end points of the slicing edge are 'end1' and 'end2' }
    end1 := bpoly[numb] ;
    FOR i := 1 TO numb
    DO BEGIN
{ Sliced area will be stored in the second storage area 'f[l2,1..newc]' }
        l2 := 3-l1 ; end2 := bpoly[i] ;
{ Calculate the functional representation of the line 'end1' to 'end2' }
{        ' F(X,Y)=ca*Y+cb*X+cc '                                        }
        ca := end2.x-end1.x ; cb := end1.y-end2.y ;
        cc := -end1.x*cb-end1.y*ca ;
{ Consider the feasible polygon one edge at a time. }
{ The edge under consideration is from 'v1' to 'v2' }
        v1 := f[l1,numc] ;
{ Calculate 'F(v1)' and determine whether it lies on, }
{ to the inside of or to the outside of the slicing edge. }
        fv1 := ca*v1.y+cb*v1.x+cc ; absfv1 := abs(fv1) ;
        IF absfv1 < epsilon
        THEN index1 := 0
        ELSE index1 := sign(fv1)*orientation ;
        numcdash := 0 ;
        FOR j := 1 TO numc
        DO BEGIN
            v2 := f[l1,j] ;
{ Calculate whether 'v2' lies on, to the inside of }
{ or to the outside of the slicing edge. }
            fv2 := ca*v2.y+cb*v2.x+cc ; absfv2 := abs(fv2) ;
            IF absfv2 < epsilon
            THEN index2 := 0
            ELSE index2 := sign(fv2)*orientation ;
{ If 'v1' lies on or to the inside of the slicing edge }
{ edge then include it in the new feasible polygon. }
            IF index1 >= 0
            THEN BEGIN
                    numcdash := numcdash+1 ;
                    f[l2,numcdash] := v1
                 END ;
{ If 'v1' and 'v2' lie on strictly opposite sides of the slicing edge }
{ then include the point of intersection in the new feasible polygon }
            IF (index1 <> 0) AND (index1 <> index2) AND
               (index2 <> 0)
            THEN BEGIN
                    delta := absfv1+absfv2 ;
                    numcdash := numcdash+1 ;
                    f[l2,numcdash].x := (absfv2*v1.x+absfv1*v2.x)/delta ;
```

```
                    f[l2,numcdash].y := (absfv2*v1.y+absfv1*v2.y)/delta
                    END ;
{ The second point of this edge will be the first of the next edge }
                    fv1 := fv2 ; absfv1 := absfv2 ;
                    index1 := index2 ; v1 := v2
                END ;
{ If the feasible polygon degenerates then no overlap exists }
                IF numcdash < 3
                THEN BEGIN intersection := 0 ; numc := 0 ; EXIT END
                ELSE BEGIN
{ The new feasible polygon becomes the next polygon to be sliced }
                    numc := numcdash ; l1 := l2 ; end1 := end2
{ Move on to the next edge of bpoly }
                END
           END ;
{ Reach here when all slicing is complete. Copy the remaining }
{ feasible polygon to the array 'cpoly' for return.}
    intersection := 1 ;
    FOR i := 1 TO numc
    DO cpoly[i] := f[l1,i]
END ; { of overlap }
```

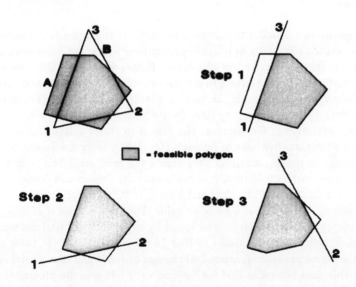

Figure 5.7

Exercise 5.11

The use of this algorithm appears a number of times in this text, particularly in the three-dimensional hidden surface removal techniques introduced in chapter 13, but it may also be used to solve a problem already mentioned — the clipping of polygonal areas in two dimensions.

When using our area-fill routine (listing 5.6) you will note that clipping within the window rectangle is automatic. This is not necessarily the case with some hardware area-filling routines. In order to draw only the part of a polygon which lies within the window area, we must draw the area of intersection between the polygon and the window rectangle. You can achieve this by adjusting the overlap routine (listing 5.8), using polygon B with four vertices (±clippedx, ±clippedy) given in anti-clockwise order.

The overlap algorithm may be used, of course, to clip around any convex polygonal area.

Exercise 5.12
The problem of blanking does not generally apply to colour graphics since an area may be blanked after the drawing is complete by simply drawing a rectangle on top, but the overlap routine could be adapted for use as a polygon-blanking algorithm and it is a useful exercise.

Animation

In this section we consider the *cartoon* methods of animating two-dimensional graphics, as used frequently in television advertising within the framework of the program technique described in chapter 4. Rather than use XOR and similar plotting methods, here we assume that the *movie* consists of a number of discrete *frames* which can be brought in view one every 1/24 second (for example, 16 mm film). Some systems may have different frame speeds – video works at 25 frames per second, for instance. The idea is to create a sequence of frames such that all consecutive pairs of frames differ slightly from one another, so that when viewed in quick succession they create the animated effect – hence the name *cartoon* method. Naturally if the scenes on consecutive frames change slowly the animation will be slow and boring, if they change too quickly then the animation will stutter and be of no value. The correct amount of change for a particular type of scene can only be found by experience and trial and error.

A ten-second movie will consist of 10 * 24 + 1 frames: note '+1', there are 24 *changes* of frame per second, hence 240 changes of frame and thus a total of 241 frames. This does not mean that we have to write 241 separate programs! If we assume that our graphics system is such that the erase primitive creates the next frame in the sequence, it is a simple matter to have a large for loop inside the scene routine which is called from the draw_a_picture routine of listing 4.2; each pass through the loop causes small changes to be made to certain parameters of construction routines, thus automating small changes in pictures in consecutive frames. Note that, if you are using 16 mm film for your movie, you will have to rotate the scene through 90° because of the mechanism used in projectors. This may be incorporated in the ABSOLUTE to OBSERVER matrix *Q*. We illustrate this idea with a number of examples.

Example 5.3

Line-drawn letters 'I', 'A' and 'N' rotate in a movie of 121 frames (numbered 0 through 120). During the movie the 'I' is to rotate 3 times about an axis through the centre of the letter into the frame. The letter 'A' consists of two parts, the outer of which is to rotate twice about the horizontal axis through its centre, while the inner remains fixed. Finally the 'N' rotates 5 times about the vertical through its centre. The example is programmed in listing 5.9 and sample frames 0, 20, 40, 60, 80, 100, 120, with 90° rotation are shown in figure 5.8.

The observer is fixed at the origin, and the rotation alpha depends on whether a 90° rotation is needed. The line segments for the 'I', 'N' and inner and outer 'A' are defined as polygons given by SETUP vertices read from disk file 'ina.dat'. With each new frame, the various ACTUAL positions of the four polygons are calculated separately (matrix P), and combined with the fixed matrix Q, to give $R = Q \times P$. Angles angi, anga and angn are used to describe the rotations of 'I', 'A' and 'N' respectively for each new frame. Rotations of vertices into the 'z-direction' are achieved by scaling! A routine poly, with R as a parameter, is then used to draw each letter in its correct OBSERVED position.

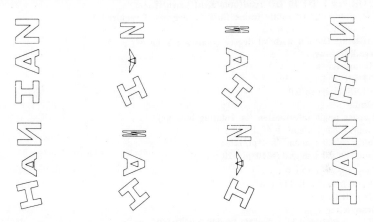

Figure 5.8

Listing 5.9

```
PROCEDURE scene ;
VAR vi,vao,vai,vn : vector2array ;
    A,B,P,R : matrix3x3 ;
    answer : char ;
    angi,angid,anga,angad,angn,angnd : real
    frame : integer ;

  PROCEDURE poly(R : matrix3x3 ; n : integer ; v : vector2array ) ;
  VAR i : integer ;
        pt : vector2 ;
```

```
BEGIN
{ Place SETUP vertices of polygon defining letter into OBSERVED }
{ position; join with lines. Move to last vertex on OBSERVED polygon }
        pt.x := R[1,1]*v[n].x+R[1,2]*v[n].y+R[1,3] ;
        pt.y := R[2,1]*v[n].x+R[2,2]*v[n].y+R[2,3] ;
        moveto(pt) ;
        FOR i := 1 TO n
        DO BEGIN
{ Join successive OBSERVED polygon vertices }
                pt.x := R[1,1]*v[i].x+R[1,2]*v[i].y+R[1,3] ;
                pt.y := R[2,1]*v[i].x+R[2,2]*v[i].y+R[2,3] ;
                lineto(pt) ;
             END
     END ; { of poly }

BEGIN
{ Read in data on letters I, A and N }
        assign(indata,'ian.dat') ; reset(indata) ;
        FOR i := 1 TO 12 DO read(indata,vi[i].x,vi[i].y) ;
        FOR i := 1 TO 8   DO read(indata,vao[i].x,vao[i].y) ;
        FOR i := 1 TO 3   DO read(indata,vai[i].x,vai[i].y) ;
        FOR i := 1 TO 10 DO read(indata,vn[i].x,vn[i].y) ;
{ Use matrix 'Q' to rotate frame thru' 90 degrees if required }
        eye.x := 0.0 ; eye.y := 0.0 ;
        writeln(' Do you wish 90 degree rotation : Y or N') ;
        readln(answer) ;
        IF answer = 'Y'
        THEN alpha := pi*0.5
        ELSE alpha := 0.0 ;
        findQ ;
{ Prepare angle information for rotating letters }
        angi := 0.0 ; angid := 6*pi/120 ;
        anga := 0.0 ; angad := 4*pi/120 ;
        angn := 0.0 ; angnd := 10*pi/120 ;
{ Loop through 120 frames }
        FOR frame := 0 TO 120
        DO BEGIN
{ Draw letter I }
                rot2(angi,A) ; tran2(2.5,0.0,B) ; mult2(B,A,P) ;
                mult2(Q,P,R) ; poly(R,12,vi) ;
{ Draw outside of A }
                scale2(1.0,cos(anga),A) ; mult2(Q,P,R) ; poly(R,8,vao) ;
{ Draw inside of A }
                poly(R,3,vai) ;
{ Draw N }
                scale2(cos(angn),1.0,A) ; tran2(-2.5,0.0,B) ;
                mult2(B,A,P) ; mult2(Q,P,R) ; poly(R,10,vn) ;
{ Update the angles }
                angi := angi+angid ; anga := anga+angad ; angn := angn+angnd ;
{ Move to next frame }
                erase
             END
     END ; { of scene }
```

FILE 'ian.dat'
```
 0.90   1.00      0.90   0.50      0.25   0.50       0.25  -0.50
 0.90  -0.50      0.90  -1.00     -0.90  -1.00      -0.90  -0.50
-0.25  -0.50     -0.25   0.50     -0.90   0.50      -0.90   1.00


 0.25   1.00      1.00  -1.00      0.50  -1.00       0.375 -0.666666
-0.375 -0.666666  -0.50  -1.00     -1.00  -1.00      -0.25   1.00


 0.00   0.333333      0.25  -0.333333      -0.25  -0.333333


 1.00   1.00     -0.50   1.00      0.50  -0.30       0.50   1.00
 1.00   1.00      1.00  -1.00      0.50  -1.00      -0.50   0.30
-0.50  -1.00     -1.00  -1.00
```

Example 5.4

Figure 5.9 shows various stages of the transformation between a square and a star. The scene procedure to achieve this movie of 121 frames is given in listing 5.10, which uses poly from listing 5.9. This must be called by the 'draw_a_ picture' routine of listing 4.2. The two planar objects are read from file 'sqstardat' as two ordered sets of 8 vertices $\{v1[i] \mid i = 1..8\}$ and $\{v2[i] \mid i = 1..8\}$, as with this example they need not be in the same orientation. Each polygonal shape is drawn by joining the vertices in the prescribed order. The animation method is to calculate and draw an intermediate SETUP set of vertices $\{vinter[i] \mid i = 1..8\}$ for each new frame. The position of these SETUP vertices in the jth frame is found by moving a proportion $j/120(=\mu)$ along the line joining the ith points from the two original figures: that is

$$vinter[i] = (1 - \mu).v1[i] + \mu.v2[i]$$

The matrix Q is then used to put the vertices directly in their OBSERVED position where they are drawn using poly.

Listing 5.10

```
PROCEDURE scene ;
VAR v1,v2,vinter : vector2array ;
    A,B,P,R : matrix3x3 ;
    answer : char ;
    mu : real
    i,frame : integer ;
BEGIN
{ Read in data on square and star }
    assign(indata,'sqstar.dat') ; reset(indata) ;
    FOR i := 1 TO 8 DO read(indata,v1[i].x,v1[i].y) ;
    FOR i := 1 TO 8 DO read(indata,v2[i].x,v2[i].y) ;
```

```
{ Use matrix 'Q' to rotate frame thru' 90 degrees if required }
   eye.x := 0.0 ; eye.y := 0.0 ;
   writeln(' Do you wish 90 degree rotation : Y or N') ;
   readln(answer) ;
   IF answer = 'Y'
   THEN alpha := pi*0.5
   ELSE alpha := 0.0 ;
   findQ ;
{ Loop thru 120 frames }
   FOR frame := 0 TO 120
   DO BEGIN
{ Find intermediate vertices in SETUP position 'vinter' }
           mu := frame/120 ;
           FOR i := 1 TO 8
           DO BEGIN
                   vinter[i].x := (1-mu)*v1[i].x+mu*v2[i].x ;
                   vinter[i].y := (1-mu)*v1[i].y+mu*v2[i].y
               END ;
           poly(Q,8,vinter) ;
{ Move to next frame }
           erase
       END
END ; { of scene }


File 'sqstar.dat'
0.0  3.0     3.0  3.0     3.0  0.0     3.0 -3.0
0.0 -3.0    -3.0 -3.0    -3.0  0.0    -3.0  3.0

3.0  0.0     1.0  1.0     0.0  3.0    -1.0  1.0
-3.0  0.0    -1.0 -1.0     0.0 -3.0     1.0 -1.0
```

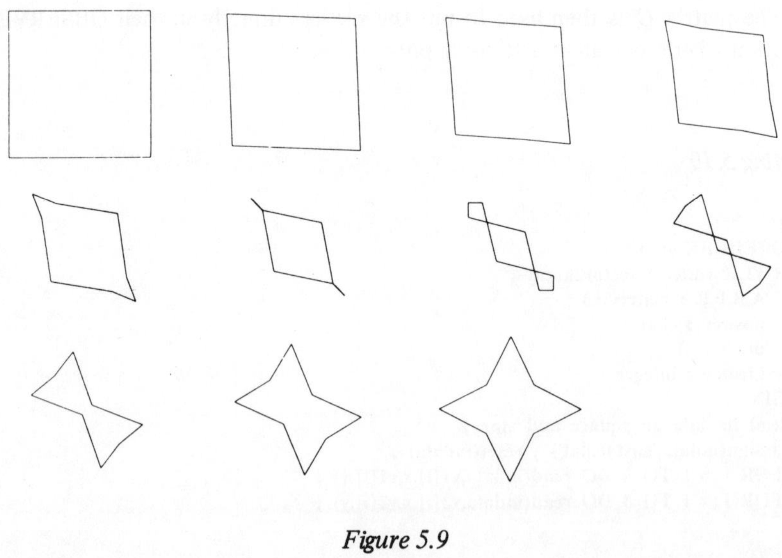

Figure 5.9

Exercise 5.13

Use this technique to create a movie of a two-dimensional scene in which objects move relative to one another (their ACTUAL position) as well as the observer changing (the OBSERVED position). These movement and observation parameters will be the values changed inside the animation loop. You can also change the size of the viewport/window scale to give the effect of zooming into a scene, or this can be achieved by scaling. Clipping may be necessary.

Exercise 5.14

You can allow a line drawing to *grow* as the movie progresses. If the complete picture is made up of a sequence of n line segments of total length d units, then the jth frame from a move of $m + 1$ frames will contain a line sequence of length $d * j/m$ units. Thus an intermediate picture will contain some lines from the complete scene, some will be missing, and one line will be partially drawn. All of this can be achieved by creating SETUP co-ordinates for the intermediate lines from a file containing data for the complete figure. For example, you can start with an empty frame and successively draw the outline of a previously *digitised* land mass, such as Australia. You could clip the scene inside a given rectangle, and change the size of the clipping rectangle as the move progresses.

Exercise 5.15

Extend this method so that it can be used with solid polygons as opposed to lines.

6 Three-dimensional Co-ordinate Geometry

Before we lead on to a study of the graphical display of objects in three-dimensional space, we first have to come to terms with the three-dimensional Cartesian co-ordinate geometry and introduce some useful procedures for manipulating objects in three-dimensional space. (For further reading we recommend books by Cohn (1961) and McCrae (1953)). As in two-dimensional space, we arbitrarily fix a point in the space, named the *co-ordinate origin* (origin for short). We then imagine three mutually perpendicular lines through this point, each line extending to infinity in both directions. These are the *x-axis*, *y-axis* and *z-axis*. Each axis is thought to have a positive and a negative half, both starting at the origin — that is, distances measured from the origin along the axis are positive on one side and negative on the other. We may think of the x and y axes in a similar way to two-dimensional space, both lying on the page of this book say, the positive x-axis horizontal and to the right of the origin, and the positive y-axis vertical and above the origin. This just leaves the position of the z-axis: it has to be perpendicular to the page (since it is perpendicular to both x and y axes). The positive z-axis can be into the page (the so-called *left-handed triad* of axes) or out of the page (the *right-handed triad*). You can realise the difference on your hands. On either hand, hold the thumb, index finger and middle finger at right angles to one another with the middle finger perpendicular to the palm of your hand: the thumb may be taken as the positive x-axis, the index finger as the positive y-axis and the middle finger the positive z-axis. See figure 6.1.

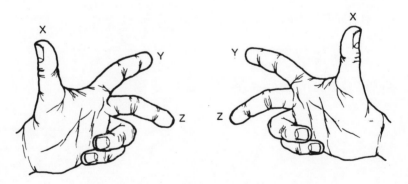

Figure 6.1

There are advantages and disadvantages with both systems, however the graphics community has standardised on the right-handed triad and so this is the axial system we will use throughout this book. What we say in the remainder of the book, using right-handed axes, has its equivalent in the left-handed system – it does not matter which notation you finally decide to use as long as you are consistent, and are aware of the implications of your choice.

We specify a general point v in space by a *co-ordinate triple* or *vector* (x, y, z), where the individual co-ordinate values are the perpendicular projections of the point on to the respective x, y and z axes. By projection we mean the unique point on the specified axis such that a line from that point to v is perpendicular to the axis.

In order to deal with three-dimensional modelling and display, we reorganise our programs in a manner similar to the two-dimensional programs of chapters 3, 4 and 5. We again will need CONST, TYPE, VAR and PROCEDURE declarations merged into the combined listings 1.1 and 1.3, together with some other useful two-dimensional routines from previous chapters. We will see in listing 7.1 a RECORD TYPE vector3 declared to hold 3-D point vectors. We also give an ARRAY TYPE vector3array which will hold up to vectorarraysize vector3 values.

Initially there are two operations we need to consider for three-dimensional vectors. Suppose we have two vectors $p_1 \equiv (x_1, y_1, z_1)$ and $p_2 \equiv (x_2, y_2, z_2)$, then a *scalar multiple* of p_1, kp_1, is obtained by multiplying the three individual co-ordinate values of p_1 by a scalar number k

$$kp_1 \equiv (k \times x_1, k \times y_1, k \times z_1)$$

and the *vector sum* of the two vectors, $p_1 + p_2$, is calculated by adding their x co-ordinates together, their y co-ordinates together and their z co-ordinates together to give a new vector

$$p_1 + p_2 = (x_1 + x_2, y_1 + y_2, z_1 + z_2)$$

Definition of a Straight Line

A straight line in three-dimensional space passing through two such points $p_1 \equiv (x_1, y_1, z_1)$ and $p_2 \equiv (x_2, y_2, z_2)$ may be defined by describing the co-ordinates of a general point $v \equiv (x, y, z)$ on the line by three equations

$$(x - x_1) \times (y_2 - y_1) = (y - y_1) \times (x_2 - x_1)$$
$$(y - y_1) \times (z_2 - z_1) = (z - z_1) \times (y_2 - y_1)$$
$$(z - z_1) \times (x_2 - x_1) = (x - x_1) \times (z_2 - z_1)$$

Although these are three equations in three unknowns, we will find that they are *linearly dependent* (inter-related) and so there is no unique solution (naturally, since we are generating a general form for points on the line, not just one point). These equations enable us to calculate two of the co-ordinates in terms of a third (see example 6.1).

As in the two-dimensional case, this is not the only way of representing a straight line. We may also use a direct extension of the vector representation introduced in chapter 3. The general point on the line is represented as a vector combination of p_1 and p_2 dependent upon the real number μ

$$v(\mu) \equiv (1 - \mu)p_1 + \mu p_2 \quad \text{where} \quad -\infty < \mu < \infty$$

that is

$$v(\mu) = ((1 - \mu) \times x_1 + \mu \times x_2, (1 - \mu) \times y_1 + \mu \times y_2, (1 - \mu) \times z_1 + \mu \times z_2))$$

The μ may be interpreted in a manner exactly analogous to the two-dimensional case and is again placed in brackets after v to demonstrate the dependence of v on its value. However, when this concept has been fully investigated then (μ) will be omitted. Note that when $\mu = 0$ the equation returns point p_1, and when $\mu = 1$ it gives p_2.

We may rewrite this vector expression

$$v(\mu) = p_1 + \mu(p_2 - p_1)$$

and like its counterpart in two dimensions, p_1 is called a *base vector* and $(p_2 - p_1)$ a *direction vector*. We normally write this as $b + \mu d$. This once again demonstrates the dual interpretation of a vector. A vector may be used to specify a unique point in three-dimensional space, or it may be considered as a general direction, namely any line parallel to that line which joins the origin to the point it represents. We can move along a line in one of two directions, so we say that the direction from the origin to the point has *positive sense*, and from the point to the origin *negative sense*. Hence vectors $d \equiv (x, y, z)$ and $-d \equiv (-x, -y, -z)$ represent the same line in space but their directions are of opposite senses. We define the *length* of a vector $d \equiv (x, y, z)$ (sometimes called its *modulus*, or *absolute value*) as $|d|$, the distance of the point vector from the origin

$$|d| \equiv \sqrt{(x^2 + y^2 + z^2)}$$

and a vector having unit length is called a *unit vector*.

So any point on the line $b + \mu d$ is found by moving to the point b and then travelling along a line which is parallel to the direction d, a distance $|\mu d|$ in the positive sense of d if μ is positive, and in the negative sense if negative. Note that any point on the line can act as a base vector b, and the direction vector d may be replaced by any non-zero scalar multiple of itself (a negative scalar multiple will reverse the sense of the line).

If the direction vector $d \equiv (x, y, z)$ with positive sense makes angles θ_x, θ_y and θ_z with the respective positive x, y and z axial directions then we have the ratio equation

$$x : y : z = \cos \theta_x : \cos \theta_y : \cos \theta_z$$

which means that

$$d \equiv (\lambda \times \cos \theta_x, \lambda \times \cos \theta_y, \lambda \times \cos \theta_z) \text{ for some } \lambda > 0$$

We know from the properties of three-dimensional geometry that

$$\cos^2 \theta_x + \cos^2 \theta_y + \cos^2 \theta_z = 1$$

Hence $\lambda = |d|$, and if the direction vector is a unit vector (that is, modulus = $\lambda = 1$), then the co-ordinates of this vector must be ($\cos \theta_x$, $\cos \theta_y$, $\cos \theta_z$). The co-ordinates of a direction vector given in this way are called the *direction cosines* of the set of lines generated by the vector. In general, if the direction vector is $d \equiv (x, y, z)$ then the direction cosines are

$$\left(\frac{x}{|d|}, \frac{y}{|d|}, \frac{z}{|d|} \right)$$

Example 6.1
Describe the line joining $(1, 2, 3)$ to $(-1, 0, 2)$, using the three methods shown so far.

The general point (x, y, z) on the line satisfies the equations

$$(x - 1) \times (0 - 2) = (y - 2) \times (-1 - 1)$$
$$(y - 2) \times (2 - 3) = (z - 3) \times (0 - 2)$$

and $\quad (z - 3) \times (-1 - 1) = (x - 1) \times (2 - 3)$

That is

$$-2x + 2y = 2 \tag{6.1}$$
$$-y + 2z = 4 \tag{6.2}$$
$$-2z + x = -5 \tag{6.3}$$

Notice that equation (6.1) is -2 times the sum of equations (6.2) and (6.3). Thus we need only consider these latter two equations, to get

$$y = 2z - 4 \quad \text{and} \quad x = 2z - 5$$

whence the general point on the line depends only on the one variable, in this case z, and it is given by $(2z - 5, 2z - 4, z)$. We easily check this result by noting that when $z = 3$ we get $(1, 2, 3)$ and when $z = 2$ we get $(-1, 0, 2)$, the two original points defining the line.

In vector form the general point on the line (depending on μ) is

$$v(\mu) = (1 - \mu)(1, 2, 3) + \mu(-1, 0, 2) = (1 - 2\mu, 2 - 2\mu, 3 - \mu)$$

Again the co-ordinates depend on just one parameter (μ), and to check the validity of this representation of a line we note that $v(0) = (1, 2, 3)$ and $v(1) = (-1, 0, 2)$.

If we put the line into base/direction vector form we see that

$$v(\mu) = (1, 2, 3) + \mu(-2, -2, -1)$$

with $(1, 2, 3)$ as the base vector and $(-2, -2, -1)$ as the direction (which incidently has modulus $\sqrt{(4 + 4 + 1)} = \sqrt{9} = 3$). We also noted that any point on the line can act as a base vector, and so we can give another form for the general point on this line, v'

$$v'(\mu) = (-1, 0 \ \ 2) + \mu(-2, -2, -1)$$

We can change the direction vector into its direction cosine form, which is $(-2/3, -2/3, -1/3)$, and represent the line in another version of the base/direction form

$$v''(\mu) = (1, 2, 3) + \mu(-2/3, -2/3, -1/3)$$

Naturally the same μ value will give different points for different representations of the line – for example, $v(3) = (-5, -4, 0)$, $v'(3) = (-7, -6, -1)$ and $v''(3) = (-1, 0, 2)$. The direction of this line makes angles $131.81° = \cos^{-1}(-2/3)$, $131.81°$ and $109.47° = \cos^{-1}(-1/3)$ with the positive x, y and z directions respectively.

The Angle between Two Direction Vectors

In order to calculate such an angle we first introduce the operator $\cdot$, the *dot product* or *scalar product*. This operates on two vectors and returns a scalar (real) result thus

$$p \cdot q = (x_1, y_1, z_1) \cdot (x_2, y_2, z_2) = x_1 \times x_2 + y_1 \times y_2 + z_1 \times z_2$$

See function dot3 in listing 6.1.

Listing 6.1

```
FUNCTION dot3(p1,p2 : vector3) : real ;
{ Returns the scalar product of the two vectors p1 and p2 }
BEGIN  dot3 := p1.x*p2.x+p1.y*p2.y+p1.z*p2.z
END ; { of dot3 }
```

If p and q are both unit vectors (that is, in direction cosine form), and θ is the angle between the lines, then $\cos \theta = p \cdot q$. The equivalent two-dimensional relationship was mentioned in chapter 3. In general, therefore, the angle between two direction vectors p and q, which we can assume meet at the origin, is

$$\cos^{-1} \left(\frac{p}{|p|} \cdot \frac{q}{|q|} \right)$$

Thus p and q are mutually perpendicular directions if and only if $p \cdot q = 0$.

Definition of a Plane

We now consider a plane in three-dimensional space. The general point $v \equiv (x, y, z)$ on the plane is given by the vector equation

$$n \cdot v = k$$

where k is a scalar, and n is a direction vector which represents the set of lines perpendicular to the plane (see example 6.2). These lines are said to be *normal* to the plane. If a is any point on the plane then naturally $n \cdot a = k$, and so by replacing k in the above equation, we may rewrite it as

$$n \cdot v = n \cdot a \quad \text{or} \quad n \cdot (v - a) = 0$$

This latter equation is self-evident from the property of the dot product, that two mutually perpendicular lines have zero dot product. For any point $v \equiv (x, y, z)$ in the plane which is not equal to a, we know that $(v - a)$ can be considered as the direction of a line in the plane. Since n is normal to the plane, and consequently perpendicular to every line in the plane, $n \cdot (v - a) = \lambda \times \cos(\pi/2) = 0$ (λ is a scalar value $= |n| \cdot |v - a|$).

Expanding the original equation of the plane with normal $n \equiv (n_1, n_2, n_3)$, we get the usual co-ordinate representation of a plane

$$(n_1, n_2, n_3) \cdot (x, y, z) = n_1 \times x + n_2 \times y + n_3 \times z = k$$

Note two planes with normals n and m (say) are parallel if and only if one normal is a scalar multiple of the other – that is, $n = \lambda m$ for some $\lambda \neq 0$.

The Point of Intersection of a Line and a Plane

Suppose the line is given by $b + \mu d$ and the plane by $n \cdot v = k$. The two either do not intersect at all (if they are parallel), intersect at an infinite number of points (if the line lies in the plane) or have a unique point of intersection which lies on both the line and the plane. We have to find the unique value of μ (if one exists) for which

$$n \cdot (b + \mu d) = k$$

that is

$$\mu = \frac{k - n \cdot b}{n \cdot d} \quad \text{provided } n \cdot d \neq 0$$

$n \cdot d = 0$ if the line and plane are parallel and so there is no unique point of intersection.

The Distance of a Point from a Plane

The distance of a point p_1 from a plane $n \cdot v = k$ is the distance of p_1 from the nearest point p_2 on the plane. Hence the normal from the plane at p_2 must pass through p_1. This normal line can be written $p_1 + \mu n$, and the μ value that defines p_2 is such that:

$$\mu = (k - n \cdot p_1)/(n \cdot n) \quad \text{from the equation above}$$

The distance of the point $p_2 \equiv p_1 + \mu n$ from p_1 is

$$\mu |n| = |k - n \cdot p_1|/|n|$$

In particular, if p_1 is the origin O then the distance of plane from the origin is $|k|/|n|$. Furthermore, if n is a direction cosine (unit) vector we see that the distance of the origin from the plane is $|k|$, the absolute value of the real number k.

Example 6.2
Find the point of intersection of the line joining $(1, 2, 3)$ to $(-1, 0, 2)$ with the plane $(0, -2, 1) \cdot v = 5$, and also find the distance of the plane from the origin.

$$b \equiv (1, 2, 3)$$
$$n \equiv (0, -2, 1)$$
$$d \equiv (-1, 0, 2) - (1, 2, 3) \equiv (-2, -2, -1)$$
$$n \cdot b = (0 \times 1 + -2 \times 2 + 1 \times 3) = -1$$
$$n \cdot d = (0 \times -2 + -2 \times -2 + 1 \times -1) = 3$$

hence the μ value of the point of intersection is $(5 - (-1))/3 = 2$, and the point vector is

$$(1, 2, 3) + 2(-2, -2, -1) \equiv (-3, -2, 1)$$

and the distance from the origin is $5/|n| = 5/\sqrt{5} = \sqrt{5}$.

The routine ilpl in listing 6.2 enables us to calculate the point of intersection of a line and a plane. The line has base vector b and direction d and the plane has real normal n and real plane constant k. The point of intersection is calculated and returned as p. b, d, n and p are all of TYPE vector3.

Listing 6.2

```
PROCEDURE ilpl(b,d,n : vector3 ; VAR p : vector3 ;
                k : real ; VAR mu : real; VAR insect : integer) ;
{ Calculates the point of intersection, 'p',of a line 'b+mu.d' }
{ and the plane with equation 'n.v=k'. }
{ 'insect' is returned as 1 if an intersection exists, 0 if not }
VAR dotprod1,dotprod2 : real ;
BEGIN
```

```
    dotprod1 := dot3(d,n) ;
{ If the line and plane are parallel then return 'insect=0' }
    IF abs(dotprod1) < epsilon
    THEN insect := 0
    ELSE BEGIN
{ Else a point of intersection does exist }
            insect := 1 ; dotprod2 := dot3(b,n) ;
            mu := (k-dotprod2)/dotprod1 ;
            p.x := b.x+mu*d.x ; p.y := b.y+mu*d.y ; p.z := b.z+mu*d.z
        END
END ; { of ilpl }
```

The Reflection of a Point in a Plane

Consider the point $p \equiv (x, y, z)$ and the infinite plane $n \cdot v = k$. We wish to find the point $p' \equiv (x', y', z')$, the reflection of p in the plane (see figure 6.2).

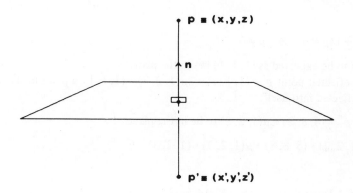

Figure 6.2

The perpendicular distance of the reflection p' from the plane is equal to the perpendicular distance of p from the plane. Furthermore, p and p' lie on the same line perpendicular to the plane but on opposite sides. The vector n is simply a direction common to all lines normal to the plane so the normal containing p and p' may be represented by $p + \mu n$, $-\infty \leqslant \mu \leqslant \infty$.

If we can find a value μ such that $p + \mu n$ lies in the plane $n \cdot v = k$ then the reflected point p' is $p + 2\mu n$. Thus the μ value of the point of intersection of the line $p + \mu n$ with the plane $n \cdot v = k$ must be found using the method above and thence the reflected point calculated.

The routine **refpp**, in listing 6.3 returns r the reflection of p in the plane $n \cdot v = k$. r, p and n are all of TYPE **vector3**.

Listing 6.3

```
PROCEDURE refpp(p,n : vector3 ; k : real ; VAR r : vector3) ;
{ Calculates 'r', the reflection of 'p' in the plane 'n.v=k' }
VAR dummy : vector3 ;
    mu : real ;
    insect : integer ;
BEGIN
    ilpl(p,n,n,dummy,k,mu,insect) ;
    r.x := p.x+2*mu*n.x ; r.y := p.y+2*mu*n.y ; r.z := p.z+2*mu*n.z
END ; { of refpp }
```

Example 6.3

What are the reflections of the points (i) $(1, 1, 1)$ and (ii) $(8, 8, 8)$ in the plane $(1, 2, 3) \cdot v = 6$?

(i) for $p'' = (1, 1, 1) + \mu(1, 2, 3)$ to lie in the plane

$$(1, 2, 3) \cdot p'' = (1, 2, 3) \cdot (1, 1, 1) + \mu(1, 2, 3) \cdot (1, 2, 3) = 6$$

that is

$$6 + 14\mu = 6 \quad \text{so} \quad \mu = 0$$

which is to be expected as $(1, 1, 1)$ lies in the plane!
So the reflected point $p' = (1, 1, 1) + 2\mu(1, 2, 3) = (1, 1, 1)$, a point in the plane being reflected into itself.

(ii) for $p'' = (8, 8, 8) + \mu(1, 2, 3)$ to lie in the plane

$$(1, 2, 3) \cdot (8, 8, 8) + \mu(1, 2, 3) \cdot (1, 2, 3) = 6$$

that is

$$48 + 14\mu = 6 \quad \text{so} \quad \mu = -42/14 = -3$$

and the point of reflection is $(8, 8, 8) - 6(1, 2, 3) = (2, -4, -10)$.

The Point of Intersection of Two Lines

Suppose we have two lines $b_1 + \mu d_1$ and $b_2 + \lambda d_2$. Their point of intersection, if it exists (if the lines are not co-planar or are parallel then they will not intersect), is identified by finding unique values for μ and λ which satisfy the vector equation (three separate co-ordinate equations)

$$b_1 + \mu d_1 = b_2 + \lambda d_2$$

Three equations in two unknowns means that for the equations to be meaningful there must be at least one pair of the equations which are independent, and the remaining equation must be a combination of these two. Two lines are parallel if one direction vector is a scalar multiple of the other. So we take two independent equations, find the values of μ and λ (we have two equations in two unknowns), and put them in the third equation to see if they are consistent. The following example 6.4 will demonstrate this method, and the routine ill3 in listing 6.4 implements it in Pascal. The first line has base and direction vectors stored as b1 and d1 respectively and the second line as b2 and d2: the calculated point of intersection is returned as p, if it exists, otherwise insect is returned as 0. Since the values used are real, equality may not be exact in the third equation because of rounding errors. We therefore check that the difference between the left-hand side and the right-hand side values is negligible ($<$ epsilon), not necessarily zero. Note that if the two independent equations are

$$a_{11} \times \mu + a_{12} \times \lambda = k_1$$
$$a_{21} \times \mu + a_{22} \times \lambda = k_2$$

then the *determinant* of this pair of equations, $\Delta = a_{11} \times a_{22} - a_{12} \times a_{21}$, will be non-zero (because the equations are not related), and we have the solutions

$$\mu = (a_{22} \times k_1 - a_{12} \times k_2)/\Delta$$
$$\lambda = (a_{11} \times k_2 - a_{21} \times k_1)/\Delta$$

Listing 6.4

```
PROCEDURE ill3(b1,d1,b2,d2 : vector3 ;
                    VAR p : vector3 ; VAR insect : integer ) ;
{ Point of intersection of two lines in 3 dimensions }
VAR bb1,bb2,dd1,dd2 : ARRAY[1..3] OF real ;
    i,i1,i2,i3 : integer ;
    delta,eq3,factor1,factor2,lambda,mu : real ;
BEGIN
{ Find independent equations }
    bb1[1] := b1.x ; bb2[1] := b2.x ; dd1[1] := d1.x ; dd2[1] := d2.x ;
    bb1[2] := b1.y ; bb2[2] := b2.y ; dd1[2] := d1.y ; dd2[2] := d2.y ;
    bb1[3] := b1.z ; bb2[3] := b2.z ; dd1[3] := d1.z ; dd2[3] := d2.z ;
    FOR i := 1 TO 3
    DO BEGIN
        i1 := i ; i2 := (i MOD 3)+1 ;
        delta := dd1[i1]*dd2[i2]-dd1[i2]*dd2[i1] ;
        IF abs(delta) > epsilon
        THEN BEGIN
{ Two independent equations , find point of intersection }
            factor1 := bb2[i1]-bb1[i1] ; factor2 := bb2[i2]-bb1[i2] ;
            mu := (dd2[i2]*factor1-dd2[i1]*factor2)/delta ;
            lambda := (dd1[i2]*factor1-dd1[i1]*factor2)/delta ;
            i3 := (i2 MOD 3) +1 ;
            eq3 := bb1[i3] + mu*dd1[i3]-bb2[i3]-lambda*dd2[i3] ;
            IF abs(eq3) > epsilon
            THEN insect := 0
            ELSE BEGIN
```

```
                insect := 1 ;
                p.x := b1.x+mu*d1.x ;
                p.y := b1.y+mu*d1.y ;
                p.z := b1.z+mu*d1.z
                END ;
        EXIT
        END
    END ;
{ No independent equations then no intersection }
    insect := 0
END ; { of ill3 }
```

Example 6.4

Find the point of intersection (if any) of

(a) $(1, 1, 1) + \mu(2, 1, 3)$ with $(0, 0, 1) + \lambda(-1, 1, 1)$
(b) $(2, 3, 4) + \mu(1, 1, 1)$ with $(-2, -3, -4) + \lambda(1, 2, 3)$.

In (a) the three equations are

$$1 + 2\mu = 0 - \lambda \tag{6.4}$$
$$1 + \mu = 0 + \lambda \tag{6.5}$$
$$1 + 3\mu = 1 + \lambda \tag{6.6}$$

From equations (6.4) and (6.5) we get $\mu = -2/3$ and $\lambda = 1/3$, which when substituted in equation (6.6) gives $1 + 3(-2/3) = -1$ on the left-hand side and $1 + 1(1/3) = 4/3$ on the right-hand side, which are obviously unequal so the lines do not intersect.

From (b) we get the equations

$$2 + \mu = -2 + \lambda \tag{6.7}$$
$$3 + \mu = -3 + 2\lambda \tag{6.8}$$
$$4 + \mu = -4 + 3\lambda \tag{6.9}$$

and from equations (6.7) and (6.8) we get $\mu = -2$ and $\lambda = 2$, and these values also satisfy equation (6.9) (left-hand side = right-hand side = 2). So the point of intersection is

$$(2, 3, 4) + -2(1, 1, 1) = (-2, -3, -4) + 2(1, 2, 3) = (0, 1, 2)$$

We now introduce a new vector operator, the *vector product* (or *cross product*) which operates on two vectors p and q (say) giving the *vector* result

$$p \times q \equiv (p_x, p_y, p_z) \times (q_x, q_y, q_z)$$
$$\equiv (p_y \times q_z - p_z \times q_y, p_z \times q_x - p_x \times q_z, p_x \times q_y - p_y \times q_x)$$

If p and q are non-parallel direction vectors then $p \times q$ is the direction vector perpendicular to both p and q. It should also be noted that this operation is *non-commutative*. This means that, in general, for given values of p and q, $p \times q \neq q \times p$; these two vectors represent directions in the same line but with opposite sense. For example, $(1, 0, 0) \times (0, 1, 0) = (0, 0, 1)$ but $(0, 1, 0) \times (1, 0, 0) = (0, 0, -1)$; $(0, 0, 1)$ and $(0, 0, -1)$ are both parallel to the z-axis (and so perpendicular to the directions $(1, 0, 0)$ and $(0, 1, 0)$) but they are of opposite sense. This can also be realised using your hands. Using right or left hand (depending on the axial system you choose) identify the palm of the hand with the plane holding the two direction vectors, with the thumb pointing along the first direction and the index finger along the second direction; the middle finger perpendicular to the palm now points along the direction of the cross product. Note that to change the order of the vectors in the cross product and thence identify the thumb with the second vector and index finger with the first vector it is necessary to twist your palm through two right angles, and so now the middle finger is pointing along the same line but in an opposite sense. A routine, **vectorproduct**, which calculates the vector product of two vectors **p** and **q**, returning **v**, is given in listing 6.5. Again **p**, **q** and **v** are all of TYPE **vector3**.

Listing 6.5

```
PROCEDURE vectorproduct(p,q : vector3 ; VAR v : vector3 ) ;
{ Calculates 'v', the vector product of two vectors 'p' and 'q' }
BEGIN
    v.x := p.y*q.z-p.z*q.y ;
    v.y := p.z*q.x-p.x*q.z ;
    v.z := p.x*q.y-p.y*q.x
END ; { of vectorproduct }
```

The Minimum Distance between Two Lines

It was mentioned above that if two lines are either parallel or non-coplanar then they do not intersect. There is therefore a minimum distance between two such lines which is greater than zero. We shall now calculate this distance. The cases where the lines are parallel and non-parallel are different. We consider first the non-parallel case.

Suppose the two lines are $a + \mu c$ and $b + \lambda d$. The minimum distance between these two lines must be measured along a line perpendicular to both. This line must, therefore, be parallel to the direction $l \equiv c \times d$.

Now, since both $a + \mu c$ and $b + \lambda d$ are perpendicular to l, they both lie in planes with l as normal. Also, since we know points on both lines (a and b) we may uniquely identify these planes: $l \cdot (v - a) = 0$ and $l \cdot (v - b) = 0$.

These planes are, of course, parallel, and so the required minimum distance is simply the distance from a point on one plane, say b, to the other plane. We have already derived a formula for this, giving the required answer

$$\frac{|(c \times d) \cdot a - (c \times d) \cdot b|}{|c \times d|}$$

$$= \frac{|(c \times d) \cdot (a - b)|}{|c \times d|}$$

If the lines are coplanar then this expression yields the result zero, since the lines must intersect as they are not parallel.

Now suppose the two lines $a + \mu c$ and $b + \lambda d$ are parallel. In this case $d \equiv \eta c$ for some $\eta \neq 0$ and consequently $|c \times d| = 0$ and the above expression is undefined.

However, both lines are normal to the same planes. Take the plane containing a with normal c (parallel to d)

$$c \cdot (v - a) = 0$$

We simply find the point of intersection, e say, of the line $b + \lambda d$ with this plane and the required distance is $|a - e|$

$$e = b + \lambda d$$

$$\text{where } \lambda = \frac{c \cdot (a - b)}{c \cdot d}$$

The routine mindist in listing 6.6 calculates the minimum distance, dist, between two lines using this method.

Listing 6.6

```
PROCEDURE mindist(a,c,b,d : vector3 ; VAR dist : real) ;
{ Finds minimum distance between two lines in 3 dimensions }
VAR aminusb,aminuse,p : vector3 ;
    lambda,pmod : real ;
BEGIN
   vecprod(c,d,p) ; pmod := sqrt(dot3(p,p)) ;
   aminusb.x := a.x-b.x ; aminusb.y := a.y-b.y ; aminusb.z := a.z-b.z ;
   IF pmod > epsilon
   THEN dist := abs(dot3(p,aminusb))/pmod
   ELSE BEGIN
           lambda := dot3(c,aminusb)/dot3(c,d) ;
           aminuse.x := a.x-b.x-lambda*d.x ;
           aminuse.y := a.y-b.y-lambda*d.y ;
           aminuse.z := a.z-b.z-lambda*d.z ;
           dist := sqrt(dot3(aminuse,aminuse))
        END
END ; { of mindist }
```

Example 6.5
Find the minimum distance between

(i) $(1, 0, 0) + \mu(1, 1, 1)$ and $(0, 0, 0) + \lambda(1, 2, 3)$

(ii) $(2, 4, 0) + \mu(1, 1, 1)$ and $(-2, -1, 0) + \lambda(2, 2, 2)$.

In (i) $\quad a \equiv (1, 0, 0) \qquad c \equiv (1, 1, 1)$
$\qquad b \equiv (0, 0, 0) \qquad d \equiv (1, 2, 3)$
$\qquad (c \times d) \equiv (1, -2, 1) \quad (a - b) \equiv (1, 0, 0)$

So the minimum distance between the lines is

$$\frac{|(1, -2, 1) \cdot (1, 0, 0)|}{|(1, -2, 1)|} = \frac{1}{\sqrt{6}}$$

In (ii) $\quad a \equiv (2, 4, 0) \qquad c \equiv (1, 1, 1)$
$\qquad b \equiv (-2, -1, 0) \qquad d \equiv (2, 2, 2)$
$\qquad (c \times d) \equiv (0, 0, 0)$ so the lines are parallel $(d = 2c)$
$\qquad c \cdot d = 6 \qquad\qquad a - b \equiv (4, 5, 0)$

$$\lambda = \frac{(1, 1, 1) \cdot (4, 5, 0)}{6} = \frac{9}{6} = \frac{3}{2}$$

$e \equiv (-2, -1, 0) + 3/2(2, 2, 2) = (1, 2, 3)$
$(a - e) \equiv (2, 4, 0) - (1, 2, 3) = (1, 2, -3)$

so the minimum distance between the lines is $\sqrt{14}$.

The Plane through Three Given Non-collinear Points

Suppose we are given three non-collinear points p_1, p_2 and p_3. Then the two vectors $p_2 - p_1$ and $p_3 - p_2$ represent the directions of two lines coincident at p_2, both of which lie in the plane containing the three points. We know that the normal to the plane is perpendicular to every line in the plane, and in particular to the two lines mentioned above. Also, because the points are not collinear, $p_2 - p_1$ is not parallel to $p_3 - p_2$ so the normal to the plane is $n \equiv (p_2 - p_1) \times (p_3 - p_2)$. See figure 6.3.

We know that p_1 lies in the plane so the equation may be written

$$((p_2 - p_1) \times (p_3 - p_2)) \cdot (v - p_1) = 0$$

The three points in the plane define a triangle, which appears from one side of the plane to be in anti-clockwise orientation and from the other side to be in clockwise orientation. The above equation imposes a consistent sense upon the normal which implies that the normal direction points towards that side of the plane from which the triangle appears in anti-clockwise orientation. (This is dependent on the use of right-handed axes; in the left-handed system the normal thus found points towards the clockwise side). The routine, **plane**, in listing 6.7 calculates the plane through three non-collinear **vector3** points.

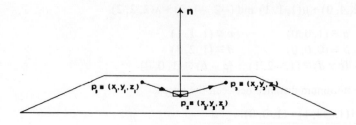

Figure 6.3

Listing 6.7

```
PROCEDURE plane(p1,p2,p3 : vector3 ; VAR n : vector3 ; VAR k : real ) ;
{ Calculates the vector equation of the plane passing through }
{ the three points 'p1', 'p2' and 'p3' }
VAR d1,d2 : vector3 ;
BEGIN
{ Calculate the direction vectors of two lines in the plane }
    d1.x := p2.x-p1.x ; d1.y := p2.y-p1.y ; d1.z := p2.z-p1.z ;
    d2.x := p3.x-p2.x ; d2.y := p3.y-p2.y ; d2.z := p3.z-p2.z ;
{ Calculate the normal to the plane using the vector product of }
{ these two lines. Calculate 'k' using point 'p1' in the plane }
    vectorproduct(d1,d2,n) ; k := dot3(n,p1)
END ; { of plane }
```

Example 6.6

Give the co-ordinate equation of the plane through the points $(0, 1, 1), (1, 2, 3)$ and $(-2, 3, -1)$.

This is given by the general point $v \equiv (x, y, z)$ where

$$(((1, 2, 3) - (0, 1, 1)) \times ((-2, 3, -1) - (1, 2, 3))) \cdot ((x, y, z) - (0, 1, 1)) = 0$$

that is

$$((1, 1, 2) \times (-3, 1, -4)) \cdot (x, y - 1, z - 1) = 0$$

so

$$(-6, -2, 4) \cdot (x, y - 1, z - 1) = 0$$

or, equivalently

$$(-6, -2, 4) \cdot v = 2$$

In co-ordinate form this is $-6x - 2y + 4z - 2 = 0$ or equivalently $3x + y - 2z = -1$.

The Point of Intersection of Three Planes

We assume that the three planes are defined by equations (6.10) to (6.12) below.

The point of intersection of these three planes, $v \equiv (x, y, z)$ must lie in all three planes and satisfy

$$n_1 \cdot v = k_1 \qquad (6.10)$$
$$n_2 \cdot v = k_2 \qquad (6.11)$$
$$n_3 \cdot v = k_3 \qquad (6.12)$$

where $n_1 \equiv (n_{11}, n_{12}, n_{13})$, $n_2 \equiv (n_{21}, n_{22}, n_{23})$ and $n_3 \equiv (n_{31}, n_{32}, n_{33})$. We can rewrite these three equations as one matrix equation

$$\begin{pmatrix} n_{11} & n_{12} & n_{13} \\ n_{21} & n_{22} & n_{23} \\ n_{31} & n_{32} & n_{33} \end{pmatrix} \times \begin{pmatrix} x \\ y \\ z \end{pmatrix} = \begin{pmatrix} k_1 \\ k_2 \\ k_3 \end{pmatrix}$$

and so the solution for v is given by the column vector

$$\begin{pmatrix} x \\ y \\ z \end{pmatrix} = \begin{pmatrix} n_{11} & n_{12} & n_{13} \\ n_{21} & n_{22} & n_{23} \\ n_{31} & n_{32} & n_{33} \end{pmatrix}^{-1} \times \begin{pmatrix} k_1 \\ k_2 \\ k_3 \end{pmatrix}$$

So any calculation requiring the intersection of three planes necessarily involves the inversion of a 3×3 matrix. The routine, invert, in lising 6.8 uses the Adjoint method of finding AINV, the inverse of matrix A. The value sing is also returned, equalling 1 if the matrix A is singular (and so has no inverse) and 0 otherwise.

Listing 6.8

```
PROCEDURE invert(A : matrix3x3 ; VAR AINV : matrix3x3 ; VAR sing : integer ) ;
{ Calculates 'AINV', the inverse of matrix 'A', using the adjoint method }
{ 'sing' is returned as 1 if 'A' is singular and has no inverse, 0 otherwise }
VAR determinant,adj : real ;
    i,i1,i2,j,j1,j2 : integer ;
BEGIN
{ Find the determinant of 'A' }
   determinant :=   A[1,1]*(A[2,2]*A[3,3]-A[2,3]*A[3,2])
                   +A[1,2]*(A[2,3]*A[3,1]-A[2,1]*A[3,3])
                   +A[1,3]*(A[2,1]*A[3,2]-A[2,2]*A[3,1]) ;
{ If 'determinant'=0 then 'A' is singular }
   IF abs(determinant) < epsilon
   THEN sing := 1
   ELSE BEGIN
{ Else the inverse is the adjoint matrix divided by determinant }
         sing := 0 ;
         FOR i := 1 TO 3
         DO BEGIN
            i1 := (i MOD 3)+1 ; i2 := (i1 MOD 3)+1 ;
            FOR j := 1 TO 3
            DO BEGIN
                j1 := (j MOD 3)+1 ; j2 := (j1 MOD 3)+1 ;
                adj := (A[i1,j1]*A[i2,j2]-A[i1,j2]*A[i2,j1]) ;
                AINV[j,i] := adj/determinant
```

```
                         END
                 END
         END
END ; { of invert }
```

Again, in the routine, i3pl, to find the point of intersection of three planes
(listing 6.9), the solution of the equations (v above), is returned as vector3 value
v; reals k1, k2 and k3 will contain the plane constants and the x, y and z co-
ordinates of the normal vectors are given as vector3 values n1, n2, and n3 respectively.

Listing 6.9

```
PROCEDURE i3pl(n1,n2,n3 : vector3 ; k1,k2,k3 : real ;
                   VAR v : vector3 ; VAR insect : integer ) ;
{ Calculates the point of intersection, 'v', of the three planes }
{ 'n1.v=k1'  ,  'n2.v=k2'  ,  'n3.v=k3' }
{ 'insect' is returned as 1 if such a point exists, 0 otherwise }
VAR N,NINV : matrix3x3 ;
        sing : integer ;
BEGIN
{ Copy the 3 normal vectors into the rows of matrix 'N' }
   N[1,1] := n1.x ; N[1,2] := n1.y ; N[1,3] := n1.z ;
   N[2,1] := n2.x ; N[2,2] := n2.y ; N[2,3] := n2.z ;
   N[3,1] := n3.x ; N[3,2] := n3.y ; N[3,3] := n3.z ;
{ Calculate the inverse of 'N' }
   invert(N,NINV,sing) ;
   IF sing=1
   THEN insect := 0
{ If 'N' is singular then no intersection }
   ELSE BEGIN
{ Otherwise calculate the intersection }
           insect := 1 ;
           v.x := NINV[1,1]*k1+NINV[1,2]*k2+NINV[1,3]*k3 ;
           v.y := NINV[2,1]*k1+NINV[2,2]*k2+NINV[2,3]*k3 ;
           v.z := NINV[3,1]*k1+NINV[3,2]*k2+NINV[3,3]*k3
        END
END ; { of i3pl }
```

Obviously if any two of the planes are parallel or the three meet in pairs in three
parallel lines, then sing equals 1 and there is no unique point of intersection.

Example 6.7
Find the point of intersection of the three planes $(0, 1, 1) \cdot v = 2, (1, 2, 3) \cdot v = 4$
and $(1, 1, 1) \cdot v = 0$.
    In the matrix form we have

$$\begin{pmatrix} 0 & 1 & 1 \\ 1 & 2 & 3 \\ 1 & 1 & 1 \end{pmatrix} \times \begin{pmatrix} x \\ y \\ z \end{pmatrix} = \begin{pmatrix} 2 \\ 4 \\ 0 \end{pmatrix}$$

The inverse of $\begin{pmatrix} 0 & 1 & 1 \\ 1 & 2 & 3 \\ 1 & 1 & 1 \end{pmatrix}$ is $\begin{pmatrix} -1 & 0 & 1 \\ 2 & -1 & 1 \\ -1 & 1 & -1 \end{pmatrix}$

and so

$$\begin{pmatrix} x \\ y \\ z \end{pmatrix} = \begin{pmatrix} -1 & 0 & 1 \\ 2 & -1 & 1 \\ -1 & 1 & -1 \end{pmatrix} \times \begin{pmatrix} 2 \\ 4 \\ 0 \end{pmatrix} = \begin{pmatrix} -2 \\ 0 \\ 2 \end{pmatrix}$$

This solution is easily checked

$(0, 1, 1) \cdot (-2, 0, 2) = 2, (1, 2, 3) \cdot (-2, 0, 2) = 4$ and
$(1, 1, 1) \cdot (-2, 0, 2) = 0$

which means that the point $(-2, 0, 2)$ lies on all three planes and so is their point of intersection.

The Line of Intersection of Two Planes

Let the two planes be $p \cdot v \equiv (p_1, p_2, p_3) \cdot v = k_1$ and
$$q \cdot v \equiv (q_1, q_2, q_3) \cdot v = k_2$$

We assume that the planes are not parallel, and so $p \neq \lambda q$ for any λ. The line common to the two planes naturally lies in each plane, and so it must be perpendicular to the normals of both planes (p and q). Thus the direction of this line must be $d \equiv p \times q$ and the line can be written in the form $b + \mu d$, where b can be any point on the line. In order to completely classify the line we have to find one such b. We find a point which is the intersection of the two planes together with a third which is neither parallel to them, nor cuts them in a common line. Choosing a plane with normal $p \times q$ will satisfy these conditions (and remember we have already calculated this vector product). We still need a value for k_3, but any will do, so we take $k_3 = 0$, assuming that this third plane goes through the origin. Thus b is given by the column vector

$$b = \begin{pmatrix} p_1 & p_2 & p_3 \\ q_1 & q_2 & q_3 \\ p_2 \times q_3 - p_3 \times q_2 & p_3 \times q_1 - p_1 \times q_3 & p_1 \times q_2 - p_2 \times q_1 \end{pmatrix}^{-1} \times \begin{pmatrix} k_1 \\ k_2 \\ 0 \end{pmatrix}$$

Example 6.8
Find the line common to the planes $(0, 1, 1) \cdot v = 2$ and $(1, 2, 3) \cdot v = 2$.

$p = (0, 1, 1)$ and $q = (1, 2, 3)$, and so
$p \times q = (1 \times 3 - 1 \times 2, 1 \times 1 - 0 \times 3, 0 \times 2 - 1 \times 1) = (1, 1, -1)$.

We require the inverse of

$$\begin{pmatrix} 0 & 1 & 1 \\ 1 & 2 & 3 \\ 1 & 1 & -1 \end{pmatrix} \text{ which is } 1/3 \begin{pmatrix} -5 & 2 & 1 \\ 4 & -1 & 1 \\ -1 & 1 & -1 \end{pmatrix}$$

and hence the point of intersection of the three planes is

$$1/3 \begin{pmatrix} -5 & 2 & 1 \\ 4 & -1 & 1 \\ -1 & 1 & -1 \end{pmatrix} \times \begin{pmatrix} 2 \\ 2 \\ 0 \end{pmatrix} = 1/3 \begin{pmatrix} -6 \\ 6 \\ 0 \end{pmatrix} = \begin{pmatrix} -2 \\ 2 \\ 0 \end{pmatrix}$$

and the line is $(-2, 2, 0) + \mu(1, 1, -1)$.

It is easy to check this result, because all the points on the line should lie in both planes

$$(0, 1, 1) \cdot ((-2, 2, 0) + \mu(1, 1, -1)) =$$
$$(0, 1, 1) \cdot (-2, 2, 0) + \mu(0, 1, 1) \cdot (1, 1, -1) = 2$$
$$\text{for all } \mu \text{ and}$$
$$(1, 2, 3) \cdot ((-2, 2, 0) + \mu(1, 1, -1)) =$$
$$(0, 1, 1) \cdot (-2, 2, 0) + \mu(1, 2, 3) \cdot (1, 1, -1) = 2$$
$$\text{for all } \mu$$

The routine, **commonline**, to solve this problem is given in listing 6.10. It is very similar to the previous routine but returns the base vector b and the direction d of the common line.

Listing 6.10

```
PROCEDURE commonline(n1,n2 : vector3 ; k1,k2 : real ;
                     VAR b,d : vector3 ; VAR insect : integer ) ;
{ Calculates the line common to the two planes 'n1.v=k1' , 'n2.v=k2' }
{ 'insect' is returned as 1 if such a line exists, 0 otherwise }
{ The base vector of the line is 'b' and direction vector 'd' }
VAR N,NINV : matrix3x3 ;
    sing : integer ;
BEGIN
{ Copy the 2 normal vectors into first two rows of matrix 'N' }
    N[1,1] := n1.x ; N[1,2] := n1.y ; N[1,3] := n1.z ;
    N[2,1] := n2.x ; N[2,2] := n2.y ; N[2,3] := n2.z ;
{ Calculate the direction vector of the line }
    vectorproduct(n1,n2,d) ;
{ Create third plane 'd.v=0', and copy into matrix 'N' }
    N[3,1] := d.x ; N[3,2] := d.y ; N[3,3] := d.z ;
{ 'b' is the point of intersection of these three planes }
{ Calculate the inverse of 'N' }
    invert(N,NINV,sing) ;
    IF sing=1
    THEN insect := 0
{ If 'N' is singular then no common line }
    ELSE BEGIN
```

```
{ Otherwise calculate the intersection }
        insect := 1 ;
        b.x := NINV[1,1]*k1+NINV[1,2]*k2 ;
        b.y := NINV[2,1]*k1+NINV[2,2]*k2 ;
        b.z := NINV[3,1]*k1+NINV[3,2]*k2
    END
END ; { of commonline }
```

Analytic Representation of a Surface

In our study of two-dimensional space in chapter 3 we noted that curves can be represented in an analytic notation. This idea can be extended into three dimensions when we study surfaces. The simplest form of surface is an infinite plane with normal $n \equiv (n_1, n_2, n_3)$, which we have seen may be given as a co-ordinate equation

$$n \cdot v - k \equiv n_1 \times x + n_2 \times y + n_3 \times z - k = 0$$

This can be rewritten in analytic form for a general point $v \equiv (x, y, z)$ on the surface

$$f(v) \equiv f(x, y, z) \equiv n_1 \times x + n_2 \times y + n_3 \times z - k \equiv n \cdot v - k$$

a simple expression in v, the variables x, y and z. It enables us to divide all the points in space into three sets, those with $f(v) = 0$ (the *zero set*), with $f(v) < 0$ (the *negative set*) and $f(v) > 0$ (the *positive set*). A point v lies on the surface if and only if it belongs to the zero set. If the surface divides space into two halves (each half being connected — that is, any two points in a given half can be joined by a curve which does not cut the surface) then these two halves may be identified with the positive and negative sets. Again beware, there are many surfaces that divide space into more than two connected volumes and then it is impossible to relate analytic representation with connected sets — for example, $f(x, y, z) \equiv \cos(y) - \sin(x^2 + z^2)$. There are, however, many useful well-behaved surfaces with this property, the sphere of radius r for example

$$f(v) \equiv r^2 - |v|^2$$

that is

$$f(x, y, z) \equiv r^2 - x^2 - y^2 - z^2$$

If $f(v) = 0$ then v lies on the sphere, if $f(v) < 0$ then v lies outside the sphere, and if $f(v) > 0$ then v lies inside it.

The analytic representation of a surface is a very useful concept. It can be used to great effect in the quad-tree, oct-tree and ray tracing algorithms discussed in chapters 15 and 17, and also to define sets of equations necessary in calculating the intersections of various objects. Furthermore, we may determine whether or not two points p and q (say) lie on the same side of a surface which divides space in two: information needed for hidden surface elimination. All we need do is compare the signs of $f(p)$ and $f(q)$. If they are of opposite signs then a line joining p and q must cut the surface. For example

Is a point on the same side of a plane as the origin?

Suppose the plane is defined (as earlier) by three non-collinear points p_1, p_2 and p_3. Then the equation of the plane is

$$((p_2 - p_1) \times (p_3 - p_2)) \cdot (v - p_1) = 0$$

We may rewrite this in analytic form

$$f(v) \equiv ((p_2 - p_1) \times (p_3 - p_2)) \cdot (v - p_1)$$

So all we need do for a point e (say) is to compare $f(e)$ with $f(O)$, where O is the origin. We assume here that neither O nor e lies in the plane.

Example 6.9

Are the origin and point $(1, 1, 3)$ on the same side of the plane defined by points $(0, 1, 1)$, $(1, 2, 3)$ and $(-2, 3, -1)$?

From example 6.6 we see that the analytic representation of the plane is

$$f(v) \equiv ((-6, -2, 4) \cdot (v - (0, 1, 1))$$

Thus

$$f(0, 0, 0) = -(-6, -2, 4) \cdot (0, 1, 1) = -2$$

and

$$f(1, 1, 3) = (-6, -2, 4) \cdot ((1, 1, 3) - (0, 1, 1)) = 2$$

Hence $(1, 1, 3)$ lies on the opposite side of the plane to the origin and so a line segment joining the two points will cut the plane at a point $(1 - \mu)(0, 0, 0) + \mu(1, 1, 3)$ where $0 \leqslant \mu \leqslant 1$.

The Orientation of a Convex Polygon in Three-dimensional Space

In chapter 5 we introduced a method for determining whether the vertices of a convex polygon were in a clockwise or anti-clockwise orientation. Again, all we need do is consider the ordered triangle formed by the first three vertices of the polygon p_1, p_2 and p_3. We saw earlier that the infinite plane containing this triangle is given by the analytic form

$$f(v) \equiv ((p_2 - p_1) \times (p_3 - p_2)) \cdot (v - p_1)$$

Obviously the orientation depends on which side of this plane you view the triangle from. One way will be clockwise, the other anti-clockwise. If the triangle is set up in the way we describe, relative to right-handed axes, and the observation point is e, then you will note that if $f(e)$ is positive then the orientation is anti-clockwise, and if $f(e)$ is negative then the orientation is clockwise. If $f(e)$ is zero then e is on the plane and the question has no meaning.

When you are constructing three-dimensional objects in later chapters you will be expected to set up facets in an anti-clockwise orientation when viewed from the outside, so this method will prove an invaluable check!

Example 6.10
This idea is programmed as orient3 in listing 6.11. Use the program to check on the orientation of the triangle formed by the vertices $(1, 0, 0)$, $(0, 1, 0)$ and $(0, 0, 1)$. Note in analytic form this is given by

$$f(v) \equiv (1, 1, 1) \cdot (v - (1, 0, 0))$$

Hence when viewed from $(1, 1, 1)$, $f(1, 1, 1) = 2$ so the triangle is anti-clockwise, and from $(0, 0, 0)$, $f(0, 0, 0) = -1$ and thus the triangle is clockwise.

Listing 6.11

```
FUNCTION orient3(p1,p2,p3,e : vector3) : integer ;
{ Returns the orientation of the polygon with consecutive vertices }
{ 'p1', 'p2' and 'p3' as viewed from vector position 'e' }
{        -1 : clockwise orientation        }
{        +1 : anti-clockwise orientation   }
{         0 : degenerate - line or point   }
VAR d1,d2,d1xd2,v : vector3 ;
BEGIN
    d1.x := p2.x-p1.x ; d1.y := p2.y-p1.y ; d1.z := p2.z-p1.z ;
    d2.x := p3.x-p2.x ; d2.y := p3.y-p2.y ; d2.z := p3.z-p2.z ;
    vectorproduct(d1,d2,d1xd2) ;
    v.x := e.x-p1.x ; v.y := e.y-p1.y ; v.z := e.z-p1.z ;
    orient3 := sign(dot3(d1xd2,v))
END ; { of orient3 }
```

The Orientation of a Convex Polygon in Two-dimensional Space

Again we consider only the first three vertices on the boundary of the polygon, $p_1 \equiv (x_1, y_1)$, $p_2 \equiv (x_2, y_2)$ and $p_3 \equiv (x_3, y_3)$. Although these are two-dimensional co-ordinates, we may assume that the points lie in the x/y plane through the origin of three-dimensional space by giving them all a z co-ordinate value of zero. We can therefore use the results of the previous section to check on the orientation of this now three-dimensional triangle. Now since the triangle lies in the x/y plane through the origin, the normal to the plane is of the form $(0, 0, r)$. The analytic form is thus

$$f(x, y, z) \equiv (0, 0, r) \cdot ((x, y, z) - p_1)$$
$$= r \times z$$

since our three-dimensional system is right-handed and we have calculated the normal so it points out of an anti-clockwise triangle. If we assume that $(x, y, z) = (0, 0, 1)$ (implying that we are observing from the positive z side of the x/y plane through the origin), then $f(x, y, z) = r$. Hence if r is positive the polygon is defined in anti-clockwise orientation and if negative clockwise.

Because the vector $(0, 0, r)$ is $(p_2 - p_1) \times (p_3 - p_2)$, the value of r is $(x_2 - x_1) \times (y_3 - y_2) - (y_2 - y_1) \times (x_3 - x_2)$ and this expression is identical to that derived in chapter 5 (see listing 5.7).

Exercise 6.1
Experiment with the methods discussed in this chapter by creating your own exercises. The answers may be readily checked using the routines given. Of course you will need to write a body of main routine that will call the necessary routines when checking your solutions.

7 Matrix Representation of Transformations in Three-dimensional Space

Transformations of co-ordinate axes in two-dimensional space were introduced in chapter 4. An extension to three-dimensional systems is an essential step before we are able to proceed to projections of three-dimensional space onto the necessarily two-dimensional graphics viewport. As in the lower dimension, there are three basic transformations: translation of origin, change of scale and axes rotation; we will ignore all other transformations such as shear. Since we have already introduced the idea of matrix representation of transformations in two dimensions, we shall move directly to a similar representation of three-dimensional transformations. It should once more be noted that certain graphics devices will have these operations in hardware. The techniques are, nevertheless, very important so a full description is given. Again the square matrices representing the transformations will be one dimension greater than the space — that is, 4×4 — and a general point in space will be represented, by a column vector, relative to some triad of co-ordinate axes

$$\begin{pmatrix} x \\ y \\ z \\ 1 \end{pmatrix}$$

We start with our library of routines used for creating the matrices representing three-dimensional transformations, and declaring them globally in listing 7.1. We also declare TYPE matrix4x4 to hold 4 by 4 matrices. Place the routines from listing 7.1 following those of listing 1.3 in your combined program.

Translation of Origin

If the origin of the new co-ordinate system is the point $t \equiv (t_x, t_y, t_z)$ relative to the old, then the general point (x, y, z) will have new co-ordinates (x', y', z') given by

$$x' = 1 \times x + 0 \times y + 0 \times z - t_x$$
$$y' = 0 \times x + 1 \times y + 0 \times z - t_y$$
$$z' = 0 \times x + 0 \times y + 1 \times z - t_z$$

so that the matrix describing the translation is

$$\begin{pmatrix} 1 & 0 & 0 & -t_x \\ 0 & 1 & 0 & -t_y \\ 0 & 0 & 1 & -t_z \\ 0 & 0 & 0 & 1 \end{pmatrix}$$

The routine tran3 for producing such a matrix A, given the parameters tx, ty and tz is given in listing 7.1.

Listing 7.1

```
{ sequence of PROCEDUREs for matrix manipulation of three-dimensional models }

TYPE
    vector3 = RECORD x,y,z : real END ;
    vector3array = ARRAY[1..vectorarraysize] OF vector3 ;
    matrix4x4 = ARRAY[1..4,1..4] OF real ;


PROCEDURE tran3(tx,ty,tz : real ; VAR A : matrix4x4 ) ;
{ Calculate 3-D axes translation matrix 'A' }
{ Origin translated by vector '(tx,ty,tz)' }
VAR i,j : integer ;
BEGIN
    FOR i := 1 TO 4
    DO BEGIN
            FOR j := 1 TO 4
            DO A[i,j] := 0.0 ;
            A[i,i] := 1.0
        END ;
    A[1,4] := -tx ;
    A[2,4] := -ty ;
    A[3,4] := -tz
END ;   { of tran3 }


PROCEDURE scale3(sx,sy,sz : real ; VAR A : matrix4x4 ) ;
{ Calculate 3-D scaling matrix 'A' given scaling vector '(sx,sy,sz)' }
{ One unit on the x axis becomes 'sx' units, one unit on the y axis}
{ becomes 'sy' units and one unit on the z axis becomes 'sz' units }
VAR i,j : integer ;
BEGIN
    FOR i := 1 TO 4
    DO FOR j := 1 TO 4
        DO A[i,j] := 0.0 ;
    A[1,1] := sx ;
    A[2,2] := sy ;
    A[3,3] := sz ;
    A[4,4] := 1.0
END ;   { of scale3 }


PROCEDURE rot3(m : integer ; theta :real ; VAR A : matrix4x4 ) ;
{ Calculates 3-D axes rotation matrix 'A'. The axes are rotated }
```

```
{ anti-clockwise through an angle 'theta' radians about an axis }
{ specified by 'm' : m=1 means x axis;   m=2   y axis;  m=3   z axis }
VAR i,j,m1,m2 : integer ;
    c,s : real ;
BEGIN
  FOR I := 1 TO 4
  DO FOR J := 1 TO 4
      DO A[i,j] := 0.0 ;
  A[m,m] := 1.0 ; A[4,4] := 1.0 ;
  m1 := (m MOD 3)+1 ; m2 := (m1 MOD 3)+1 ;
  c := cos(theta) ; s := sin(theta) ;
  A[m1,m1] := c ; A[m2,m2] :=  c ;
  A[m1,m2] := s ; A[m2,m1] := -s
END ; { of rot3 }

PROCEDURE mult3(A,B : matrix4x4 ; VAR C : matrix4x4 ) ;
{ Calculates the matrix product 'C' of two matrices 'A' and 'B' }
VAR i,j,k : integer ;
    ab : real ;
BEGIN
  FOR I := 1 TO 4
  DO FOR J := 1 TO 4
      DO BEGIN
          ab := 0 ;
          FOR k := 1 TO 4
          DO ab := ab+A[i,k]*B[k,j] ;
          C[i,j] := ab
        END ;
END ; { of mult3 }


PROCEDURE genrot(phi : real ; b,d : vector3 ; VAR A : matrix4x4 ) ;
{ Calculates the matrix 'A' representing the rotation of axes through }
{ an angle 'phi' about a general line with base 'b' and direction 'd' }
VAR F,G,H,W,FI,GI,HI,S,T : matrix4x4 ;
    beta,theta,v : real ;
BEGIN
  tran3(b.x,b.y,b.z,F) ; tran3(-b.x,-b.y,-b.z,FI) ;
  theta := angle(d.x,d.y) ;
  rot3(3,theta,G) ; rot3(3,-theta,GI) ;
  v := sqrt(d.x*d.x+d.y*d.y) ; beta := angle(d.z,v) ;
  rot3(2,beta,H) ; rot3(2,-beta,HI) ;
  rot3(3,phi,W) ;
  mult3(G,F,S)  ; mult3(H,S,T)   ; mult3(W,T,S) ;
  mult3(HI,S,T) ; mult3(GI,T,S) ; mult3(FI,S,A)
END ; { of genrot }
```

Change of Scale

If the units on the old x, y and z axes are changed to Sx, Sy and Sz units respectively on the new, then the new co-ordinates of the general point (x, y, z) become (x', y', z')

$$x' = Sx \times x + 0 \times y + 0 \times z + 0$$
$$y' = 0 \times x + Sy \times y + 0 \times z + 0$$

$$z' = 0 \times x + 0 \times y + Sz \times z + 0$$

giving the matrix

$$\begin{pmatrix} Sx & 0 & 0 & 0 \\ 0 & Sy & 0 & 0 \\ 0 & 0 & Sz & 0 \\ 0 & 0 & 0 & 1 \end{pmatrix}$$

and the routine scale3 (listing 7.1) to create this matrix, A.

Rotation of Co-ordinate Axes

In three-dimensional space, rotation by a given angle implies a torque about a line (the *axis of rotation*). There are obviously an infinite number of directions which this line may take and each direction will produce a different form of transformation. We begin, therefore, by considering only the simplest cases, where the axis of rotation is coincident with one of the co-ordinate axes. If the positive half of the axis in question goes out of the page, then the other two axes appear to rotate in an anti-clockwise orientation. If a clockwise rotation by an angle θ is required then an anti-clockwise rotation by an angle $-\theta$ must be used.

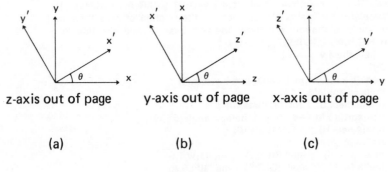

z-axis out of page y-axis out of page x-axis out of page

(a)   (b)   (c)

Figure 7.1

Rotation by an angle θ about the z-axis
Referring to figure 7.1a, the axis of rotation being perpendicular to the page (the positive z-axis is out of the page since we are using right-handed axes), the problem is reduced to a rotation of the x and y axes in two dimensions, the z co-ordinates remaining unchanged. Thus, using the formulae from chapter 4, we obtain the new co-ordinates, (x', y', z') of the general point (x, y, z) as follows

$$x' = \cos \theta \times x + \sin \theta \times y$$
$$y' = -\sin \theta \times x + \cos \theta \times y$$
$$z' = z$$

and the matrix:

$$\begin{pmatrix} \cos \theta & \sin \theta & 0 & 0 \\ -\sin \theta & \cos \theta & 0 & 0 \\ 0 & 0 & 1 & 0 \\ 0 & 0 & 0 & 1 \end{pmatrix}$$

Rotation by an angle θ about the y-axis

Referring to figure 7.1b, we now have the positive y-axis out of the page and, since we are using right-handed axes, the positive z-axis is horizontal and to the right of the origin and the positive x-axis is above the origin. This leads us to the equations

$$z' = \cos \theta \times z + \sin \theta \times x$$
$$x' = -\sin \theta \times z + \cos \theta \times x$$
$$y' = y$$

and rearranging

$$x' = \cos \theta \times x - \sin \theta \times z$$
$$y' = y$$
$$z' = \sin \theta \times x + \cos \theta \times z$$

which gives the matrix

$$\begin{pmatrix} \cos \theta & 0 & -\sin \theta & 0 \\ 0 & 1 & 0 & 0 \\ \sin \theta & 0 & \cos \theta & 0 \\ 0 & 0 & 0 & 1 \end{pmatrix}$$

Rotation by an angle θ about the x-axis

Referring to figure 7.1c, we find, in a similar manner, that the co-ordinates of the general point (x, y, z) become (x', y', z') as follows

$$y' = \cos \theta \times y + \sin \theta \times z$$
$$z' = -\sin \theta \times y + \cos \theta \times z$$
$$x' = x$$

which, rearranged, become

$$x' = x$$
$$y' = \cos \theta \times y + \sin \theta \times z$$
$$z' = -\sin \theta \times y + \cos \theta \times z$$

and thus the matrix is

$$\begin{pmatrix} 1 & 0 & 0 & 0 \\ 0 & \cos\theta & \sin\theta & 0 \\ 0 & -\sin\theta & \cos\theta & 0 \\ 0 & 0 & 0 & 1 \end{pmatrix}$$

A routine rot3 to produce A, any one of these three matrices, given the angle theta (in radians) and the axis number m (m = 1 for x-axis, m = 2 for y-axis and m = 3 for z-axis) is given as listing 7.1.

Exercise 7.1: Other transformations
We saw in chapter 4 that there are transformations other than the three we have mentioned. Write your own routine that returns the three-dimensional equivalent of the shear transformation, which will give a matrix A in the form of an identity matrix except for one extra non-zero entry A[i, j], where $1 \leqslant i, j \leqslant 3$ and $i \neq j$.

Combining Transformations

As with the two-dimensional case, we shall combine sequences of such transformations and hence require a routine to multiply two matrices A and B giving a product matrix C (see listing 7.4). Remember that we are pre-multiplying the matrices and so the right-hand matrix B refers to the initial transformation and the left-hand matrix A refers to the second. Remember also that matrix multiplication is non-commutative: $A \times B$ is not necessarily equal to $B \times A$.

Inverse Transformations

Before we can consider the general rotation of axes we must look at inverse transformations in three-dimensional space. These are exactly equivalent to their two-dimensional counterparts. The inverse of a transformation represented by a matrix A is represented by the inverse of A, A^{-1}. The three basic transformations are inverted as follows

(1) A translation of axes by (tx, ty, tz) is inverted with a translation by (−tx, −ty, −tz).
(2) A change of scale by sx, sy and sz on the x, y and z axes respectively is inverted with a change of scale by 1/sx, 1/sy and 1/sz.
(3) A rotation by an angle θ about a given axis is inverted with a rotation by an angle $-\theta$ about the same axis.
(4) If the transformation matrix is the product of a number of translation, scaling and rotation matrices $A \times B \times C \times \ldots \times L \times M \times N$, then the inverse transformation is

$$N^{-1} \times M^{-1} \times L^{-1} \times \ldots \times C^{-1} \times B^{-1} \times A^{-1}$$

The inverse matrices need not, of course, be calculated directly but may instead be obtained by calling the respective transformation matrix creation routine with the inverse parameters given above.

Rotation of Axes by an Angle ϕ about a General Axis $b + \mu d$

Assume $b \equiv (b_x, b_y, b_z)$ and $d \equiv (d_x, d_y, d_z)$. The idea is to transform the axes so that the line $b + \mu d$ becomes coincident with the z-axis, with the point b at the origin and sense of direction d along the positive z-axis. The rotation may then be executed about this new z-axis, and the axis of rotation subsequently transformed back to its original position. We break down the task into a number of subtasks

(a) The co-ordinate origin is translated to the point b so that the axis of rotation now passes through the origin. This is achieved by the matrix F

$$
F = \begin{pmatrix} 1 & 0 & 0 & -b_x \\ 0 & 1 & 0 & -b_y \\ 0 & 0 & 1 & -b_z \\ 0 & 0 & 0 & 1 \end{pmatrix}
\qquad
F^{-1} = \begin{pmatrix} 1 & 0 & 0 & b_x \\ 0 & 1 & 0 & b_y \\ 0 & 0 & 1 & b_z \\ 0 & 0 & 0 & 1 \end{pmatrix}
$$

The axis of rotation is now of the form μd. We now require the axis of rotation to be along the z-axis. This is achieved by the next two steps.

(b) The axes are rotated about the z-axis by an angle $\theta = \tan^{-1}(d_y/d_x)$. This is represented by the matrix G

$$
G = \frac{1}{v} \begin{pmatrix} d_x & d_y & 0 & 0 \\ -d_y & d_x & 0 & 0 \\ 0 & 0 & v & 0 \\ 0 & 0 & 0 & v \end{pmatrix}
\qquad
G^{-1} = \frac{1}{v} \begin{pmatrix} d_x & -d_y & 0 & 0 \\ d_y & d_x & 0 & 0 \\ 0 & 0 & v & 0 \\ 0 & 0 & 0 & v \end{pmatrix}
$$

where the positive number v is given by $v^2 = d_x^2 + d_y^2$. The axis of rotation, relative to the resultant co-ordinate axes, is now a line lying in the x/z plane passing through the point $(v, 0, d_z)$,

(c) The axes are then rotated about the y-axis by an angle $\beta = \tan^{-1}(v/d_z)$, a transformation represented by matrix H

$$
H = \frac{1}{w} \begin{pmatrix} d_z & 0 & -v & 0 \\ 0 & w & 0 & 0 \\ v & 0 & d_z & 0 \\ 0 & 0 & 0 & 0 \end{pmatrix}
\qquad
H^{-1} = \frac{1}{w} \begin{pmatrix} d_z & 0 & v & 0 \\ 0 & w & 0 & 0 \\ -v & 0 & d_z & 0 \\ 0 & 0 & 0 & 1 \end{pmatrix}
$$

where w is the positive number given by

$$
w^2 = v^2 + d_z^2 = d_x^2 + d_y^2 + d_z^2
$$

So the co-ordinates of the point $(v, 0, d_z)$ are transformed to $(0, 0, w)$, hence the axis of rotation is along the z-axis. Thus the combination $H \times G \times F$

transforms the z-axis to the line $b + \mu d$ with the point b at the origin and d along the positive z-axis.

(d) The problem of rotating the co-ordinate axes about a general line has thus been reduced to rotating space about the z-axis. This is achieved by matrix W which rotates the triad anti-clockwise through an angle ϕ about the z-axis

$$W = \begin{pmatrix} \cos\phi & \sin\phi & 0 & 0 \\ -\sin\phi & \cos\phi & 0 & 0 \\ 0 & 0 & 1 & 0 \\ 0 & 0 & 0 & 1 \end{pmatrix}$$

(e) The required rotation, however, is meant to be relative to the original axis positions so the transformations which were used to transform the axes to a suitable position for the rotation, F, G and H, must be inverted; therefore we pre-multiply by H^{-1}, G^{-1} and finally F^{-1}.

Thus the final matrix P which rotates axes by the angle ϕ about the axis $b + \mu d$ is $P = F^{-1} \times G^{-1} \times H^{-1} \times W \times H \times G \times F$. Naturally some of these matrices may reduce to the identity matrix in some special cases. For example, if the axis of rotation goes through the origin then F and F^{-1} are identical to the identity matrix I and can be ignored. The general case of matrix P is created by the routine genrot given in listing 7.1.

Example 7.1
What are the new co-ordinates of the points $(0, 0, 0)$, $(1, 0, 0)$, $(0, 1, 0)$, $(0, 0, 1)$ and $(1, 1, 1)$ relative to co-ordinate axes obtained by rotating the existing system through $\pi/4$ radians clockwise about an axis $(1, 0, 1) + \mu(3, 4, 5)$?

Using the above theory we note that

$$F = \begin{pmatrix} 1 & 0 & 0 & -1 \\ 0 & 1 & 0 & 0 \\ 0 & 0 & 1 & -1 \\ 0 & 0 & 0 & 1 \end{pmatrix} \qquad F^{-1} = \begin{pmatrix} 1 & 0 & 0 & 1 \\ 0 & 1 & 0 & 0 \\ 0 & 0 & 1 & 1 \\ 0 & 0 & 0 & 1 \end{pmatrix}$$

$$G = \frac{1}{5} \begin{pmatrix} 3 & 4 & 0 & 0 \\ -4 & 3 & 0 & 0 \\ 0 & 0 & 5 & 0 \\ 0 & 0 & 0 & 5 \end{pmatrix} \qquad G^{-1} = \frac{1}{5} \begin{pmatrix} 3 & -4 & 0 & 0 \\ 4 & 3 & 0 & 0 \\ 0 & 0 & 5 & 0 \\ 0 & 0 & 0 & 5 \end{pmatrix}$$

$$H = \frac{1}{\sqrt{2}} \begin{pmatrix} 1 & 0 & -1 & 0 \\ 0 & \sqrt{2} & 0 & 0 \\ 1 & 0 & 1 & 0 \\ 0 & 0 & 0 & \sqrt{2} \end{pmatrix} \qquad H^{-1} = \frac{1}{\sqrt{2}} \begin{pmatrix} 1 & 0 & 1 & 0 \\ 0 & \sqrt{2} & 0 & 0 \\ -1 & 0 & 1 & 0 \\ 0 & 0 & 0 & \sqrt{2} \end{pmatrix}$$

$$W = \frac{1}{\sqrt{2}} \begin{pmatrix} 1 & -1 & 0 & 0 \\ 1 & 1 & 0 & 0 \\ 0 & 0 & \sqrt{2} & 0 \\ 0 & 0 & 0 & \sqrt{2} \end{pmatrix}$$

since a clockwise rotation through $\pi/4$ radians is equivalent to an anti-clockwise rotation through $-\pi/4$, and

$$P = \frac{1}{50\sqrt{2}} \begin{pmatrix} 41 + 9\sqrt{2} & -12 - 13\sqrt{2} & -15 + 35\sqrt{2} & -26 + 6\sqrt{2} \\ -12 + 37\sqrt{2} & 34 + 16\sqrt{2} & -20 + 5\sqrt{2} & 32 - 42\sqrt{2} \\ -15 - 5\sqrt{2} & -20 + 35\sqrt{2} & 25 + 25\sqrt{2} & -10 + 30\sqrt{2} \\ 0 & 0 & 0 & 50\sqrt{2} \end{pmatrix}$$

where $P = F^{-1} \times G^{-1} \times H^{-1} \times W \times H \times G \times F$ is the matrix representation of the required transformation. Pre-multiplying the column vectors equivalent to $(0, 0, 0)$, $(1, 0, 0)$, $(0, 1, 0)$, $(0, 0, 1)$ and $(1, 1, 1)$ by P and changing the resulting column vectors back into row form and taking out a factor $1/50\sqrt{2}$ gives the respective co-ordinates

$(-26 + 6\sqrt{2}, 32 - 42\sqrt{2}, -10 + 30\sqrt{2})$, $(15 + 15\sqrt{2}, 20 - 5\sqrt{2}, -25 + 25\sqrt{2})$, $(-38 - 7\sqrt{2}, 66 - 26\sqrt{2}, -30 + 65\sqrt{2})$, $(-41 + 41\sqrt{2}, 12 - 37\sqrt{2}, 15 + 55\sqrt{2})$ and $(-12 + 37\sqrt{2}, 34 + 16\sqrt{2}, -20 + 85\sqrt{2})$

Placing Objects in Space

Scenes may be constructed in three dimensions in a manner precisely analogous to that described in chapter 4 for two-dimensional scenes. We define an arbitrary right-handed triad of axes, which we call the ABSOLUTE system, and we specify the co-ordinates of each vertex relative to this triad. Again these co-ordinates may be defined in a simple SETUP position and then moved, using matrix transformations, to their ACTUAL position. A detailed description is given in the next section. The matrices representing these transformations of vertices in space may be calculated using the routines which we have developed for transforming axis systems but, as before, the parameters used to call the routines must change as follows.

Translation
A vertex (x, y, z) is to be moved by a vector $t \equiv (t_x, t_y, t_z)$ to $(x + t_x, y + t_y, z + t_z)$. This is exactly equivalent to keeping the vertex fixed and translating the origin of the axes to $(-t_x, -t_y, -t_z)$. Thus the matrix representing this transformation may be calculated by

    tran3(−tx, −ty, −tz, A);

Change of scale and reflection
The origin is fixed and a general point (x, y, z) is moved to $(Sx \times x, Sy \times y, Sz \times z)$. This transformation is equivalent to changing the scale of the co-ordinate axes so that 1 unit on the x-axis becomes Sx units, 1 unit on the y-axis becomes Sy units and 1 unit on the z-axis becomes Sz units. The transformation matrix may thus be calculated by

scale3(sx, sy, sz, A);

Furthermore, if one of the co-ordinates is multiplied by a negative factor Sx, Sy or Sz, this corresponds to a reflection in the plane containing the other two axes. For example, $Sx = 1$, $Sy = 1$ and $Sz = -1$ gives a reflection in the x/y plane.

Rotating an object about a co-ordinate axis

Rotating an object about a co-ordinate axis anti-clockwise through an angle θ (theta) is equivalent to keeping the object fixed and rotating the axis system through an angle θ clockwise about the same axis, or, alternatively, by an angle $-\theta$ anti-clockwise. The rotation matrix is therefore returned by

rot3(m, −theta A);

where m is the index of the co-ordinate axis about which the rotation occurs.

Rotation of vertices about a general axis may be achieved in exactly the same way we achieved a rotation of axes earlier. Matrices F, G and H are used to transform the co-ordinate axes into such a position that the axis of rotation is coincident with the z-axis. Then space (not axes) are rotated with the matrix W so that the vertices move about this new z-axis. Finally H^{-1}, G^{-1} and F^{-1} replace the axes to their original positions. The complete rotation, as before, achieved by $F^{-1} \times G^{-1} \times H^{-1} \times W \times H \times G \times F$.

SETUP and ACTUAL Positions

In order to define a scene consisting of an object in some position and orientation in three-dimensional space, we use exactly the same method as was used for two-dimensional space. The co-ordinates of the vertices of the object are defined in some simple way, usually about the origin. This we call the *SETUP position*. Lines and facets within the object are defined by specifying the vertices forming their end-points or corners.

Each vertex of the object is moved from its SETUP position to the desired position in space by pre-multiplying the column vector holding its co-ordinates by the matrix representing the required transformation. (Naturally, each vertex undergoes the same transformation.) Again, this new position is called the *ACTUAL position*. Co-ordinates are still specified with respect to the ABSOLUTE system. The line and facet relationships are preserved with the transformed vertices. The matrix which relates the SETUP to ACTUAL position will be called P throughout and may be calculated using one of, or a combination of, the transformations described above.

We must reiterate that the co-ordinates of all vertices in both the SETUP and ACTUAL positions are defined with respect to the same set of axes − those of the ABSOLUTE system.

Storing Information about Scenes

The data representing objects in a scene undergoes various manipulations between its creation and the eventual drawing and so may need to be stored in an easily accessible form in a database. The database itself is declared in listing 7.2. The CONST, TYPE and VAR declaration must be merged into the program containing listings 1.1, 1.3 etc., as indicated by the comments in listing 1.1. The evaluation of a section of the database relevant to one occurrence of one particular object will be achieved by a call to a *Construction Routine* for that object, which will normally have a SETUP to ACTUAL matrix *P* as a parameter in order to place the object in its correct ACTUAL position. As usual, the SETUP information can be input from file. If the same ACTUAL scene is required over and over again, then it is possible to skip over the SETUP stage and read in the ACTUAL position of objects in the scene with a routine we name **datain**. Remember, if required, **datain** can read vertex information in SETUP and/or ACTUAL position.

As with two dimensions, we use arrays to store this information. When required, we use global arrays declared in listing 7.2 to store this information. The three-dimensional scene is assumed to contain **nov** vertices. The ACTUAL x, y and z co-ordinates of these vertices are stored in an array **act[1..maxv]** with elements of RECORD TYPE **vector3** (that is, **act** is of TYPE **vertex3array**), where **maxv** is not less than **nov**. A vertex with co-ordinates (**act[j].x, act[j].y, act[j].z**) is said to have index **j**. Unlike in two-dimensions, we do not store information about lines, but should you require it, you yourself can add **nol** lines stored in an array **line[1..maxl]** with elements of RECORD TYPE **linepair**. The value of **maxl** must not be less than **nol**, and values **line[i].front** and **line[i].back** indicate respectively the indices of the **front** and **back** vertices of the ith line (compare this with listing 4.2). Our objects will be defined in terms of facets, whose description will be far more complex than simple vertices: a vertex always has three components, the x, y and z co-ordinates, but a facet may have any number of sides and hence any number of vertices around its boundary, as well as peculiar colour, reflective and refractive properties etc. Lines may be considered as edges of facets; in fact a single line may be described as a degenerate one or two-sided facet. We saw in chapter 4 with the two-dimensional equivalent that the most efficient method of representing a facet without imposing unreasonable limits upon the number of vertices around the boundary involves the use of a linear list implemented with three arrays. A large array of integers, **faclist[1..maxlist]**, contains a list of vertices in the ACTUAL array and each of **nof** facets is defined by two integer pointers to this list, contained in arrays **facfront[1..maxf]** and **size[1..maxf]**; **maxf** is not less than **nof**, the number of facets in the scene. The pointer to the ith facet, **facfront[i]**, points to the element of the **faclist** array preceding that which holds the index of the first vertex of that facet; thus **facfront[1] = 0**. The value **size[i]** contains the number of vertices on the boundary of the ith facet, and these in turn are stored in the faclist array as faclist[facfront[i] + 1], faclist[facfront[i] + 2], . . . , faclist-[facfront[i] + size[i]]. The only constraint thus placed upon the number of vertices on the boundary of a facet is that the total number on all facets must not exceed the dimension of the faclist array. An integer variable last indicates the position within faclist of the last vertex of the last facet; this is useful in updating the database.

We also introduce the idea of attributes associated with facets. Initially this will involve only the colour in which they are to be drawn but several more attributes will be introduced when more complex pictures of three-dimensional objects are considered. These attributes will also be stored in arrays relating to the facets. The colour of facet i will be stored in the array colour[1..maxf] as colour[i].

Two further variables are stored: the integer counts ntv and ntf. These are not used yet, but in later chapters they will represent respectively the total numbers of vertices and facets in the scene, inclusive of any extra which may be created during the processing of the scene.

The construction routines that follow will be used to update the initially empty database of facets and vertices in their ACTUAL position; the placement of an observer and the drawing of objects will be left to other routines including transform, findQ, look3 and observe of listing 7.2 together with a special version of routine draw_a_picture which initialises the database before calling a routine scene which will control the construction of the complete scene and the way it is displayed. Procedure draw_a_picture links the modelling and display routines that follow to the primitive routines of listing 1.1 and the graphics library of listing 1.3. In order for you to construct and draw three-dimensional scenes, you need only write a scene routine, and to help you in this task a number of example scene routines will follow.

The Structure of the scene Construction

All these ideas must now be put together in a Pascal program for modelling and drawing a three-dimensional scene. We can assume that the previously defined routines are properly declared and that draw_a_picture calls the scene routine after the scale of the graphics WINDOW has been created (in the body of the main program, listing 1.3), the database has been cleared, data on a cube has been input and two stack heaps have been initialised (in the body of draw_a_picture, listing 7.2). Note that this listing 7.2 includes a routine transform for transforming a vector by a matrix, routines cubesetup and cube for creating the data for a cube (see example 7.2), and the arrays (heap, permheap), free-pointers (free, permfree) and procedures (heapset, pop, push, permheapset and pushperm) for manipulating a heap data structures needed in later chapters and explained in chapter 2. Two very simple example scene routines are given in this chapter (listing 7.3 and 7.4) which merely print out data on a scene containing just one cube. In general the PROCEDURE scene must model (via construction routines declared within scene), observe (via findQ, look3 and observe: see chapter 8) and display (via project, drawit etc. declared within scene) the objects in the three-dimensional scene, before finish finally 'flushes the buffers'. This general situation takes the form of four definite stages.

Listing 7.2

```
{ three dimensional data base and model-independent transformations }

CONST
    maxv=400 ; maxf=400 ; maxlist = 2000 ; maxheap=2000 ;

TYPE
    vertex3array = ARRAY[1..maxv] OF vector3 ;
    vertex2array = ARRAY[1..maxv] OF vector2 ;
    facetarray   = ARRAY[1..maxf] OF integer ;
    heapcell = RECORD info,pointer : integer END ;

VAR  { data base variables }
    nov,ntv,nof,ntf,last : integer ;  {COUNTS }
    act,obs,setup : vertex3array ; {ACTUAL, OBSERVED and SETUP}
    pro : vertex2array ; {PROJECTED vertices}
    colour,size,facfront,nfac,super,firstsup : facetarray ;
    faclist : ARRAY[1..maxlist] OF integer ; { FACETS }
{ heap and permanent heap variables }
    heap,permheap : ARRAY[1..maxheap] OF heapcell ;
    free,permfree : integer ;
{ variables for observation and projection }
    zero,eye,direct : vector3 ; Q : matrix4x4 ; ppd : real ;
{ data for setting up a cube of side 2 }
    cubevert : ARRAY[1..8] OF vector3 ;
    cubefacet : ARRAY[1..6,1..4] OF integer ;


PROCEDURE transform(v : vector3 ; A : matrix4x4 ; VAR w : vector3) ;
{ transform column vector 'v' using matrix 'A' into column vector 'w' }
BEGIN
    w.x := A[1,1]*v.x + A[1,2]*v.y + A[1,3]*v.z + A[1,4] ;
    w.y := A[2,1]*v.x + A[2,2]*v.y + A[2,3]*v.z + A[2,4] ;
    w.z := A[3,1]*v.x + A[3,2]*v.y + A[3,3]*v.z + A[3,4]
END ; { of transform }

PROCEDURE cubesetup ;
{ Procedure to read data on cube from file 'cube.dat' }
VAR i,j : integer ;
BEGIN
    assign(indata,'cube.dat') ; reset(indata) ;
    FOR i:= 1 TO 8
    DO read(indata,cubevert[i].x,cubevert[i].y,cubevert[i].z) ;
    FOR i:= 1 TO 6
    DO FOR j:= 1 TO 4
        DO read(indata,cubefacet[i,j]) ;
    close(indata)
END ; { of cubesetup }
```

```
PROCEDURE cube(P : matrix4x4) ;
{ Construction routine for a rectangular block. Initially a cube }
{ the block is distorted by the scaling matrix component of 'P' }
{ Assume cube has logical colour 3 }
VAR i,j : integer ;
BEGIN
{ Update facet data base with 6 new facets }
   FOR i := 1 TO 6
   DO BEGIN
         FOR j := 1 TO 4
         DO faclist[last+j] := cubefacet[i,j]+nov ;
         nof := nof+1 ; facfront[nof] := last ; size[nof] := 4 ;
         last := last+size[nof] ;
         colour[nof] := 3 ; nfac[nof] := nof ;
         super[nof] := 0 ; firstsup[nof] := 0
   END ;
{ Update vertex data base with 8 new vertices in ACTUAL position }
   FOR i := 1 TO 8
   DO BEGIN
         nov := nov+1 ; transform(cubevert[i],P,act[nov])
   END
END ; { of cube }


PROCEDURE heapstart ;
{ Initialise the 'heap'. At first no 'info'rmation is stored }
{ Only 'pointer', which points to next cell in the heap }
VAR i : integer ;
BEGIN
   free := 1 ;
   FOR i := 1 TO maxheap-1
   DO heap[i].pointer := i+1 ;
   heap[maxheap].pointer := 0
END ; { of heapstart }


PROCEDURE push(VAR stackname : integer ; value : integer) ;
{ Routine to 'push' the integer 'value' onto the stack-type }
{ linear list 'stackname' which is stored on a 'heap' }
VAR location : integer ;
BEGIN
{ create new node for stackname }
   IF free=0
   THEN BEGIN
         writeln(' Heap size exceeeded') ;
         EXIT
      END
   ELSE BEGIN
{ Obtain 'location' from 'heap', and delete it from 'free' list }
         location := free ; free := heap[free].pointer ;
{ Add 'location' to front of 'stackname', store 'value' there }
         heap[location].info := value ;
         heap[location].pointer := stackname ;
         stackname := location
      END
END ; { of push }
```

```
PROCEDURE pop(VAR stackname,value : integer) ;
{ Routine to 'pop' the first 'value' from the linear list 'stackname' }
VAR location : integer ;
BEGIN
{ 'value' is stored at the front of list 'stackname' }
   IF stackname = 0
   THEN BEGIN
            writeln(' Stack is empty') ; value := -9999
        END
   ELSE BEGIN
            location := stackname ; value := heap[stackname].info ;
{ Delete front element of stackname, and dispose }
            stackname := heap[stackname].pointer ;
            heap[location].pointer := free ;
            free := location
        END
END ; { of pop }


PROCEDURE permheapstart ;
{ Routine to initialise the permanent heap. At first no information }
{ is stored and each 'pointer' points to the next cell in the heap }
VAR i : integer ;
BEGIN
   permfree := 1 ;
   FOR i := 1 TO maxheap-1
   DO permheap[i].pointer := i+1 ;
   permheap[maxheap].pointer := 0
END ; { of permheapstart }


PROCEDURE pushperm(VAR stackname : integer ; value : integer) ;
{ Routine to 'push' the integer 'value' onto the stack-type }
{ linear list 'stackname' which is stored on the permanent 'heap' }
VAR location : integer ;
BEGIN
{ create new node for stackname }
   IF permfree = 0
   THEN BEGIN
            write(' Heap size exceeded') ; EXIT
        END
   ELSE BEGIN
{ Obtain 'location' from 'heap', and delete it from 'free' list }
            location := permfree ;
            permfree := permheap[permfree].pointer ;
{ Add 'location' to front of 'stackname', store 'value' there }
            permheap[location].info := value ;
            permheap[location].pointer := stackname ;
            stackname := location
        END
END ; { of pushperm }

PROCEDURE dataout ;
{ Routine to output an ACTUAL scene to file 'model.out' }
VAR front,i,j : integer ;
BEGIN
   assign(outdata,'model.out') ; rewrite(outdata) ;
```

```
    writeln(outdata,nov:5,nof:5) ;
    FOR i := 1 TO nov
    DO writeln(outdata,act[i].x,act[i].y,act[i].z) ;
    FOR i := 1 TO nof
    DO BEGIN
           front := facfront[i] ;
           writeln(outdata,size[i]:5,colour[i]:5,super[i]:5) ;
           FOR j := 1 TO size[i]
           DO write(outdata,faclist[front+j]:5) ;
           writeln(outdata)
        END ;
    close(outdata)
END ; { of dataout }



PROCEDURE datain ;
{ Routine to input an ACTUAL scene from file 'model.in' }
VAR front,i,j : integer ;
BEGIN
    assign(indata,'model.in') ; reset(indata) ;
    read(indata,nov,nof) ;
    FOR i := 1 TO nov
    DO read(indata,act[i].x,act[i].y,act[i].z) ;
    FOR i := 1 TO nof
    DO BEGIN
           read(indata,size[i],colour[i],super[i]) ;
           FOR j := 1 TO size[i]
           DO read(indata,faclist[last+j]) ;
           nfac[i] := i ; facfront[i] := last ; last := last+size[i] ;
{ See chapter 9 for explanation of storing superficial facets }
           IF super[i] < > 0
           THEN pushperm(firstsup[super[i]],i)
        END ;
    close(indata)
END ; { of datain }



{   Other routines including .......
    PROCEDURE findQ ;
    PROCEDURE look3 ;
    PROCEDURE observe ;
    PROCEDURE project ;
    PROCEDURE scene ;                                  }


PROCEDURE draw_a_picture ;
BEGIN
    zero.x := 0 ; zero.y := 0.0 ; zero.z := 0.0 ;
{ Initialise vertex, line and facet counts }
    nov := 0 ; nof := 0 ; last := 0 ;
{ Prepare heap and setup cube data base }
    heapstart ; permheapstart ; cubesetup ;
{ Construct and draw scene }
    scene
END ; { of draw_a_picture }
```

File 'cube.dat'
```
 1   1   1
 1  -1   1
 1  -1  -1
 1   1  -1
-1   1   1
-1  -1   1
-1  -1  -1
-1   1  -1
 1   2   3   4
 1   4   8   5
 1   5   6   2
 3   7   8   4
 2   6   7   3
 5   8   7   6
```

The CONST declaration is used to define the upper indices maxv, maxf and maxlist:

CONST maxv = 400; maxf = 400; maxlist = 2000; maxheap = 2000;

These values are arbitrarily chosen, and for very complex models these values may be greatly increased. We also introduce maxheap, the size of a heap data structure here (see chapter 2). The counts of vertices and facets for a particular scene or model are also declared here

{VAR} nov,ntv,nof,ntf,last : integer;

and the ACTUAL co-ordinate vertices of the scene, act, are declared along with other interpretations of these co-ordinates, setup and obs (see later) thus:

{VAR} act, obs, setup : vertex3array;

where

{TYPE} vertex3array = ARRAY[1..maxv] OF vector3;

Care must be taken to ensure that all the vertices of a declared facet are coplanar. If this is so in SETUP position then it is maintained through any combination of affine transformations. Other arrays must be declared in the global database to hold a description of these facets.

{TYPE} facetarray = ARRAY[1..maxf] OF integer;
{VAR} colour,size,facfront,nfac,super,firstsup : facetarray;
{VAR} faclist : ARRAY[1..maxlist] OF integer;

The array nfac[1..maxf] holds a pointer for each facet. Later when we draw facets, it will be necessary to use clipping on the three-dimensional facet data. Hence the original facet will have pieces clipped off, and the visible portion of each may be represented by a new set of vertices and a new facet (hence the need for ntv and ntf, which will be initialised in the drawit routine). For any clipped facet i, nfac[i] will allow us to point at the list of entries facfront [nfac[i]] + 1,..., facfront [nfac[i]] + size [nfac[i]]

of the faclist array which indicate the polygon vertices representing the clipped part of facet i. Initially we assume that no facets are clipped, and hence nfac[i] will equal i for all facets of the object and entries

facfront[i] + 1, . . . ,facfront[i] + size[i]

hold the vertex indices of the original facet i. This will not necessarily be the case later, so it is advisable for us to draw some distinction now between (1) the vertex entries of a facet prior to clipping, and (2) the vertex entries after clipping. This distinction will be clarified in chapter 14. Arrays needed to store information on superficial facets (super and firstsup: see chapter 9) are also declared here.

Remember that, if they are required, the SETUP *x*, *y* and *z* co-ordinates of the vertices and facet information of any particular object type are stored in the special arrays, specific to that object in a manner similar to those declared above, with values either read from file or perhaps implied by the program listing: see the cube data in listing 7.2. Note we have already declared space for SETUP vertices, setup[1..maxv] above. As our drawing of scenes gets more sophisticated, then more attributes will be needed for the objects and hence expanded and extended entries will be needed for the database. *When new entries are introduced in the text, you must remember to amend the database declarations accordingly.*

(1) If required the necessary SETUP information is created within construction routines using data read by a datain routine.
(2) The main body of scene calculates the SETUP to ACTUAL information for each object within the scene and calls the corresponding construction routine to place that object in the ACTUAL position. Alternatively the complete ACTUAL scene can be read from disk using a datain routine (listing 7.2).
(3) An observer is defined, and the OBSERVED positions of vertices in the scene are calculated (routines findQ, look3 and observe: listing 8.1).
(4) The three-dimensional scene cannot be drawn directly as in two dimensions, the routine drawit must first call project which projects the scene onto a two-dimensional window before constructing a view on the viewport.

Organised in this modular way, users will only have to write specific scene routines and perhaps datain, drawit and construction routines, and these will be merged with the routines of listings 1.1, 1.3 and 7.1 via the draw_a_picture routine which calls scene. Even these will be in a form similar to the examples we give, so this should not prove too difficult.

There will be situations when the SETUP information can be programmed directly into the construction routines and there will be no need to have an explicit datain routine. In chapter 9, for example, an ellipsoid is constructed by routine ellipsoid (listing 9.7). What is important is that the reader recognises the various stages in construction and drawing.

Listing 7.3

```
PROCEDURE scene ;
{ Construct scene of one cube }
VAR P : matrix4X4 ;
BEGIN
{ Place Cube as per Example 7.2 in its SETUP position }
   tran3(0.0,0.0,0.0,P) ; cube(P) ; dataout
END ; { of scene }
```

Example 7.2
In order that our explanations of the display algorithms are not obscured by too complicated objects, we will start all our display descriptions by using a cube. Then when these ideas are understood we can add complexity into the scenes with other objects. Since the cube is such a useful object we create special SETUP array cubevert[1..8] for the vertices and cubefacet[1..6, 1..4] for the facets and initialise them with a call to the cubesetup routine (listing 7.2). The construction routine cube is then used to read the information from file 'cube.dat' and then add a single example of a cube in ACTUAL position to the database, the SETUP co-ordinates of the cube are the 8 vertices $(1, 1, 1)$; $(1, -1, 1)$; $(1, -1, -1)$; $(1, 1, -1)$; $(-1, 1, 1)$; $(-1, -1, 1)$; $(-1, -1, -1)$ and $(-1, 1, -1)$: numbered 1 through 8. The six facets are thus the sets of four vertices 1, 2, 3, 4; 1, 4, 8, 5; 1, 5, 6, 2; 3, 7, 8, 4; 2, 6, 7, 3 and 5, 8, 7, 6; see figure 7.2. The peculiar ordering of the vertex indices in the facet definitions is to ensure that when viewed from outside the object, the vertices occur in an anti-clockwise orientation, an order

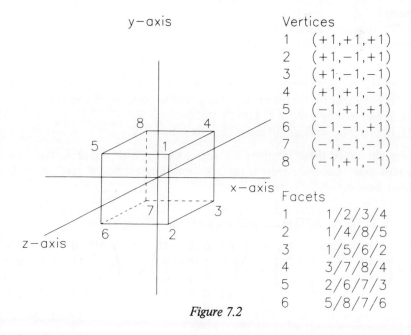

Vertices	
1	$(+1,+1,+1)$
2	$(+1,-1,+1)$
3	$(+1,-1,-1)$
4	$(+1,+1,-1)$
5	$(-1,+1,+1)$
6	$(-1,-1,+1)$
7	$(-1,-1,-1)$
8	$(-1,+1,-1)$

Facets	
1	1/2/3/4
2	1/4/8/5
3	1/5/6/2
4	3/7/8/4
5	2/6/7/3
6	5/8/7/6

Figure 7.2

needed for later hidden surface algorithms. If you are not sure if your vertices are in the correct order you should check using the program listing 6.11. In this example we enter the construction routine with an identity matrix, so that the cube is placed in ACTUAL position identical to its SETUP position. Since we are not yet in a position to draw a three-dimensional scene, listing 7.3 includes a scene routine which takes the cube and places it in this simple ACTUAL position and then just stores the ACTUAL scene on disk using the dataout routine. (The inverse datain routine that recreates this ACTUAL scene from disk, in the same format generated by dataout, is also given. This will be used in the example 8.1.)

Listing 7.4

```
PROCEDURE scene ;
{ Construct scene of one cube }
VAR A,B,C,D,P : matrix4x4 ;
    alpha : real ;
BEGIN
{ Place Cube as per Example 7.3 }
    alpha := -0.927295218 ; rot3(3,-alpha,A) ;
    tran3(1.0,0.0,0.0,B) ; rot3(2,alpha,C) ;
    mult3(B,A,D) ; mult3(C,D,P) ; cube(P) ;
{ printout database }
    dataout
END ; { of scene }
```

Example 7.3

In this example we place the cube in ACTUAL position (scene listing 7.4) with the following three transformations

(1) Rotate the cube by an angle $\alpha = -0.927295218$ radians about the z-axis: matrix A. This example is contrived so that $\cos \alpha = 3/5$ and $\sin \alpha = -4/5$, in order that the rotation matrix consists of uncomplicated elements.
(2) Translate it by a vector $(-1, 0, 0)$: matrix B.
(3) Rotate it by an angle $-\alpha$ about the y-axis: matrix C.

Remember that these rotations are anti-clockwise with regard to the right-handed axes. Also note these three transformations are not of axes but of the object itself.

The SETUP to ACTUAL matrix is thus $P = C \times B \times A$, where

$$A = \begin{pmatrix} 3/5 & 4/5 & 0 & 0 \\ -4/5 & 3/5 & 0 & 0 \\ 0 & 0 & 1 & 0 \\ 0 & 0 & 0 & 1 \end{pmatrix} \quad B = \begin{pmatrix} 1 & 0 & 0 & -1 \\ 0 & 1 & 0 & 0 \\ 0 & 0 & 1 & 0 \\ 0 & 0 & 0 & 1 \end{pmatrix} \quad C = \begin{pmatrix} 3/5 & 0 & 4/5 & 0 \\ 0 & 1 & 0 & 0 \\ -4/5 & 0 & 3/5 & 0 \\ 0 & 0 & 0 & 1 \end{pmatrix}$$

and P is given by

$$P = \frac{1}{25}\begin{pmatrix} 9 & 12 & 20 & -15 \\ -20 & 15 & 0 & 0 \\ -12 & -16 & 15 & 20 \\ 0 & 0 & 0 & 25 \end{pmatrix}$$

So the above eight vertex SETUP co-ordinates are transformed to the co-ordinate triples $(26/25, -5/25, 7/25)$; $(2/25, -35/25, 39/25)$; $(-38/25, -35/25, 9/25)$; $(-14/25, -5/25, -23/25)$; $(8/25, 35/25, 31/25)$; $(-16/25, 5/25, 63/25)$; $(-56/25, 5/25, 33/25)$ and $(-32/25, 35/25, 1/25)$.

For example, $(1, 1, 1)$ is transformed into $(26/25, -5/25, 7/25)$ because

$$\frac{1}{25}\begin{pmatrix} 9 & 12 & 20 & -15 \\ -20 & 15 & 0 & 0 \\ -12 & -16 & 15 & 20 \\ 0 & 0 & 0 & 25 \end{pmatrix} \times \begin{pmatrix} 1 \\ 1 \\ 1 \\ 1 \end{pmatrix} = \frac{1}{25}\begin{pmatrix} 26 \\ -5 \\ 7 \\ 25 \end{pmatrix}$$

The values can be checked by printing out the array values by using dataout.

Exercise 7.2
Use the SETUP information of the cube and a scaling matrix as part of the SETUP to ACTUAL matrix P so that the cube construction routine places a rectangular block a units long, by b units high by c units deep in its ACTUAL position using a matrix P.

Exercise 7.3
Create construction routines for

(1) A tetrahedron: four vertices $(1, 1, 1)$; $(-1, 1, -1)$; $(-1, -1, 1)$ and $(1, -1, -1)$ (labelled 1 through 4) and four facets $1, 2, 3$; $1, 3, 4$; $1, 4, 2$ and $4, 3, 2$.
(2) An icosahedron: $\tau = (1 + \sqrt{5})/2$: twelve vertices $(0, 1, -\tau)$; $(\tau, 0, -1)$; $(1, \tau, 0)$; $(0, -1, -\tau)$; $(\tau, 0, 1)$; $(-1, \tau, 0)$; $(0, 1, \tau)$; $(-\tau, 0, -1)$; $(1, -\tau, 0)$; $(0, -1, \tau)$; $(-\tau, 0, 1)$ and $(-1, -\tau, 0)$. The facets are $1, 3, 2$; $1, 2, 4$; $1, 4, 8$; $1, 8, 6$; $1, 6, 3$; $2, 3, 5$; $2, 9, 4$; $4, 12, 8$; $8, 11, 6$; $3, 6, 7$; $2, 5, 9$; $4, 9, 12$; $8, 12, 11$; $6, 11, 7$; $3, 7, 5$; $5, 10, 9$; $9, 10, 12$; $12, 10, 11$; $11, 10, 7$; $7, 10, 5$.
(3) Find your own data for such Archimedean solids as the octahedron, rhombic dodecahedron, pentagonal dodecahedron, cuboctahedron etc.

Far greater consideration will be given in chapter 9 to the creation of object data, but for the moment we need worry only about its form, as the next chapter will discuss the representation of a three-dimensional scene on a graphics viewport, using the simple cube to illustrate the ideas.

8 The Observer and the Orthographic Projection

We now address the problem of representing views of three-dimensional scenes on the graphics viewport. There are three major stages. In chapter 7 we saw how to construct a model of a three-dimensional scene in ACTUAL position. In this chapter we consider observing the scene and the display of a corresponding view. The display of the scene is co-ordinated by routine drawit which may take a number of different forms, depending on the type of image required (line drawing, colour etc). This routine will be called at the end of the scene routine after the construction of the model and the positioning of the observer. We shall deal with the observer before going on to consider the drawit display.

We shall assume that the information about the scene to be drawn is stored in terms of vertex co-ordinates in ACTUAL position specified relative to the ABSOLUTE co-ordinate system.

The eye (note only one eye!) is placed at a vector3 position eye relative to the ABSOLUTE axes looking in a fixed vector3 direction direct, say. These values are declared in the global database. The head can also be tilted, but more of this later. We use matrix transformations to calculate the co-ordinates of the vertices relative to a triad of axes, called the *OBSERVER system*, which has the eye at the origin and direction of view along the negative z-axis. (It would make more sense to use left-handed axes here in order that the observer looks along the positive z-axis, but because of standardisation we remain with the right-handed system!) These new co-ordinate values are called the *OBSERVED co-ordinates* of the vertices. The matrix which represents the transformation from ABSOLUTE to OBSERVER systems will be called Q throughout this book and is also declared in the global database. We also declare variables ppd and eyedist which are needed for perspective and stereoscopic projections later.

Construction of the ABSOLUTE to OBSERVER Transformation Matrix Q

The OBSERVER system has origin eye relative to the ABSOLUTE system with negative z-axis parallel to and with the same sense as the direction vector direct. See figure 8.1. If the observer wishes to look at the ABSOLUTE origin then direct.x = −eye.x, direct.y = −eye.y and direct.z = −eye.z.

Given a point with co-ordinates specified relative to the ABSOLUTE system, we want to determine its co-ordinates relative to the OBSERVER system. These

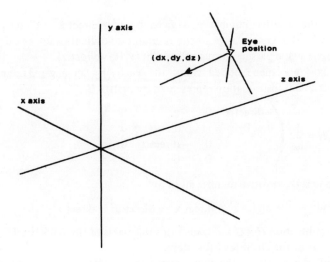

Figure 8.1

co-ordinates may be found by pre-multiplying a column vector holding the ABSOLUTE co-ordinates by a matrix which represents the series of steps required to transform the ABSOLUTE axes into the OBSERVER axes. The calculation of this matrix is similar to that considered in chapter 7. The rotation of a point about a general line $b + \mu d$ involved the transformation of the axis system so that the origin moved to b and the positive z-axis had direction d. In this case, therefore, we take $b \equiv$ (eye.x, eye.y, eye.z) and $d \equiv$ (−direct.x, −direct.y, −direct.z), and carry out the equivalent steps (NOTE the minus signs!).

(1) The co-ordinate origin is translated to the point b so that the axis of rotation now passes through the origin. This is achieved by the matrix F

$$F = \begin{pmatrix} 1 & 0 & 0 & -\text{eye.x} \\ 0 & 1 & 0 & -\text{eye.y} \\ 0 & 0 & 1 & -\text{eye.z} \\ 0 & 0 & 0 & 1 \end{pmatrix}$$

The OBSERVER z-axis is now of the form $\mu d \equiv \mu$ (−direct.x, −direct.y, −direct.z) relative to the transformed system. We now require the z-axis of the OBSERVER system and that of the transformed ABSOLUTE system to be coincident. This is achieved by the next two steps.

(2) The axes are rotated about the z-axis by an angle $\alpha = \tan^{-1}$ (−direct.y/ −direct.x). This is represented by the matrix G

$$G = \frac{1}{v} \begin{pmatrix} -\text{direct.x} & -\text{direct.y} & 0 & 0 \\ \text{direct.y} & -\text{direct.x} & 0 & 0 \\ 0 & 0 & v & 0 \\ 0 & 0 & 0 & v \end{pmatrix}$$

where the positive number v is given by $v^2 = \text{direct.x}^2 + \text{direct.y}^2$. The OBSERVER z-axis, relative to the resultant co-ordinate axes, is a line lying in the x/z plane passing through the point $(v, 0, -\text{direct.z})$,

(3) The axes are then rotated about the y-axis by an angle $\beta = \tan^{-1} (v/-\text{direct.z})$ a transformation represented by matrix H

$$H = \frac{1}{w} \begin{pmatrix} -\text{direct.z} & 0 & -v & 0 \\ 0 & w & 0 & 0 \\ v & 0 & -\text{direct.z} & 0 \\ 0 & 0 & 0 & w \end{pmatrix}$$

where w is the positive number given by

$$w^2 = v^2 + \text{direct.z}^2 = \text{direct.x}^2 + \text{direct.y}^2 + \text{direct.z}^2$$

The combination $H \times G \times F$ transforms the z-axis of the ABSOLUTE system into the z-axis of the OBSERVER system.

Although the z-axes of the two systems are coincident, this does not mean that the triads are identical. Nothing has been said about the positions of the x and y axes of the OBSERVER triad. You cannot assume that the ABSOLUTE and OBSERVER x/y axes are parallel: far from it. The rotation transformations used to relate ABSOLUTE and OBSERVER axes can induce a torque. There is a simple physical demonstration of this phenomenon using three rotations. Place your right arm at your side, palm inwards. Hold the arm stiff and lift it directly in front of you to shoulder level. Now move the arm, keeping at shoulder level, until it is to the right of your body. Then, still with the arm stiff, drop it to your side. The arm has returned to its original direction but it has twisted through a right angle.

These rotations of the arm were all right angles, arbitrary rotations can introduce quite peculiar torques. We therefore have to standardise in order to avoid spurious torques which are by-products of the rotations used in the method of linking the two systems and which have nothing to do with the observer or the scene. Since the OBSERVER system represents the position and orientation of the viewer's head we adopt the convention that the y-axis is in the vertical plane, parallel to the y/z plane of the ABSOLUTE system, which means that the OBSERVER is standing upright. This convention is called *maintaining the vertical* and results in a vertical line, with general point eye $+ \mu(0, 1, 0)$ relative to the ABSOLUTE system, being transformed to $(0, 0, 0) + \mu(0, y', z')$ relative to the OBSERVER system. Pre-multiplication of such a point on this line by the matrix $E = H \times G \times F$ gives the new co-ordinates $\mu/v \times w)$ (direct.y × direct.z, $-w \times \text{direct.x}, -v \times \text{direct.y}) = (p, q, r)$ way. So, inorder that the vertical be maintained, we must further rotate the system about the z-axis (leaving z co-ordinates unchanged) so that the vector (p, q, r) has a new x co-ordinate of zero. This is achieved by rotation of axes about the z-axis through an angle $\gamma = -\tan^{-1} (-\text{direct.y} \times \text{direct.z}/w \times \text{direct.x}) = -\tan^{-1} (p/q)$ which is represented by the matrix U

$$U = \frac{1}{t} \begin{pmatrix} q & -p & 0 & 0 \\ p & q & 0 & 0 \\ 0 & 0 & t & 0 \\ 0 & 0 & 0 & t \end{pmatrix}$$

where $t^2 = p^2 + q^2$ and thus

$$U \times \begin{pmatrix} p \\ q \\ r \\ 1 \end{pmatrix} = \frac{1}{t} \begin{pmatrix} q & -p & 0 & 0 \\ p & q & 0 & 0 \\ 0 & 0 & t & 0 \\ 0 & 0 & 0 & t \end{pmatrix} \times \begin{pmatrix} p \\ q \\ r \\ 1 \end{pmatrix} = \begin{pmatrix} 0 \\ t \\ r \\ 1 \end{pmatrix}$$

Thus the complete transformation from co-ordinates in SETUP position to those in OBSERVED position is achieved by pre-multiplication with the matrix $R = Q \times P$ where P is the SETUP to ACTUAL transformation matrix and $Q = U \times H \times G \times F$, the ABSOLUTE to OBSERVER matrix.

The procedures look3 and findQ (listing 8.1), given eye and direct, generate the matrix Q. The transformation of vertices from ABSOLUTE to OBSERVER systems is also given in this listing as routine observe.

The OBSERVED co-ordinates of vertices, obs, are declared in the global data-base alongside act and setup.

Listing 8.1

```
PROCEDURE findQ ;
{ Calculates the observation matrix 'Q' for a given observer }
VAR E,F,G,H,U : matrix4x4 ;
    alpha,beta,gamma,v,w : real ;
BEGIN
{ Calculate translation matrix 'F' }
   tran3(eye.x,eye.y,eye.z,F) ;
{ Calculate rotation matrix 'G' }
   alpha := angle(-direct.x,-direct.y) ; rot3(3,alpha,G) ;
{ Calculate rotation matrix 'H' }
   v := sqrt(direct.x*direct.x+direct.y*direct.y) ;
   beta := angle(-direct.z,v) ; rot3(2,beta,H) ;
{ Calculate rotation matrix 'U' }
   w := sqrt(v*v+direct.z*direct.z) ;
   gamma := angle(-direct.x*w,direct.y*direct.z) ;
   rot3(3,-gamma,U) ;
{ Combine the transformations to find 'Q' }
   mult3(G,F,Q) ; mult3(H,Q,E) ; mult3(U,E,Q)
END ;  { of findQ }

PROCEDURE look3 ;
{ Read in vector 'eye' looking in direction vector 'direct' }
{ then calculate the observation matrix 'Q' }
```

```
BEGIN
{ Read in observation data }
    writeln(' Type in eye position and direction of view') ;
    readln(eye.x,eye.y,eye.z,direct.x,direct.y,direct.z) ;
    findQ
END ;   { of look3 }

PROCEDURE observe ;
VAR i : integer ;
BEGIN
    FOR i := 1 TO nov
    DO transform(act[i],Q,obs[i])
END ;   { of observe }
```

Exercise 8.1

If required, you can extend this program to deal with the situation where the head is tilted through an angle ϕ from the vertical. This is achieved by further rotating the axes by $+\phi$ about the z-axis. Thus matrix U should rotate about the z-axis by an angle $\gamma + \phi$.

Exercise 8.2

Rewrite the look3 and findQ routines so that the position of the observer, the direction of view and tilt of the head are given in spherical polar co-ordinates.

Henceforth, throughout our discussion of projections, all three-dimensional co-ordinate values should be understood to refer to the OBSERVER system unless otherwise stated. These ideas will be graphically illustrated in example 8.1, after we have described how to project a three-dimensional scene onto a graphics viewport.

Projections: the View Plane, the Window and the Viewport

The viewport is two dimensional (a plane) so, in order to create an image of a three-dimensional scene, a mapping from three-dimensional space onto this plane is required.

What the eye sees when looking at a three-dimensional scene is a *projection* of the vertices, lines and facets of the object onto a *view plane* which is perpendicular to the line of sight. A projection is defined by a set of lines which we call *the lines of projection*. The projection of a point onto a plane is the point of intersection of the plane with the unique line of projection which passes through the point. The projection of a line onto a plane is the line in the plane joining the projections of its two end-points. The projection of a facet onto a plane is the polygon formed by the projection of its vertices.

In the OBSERVER system we note that the view plane is of the form $z = -d$ (for some $d \geq 0$) – a plane parallel to the x/y plane. Vertices are projected onto this plane by some method (via a routine **project**), producing projected points with co-ordinates of the form $(xp, yp, -d)$ where xp and yp depend upon the type of projection and d is the fixed perpendicular distance of the view plane from the eye. The projected values of the **obs** vertices from the database are also declared globally in listing 7.2.

    {VAR} pro : vertex2array;

The problem is thus reduced to that of representing in the graphics viewport the two-dimensional image which is projected onto the view plane. Apart from the extra projection step, this is exactly equivalent to the graphical representation of two-dimensional space which we discussed in chapter 4. Recall that we identified the viewport with a rectangular area of the two-dimensional Cartesian plane which we called the *window*. Points within this window were identified with pixels within the viewport using two functions **fx** and **fy** which transformed their Cartesian x and y co-ordinates to pixel co-ordinates. In order to follow this process for the representation of a view of three-dimensional space we must simply specify a window and co-ordinate system on the view plane. We define such a two-dimensional co-ordinate system, which we call the WINDOW system, simply by saying that a point on the view plane with OBSERVED co-ordinates $(xp, yp, -d)$ has WINDOW co-ordinates (xp, yp). Thus the x and y axes of the WINDOW system are lines in the view plane which are parallel to the x and y axes (respectively) of the OBSERVER system and its origin is on the OBSERVER z-axis at $z = -d$. The window itself is defined in a manner exactly equivalent to that in two dimensions – as a rectangle, centred on the origin, with edges of length **horiz** parallel to the x-axis and **vert** parallel to the y-axis. We then identify the x and y co-ordinates of points in the window with pixels in the viewport. Once the vertices have been projected onto the view plane and thence onto the viewport, we can construct the projection of facets. The facet definitions in terms of vertex indices are preserved whatever position (SETUP, ACTUAL or OBSERVED) or co-ordinate system (ABSOLUTE, OBSERVER, WINDOW or viewport) we use. Since facets are defined in terms of pointers to vertex indices we may use precisely the same definition for the projected facets with the understanding that the pointers then refer to the WINDOW co-ordinates and hence the viewport representation of these vertices as opposed to the ABSOLUTE or OBSERVER systems.

We are now ready to consider the projection of the vertices onto the view plane in routine **project**. As yet we have neither defined the position of the view plane (the value d), nor have we described the type of projection of three-dimensional space onto the plane. These requirements are closely related. In this book we will consider three possible projections – in a later chapter we will deal with the *perspective* and *stereoscopic* projections, but first we introduce the simplest projection – the *orthographic*, sometimes called the *axonometric* or *orthogonal* projection.

The Orthographic Projection

A *parallel projection* is a projection under which points in three-dimensional space are projected along a fixed direction onto any plane: it is characterised by having parallel lines of projection. The orthographic projection is a special case whereby the lines of projection are perpendicular to the plane (it is sometimes referred to simply as *the* parallel projection). We can choose the view plane to be *any* plane with normal vector along the line of sight. This means that we can choose any plane parallel to the x/y plane of the OBSERVER system and for simplicity we take the plane through the origin, given by the equation $z = 0$. The vertices of the object are thus projected onto the view plane by the simple expedient of setting their z co-ordinates to zero. Thus any two different points with OBSERVED co-ordinates (x, y, z) and (x, y, z') say (where $z \neq z'$), are projected onto the same point $(x, y, 0)$ on the view plane, and hence the point (x, y) in the WINDOW system. Although we can use the x and y co-ordinates of the **obs** values as the projected co-ordinates in this case, this will not be so in general. To maintain consistency we copy these into the **pro** array in routine **project**. The orthographic **project** is given in listing 8.2. Note that the routine calculates the projection of all **ntv** vertices and hence **ntv** must be evaluated before the call to **project**, which in turn must be declared before it is called.

Listing 8.2

```
PROCEDURE project ;
{ Orthographic projection of OBSERVED vertices }
VAR i : integer ;
BEGIN
    FOR i := 1 TO ntv
    DO BEGIN
            pro[i].x := obs[i].x ; pro[i].y := obs[i].y
        END
END ; { of project }
```

Drawing a Scene

Most of the remainder of this book will be dealing with the drawing of projections of three-dimensional scenes. This will include discussions of hidden line and surface removal, three-dimensional clipping, shading, shadows etc. The necessary routines are declared before and called as required from a controlling routine, **drawit**. Such a routine will be employed in a number of different forms throughout the book. In the simplest case (listing 8.3) **drawit** will call **project** followed by another routine **wireframe** which will draw a line diagram of the scene.

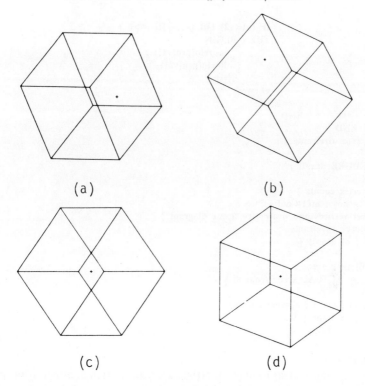

(a) (b)

(c) (d)

Figure 8.2

Listing 8.3

```
PROCEDURE wireframe ;
{ Drawing wire diagram of closed objects + superficial facets }
VAR i,j,k,v1,v2 : integer ;
BEGIN
{ View each facet 'i' in turn }
    FOR i := 1 TO ntf
    DO BEGIN
            j := nfac[i] ;
            IF j <> 0
            THEN BEGIN
                    v1 := faclist[facfront[j] + size[j]] ;
{ For facet 'i' consider the size[j] lines on its boundary }
                    FOR k := 1 TO size[j]
                    DO BEGIN
{ Typical line joins vertex index 'v1' to vertex index 'v2' }
{ Only join vertices if 'v1 < v2' on non-superficial facet }
{ If objects in the figure are not closed then rewite the }
{ code so that lines are drawn in both directions! }
                            v2 := faclist[facfront[j] + k] ;
```

```
                    IF (v1 < v2) OR (super[i] < > 0 )
                    THEN BEGIN
                           moveto(pro[v1]) ;
                           lineto(pro[v2])
                         END ;
                    v1 := v2
                  END
               END
         END
END ; { of wireframe }


PROCEDURE drawit ;
BEGIN
{ Set vertex counts }
    ntv := nov ; ntf := nof ;
{ Project vertices and draw wire frame diagram }
    project ; wireframe
END ; { of drawit }


PROCEDURE scene ;
{ Read in ACTUAL scene from disk }
BEGIN
    datain ; look3 ; observe ; drawit
END ; { of scene }
```

Example 8.1

We use the above ideas to draw an orthographic projection of either of the cubes defined in example 7.2 or 7.3. Line-figures such as those in figure 8.2 are called *wire diagrams* or *skeletons* (for obvious reasons) and are drawn by a routine wireframe. The required scene, drawit and wireframe routines are given in listing 8.3. The scene routine uses datain to read in the scene from disk, where it was stored by dataout (listing 7.2)

In SETUP position (relative to the ABSOLUTE co-ordinate system) the cube consisted of eight vertices $(1, 1, 1)$, $(1, -1, 1)$, $(1, -1, -1)$, $(1, 1, -1)$, $(-1, 1, 1)$, $(-1, -1, 1)$, $(-1, -1, -1)$ and $(-1, 1, -1)$: labelled numerically 1 to 8. The twelve lines, each of which is an edge common to two adjacent facets join vertices 1 to 2, 2 to 3, 3 to 4, 4 to 1; 5 to 6, 6 to 7, 7 to 8, 8 to 1; 1 to 5, 2 to 6, 3 to 7 and 4 to 8. We do not have the line information stored explicitly, however it can be derived from the facet data. Since each line occurs twice in the data of a closed convex body and we have oriented the facets anti-clockwise, then if an edge on one facet joins vertex I to vertex J, then on an adjacent facet there will be an edge joining J to I. Therefore, if, in wireframe (listing 8.3), we go round the edges of all the facets in anti-clockwise order, only drawing a line between consecutive projected vertices if the larger vertex index follows the smaller, then we will draw each line once but only once. The line is assumed to be drawn in the current logical colour. wireframe only works with *closed objects*, that is it is impossible to get inside an object other than by passing through a surface facet. If you wish to draw non-closed objects, then wireframe must be rewritten so that each edge line of every facet is drawn, irrespective of the order of the vertex indices!

Figure 8.2a shows the simplest possible example of an orthographic projection of the cube, where both the SETUP to ACTUAL matrix and the ABSOLUTE to OBSERVER matrix are identity matrices (example 7.2) — that is, the cube stays in its SETUP position and the observer is looking along the negative z-axis. We get a square. Pairs of parallel lines from the front and back of the cube project into the same line on the viewport.

Figure 8.2b shows the cube from example 7.3 drawn in its ACTUAL position but viewed with the observer on the z-axis looking along it in the negative direction (matrix Q is then the identity matrix). We calculated the eight ACTUAL co-ordinate triples to be (26/25, −5/25, 7/25), (2/25, −35/25, 39/25), (−38/25, −35/25, 9/25), (−14/25, −5/25, −23/25), (8/25, 35/25, 31/25), (−16/25, 5/25, 63/25), (−56/25, 5/25, 33/25) and (−32/25, 35/25, 1/25). Since we assume the ABSOLUTE to OBSERVER matrix Q to be the identity matrix, the projected WINDOW co-ordinates of the vertices are thus: (26/25, −5/25), (2/25, −35/25), (−38/25, −35/25), (−14/25, −5/25), (8/25, 35/25), (−16/25, 5/25), (−56/25, 5/25) and (−32/25, 35/25). These WINDOW co-ordinates are identified with pixels in the viewport and the lines defined above are drawn by joining (with straight lines) the projections of the vertices in the correct combinations.

Figure 8.2d shows the image produced of the cube in example 7.2 using these methods with the observer at the ABSOLUTE position (1, 2, 3) looking towards the origin in the direction (−1, −2, −3), with the vertical maintained. Figure 8.2c shows the image produced by the same process with the maintenance of vertical omitted. Note that this technique works in all cases except where direct.x = direct.z = 0 is the vertical direction, and naturally maintaining the vertical makes no sense. In this case the program would not fail; the final transformation is just an illogical step, producing an arbitrary rotation.

Listing 8.4

```
{ PROCEDUREs wireframe and drawit from listing 8.3 }

PROCEDURE scene ;
{ A scene consisting of two cubes }
VAR A,B,P : matrix4x4 ;
BEGIN
{ First Cube }
    scale3(1.0,1.0,1.0,P) ; cube(P) ;
{ Second cube }
    scale3(1.5,1.5,1.5,A) ; tran3(-4.0,-2.0,-4.0,B) ;
    mult3(B,A,P) ; cube(P) ;
{ Observe, project and draw object }
    look3 ; observe ; drawit
END ; { of scene }
```

Example 8.2

Listing 8.4 creates a scene consisting of two cubes, one of side 2 placed in its SETUP position, the other with side 3 translated to (4, 2, 4). Note the complete program uses cubesetup, cube (listing 7.2), findQ, look3, observe (listing 8.1), project (listing 8.2) and drawit and wireframe (listing 8.3), as well as the necessary routines from listings 1.1, 1.3, 7.1 and 7.2. We noted earlier how the call to scene inside routine draw_a_picture links the modelling and display to the primitive graphics routines.

Pictures containing a number of similar objects can be drawn with a minimum of extra effort. A scene such as figure 8.3 containing two cubes, for example, may be constructed using listing 8.3 by calling the cube routine from listing 7.2 twice within the scene routine, on each occasion with a different matrix P. This is what we call the *building block* method. Each construction routine creates a block which is included in the model for the scene. Information relating to the observer is introduced and look3 and findQ calculate the matrix Q which is used by observe to calculate the OBSERVED co-ordinates of each vertex. Finally, drawit calls project to project these vertices onto the view plane before calling wireframe to draw a picture.

This modular approach of solving the problem of defining and drawing a picture does greatly clarify the situation for beginners, enabling them to ask the right questions about constructing a required scene. Also when dealing with multiple views (for example, in animation), this approach will minimise problems in scenes where not only are the objects moving relative to one another, but also the observer itself is moving.

In summary, the orthographic projection of each object in a three-dimensional scene is produced by the following process

(1) Define objects in the scene in their SETUP position with the co-ordinates of vertices specified in relation to the ABSOLUTE axes. The facets of the scene may also be defined at this stage.

(2) Calculate the matrix P which moves the vertices of each object to their ACTUAL position, the co-ordinates still relating to the ABSOLUTE system, by pre-multiplication of their SETUP co-ordinates. These co-ordinates are stored in array act. If a scene is to be made up of a number of different objects, steps (1) and (2) may be repeated for each, the arrays being updated at every pass.

(3) Calculate the matrix Q given the position of the eye relative to the ABSOLUTE system, and a direction of view, vector3 values eye and direct. Calculate the OBSERVED co-ordinates of the vertices relative to the OBSERVER axes with eye at the origin and the negative z-axis along the direction direct, by pre-multiplying the co-ordinates of the ACTUAL position by Q. These OBSERVED co-ordinates are stored in the x/y co-ordinates of array obs.

(4) Calculate the WINDOW co-ordinates of the vertices on the view plane, pro. For the orthographic projection this simply involves taking their x and y

OBSERVED co-ordinates, which are already stored in the array **obs**. Identify the projected co-ordinates with the co-ordinate system of the viewport and plot the points using the real-to-pixel functions of chapter 1. The lines may also be drawn by joining their projected end-points. For the moment you will draw only the facet edges and not the facets themselves in pictures of three-dimensional scenes. Facets will be considered in later chapters.

Exercise 8.3
If you require only a single view of a scene, rather than use the intermediate storage of the ACTUAL and OBSERVED positions, it is more efficient to go directly from SETUP position to projected WINDOW co-ordinates. Now each construction routine must be called with matrix parameter $R = Q \times P$, and the vertices immediately projected into **pro**. Cannibalise the programs from this chapter in such a way.

Figure 8.3

9 Generation of Model Data

The previous chapter introduced our method for constructing and drawing scenes: a routine **scene** is used to construct data about a three-dimensional scene via construction routines, some input from file. Then the vertices are transformed into the OBSERVED position, and the routine **drawit** is called to display the scene. In the following chapters we will give a number of different types of **drawit**, **project** and facet display routines, dependent only on the projection and type of picture you require: line drawing, colour with/without shading, shadows etc. All the reader need do is create the relevant **scene** and construction routines and call the correct **drawit** routine.

All? As you go further into computer graphics you will discover that the vast majority of human effort in this subject is put into the construction of data and not in the display algorithms. Any technique that will ease this burden is obviously of great advantage. In this chapter we shall introduce you to some *tricks of the trade*, which may help you in specific cases, and lead you into the correct approach to the construction of data.

Using File Input with Construction Routines

In the previous chapter we saw how the method of building blocks can be used to construct scenes using just a few elementary construction routines and limited SETUP files. We shall see that even this simple idea can give rise to very complicated scenes.

Example 9.1
To illustrate this method further we give a **scene** routine that draws figure 9.1a, two peculiarly shaped pyramids on a thin rectangular table top. A file 'pyramid.dat' holds the information needed to define a pyramid with a square base of side 2 units and height 1 unit. The construction routine **pyramid** uses the SETUP-to-ACTUAL matrix P to place in the database the data for a pyramid in its proper ACTUAL position. The scale of the pyramid can be changed by introducing a scaling matrix into the definition of P. Note that the ACTUAL positions of each object are individually stated in the definition of the various P matrices in the **scene** of listing 9.1. Everything is given in absolute terms, the relative positions of the objects are not considered.

The drawit, project and wireframe routines to achieve figure 9.1a are taken from listings 8.2 and 8.3. Figure 9.1b is the same scene drawn in perspective and with the hidden lines removed: project now comes from listing 11.1, and drawit from listing 10.1 calls hidden (listing 12.1). You will note that all other routines remain unchanged, which demonstrates the power and ease of use of this modular approach.

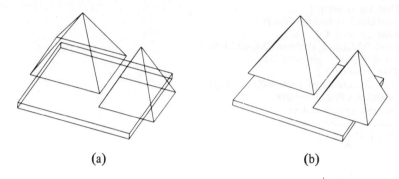

(a)   (b)

Figure 9.1

Listing 9.1

```
PROCEDURE scene ;
{ Construct scene of two pyramids on a tabletop }
VAR A,B,P : matrix4x4 ;

    PROCEDURE pyramid(P : matrix4x4 ; col : integer) ;
{ Construction routine for a pyramid. Initially of unit height and, }
{ base 2 by 2, the block is distorted by the scaling matrix component }
{ of 'P'. Pyramid has logical colour 'col' }
    VAR i,j,invalue : integer ;
    BEGIN
        assign(indata,'pyramid.dat') ; reset(indata) ;
{ Update facet data base with 5 new facets. All are triangular }
        FOR i := 1 TO 5
        DO BEGIN
            FOR j := 1 TO 3
            DO BEGIN read(indata,invalue) ;
                    faclist[last+j] := invalue+nov
                END ;
            nof := nof+1 ; facfront[nof] := last ; size[nof] := 3 ;
            last := last+size[nof] ;
            colour[nof] := col ; nfac[nof] := nof ;
            super[nof] := 0 ; firstsup[nof] := 0
        END ;
{ Don't forget the 4 vertices on last facet }
        size[nof] := 4 ; faclist[facfront[nof]+4] := 2+nov ;
{ Update vertex data base with 5 new vertices in ACTUAL position }
```

```
      last := last+1 ;
      FOR i := 1 TO 5
      DO BEGIN
              read(indata,setup[i].x,setup[i].y,setup[i].z) ;
              nov := nov+1 ; transform(setup[i],P,act[nov])
          END ;
      close(indata)
END ; { of pyramid }
BEGIN
{ First the tabletop }
   scale3(4.0,0.2,4.0,P) ; cube(P) ;
{ Then pyramid 1 }
   scale3(2.5,4.0,2.5,A) ; tran3(2.0,-0.2,2.0,B) ;
   mult3(B,A,P) ; pyramid(P,1) ;
{ Then pyramid 2 }
   scale3(2.0,4.0,2.0,A) ; tran3(-3.0,-0.2,0.0,B) ;
   mult3(B,A,P) ; pyramid(P,2) ;
{ Observe, project and draw }
   look3 ; observe ; drawit
END ; { of scene }
```

File 'pyramid.dat'

```
1   2   3
1   3   4
1   4   5
1   5   2
5   4   3
  0.0   1.0    0.0
  1.0   0.0   -1.0
 -1.0   0.0   -1.0
 -1.0   0.0    1.0
  1.0   0.0    1.0
```

Exercise 9.1

Use this method to draw arbitrary scenes consisting not only of cubes and pyramids, but also the icosahedron, and other Archimedean solids mentioned in chapter 7.

Graph Paper Construction

So far we have not considered how to construct the data stored in the files, neither the co-ordinates of the vertices nor their order in defining facets. With objects like a cube or pyramid this information is relatively easy to visualise, but what if an object like one of the idealised houses in figure 9.2b is required? A popular method is to draw rough sketches on squared graph paper of partial orthographic views of the SETUP object from the x, y and z directions as in figure 9.2a. As in this diagram, vertices are indicated by their index number in the database – each may occur in a number of different projections, and the *x*, *y* and *z* co-ordinates can be read directly from the graph paper. The orientation of the facets can also be taken from the graph paper. Note that facets representing the windows and doors must be included. In this model they are considered to be *superficial*, simply lying on the surface of another larger *host facet*. So although they have an existence in their own right, each must be associated with its relevant host facet. This is achieved by the array attribute **super** stored in the global database. **super**[i] has a value j if the ith facet is superficial to the jth facet, otherwise **super**[i] is set to zero. Furthermore each facet j is allocated a linked list of indices of all the facets that are superficial to facet j. This list is stored using a heap such as that described in chapter 2. We call this heap the *Permanent Heap*, since the information stored therein remains unchanged once created. Later we shall introduce a *Dynamic Heap* on which the information may change during processing. The permanent heap is implemented using an array of **heapcell** elements (each a record of two integer fields **info** and **pointer**) named **permheap** declared in listing 7.2. The size of the array is defined by CONSTant **maxheap**; **permfree** is the free list pointer. **firstsup**[j] refers to the cell in the heap which contains the first element in the list of facets superficial to facet j. Hence **super**[**firstsup**[j]] .**info** is the index of the first facet in the list and **super**[**firstsup**[j]] .**pointer** points to the next element in the list. The routines for initialising the permanent heap **permheapset** and for pushing an entry onto a list contained in this heap (**pushperm**) are found in listing 7.2. Note that any program using superficial facets *must* contain a call to **permheapstart** in the **scene** routine before any call to **pushperm**.

Example 9.2
Figure 9.2b shows four such houses defined by data (from file'**house.dat**') containing superficial facets for doors and windows. They are placed in position by **scene** (listing 9.2), projected by **project** (listing 11.1: perspective) and drawn with the hidden line **drawit** (listing 12.1). We could have used the orthographic wireframe **drawit** of listing 8.3. Both of these display routines assume that all objects in the scene are closed: you will have to change the listings slightly if you wish to draw non-closed objects (see chapter 8).

Listing 9.2

```
PROCEDURE scene ;
{ Create ACTUAL scene of 4 houses }
CONST piby2 = 1.5707963268 ;
VAR A,B,P : matrix4x4 ;

    PROCEDURE house(P : matrix4x4) ;
{ Construction routine for idealised house }
    VAR i,j,host,invalue,nofstore : integer ;
    BEGIN
        assign(indata,'house.dat') ; reset(indata) ;
```

```
{ Update facet data base with 19 new facets }
{ First the 'faclist' array, then 'facfront' etc. }
      FOR i := 1 TO 79
      DO BEGIN
                read(indata,invalue) ;
                faclist[last+i] := invalue+nov
            END ;
      nofstore := nof ;
      FOR i := 1 TO 19
      DO BEGIN
                nof := nof+1 ; facfront[nof] := last ;
                read(indata,size[nof]) ;
                last := last+size[nof] ; nfac[nof] := nof ;
{ Deal with superficial facets }
                IF i<8 THEN colour[nof] := 3 ELSE colour[nof] := 4 ;
                read(indata,super[nof]) ; firstsup[nof] := 0 ;
                IF super[nof] < >0
                THEN BEGIN
                        host := super[nof]+nofstore ;
                        super[nof] := host ;
                        pushperm(firstsup[host],nof)
                     END
            END ;
{ Update vertex data base with 59 new vertices in ACTUAL position }
      FOR i := 1 TO 59
      DO BEGIN
                read(indata,setup[i].x,setup[i].y,setup[i].z) ;
                nov := nov+1 ; transform(setup[i],P,act[nov])
            END ;
      close(indata)
   END ; { of house }

BEGIN
{ Create four houses }
   tran3(0.0,0.0,12.0,P) ; house(P) ;

   rot3(2,-piby2,A) ; tran3(12.0,0.0,0.0,B) ;
   mult3(B,A,P) ; house(P) ;

   rot3(2,pi,A) ; tran3(0.0,0.0,-12.0,B) ;
   mult3(B,A,P) ; house(P) ;

   rot3(2,piby2,A) ; tran3(-12.0,0.0,0.0,B) ;
   mult3(B,A,P) ; house(P) ;

   look3 ; observe ; drawit
END ; { of scene }
```

File 'house.dat'

1	2	6	5		5	6	7	10		2	3	8	7	6		3	4	9	8
8	9	10	7		4	1	5	10	9	4	3	2	1			11	12	13	14
15	16	17	18		19	20	21	22		23	24	25	26		27	28	29	30	
31	32	33	34		35	36	37	38		39	40	41	42		43	44	45	46	47
48	49	50	51		52	53	54	55		56	57	58	59						

| 4 0 | 4 0 | 5 0 | 4 0 | 4 0 | 5 0 | 4 0 | 4 1 | 4 1 | 4 1 |
| 4 1 | 4 3 | 4 4 | 4 4 | 5 4 | 4 4 | 4 4 | 4 6 | 4 6 | |

-6	0	4	6	0	4	6	0 -4	-6	0 -4	-6	8 4
6	8	4	6	11	0	6	8 -4	-6	8 -4	-6	11 0
-4	1	4	-1	1	4	-1	3 4	-4	3 4	-4	5 4
-1	5	4	-1	7	4	-4	7 4	0	0 4	5	0 4
5	4	4	0	4	4	1	5 4	4	5 4	4	7 4
1	7	4	6	5	-1	6	5 -3	6	7 -3	6	7 -1
5	1	-4	2	1	-4	2	3 -4	5	3 -4	5	5 -4
2	5	-4	2	7	-4	5	7 -4	1	0 -4	-1	0 -4
-1	3	-4	0	4	-4	1	3 -4	-2	1 -4	-5	1 -4
-5	3	-4	-2	3	-4	-2	5 -4	-5	5 -4	-5	7 -4
-2	7	-4	-6	0	1	-6	0 3	-6	3 3	-6	3 1
-6	5	1	-6	5	3	-6	7 3	-6	7 1		

Exercise 9.2
Extend the house database to include a chimney, curtains on the windows etc. Produce a construction routine for a second style of house. Add garages. Put a housing estate of both types of house on a large gridded rectangular area.

Using the datain routine

Very often the same scene will be required over and over again. We have seen that, rather than regenerate the data each time it is needed, it makes more sense to create it once, and store the information on backing store with a dataout routine (listing 7.2). You can create the scene directly by typing data from the keyboard into such a file. When it is needed this data can be read directly into the database by a datain routine (listing 7.2) and drawn, with a minimum of transformations needed. The information may be stored in SETUP or more usually in ACTUAL position. You will then use the scene routine of listing 8.3 to initiate the graphics process, using findQ, look3, observe and the relevant routines drawit, project etc.

Example 9.3
Figure 9.3 shows an interpenetrant cube (the shape of a Fluorite crystal) constructed from the file information given in listing 9.3. Note that by calling the relevant drawit and project routines the object can be drawn in orthographic, perspective or stereoscopic projection, as a wire diagram or with the hidden lines removed; later we will see how it can be drawn in colour, with shadows etc.

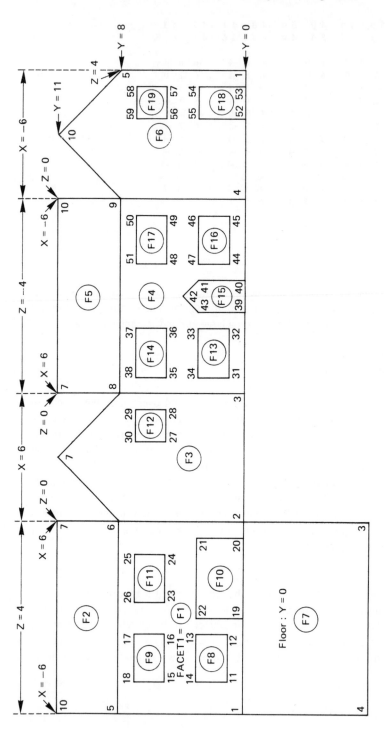

Figure 9.2(a)

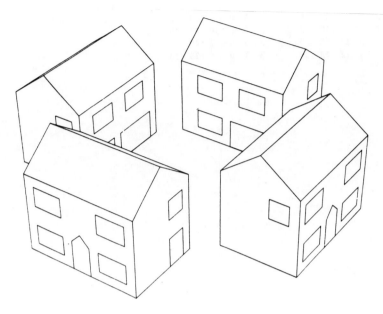

Figure 9.2(b)

Listing 9.3

20   36

3.0	3.0	-3.0		-3.0	3.0	-3.0		-3.0	-3.0	-3.0
3.0	-3.0	-3.0		-3.0	-3.0	3.0		3.0	-3.0	3.0
3.0	3.0	3.0		-3.0	3.0	3.0		-3.0	0.0	-3.0
0.0	-3.0	-3.0		3.0	-3.0	0.0		3.0	0.0	3.0
0.0	3.0	3.0		-3.0	3.0	0.0		5.0	-1.0	1.0
-1.0	5.0	1.0		-1.0	-1.0	-5.0		-5.0	1.0	-1.0
1.0	-5.0	-1.0		1.0	1.0	5.0				

3	3	0	1	11	4		3	3	0	11	12	6
3	3	0	1	7	12		3	3	0	7	1	13
3	3	0	13	14	8		3	3	0	14	1	2
3	3	0	2	1	9		3	3	0	3	9	10
3	3	0	1	4	10		3	3	0	8	14	5
3	3	0	14	2	9		3	3	0	3	5	9
3	3	0	3	10	5		3	3	0	4	11	10
3	3	0	6	5	11		3	3	0	5	6	12
3	3	0	12	7	13		3	3	0	13	8	5
3	3	0	1	15	11		3	3	0	15	12	11
3	3	0	1	12	15		3	3	0	13	1	16
3	3	0	13	16	14		3	3	0	16	1	14
3	3	0	9	1	17		3	3	0	10	9	17
3	3	0	1	10	17		3	3	0	5	14	18

3	3	0	18	14	9		3	3	0	5	18	9
3	3	0	10	19	5		3	3	0	10	11	19
3	3	0	11	5	19		3	3	0	12	20	5
3	3	0	12	13	20		3	3	0	5	20	13

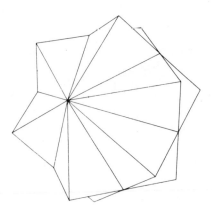

Figure 9.3

Exercise 9.3

Save the data for the houses in example 9.2 on backing store with **dataout**. Then use the **scene** routine of listing 8.3 to read it back into memory and draw figure 9.2.

Relative Positioning of Objects

Thus far all objects have been considered independent of one another and they are placed in position by a **scene** routine. We often need to create complex objects with component parts that are themselves objects with their own construction files.

Example 9.4

Take, for example, the hollow cube shown in figure 9.4. It consists of twenty blocks, twelve rectangular prisms and eight cubes. Each has a well-defined position relative to every other. In order to create a SETUP position for this hollow cube, we can imagine each block being moved into an ACTUAL position around the origin, by its own unique SETUP-to-ACTUAL matrix. Pre-multiplying each of these twenty matrices by the SETUP-to-ACTUAL matrix of the whole object will enable us to calculate the final ACTUAL position of its component vertices. Also note that in certain geometrically defined objects (such as this hollow cube) it may be possible to calculate these matrices implicitly (within a loop) rather than to type them in explicitly. See how the cube data from listing 7.2 is used in listing 9.4 to achieve this.

Listing 9.4

```
PROCEDURE scene ;
{ Construct SCENE of one hollowed cube in SETUP position }
VAR P : matrix4x4 ;

    PROCEDURE hollow(P1 : matrix4x4) ;
{ Routine to place hollowed cube in ACTUAL position }
{ 'P1' is matrix that moves hollow cube into position }
{ 'P2' is matrix that moves each component prism into an ACTUAL }
{ position which is SETUP for the hollow cube }
{ 'P = P1xP2' places component into ACTUAL position for final scene }
    VAR A,B,P,P2 : matrix4x4 ;
        i : integer ;
    BEGIN
{ Setup the 8 corner cubes }
        FOR i := 1 TO 8
        DO BEGIN
            tran3(4.0*cubevert[i].x,4.0*cubevert[i].y,4.0*cubevert[i].z,P2) ;
            mult3(P1,P2,P) ; cube(P)
        END ;
{ Setup the 12 rectangular prisms which join corner cubes }
        FOR i := 1 TO 4
        DO BEGIN
            scale3(3.0,1.0,1.0,A) ;
            tran3(0.0,4.0*cubevert[i].y,4.0*cubevert[i].z,B) ;
            mult3(A,B,P2) ; mult3(P1,P2,P) ; cube(P) ;
            scale3(1.0,3.0,1.0,A) ;
            tran3(4.0*cubevert[i].y,0.0,4.0*cubevert[i].z,B) ;
            mult3(A,B,P2) ; mult3(P1,P2,P) ; cube(P) ;
            scale3(1.0,1.0,3.0,A) ;
            tran3(4.0*cubevert[i].z,4.0*cubevert[i].y,0.0,B) ;
            mult3(A,B,P2) ; mult3(P1,P2,P) ; cube(P) ;
        END
    END ; { of hollow }

BEGIN
    tran3(0.0,0.0,0.0,P) ; hollow(P) ;
    look3 ; observe ; drawit
END ; { of scene }
```

Exercise 9.4

Much of the data created in the previous example is redundant. Certain facets occur twice, perhaps in different orientations, being common to two different component blocks; these lie inside the body anyway and may be ignored. Also the same absolute vertex may be referred to by different indices; it may have

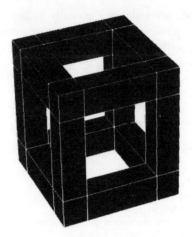

Figure 9.4

been created separately in different blocks. Write a routine which runs through the database and removes such inefficient duplication. Also see exercise 12.2.

Example 9.5
In example 9.4 all the vertices come ultimately from transforming vertices given in a SETUP file. There are some cases where new vertices can be created in construction routines, with positions given relative to other vertex values, perhaps explicitly defined in a procedure. The stellar body shown in figure 9.5 and programmed in listing 9.5, for example. This is a cube with pyramids added to each face. Note that six new vertices are added to the database and that the original cube faces are not included in the final object, since they will be totally obscured by the pyramids. Their orientation, however, is used to orientate the stars facets.

Listing 9.5

```
PROCEDURE scene ;
{ Construct SCENE of one stellar body in SETUP position }
VAR P : matrix4x4 ;

    PROCEDURE star(P : matrix4x4 ; d : real ) ;
{ Routine to place a stellar body in ACTUAL position }
    VAR i,j,v1,v2 : integer ;
        A,S : matrix4x4 ;
        vec : ARRAY[1..6] OF vector3 ;
    BEGIN
{ For each side of a cube, update data base with 4 new facets }
        FOR i := 1 TO 6
{ Go round the edges of each cube facet }
            DO BEGIN
```

```
              v1 := cubefacet[i,4]+nov ;
              FOR j := 1 TO 4
              DO BEGIN
                     v2 := cubefacet[i,j]+nov ;
{ Add a triangular facet to data base }
                     nof := nof+1 ; faclist[last+1] := v1 ;
                     faclist[last+2] := v2 ; faclist[last+3] := nov+8+i ;
                     facfront[nof] := last ; size[nof] := 3 ;
                     last := last+size[nof] ; colour[nof] := 3 ;
                     nfac[nof] := nof ; super[nof] := 0 ;
                     firstsup[nof] := 0 ; v1 := v2
              END
       END ;
{ Update vertex data base with 8 cube corners in ACTUAL position }
       FOR i := 1 TO 8
       DO BEGIN
              nov := nov+1 ; transform(cubevert[i],P,act[nov])
       END ;
{ Update vertex data base with 6 stellar points in ACTUAL position }
       vec[1].x := 1.0 ; vec[1].y := 0.0 ; vec[1].z := 0.0 ;
       vec[2].x := 0.0 ; vec[2].y := 1.0 ; vec[2].z := 0.0 ;
       vec[3].x := 0.0 ; vec[3].y := 0.0 ; vec[3].z := 1.0 ;
       vec[4].x := 0.0 ; vec[4].y := 0.0 ; vec[4].z := -1.0 ;
       vec[5].x := 0.0 ; vec[5].y := -1.0 ; vec[5].z := 0.0 ;
       vec[6].x := -1.0 ; vec[6].y := 0.0 ; vec[6].z := 0.0 ;
{ Data for stellar points must be scaled by D }
       scale3(D,D,D,A) ; mult3(A,P,S) ;
       FOR i := 1 TO 6
       DO BEGIN
              nov := nov+1 ; transform(vec[i],S,act[nov])
       END
   END ; { of star }

BEGIN
{ Construct scene of one stellar body in SETUP position }
   tran3(0.0,0.0,0.0,P) ; star(P,5.0) ;
   look3 ; observe ; drawit
END ; { of scene }
```

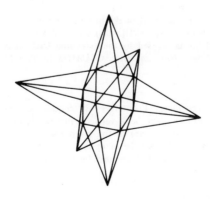

Figure 9.5

Exercise 9.5
Draw stellar bodies based on a tetrahedron, icosahedron etc.

Extrusion

We are all used to drawing pictures in two dimensions, but three dimensions is another matter. Therefore any method that will enable us to extend a two-dimensional object into three dimensions will be of enormous value. We will consider two methods here. The first, *extrusion*, takes a two-dimensional polygonal convex facet of say n ordered vertices stored in a **vector2array** v, {(v[i] .x, v[i] .y) | i = 1..n}, and gives it thickness d. This will result in a three-dimensional object of 2 + n facets, the front and back facets (each of n sides) and n four-sided facets, which are created by each of the n edges of the original face being extruded in the negative z direction of the ABSOLUTE right-handed co-ordinate system. The whole process is programmed in listing 9.6. When viewed from outside the object, each of the final 2 + n facets in three-dimensional space will have the same orientation as the original two-dimensional polygon.

Example 9.6
Figure 9.6a shows the line-drawn letter H (**scene** and **extrude** routines of listing 9.6) consisting of 3 two-dimensional facets after it is extruded into three dimensions. The data for this letter is on file 'letterH.dat'. Figure 9.6b shows it drawn in perspective and in colour with the hidden surfaces removed using **drawit** from listing 10.1.

Listing 9.6

```
PROCEDURE extrude(P : matrix4x4 ; d : real ; col,n : integer ;
                  v : vector2array ) ;
{ Extrude in colour 'col', a 2-D polygon defined in a given }
{ orientation by 'n' vertices    '(v[i].x,v[i].y,0.0) : i=1..n' }
{ The new vertices and facets created by the extruding backwards }
{ by a distance 'd' are used to extend the ACTUAL data base }
VAR i,j,lasti : integer ;
    v3 : vector3 ;
BEGIN
{ First add front and back facets. Front face will contain vertices }
{ with indices 'nov+1,..,nov+n'. The back vertices 'nov+n+1,..,nov+2n' }
{ The vertices of the front polygon are in the given orientation }
{ so the equivalent back polygon will be of opposite orientation }
{ Hence the orientation of the back face must be reversed }
    FOR i := 1 TO n
    DO BEGIN
           faclist[last+i] := nov+i ;
           faclist[last+n+i] := nov+2*n+1-i ;
```

Plate I

Plate II

Plate III

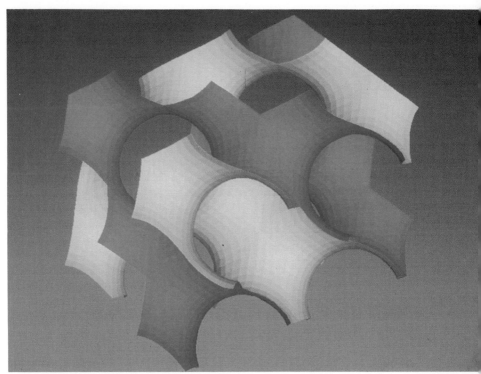

Plate IV

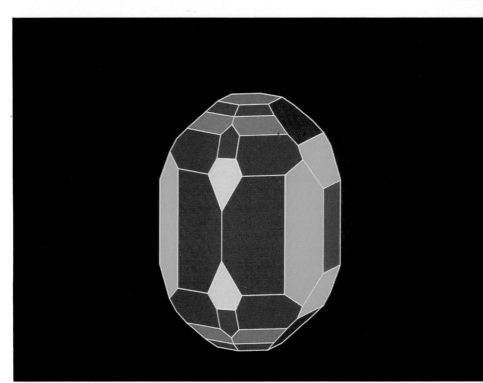

Plate V

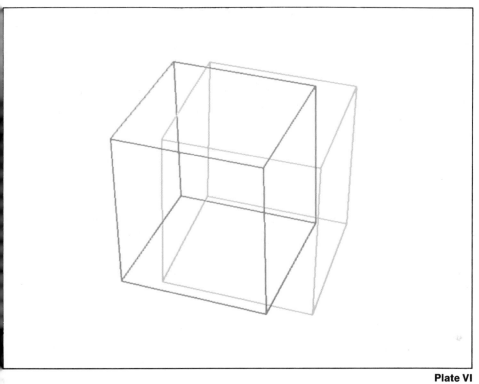

Plate VI

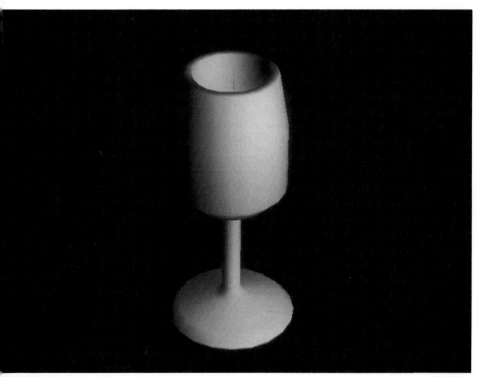

Plate VII

Plate VIII

Plate IX

Plate X

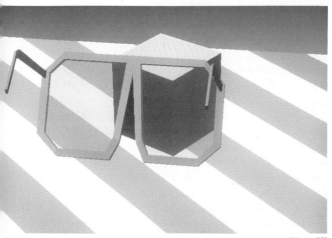

Plate XI

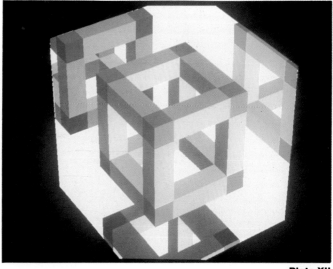

Plate XII

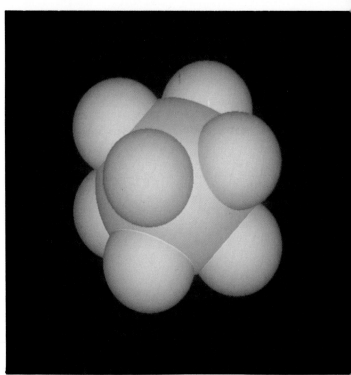

Plate XI

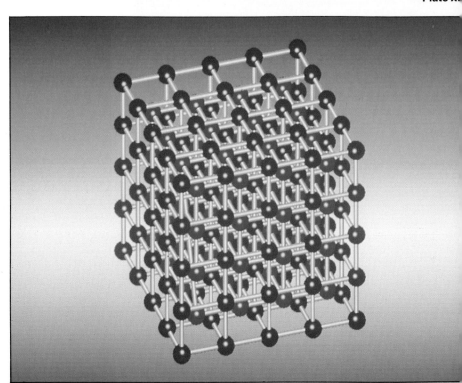

Plate XII

Plate XV

Plate XVI

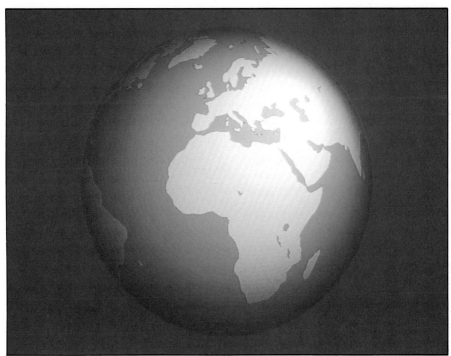

Plate XVII

Plate XVIII

```
        END ;
      facfront[nof+1] := last ; facfront[nof+2] := last+n ;
      size[nof+1] := n ; size[nof+2] := n ;
      nfac[nof+1] := nof+1 ; nfac[nof+2] := nof+2 ;
      super[nof+1] := 0 ; super[nof+2] := 0 ;
      firstsup[nof+1] := 0 ; firstsup[nof+2] := 0 ;
      colour[nof+1] := col ; colour[nof+2] := col ;
      last := last+2*n ; nof := nof+2 ;
{ For each line on the front face there is a quadrilateral side face }
{ If the line joins vertex 'in-1' to 'i' of the original polygon (given }
{ orientation), then the side face will have ACTUAL vertices with indices }
{ 'nov+i,nov+i-1,nov+n+i-1,nov+n+i' (quadrilateral : same orientation) }
      lasti := n ;
      FOR i := 1 TO n
      DO BEGIN
            faclist[last+1] := nov+i ; faclist[last+2] := nov+lasti ;
            faclist[last+3] := nov+n+lasti ; faclist[last+4] := nov+n+i ;
            nof := nof+1 ; facfront[nof] := last ;
            size[nof] := 4 ; nfac[nof] := nof ;
            super[nof] := 0 ; firstsup[nof] := 0 ;
            colour[nof] := col ; last := last+4 ;
            lasti := i
      END ;
{ Now set the ACTUAL vertices }
      FOR i := 1 TO n
      DO BEGIN
            v3.x := v[i].x ; v3.y := v[i].y ; v3.z := 0.0 ;
{ Front face vertices in ACTUAL position }
            nov := nov+1 ; transform(v3,P,act[nov]) ;
{ Back face vertices }
            v3.z := -d ; transform(v3,P,act[nov+n]) ;
      END ;
      nov := nov+n
END ; { of extrude }

PROCEDURE scene ;
{ Extruding 2-D object (a letter H) into 3-D space }
VAR letterH : vector2array ;
    i,j : integer ;
    P : matrix4x4 ;
BEGIN
{ Place in SETUP position }
    tran3(0.0,0.0,0.0,P) ;
    assign(indata,'letterH.dat') ; reset(indata) ;
{ Setup three rectangles from the data file 'letterH.dat' }
    FOR i := 1 TO 3
    DO BEGIN
            FOR j := 1 TO 4
            DO read(indata,letterH[j].x,letterH[j].y) ;
{ Extrude then to a depth 2 in colour 1 }
            extrude(P,2.0,1,4,letterH)
      END ;
    look3 ; observe ; drawit
END ; { of scene }
```

File 'letterH.dat'

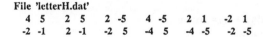

```
 4  5    2  5    2 -5    4 -5    2  1   -2  1
-2 -1    2 -1   -2  5   -4  5   -4 -5   -2 -5
```

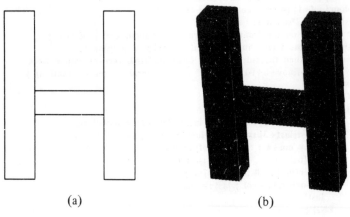

(a)　　　　　　　　　　　　　　　(b)

Figure 9.6

Exercise 9.6

Try other letters of alphabet. Run the program with the hidden line routine from listing 12.1 and the **drawit** of listing 10.1.

Body of Revolution

Another method of turning two-dimensional information into a three-dimensional object is the *body of revolution*. This routine is given an ordered sequence of **nvert** two-dimensional vertices stored in the **vector2array v** which, taken in order, define **nvert** − 1 lines. These may be considered to be three-dimensional vertices and lines lying in the x/y plane through the origin. Each line is now rotated anti-clockwise by angles $2\pi i/$**nhoriz** radians ($1 \leqslant i \leqslant$ **nhoriz**) around the vertical y-axis into **nhoriz** positions. A line defined by a pair of vertices, neither being on the axis, will define **nhoriz** quadrilateral facets; those with one vertex on the axis will create **nhoriz** triangular facets; and those with both vertices on the axis are degenerate and ignored. The routine **bodyrev** in listing 9.7 creates the data for a body of revolution. If the last vertex is joined to the first then this creates a polygon whose vertices are in the same orientation as the facets on the body of revolution, so if you wish to create facets which are oriented anti-clockwise when viewed from outside you must ensure that your initial polygon is also anti-clockwise.

Example 9.7

Figure 9.7 shows an *ellipsoid* created by the construction routine **ellipsoid**, using **bodyrev**. All data is created by a program from a semicircle of unit radius (listing 9.7) and is not read from file. The routine actually generates a unit *sphere*, but a scaling matrix included in the SETUP-to-ACTUAL matrix can distort it into an arbitrary sized ellipsoid. A **scene** routine is given which creates such a shape. Figure 9.8, a goblet, was drawn by the **scene** and **goblet** routines from listing 9.8 using the same **bodyrev** routine. Data is read from file '**goblet.dat**'. Note that this technique creates data for the surface of the object only. If the vertex sequence is not closed or does not start and end on the *y*-axis, then it will be possible to look up inside the object, and this could cause problems with the hidden line and surface algorithms that follow.

Listing 9.7

```
PROCEDURE bodyrev(P : matrix4x4 ; col,nvert,nhoriz : integer ;
                  v : vector2array) ;
{ Routine to form Body of Revolution by rotating a section of 'nvert' }
{ points '(v[i].x,v[i].y,0)' around the vertical y axis. Each point in }
{ the section is rotated into 'nhoriz' points around the axis }
{ (or degenerates into one point on the axis). The method is to take }
{ consecutive pairs of vertices from the section, rotate each into }
{ 'nhoriz'(or 1) positions in a horizontal slice, and then form }
{ 'nhoriz' facets with each pair of slices. The vertices in the slices }
{ are first stored in SETUP position. At any one time we have two slices, }
{ a top and a bottom slice. 'index1' and 'index2' hold the indices of the }
{ vertices of these two slices. Body is logical colour 'col'. Finally }
{ ACTUAL vertices are stored. Orientation of the facets the same as in }
{ the original polygon. Maximum polygon size is 100. }
VAR theta,thetadiff : real ;
    i,j,newnov : integer ;
    c,s : ARRAY[1..100] OF real ;
    index1,index2 : ARRAY[1..101] OF integer ;
BEGIN
{ Store the sines and cosines of 'nhoriz' angles around axis }
    theta := 0.0 ; thetadiff := 2*pi/nhoriz ;
    FOR i := 1 TO nhoriz
    DO BEGIN
          c[i] := cos(theta) ; s[i] := sin(theta) ;
          theta := theta+thetadiff
       END ;
{ Update ACTUAL data base with new SETUP vertices }
    newnov := nov ;
    IF abs(v[1].x) < epsilon
    THEN BEGIN
{ Top slice is degenerate, so only one slice vertex created }
          newnov := newnov+1 ; setup[newnov].x := 0.0 ;
          setup[newnov].y := v[1].y ; setup[newnov].z := 0.0 ;
          FOR i := 1 TO nhoriz+1
          DO index1[i] := newnov
       END
```

```
        ELSE BEGIN
{ Create 'nhoriz' vertices for top slice }
                FOR i := 1 TO nhoriz
                DO BEGIN
                        newnov := newnov+1 ;
                        setup[newnov].x :=  v[1].x*c[i] ;
                        setup[newnov].y :=  v[1].y ;
                        setup[newnov].z := -v[1].x*s[i] ;
                        index1[i] := newnov
                    END ;
                index1[nhoriz+1] := index1[1]
            END ;
{ Run through 'nvert-1' lines }
        FOR j := 2 TO nvert
        DO BEGIN
                IF abs(v[j].x) < epsilon
                THEN BEGIN
{ Bottom slice is degenerate, so only one slice vertex created }
                        newnov := newnov+1 ; setup[newnov].x := 0.0 ;
                        setup[newnov].y := v[j].y ; setup[newnov].z := 0.0 ;
                        FOR i := 1 TO nhoriz+1
                        DO index2[i] := newnov
                    END
                ELSE BEGIN
{ Create 'nhoriz' vertices for bottom slice }
                        FOR i := 1 TO nhoriz
                        DO BEGIN
                                newnov := newnov+1 ;
                                setup[newnov].x :=  v[j].x*c[i] ;
                                setup[newnov].y :=  v[j].y ;
                                setup[newnov].z := -v[j].x*s[i] ;
                                index2[i] := newnov
                            END ;
                        index2[nhoriz+1] := index2[1]
                    END ;
{ Create facets }
                IF index1[1] < >index1[2]
                THEN IF index2[1] =index2[2]
                    THEN BEGIN
{ bottom slice is degenerate, top isn't }
{ 'nhoriz' oriented triangles formed by degenerate bottom slice }
                        FOR i := 1 TO nhoriz
                        DO BEGIN
                                nof := nof+1 ; size[nof] := 3 ;
                                facfront[nof] := last ;
                                faclist[last+1] := index1[i+1] ;
                                faclist[last+2] := index2[i] ;
                                faclist[last+3] := index1[i] ;
                                last := last+size[nof] ;
                                nfac[nof] := nof ; colour[nof] := col ;
                                super[nof] := 0 ; firstsup[nof] := 0
                            END
                        END
                    ELSE BEGIN
{ neither slice is degenerate }
{ 'nhoriz' oriented quadrilaterals formed by top and bottom slices }
                        FOR i := 1 TO nhoriz
                        DO BEGIN
```

```
                              nof := nof+1 ; size[nof] := 4 ;
                              facfront[nof] := last ;
                              faclist[last+1] := index1[i+1] ;
                              faclist[last+2] := index2[i+1] ;
                              faclist[last+3] := index2[i] ;
                              faclist[last+4] := index1[i] ;
                              last := last+size[nof] ;
                              nfac[nof] := nof ; colour[nof] := col ;
                              super[nof] := 0 ; firstsup[nof] := 0
                         END
                    END
          ELSE IF index2[1] < >index2[2]
{ top slice is degenerate, bottom isn't }
{ 'nhoriz' oriented triangles formed by degenerate top slice }
                    THEN FOR i := 1 TO nhoriz
                         DO BEGIN
                              nof := nof+1 ; size[nof] := 3 ;
                              facfront[nof] := last ;
                              faclist[last+1] := index2[i+1] ;
                              faclist[last+2] := index2[i] ;
                              faclist[last+3] := index1[i] ;
                              last := last+size[nof] ;
                              nfac[nof] := nof ; colour[nof] := col ;
                              super[nof] := 0 ; firstsup[nof] := 0
                         END ;
  { Copy bottom slice into top slice and loop }
          FOR i := 1 TO nhoriz+1
          DO index1[i] := index2[i] ;
      END ;
{ Put SETUP vertices in ACTUAL position }
   FOR i := nov+1 TO newnov
   DO transform(setup[i],P,act[i]) ;
   nov := newnov
END ; { of bodyrev }


PROCEDURE ellipsoid(P : matrix4x4 ; col : integer ) ;
{ Construct an ellipsoid. First a semicircle of 21 points. If }
{ last point is joined to first we get anticlockwise polygon }
VAR v : vector2array ;
    theta,thetadiff : real ;
    i : integer ;
BEGIN
   theta := -pi*0.5 ; thetadiff := theta*0.1 ;
   FOR i := 1 TO 21
   DO BEGIN
         v[i].x := cos(theta) ; v[i].y := sin(theta) ;
         theta := theta+thetadiff
      END ;
{ Call Body of Revolution with 20 rotations }
   bodyrev(P,col,21,20,v)
END ; { of ellipsoid }

PROCEDURE scene ;
{ An ellipsoid with x,y and z axes 3,2,1 respectively }
VAR P : matrix4x4 ;
BEGIN
   scale3(3.0,2.0,1.0,P) ; ellipsoid(P,3) ;
   look3 ; observe ; drawit
END ; { of scene }
```

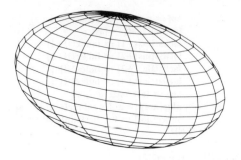

Figure 9.7

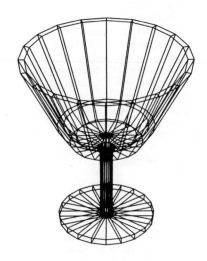

Figure 9.8

Listing 9.8

```
PROCEDURE goblet(P : matrix4x4 ; col : integer) ;
{ Construct a goblet in ACTUAL position }
VAR gobdat : vector2array ;
    i : integer ;
BEGIN
{ read in silhouette of goblet into 'goblet.dat' }
  assign(indata,'goblet.dat') ; reset(indata) ;
  FOR i := 1 TO 12
  DO read(indata,gobdat[i].x,gobdat[i].y) ;
  close(indata) ;
{ Body of Revolution with 20 rotations }
```

```
    bodyrev(P,col,12,20,gobdat)
END ; { of goblet }

PROCEDURE scene ;
{ Create a goblet in SETUP position }
VAR P : matrix4x4 ;
BEGIN
    tran3(0.0,0.0,0.0,P) ; goblet(P,3) ;
    look3 ; observe ; drawit
END ; { of scene }
```

File 'goblet.dat'

0.0	-16.0	8.0	-16.0	8.0	-15.0	1.0	-15.0
1.0	-2.0	6.0	-1.0	8.0	2.0	14.0	14.0
13.0	14.0	7.0	2.0	5.0	0.0	0.0	0.0

Exercise 9.7
Combine the body of revolution and extrusion techniques to construct the body
and fins respectively of the rocket of figure 9.9 drawn using drawit from listing
10.1.

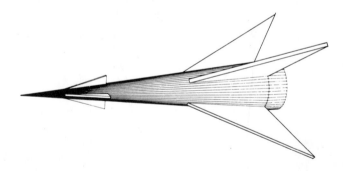

Figure 9.9

Exercise 9.8
Extend the body of revolution method to create a *body of rotation*. Now the
two-dimensional line sequence rotates about the central axis, but with each
small rotation the defining line also moves a small distance vertically. Create
pictures like the helix of figure 9.10 with this technique.

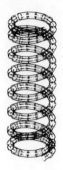

Figure 9.10

Exercise 9.9
Write a routine which creates handles and spouts for figures created by the body of revolution method. This routine must be given line sequences that form a silhouette, which can be turned into facet data for a handle or spout by imposing a circular or some other such cross-section on the data. See figure 9.11.

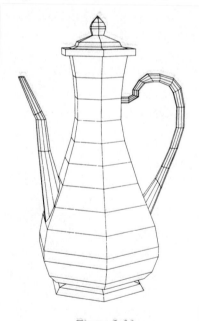

Figure 9.11

Three-dimensional Animation

We can use the techniques introduced in chapter 5 to animate three-dimensional scenes. Again a loop in **scene**, called from **draw_a_picture** (listing 7.2), is used to create individual frames for the movie. The ACTUAL position of the objects can change, as well as the position of the observer. The parameters for calculating the corresponding matrices are evaluated inside the loop. For a moving observer, the usual questions in scene requesting the observer position must be replaced by a calculation which positions the observer for any given frame in the animation.

Example 9.8
Listing 9.9 creates a movie of 121 frames of a SETUP cube rotating about the horizontal ABSOLUTE x-axis through its centre once every 60 frames, while the observer moves in a complete horizontal circle centred at the ABSOLUTE origin once during the film.

Listing 9.9

```
PROCEDURE scene ;
{ Animation : cube and observer moving independently }
VAR AI,P,QE,S : matrix4x4 ;
    answer : char ;
    angcube,diffcube,angobs,diffobs : real ;
    frame : integer ;
BEGIN
    writeln(' Do you wish 90 degree rotation : Y or N') ;
    readln(answer) ;
    IF answer = 'y'
    THEN BEGIN
{ Identity matrix stored as 'AI' }
            rot3(3,-pi*0.5,QE) ; tran3(0.0,0.0,0.0,AI)
        END ;
{ Initialise angular values }
    angcube := 0.0 ; diffcube := pi/60.0 ;
    angobs := 0.0 ; diffobs := pi/30.0 ;
{ Loop thru 120 frames }
    FOR frame := 0 TO 120
    DO BEGIN
{ Position cube }
            rot3(1,angcube,P) ; cube(P) ;
{ Position observer }
            eye.x := cos(angobs) ; eye.y := 0.0 ; eye.z := sin(angobs) ;
            direct.x := -eye.x ; direct.y := -eye.y ; direct.z := -eye.z ;
            findQ ;
{ Rotate picture thru 90 degrees if required }
            IF answer = 'y'
            THEN BEGIN
{ Copy new observed matrix back into 'Q' }
                    mult3(QE,Q,S) ; mult3(AI,S,Q)
                END ;
{ Draw the scene and move to next frame }
            observe ; drawit ; erase ;
{ Reset the data base }
            nov := 0 ; nof := 0 ; last := 0 ;
{ update angular values }
```

```
        angcube := angcube+diffcube ;  angobs := angobs+diffobs
    END
END ; { of scene }
```

Exercise 9.10

Animate a scene which includes an icosahedron spinning and moving through space, while the observer looking at the centre of the icosahedron is also moving away on a spiral orbit.

10 Simple Hidden Line and Surface Algorithms

We are now able to draw wire diagrams representing any scene. We would like, however, to consider solid objects, in which case the facets at the front will obviously restrict the view of the facets (and boundary lines) at the back. In order to produce such a picture we must introduce an algorithm which determines which parts of a surface or line are visible and which are not. Such algorithms are called hidden surface or hidden line algorithms, depending upon their purpose. There are many of these algorithms, some elementary for specially restricted situations, others very sophisticated for viewing general complicated scenes (Sutherland *et al.*, 1974). In this book we shall consider a variety of approaches ranging from the very simplest types in this chapter, to examples of general-purpose algorithms in chapters 12 and 13.

The algorithms described in this chapter enable us for the first time to produce colour pictures of three-dimensional scenes. We introduce a new routine seefacet(k) which will be called to display facet k and all associated superficial facets. This routine will call a further new routine, facetfill, which will initiate the filling of an area of pixels. For the moment this will just be an ordinary area-fill (see chapter 1), but later on we will introduce variants that will allow *smooth shading, surface texture* etc. We must structure the calls to display routines so that they are consistent throughout the more complex applications that will follow. Recall that routine drawit co-ordinates the calls to all routines used in the display of a scene. The routines which eliminate hidden surfaces or lines will be called hidden and these will, in turn, call seefacet to display each visible facet. The new drawit is given in listing 10.1.

Listing 10.1

```
PROCEDURE drawit ;
BEGIN
{ Set vertex counts, project and draw }
    ntv := nov ; ntf := nof ; project ; hidden
END ; { of drawit }
```

All of the hidden line and hidden surface algorithms we consider will operate upon the OBSERVED co-ordinate data of vertices and facets of objects in a three-dimensional scene.

The first algorithm we shall look at may be used for both line and surface drawings of closed convex bodies. A *convex body* is one in which any line segment joining two internal points lies entirely within the body — a direct extension of the definition of a convex polygon in two dimensions. If such a body is *closed* then it is impossible to get inside without crossing through its surface. One example of a closed convex body is the extrusion of a convex two-dimensional polygon into three-dimensional space. In order to simplify the hidden surface algorithm we impose a restriction on the order in which vertices defining each facet are stored. For any facet i, nfac[i] gives the index of the stored polygon representing facet i. Suppose nfac[i] equals j, then facfront[j] points to the start of a list of size[j] vertex indices stored in array faclist. (All declared in listing 7.2.) The vertex indices must be in the order in which they occur around the edge of the facet, and when viewed from the *outside* of an object they must be in an anti-clockwise orientation. Naturually from the *inside* of the object the vertices taken in this same order would appear clockwise! As before, we will also assume that facets intersect only at common edges. Since no lines are given explicitly in the data, individual lines not related to facets must be added as trivial two-sided facets. We can check that the facets are actually stored as anti-clockwise sets of vertices by referring to listing 6.11 during the SETUP stage of the scene definition.

Exercise 10.1
Use listing 6.11 to check that the programs from previous chapters do indeed create facets with vertices in the correct anti-clockwise orientation.

A Hidden Surface Algorithm for a Single Closed Convex Body

We orthographically project (or use perspective, see chapter 11) all the vertices of each facet onto the view plane, noting that a projection of a convex polygon with n sides in three-dimensional space is an n-sided convex polygon in the view plane (or degenerates to a line if the three-dimensional polygon is parallel to the lines of projection). Taking the projected vertices of any facet in the same order as the original, we find that either the new two-dimensional polygon is in anti-clockwise orientation, in which case we are looking at the outside of the facet, or the new vertices are clockwise and we are looking at the underside. The orientation of a two-dimensional facet is calculated by the function orient in listing 10.2 in a manner similar to that used in listing 5.7. In this routine we introduce a method required in a number of later routines when they have to be used with different co-ordinate systems: the array holding the vertex co-ordinates is passed as parameters, rather than as global variables and thus the routines are independent of the co-ordinate system. We are assuming that the observer is outside the closed convex body and hence is able to see only the outside of facets, the view of their underside being blocked by the bulk of the object. Therefore we need only draw the anti-clockwise polygonal facets – a very simple algorithm, which can be implemented directly in a construction routine or via a **hidden** routine. Note that if we only draw the edges of the visible facets, and do not fill in the facets in colour, then the above method gives us a simple hidden line algorithm. Plate V shows a topaz crystal drawn using this method.

Listing 10.2

```
FUNCTION orient(f : integer ; v : vertex2array) : integer ;
{ Finds orientation of facet 'f' when projected into 2-D co-ordinate }
{ system defined by array v of 2-D vertices }
{ 1 = anticlockwise, -1 = clockwise, 0 = degenerate }
VAR i,ind1,ind2,ind3 : integer ;
    dv1,dv2 : vector2 ;
BEGIN
   i := nfac[f] ;
   IF i = 0
   THEN orient := 0
   ELSE BEGIN
           ind1 := faclist[facfront[i]+1] ;
           ind2 := faclist[facfront[i]+2] ;
           ind3 := faclist[facfront[i]+3] ;
           dv1.x := v[ind2].x-v[ind1].x ;
           dv1.y := v[ind2].y-v[ind1].y ;
           dv2.x := v[ind3].x-v[ind2].x ;
           dv2.y := v[ind3].y-v[ind2].y ;
           orient := sign(dv1.x*dv2.y-dv2.x*dv1.y)
        END
END ; { of orient }
```

Listing 10.3

```
PROCEDURE hidden ;
{ Drawing a convex body with hidden surfaces removed }
VAR i : integer ;
BEGIN
{ Take each facet 'i' in turn }
   FOR i := 1 TO nof
{ Deal only with host facets }
   DO IF super[i] = 0
        THEN IF orient(i,pro) = 1
                THEN seefacet(i)
END ; { of hidden }
```

Listing 10.4

```
PROCEDURE facetfill(k : integer) ;
VAR v : vector2array ;
    i,index,j : integer ;
BEGIN
{ Store projected vertices of facet in array 'v' }
   j := nfac[k] ;
   FOR i := 1 TO size[j]
   DO BEGIN
          index := faclist[facfront[j]+i] ;
          v[i].x := pro[index].x ; v[i].y := pro[index].y
       END ;
{ Draw the facet in given colour }
   setcol(colour[k]) ; polyfill(size[j],v) ;
{ Colour edge lines in black }
   setcol(0) ; moveto(v[size[j]]) ;
   FOR i := 1 TO size[j]
   DO lineto(v[i])
END ; { of facetfill }

PROCEDURE seefacet(k : integer) ;
{ Colour host facet 'k' and all superficial facets }
VAR ipt,supk : integer ;
BEGIN
{ colour in facet 'k' }
   facetfill(k) ; ipt := firstsup[k] ;
   WHILE ipt < > 0
   DO BEGIN
{ colour in superficial facets 'supk' }
          supk := permheap[ipt].info ; facetfill(supk) ;
{ find next superficial facet }
          ipt := permheap[ipt].pointer
       END
END ; { of seefacet }
```

Example 10.1
Listing 10.3 holds the **hidden** routine that can be used for both orthographic and perspective (see chapter 11) projections. Listing 10.4 gives the necessary **seefacet** and **facetfill** routines. Ensure that all calls to these routines are within the scope of their declaration. Figure 10.1 shows the cube of example 7.2 orthographically projected and drawn with hidden surfaces suppressed. This routine can be used with any convex body! For example, figure 10.2 shows a convex body of rotation (a sphere) with the hidden surfaces suppressed, while figure 10.3 shows an extruded convex polygon.

Example 10.2
Note how the algorithm in listing 10.3 also works for data containing superficial facets which are not considered in **hidden**. Figure 10.4 shows a die constructed by the **scene** and **die** construction routine of listing 10.5 and also the file 'die.dat'. Note the implied need of **cubesetup** and **cube** from listing 7.2.

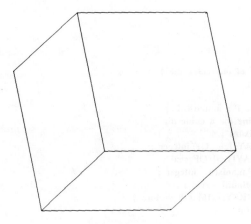

Figure 10.1

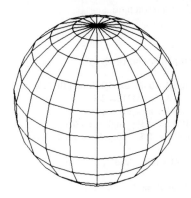

Figure 10.2

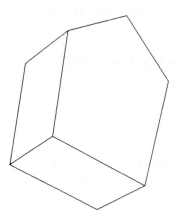

Figure 10.3

Listing 10.5

```
PROCEDURE scene ;
{ Construct SCENE of one cubic die }
VAR P : matrix4x4 ;

    PROCEDURE die(P : matrix4x4) ;
{ Construction routine for a cubic die }
    VAR A,B : matrix4x4 ;
        axis : ARRAY[1..6] OF integer ;
        angl : ARRAY[1..6] OF real ;
        face,i,index,j,n,nofsto : integer ;
        rad,theta,thetadiff : real ;
        corner : ARRAY[1..16] OF vector3 ;
        vertex : vector3 ;
    BEGIN
{ read in data about position of dots on six faces }
{ Place all 21 dots on face X=1 }
        assign(indata,'die.dat') ; reset(indata) ;
        FOR i := 1 TO 21
        DO BEGIN
                setup[i].x := 1.0 ;
                read(indata,setup[i].y,setup[i].z)
            END ;
{ Rotate face X=1 by pi*angl[j] about axis[j] into j'th face }
        axis[1] := 3 ; axis[2] := 3 ; axis[3] := 2 ;
        axis[4] := 2 ; axis[5] := 3 ; axis[6] := 3 ;
        angl[1] :=   0.0 ; angl[2] := -0.5 ; angl[3] := 0.5 ;
        angl[4] := -0.5 ; angl[5] :=   0.5 ; angl[6] := 1.0 ;
        nofsto := nof ;
{ Each dot will be a 'n-gon' of radius 'rad' }
        n := 16 ; rad := 0.15 ;
{ Form the corners of the 'n-gon' on face X=1 }
        theta := 0.0 ; thetadiff := 2*pi/n ;
        FOR i := 1 TO n
        DO BEGIN
                corner[i].y := rad*cos(theta) ; corner[i].z := rad*sin(theta) ;
                corner[i].x := 1.0 ; theta := theta+thetadiff
            END ;
{ First form the cube }
        cube(P) ;
{ Then look at dot 'index' on each of the six faces }
        index := 0 ;
        FOR face := 1 TO 6
        DO BEGIN
{ Store matrix 'B' for rotating dots onto correct face }
                rot3(axis[face],angl[face]*pi,A) ; mult3(P,A,B) ;
                FOR i := 1 TO face
                DO BEGIN
                        index := index+1 ;
{ Update facet data base with each new dot facet }
                        FOR j := 1 TO n
                        DO faclist[last+j] := nov+j ;
                        nof := nof+1 ; facfront[nof] := last ;
```

```
            size[nof] := n ; last := last+size[nof] ;
            colour[nof] := 0 ; nfac[nof] := nof ;
            super[nof] := nofsto+face ; firstsup[nof] := 0 ;
            pushperm(firstsup[nofsto+face],nof) ;
{ Now store the vertices }
                FOR j := 1 TO n
                DO BEGIN
                    vertex.x := 1.0 ;
                    vertex.y := corner[j].y+setup[index].y ;
                    vertex.z := corner[j].z+setup[index].z ;
                    nov := nov+1 ; transform(vertex,B,act[nov])
                    END
            END
        END
    END ; { of die }

BEGIN
{ Place Die in its SETUP position }
    tran3(0.0,0.0,0.0,P) ; die(P) ;
    look3 ; observe ; drawit
END ; { of scene }
```

File 'die.dat'

0.0	0.0	-0.5	-0.5	0.5	0.5
-0.5	-0.5	0.0	0.0	0.5	0.5
-0.5	0.5	-0.5	-0.5	0.5	-0.5
0.5	0.5	0.5	0.5	0.5	-0.5
-0.5	-0.5	-0.5	0.5	0.0	0.0
-0.5	-0.5	0.0	-0.5	0.5	-0.5
0.5	0.5	0.0	0.5	-0.5	0.5

Figure 10.4

Exercise 10.2
Write a construction routine that places superficial flags or alphabetic characters
on the side of a cube. Do the same for the octahedron and icosahedron.

Example 10.3
As with two-dimensional objects, there is no need to go through the whole process, we can short-cut the storage of data by including projection and drawing as
part of the construction routine. See an alternative cube routine in listing 10.6
for such a method of drawing the cube of figure 10.1.

Listing 10.6

```
PROCEDURE cube(R : matrix4x4) ;
{ Construction routine for rectangular block in OBSERVED position }
{ Initially a cube, block is distorted by scaling matrix component }
{ of 'R'. Assume cube has logical colour 3 with black edges }
{ Cube is drawn with orthographic projection }
VAR i,index1,index2,index3,j : integer ;
    dv1,dv2 : vector2 ;
    v : vector2array ;
BEGIN
    FOR i := 1 TO 8
    DO transform(cubevert[i],R,setup[i]) ;
    FOR i := 1 TO 6
    DO BEGIN
            index1 := cubefacet[i,1] ;
            index2 := cubefacet[i,2] ;
            index3 := cubefacet[i,3] ;
            dv1.x := setup[index2].x-setup[index1].x ;
            dv1.y := setup[index2].y-setup[index1].y ;
            dv2.x := setup[index3].x-setup[index2].x ;
            dv2.y := setup[index3].y-setup[index2].y ;
{ Draw facet if visible }
            IF dv1.x*dv2.y-dv2.x*dv1.y > 0.0
            THEN BEGIN
                    FOR j := 1 TO 4
                    DO BEGIN
                            v[j].x := setup[cubefacet[i,j]].x ;
                            v[j].y := setup[cubefacet[i,j]].y
                        END ;
{ Draw the facet in colour 3 }
                    setcol(3) ; polyfill(4,v) ;
{ Colour edge lines in black }
                    setcol(0) ; moveto(v[4]) ;
                    FOR j := 1 TO 4
                    DO lineto(v[j])
                END
        END
END ; { of cube }

PROCEDURE scene ;
VAR P,R : matrix4x4 ;
```

```
BEGIN
    look3 ; scale3(1.0,2.0,3.0,P) ;
    mult3(Q,P,R) ; cube(R)
END ; { of scene }
```

Exercise 10.3
Rewrite the body of revolution construction routine so that a single convex body of rotation is created with the visible facets being drawn as soon as they are calculated.

The Painter's Algorithm (or the Back-to-Front Method)

The call for pictures of convex solids is limited, so we now look at another simple algorithm that can be used with non-convex figures. When using raster graphics devices in normal REPLACE mode (not XOR nor other logical plotting modes) you will have noticed that when colouring a new area, all the colours previously placed in that section of the viewport will be obliterated. This furnishes us with a very simple hidden surface algorithm, namely we draw the areas furthest from the eye first and the nearest last. Exactly what we mean by furthest/nearest is not that straightforward. However, there are certain situations (for example, the next section) where this phrase has a very simple meaning and the algorithm is easy to implement. See chapter 13 for a more general painter's algorithm.

Drawing a Special Three-dimensional Surface

We consider the construction of a restricted type of three-dimensional surface in which the y co-ordinate of each point on the surface is given by a single-valued function F of the x and z co-ordinates of that point. The method may be used with orthographic, perspective or stereoscopic projections. f will be included as a function in the program listing 10.7. Since it is impossible to draw every point on the surface we have to approximate by considering a subset of these surface points. We choose those points with x/z co-ordinate on a *grid*, in other words, when orthographically viewed directly from above (thus ignoring the y values), the points form a rectangular grid. This grid is composed of nx by nz rectangles in the x/z plane. The x co-ordinates of the vertices are equi-spaced and vary between xmin and xmax (xmin < xmax) and the equi-spaced z values vary between zmin and zmax (zmin < zmax). There are thus $(nx + 1) \times (nz + 1)$ vertices (X_i, Z_j) in the grid where

$$X_i = \text{xmin} + i \times \text{xstep where } 0 \leqslant i \leqslant nx \text{ and xstep} = (\text{xmax} - \text{xmin})/nx$$
$$Z_j = \text{zmin} + j \times \text{zstep where } 0 \leqslant j \leqslant nz \text{ and zstep} = (\text{zmax} - \text{zmin})/nz$$

The equivalent ACTUAL point on the surface is (X_i, Y_{ij}, Z_j) where $Y_{ij} = f(X_i, Z_j)$. Every one of the $(nx + 1) \times (nz + 1)$ points generated in this way is joined to its four immediate neighbours along the grid (that is, those with equal x or equal z values), unless it lies on the edge in which case it is joined to three, or in the case of corners to two neighbours.

The approximation to the surface may then be formed by $nx \times nz$ sets of four grid vertices

$$\{(X_i, Z_j); (X_i, Z_{j+1}); (X_{i+1}, Z_{j+1}); (X_{i+1}, Z_j) \,|\, 0 \leqslant i < nx \text{ and } 0 \leqslant j < nz\}$$

Note that the four surface points corresponding to such a set of four vertices may not be coplanar, so strictly we should *not* call the surface area bounded by these vertices a four-sided facet, instead we call it a *patch*. The patch may undulate, so not all the surface area of the patch need be visible from a given view point — in fact it may even be partially visible. We devise a very simple method to eliminate the hidden surfaces by working from the back of the surface to the front. To simplify the algorithm we assume that the eye is always in the positive quadrant — that is eye.x > 0 and eye.z > 0 — and that the eye is always looking at the origin (direct = − eye). If the function f is asymmetrical and we wish to view it from another quadrant then we simply change the sign of x and/or z in the function. We can then transform the vertices on the surface into OBSERVED co-ordinates before projecting them onto the window and viewport.

We start by looping through the set of nz patches generated from the consecutive fixed-z ACTUAL grid lines $z = Z_i$ and $z = Z_{i+1}$ from the back ($i = 0$) to the front ($i = nz - 1$); naturally the term 'back-to-front' is used in the sense of the OBSERVER co-ordinate system, but the choice of eye.x and eye.z implies this. Within each set (defined by i: $0 \leqslant i < nz$) we loop through the individual patches generated by the intersection of the fixed-z lines with the fixed-x grid lines starting at $x = X_0$ and $x = X_1$, working through to $x = X_{nx-1}$ and $x = X_{nx}$. For each x and z value of a grid point we calculate a y value for the point on the patch using the mathematical function f. We can then project the ACTUAL patch vertices corresponding to the grid points $\{(X_i, Z_j); (X_{i+1}, Z_j);$ $(X_i, Z_{j+1}); (X_{i+1}, Z_{j+1})\}$ via their OBSERVED co-ordinates onto the view plane: to points p_1, p_2, p_3, p_4 say. We consider the polygonal area bounded by these four projected points, taken in the same order as defined in the above set. This polygonal area will either be considered as two triangles because two of the edges of the patch intersect, or a quadrilateral, not necessarily convex, which itself can be considered as two triangles. We distinguish between the possibilities by

(1) Finding a point p_5 (if one exists) which is the intersection of the line segments from p_1 to p_2 with the segment from p_3 to p_4. Then the two triangles formed by p_1, p_3 and p_5 and by p_2, p_4 and p_5 are drawn.

(2) If no proper intersection exists in case (1) then we find a point p_5 (if one

exists) which is the intersection of the line segments from p_1 to p_3 with the segment from p_2 to p_4. Then the two triangles formed by p_1, p_2 and p_5 and by p_3, p_4 and p_5 are drawn.

(3) If neither case (1) nor (2) is relevant, then the patch is a quadrilateral which can be drawn as two triangles formed by p_1, p_2 and p_4 and by p_1, p_3 and p_4.

All other combinations are topologically impossible. Having thus drawn the two triangles or the quadrilateral (defined as two triangles to avoid problem of non-convexity) in the correct back-to-front construction (because eye.x and eye.z are positive), we get a correct hidden surface picture. Again note how the drawing is achieved inside the construction routine.

Example 10.4
This method is programmed in listing 10.7. As an example of its use, figure 10.5 shows the function $y = 4\sin(t)/t$ where $t = \sqrt{(x^2 + z^2)}$.

Listing 10.7

```
PROCEDURE scene ;

    FUNCTION f(x,z : real) : real ;
{ Required function 'y=4sin(sqrt(x*x+z*z))/sqrt(x*x+z*z)' }
    VAR t : real ;
    BEGIN
        t := sqrt(x*x+z*z) ;
        IF abs(t) < epsilon
        THEN f:= 4.0
        ELSE f:= 4.0*sin(t)/t
    END ; { of f }

    PROCEDURE triangle(v1,v2,v3 : vector2) ;
{ Draw a triangle with corners 'v1','v2' and 'v3' }
    VAR poly : vector2array ;
    BEGIN
        poly[1].x := v1.x ; poly[1].y := v1.y ;
        poly[2].x := v2.x ; poly[2].y := v2.y ;
        poly[3].x := v3.x ; poly[3].y := v3.y ;
        setcol(1) ; polyfill(3,poly) ; setcol(4) ; moveto(poly[3]) ;
        lineto(poly[1]) ; lineto(poly[2]) ; lineto(poly[3])
    END ; { of triangle }

    PROCEDURE quadrilateral(v1,v2,v4,v3 : vector2) ;
{ Draw a quadrilateral with corners 'v1','v2','v4' and 'v3' }
    VAR poly : vector2array ;
    BEGIN
        poly[1].x := v1.x ; poly[1].y := v1.y ;
        poly[2].x := v2.x ; poly[2].y := v2.y ;
        poly[3].x := v4.x ; poly[3].y := v4.y ;
        poly[4].x := v3.x ; poly[4].y := v3.y ;
```

```
        setcol(1) ; polyfill(4,poly) ; setcol(4) ; moveto(poly[4]) ;
        lineto(poly[1]) ; lineto(poly[2]) ;
        lineto(poly[3]) ; lineto(poly[4])
    END ; { of quadrilateral }

    PROCEDURE patch(v1,v2,v3,v4 : vector2 ) ;
{ Find intersection of lines 'v1' to 'v2' and 'v3' to 'v4' }
    VAR denom,mu : real ;
        v5 : vector2 ;
    BEGIN
        denom := (v2.x-v1.x)*(v4.y-v3.y)-(v2.y-v1.y)*(v4.x-v3.x) ;
        IF abs(denom) > epsilon
        THEN BEGIN
                mu := ((v3.x-v1.x)*(v4.y-v3.y)-(v3.y-v1.y)*(v4.x-v3.x))/denom ;
{ If intersection between lines 'v1' to 'v2' and 'v3' to 'v4', call it 'v5' }
{ and form triangles 'v1;v3;v5' }
                IF (mu >= 0) AND (mu<=1)
                THEN BEGIN
                        v5.x := (1-mu)*v1.x+mu*v2.x ;
                        v5.y := (1-mu)*v1.y+mu*v2.y ;
                        triangle(v1,v3,v5) ; triangle(v2,v4,v5) ;
                        EXIT
                    END
            END ;
{ Else find intersection of lines 'v1' to 'v3' and 'v2' to 'v4' }
        denom := (v3.x-v1.x)*(v4.y-v2.y)-(v3.y-v1.y)*(v4.x-v2.x) ;
        IF abs(denom) > epsilon
        THEN BEGIN
                mu := ((v2.x-v1.x)*(v4.y-v2.y)-(v2.y-v1.y)*(v4.x-v2.x))/denom ;
{ If intersection between 'v1' and 'v2', call it 'v5' and form }
{ triangles 'v1;v2;v5' and 'v3;v4;v5' }
                IF (mu >= 0) AND (mu<=1)
                THEN BEGIN
                        v5.x := (1-mu)*v1.x+mu*v3.x ;
                        v5.y := (1-mu)*v1.y+mu*v3.y ;
                        triangle(v1,v2,v5) ; triangle(v3,v4,v5) ;
                        EXIT
                    END
            END ;
{ There are no proper intersections so form quadrilateral 'v1;v2;v4;v3' }
        quadrilateral(v1,v2,v4,v3)
    END ; { of patch }

    PROCEDURE drawit ;
{ Draw a mathematical function 'f' }
    CONST maxgrid = 100 ;
    VAR v : ARRAY[1..2,1..maxgrid] of vector2 ;
        xi,xmin,xmax,xstep,yij : real ;
        zj,zmin,zmax,zstep : real ;
        i,im1,j,nx,nx1,nz : integer ;
    BEGIN
{ Grid from 'xmin' to 'xmax' in 'nx' steps and 'zmin' to 'zmax' in 'nz' steps }
        writeln(' Type in xmin, xmax, nx') ; readln(xmin,xmax,nx) ;
        nx1 := nx+1 ; xstep := (xmax-xmin)/nx ;
        writeln(' Type in zmin, zmax, nz') ; readln(zmin,zmax,nz) ;
```

```
       zstep := (zmax-zmin)/nz ; xi := xmin ; zj := zmin ;
{ Calculate grid points on first fixed-z line, find the y-height }
{ and transform the points '(xi,yij,zj)' into OBSERVED position }
{ OBSERVED first set stored in 'v[1,1..nx1]'. }
       FOR i := 1 TO nx1
       DO BEGIN
              yij := f(xi,zj) ;
              v[1,i].x := Q[1,1]*xi+Q[1,2]*yij+Q[1,3]*zj ;
              v[1,i].y := Q[2,1]*xi+Q[2,2]*yij+Q[2,3]*zj ;
              xi := xi+xstep
       END ;
{ Run through consecutive fixed-z lines (the second set) }
       FOR j := 1 TO nz
       DO BEGIN
              im1 := 1 ; xi := xmin ; zj := zj+zstep ;
{ Calculate grid points on this second set, find the y-height }
{ and transform the points '(xi,yij,zj)' into OBSERVED position }
{ OBSERVED second set stored in 'v[2,1..nx1]'. }
              FOR i := 1 TO nx1
              DO BEGIN
                     yij := f(xi,zj) ;
                     v[2,i].x := Q[1,1]*xi+Q[1,2]*yij+Q[1,3]*zj ;
                     v[2,i].y := Q[2,1]*xi+Q[2,2]*yij+Q[2,3]*zj ;
                     xi := xi+xstep
              END ;
{ Run through the 'nx' patches formed by these two sets }
              FOR i := 1 TO nx
              DO patch(v[1,i],v[1,i+1],v[2,i],v[2,i+1]) ;
{ Copy second fixed-z set into first set }
              FOR i := 1 TO nx1
              DO BEGIN
                     v[1,i].x := v[2,i].x ; v[1,i].y := v[2,i].y
              END
       END
   END ; { of drawit }

BEGIN
   look3 ; drawit
END ; { of scene }
```

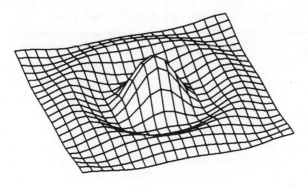

Figure 10.5

Exercise 10.4
Change the functions f used by this program. For example, use $f = 4\sin(t)$ where $t = \sqrt{(x^2 + z^2)}$.

Exercise 10.5
Use the knowledge of the orientation of the original grid rectangle and the orientation of the implied two triangles for each patch to extend the above program so that it draws the top side of the surface in a different colour to the underside.

Other Methods

There are many other simple methods, variations on a theme and even hybrid algorithms, that can prove efficient for suppressing hidden surfaces in three-dimensional scenes with special properties; see project 22 (chapter 18).

There are some situations (such as project 20 of chapter 18) when a *front-to-back* method can be used. Now instead of the back-to-front painter's method, the graphics viewport is cleared and the polygon area-fill must only colour pixels which have not already been coloured. Thus going from front to back furnishes a hidden surface algorithm. We still have to define what we mean by 'front' and 'back' of course! A variation on this method proves quite efficient in certain line-drawing problems, as in project 20 of chapter 18.

Probably the simplest conceptual approach, but which is relatively expensive on processing power for less complex models, is the so-called *Z-buffer* algorithm. In the extreme case each pixel in the viewport is given a depth value stored in the z-buffer along with a facet index. We can imagine a rectangular (orthographic) or pyramidal (perspective) prism leading from the eye, to the pixel and off to minus infinity. The z value of the intersection of the axis of this prism with each facet is calculated in turn and compared with the buffer value. The larger value (closer to the eye) is placed in the buffer. When every facet has been considered the buffer holds the z value of the intersection nearest the eye and the facet index, giving a simple hidden surface algorithm for each pixel.

In very special cases only subsets of the pixels need be sampled to achieve a hidden surface algorithm, but you will have to be very careful with your scene definition if you hope to avoid referencing all the pixels in the viewport.

Another approach, the *scan-line algorithms*, considers one scan line of a raster screen at a time, and uses information about polygonal facets in the scene to colour these scan lines correctly, giving a correct hidden surface picture.

Yet another way is to *seed* each facet with a single point in the facet: the so-called *depth-sort algorithm*. When transformed into OBSERVED position, the seed points are put into an order of increasing distance from the eye, and this order is used by the painter's algorithm. This is not a very satisfactory method because it will often give incorrect displays of scenes which contain a wide variety of facet sizes.

The ray tracing technique (Appel, 1968; Mathematical Applications Group, 1968) involves defining a ray from the eye to each pixel on the viewport, and then following each ray in turn through space, taking into account reflection, refraction etc. The amount of reflection and refraction will of course depend on the various properties of the surfaces met by the ray in its travels (see chapter 15). Each ray could be divided up into its red, green, blue components, each with its own refractive properties, and these followed individually, to be combined ultimately to give the colour of the pixel. Since each surface can introduce both refraction and reflection of a ray, the initial ray can give rise to a complex network of subrays. If the ray is not halted by a non-reflecting surface then some stage must be reached when the tracing stops (a decision based on ray intensity), and the complete network of rays used to evaluate the colour of the corresponding pixel. The definition of surfaces can be considered as a polygonal mesh, or more usually is defined as a combination of primitive surfaces such as spheres, cylinders etc. (see chapter 17).

11 Perspective and Stereoscopic Projections

PERSPECTIVE

The orthographic projection has the property that parallel lines in three-dimensional space are projected into parallel lines on the view plane. Although they have their uses, such views do look odd! Our view of space is based upon the concept of *perspective*. Our brains attempt to interpret orthographic figures as if they are perspective views, making the cubes of figure 8.1, for instance, look distorted.

Not wanting to linger on such distorted views, we have already referred to the perspective version of **project** in chapter 9, where we noted the need for visual realism. It is obviously essential to produce a projection which displays perspective phenomena – that is, parallel lines should meet on the horizon and an object should appear smaller as it moves away from the observer. The drawing-board methods devised by artists over the centuries are of no value to us, but the three-dimensional co-ordinate geometry introduced in chapter 6 furnishes us with a relatively straightforward technique.

What is Perspective Vision?

To produce a perspective view we introduce a very simple definition of what we mean by vision. We imagine every visible point in space sending out a ray which enters the eye. Naturally the eye cannot see all of space, it is limited to a cone of rays which fall on the retina, the so-called *cone of vision*, which is outlined by the dashed lines of figure 11.1. These rays are the lines of projection. The axis of the cone is called the *direction of vision* (or the *straight-ahead ray*). In the work that follows we assume that all co-ordinates relate to the OBSERVER right-handed co-ordinate system with the eye at the origin and the straight-ahead ray identified with the negative z-axis.

We place the view plane (which we call the *perspective plane* in this special case) perpendicular to the axis of the cone of vision at a distance d from the eye (that is, the plane $z = -d$). In order to form the perspective projection we mark the points of intersection of each ray with this plane. Since there is an infinity of such rays this appears to be an impossible task. Actually the problem is not that great because we need only consider the rays which emanate from the

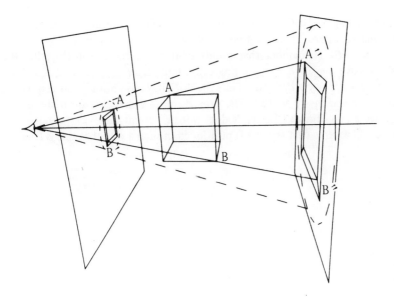

Figure 11.1

important points in the scene — for example, the corner vertices of polygonal facets. Once the projections of the vertices onto the perspective screen have been determined, the problem is reduced to that of representing the perspective plane (the view plane) on the graphics viewport. The solution to this problem was discussed in chapter 8 with regard to the orthographic projection and exactly the same process may be followed here — a two-dimensional co-ordinate system, the WINDOW system, is defined on the view plane together with a rectangular window which is identified with the viewport. The image is drawn by joining the pixels corresponding to the end-points of lines or the vertices of facets in exactly the same manner as that used in the representation of a two-dimensional scene.

Figure 11.1 shows a cube observed by an eye and projected onto two different view planes, the whole scene also being drawn in perspective! Two example rays are shown: the first from the eye to A, one of the nearest corners of the cube to the eye, and the second to B, one of the far corners. The perspective projections of these points onto the near plane are A' and B', and onto the far plane A'' and B''. Note that the projections will have the same shape and orientation, but they will be of different sizes.

Calculation of the Perspective Projection of a Point

We let the perspective plane by a distance d from the eye (variable **ppd** in later programs). Consider a point $p \equiv (x, y, z)$ (with respect to the OBSERVER system) which sends a ray into the eye. We must calculate the point $p' \equiv (x', y', -d)$ where this ray cuts the view plane (the $z = -d$ plane) and thus we determine the corresponding WINDOW co-ordinates (x', y'). First consider the value of y' by referring to figure 11.2. By *similar triangles* we see that $y'/d = y/|z|$, that is $y' = -y \times d/z$ (remember that points in front of the eye in the OBSERVER system have negative z co-ordinates). Similarly $x' = -x \times d/z$ and hence $p' = (-x \times d/z, -y \times d/z, -d)$. Thus the WINDOW co-ordinates corresponding to p are $(-x \times d/z, -y \times d/z)$. The projection only makes sense if the point has negative z co-ordinate (that is, it does not lie behind the eye). So until chapter 14 we will assume that the eye is positioned in such a way that this is true.

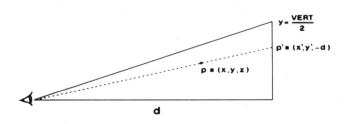

Figure 11.2

Example 11.1

Calculate the perspective projection of a cube with eight vertices $(0, 0, -4)$ + $(\pm 1, \pm 1, \pm 1)$ on the perspective plane $z = -4$, where the eye is origin and the direction of vision is along the negative z-axis.

The projected co-ordinates are calculated by the above method since the co-ordinates are already specified relative to the OBSERVER axes (ABSOLUTE system $\equiv$ OBSERVER system). For example, $(1, 1, -3)$ is projected to $(-1 \times 4/-3, -1 \times 4/-3, -4) = (4/3, 4/3, -4)$ which becomes $(4/3, 4/3)$ in the WINDOW system. So we get the eight projections

$$(1, 1, -3) \text{ to } (4/3, 4/3), \quad (1, -1, -3) \quad \text{to } (4/3, -4/3)$$
$$(-1, 1, -3) \text{ to } (-4/3, 4/3), (-1, -1, -3) \quad \text{to } (-4/3, -4/3)$$
$$(1, 1, -5) \text{ to } (4/5, 4/5), \quad (1, -1, -5) \quad \text{to } (4/5, -4/5)$$
$$(-1, 1, -5) \text{ to } (-4/5, 4/5), (-1, -1, -5) \quad \text{to } (-4/5, -4/5)$$

which are identified with points in the viewport, and the resulting diagram is shown in figure 11.3a.

Properties of the perspective transformation

(1) The perspective transformation of a straight line (Γ_3 say) is a straight line (Γ_2 say) or a point. This is obvious because the origin (the eye) and the line Γ_3 form a plane (Ω say) in three-dimensional space and all the rays emanating from points on Γ_3 lie in this plane. (If Γ_3 enters the eye, Ω degenerates into the line Γ_3 which is projected into a single point.) Naturally Ω cuts the

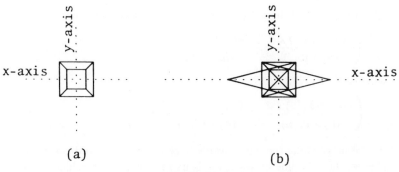

Figure 11.3

perspective plane in a line Γ_2 (or degenerates to a point) and so the perspective projection of a point on the original line Γ_3 now lies on the new line Γ_2. It is important to realise that a line does not become curved in this type of perspective projection. Furthermore, we may deduce that the projection of a straight line segment joining two points p_1 and p_2 is a straight line segment in the perspective plane which joins the perspective projections of p_1 and p_2.

(2) The perspective transformation of a three-dimensional facet (a closed sequence of coplanar line segments) is a two-dimensional facet in the perspective plane. If the facet is an area bounded by n coplanar line segments then the transform of this facet is naturally an area in the $z = -d$ plane bounded by the transforms of the n line segments since their end-points are the projections of the vertices of the projected facet, each of which is common to two edges. Again note, no curves are introduced in the projection: if they were then the task of producing perspective pictures would be far more complicated.

(3) The projection of a convex facet is also convex. Suppose facet F1 is projected onto facet F2 in the view plane. Since the projection of a closed facet is also closed and lines are projected into lines, then points inside F1 are projected into points inside F2. Suppose F2 is not convex. Then there exist two points p_1 and p_2 inside F2 such that the line segment joining them goes outside this facet. Hence there is at least one point p on this line segment lying outside F2. If p_1 and p_2 are projections of points q_1 and q_2 from F1, then p is the projection of some point q on the line joining q_1 and q_2. Since the F1 is convex then q must be inside F1, but then p must be inside F2, thus contradicting the assumption that F2 is not convex and so F2 must be convex and our proposition is proved.

(4) All infinitely long parallel lines appear to meet at one point, their so-called *vanishing point*. If we take a general line (with base vector b) from a set of parallel lines with direction vector h then

$$b + \mu h \equiv (b_x, b_y, b_z) + \mu(h_x, h_y, h_z)$$

where $h_z < 0$, and the perspective transform of a general point on this line is

$$\left(\frac{-(b_x + \mu h_x) \times d}{(b_z + \mu h_z)}, \frac{-(b_y + \mu h_y) \times d}{(b_z + \mu h_z)} \right)$$

which can be rewritten as

$$\left(\frac{-(h_x + b_x/\mu) \times d}{(h_z + b_z/\mu)}, \frac{-(h_y + b_y/\mu) \times d}{(h_z + b_z/\mu)} \right)$$

As we move along the line towards large negative z co-ordinates, that is as $\mu \to \infty$, then the line moves towards its vanishing point, which is therefore given by $(-d \times h_x/h_z, -d \times h_y/h_z)$. This vanishing point is independent of b, the base point of the line, and hence all lines parallel to the direction h have the same vanishing point. Of course the case $h_z > 0$ is ignored because the line would disappear outside the cone of vision as $\mu \to \infty$.

(5) The vanishing points of all lines in parallel planes are collinear. Suppose that the set of parallel planes have a common normal direction $n \equiv (n_x, n_y, n_z)$. If a general line in one of these planes has direction $h \equiv (h_x, h_y, h_z)$, then h is perpendicular to n (all lines in these planes are perpendicular to the normal n). Thus $n \cdot h = 0$, which in co-ordinate form is

$$n_x \times h_x + n_y \times h_y + n_z \times h_z = 0$$

which, dividing by h_z, gives

$$n_x \times h_x/h_z + n_y \times h_y/h_z + n_z = 0$$

and so the vanishing point $(-d \times h_x/h_z, -d \times h_y/h_z)$ lies on the straight line

$$n_x \times x + n_y \times y - n_z \times d = 0$$

and the statement is proved. This concept is very familiar to us — the vanishing points of all lines in horizontal planes lie on the horizon!

Example 11.2
Find the vanishing points of the edges of the cube in example 11.1, and of the diagonals of its top and bottom planes.

We divide the twelve edges of the cube into three sets of four edges, each set being parallel to the x, y and z axis respectively and so having direction vectors $(1, 0, 0)$, $(0, 1, 0)$ and $(0, 0, -1)$. The first two sets have zero z values, and so their extended edges disappear outside the cone of vision and are ignored, whereas the third direction has vanishing point $(-4 \times 0/-1, -4 \times 0/-1) = (0, 0)$ on the view plane. On the top and bottom faces the diagonals have directions $(-1, 0, -1)$, the major diagonal, and $(1, 0, -1)$, the minor diagonal. The major diagonal on the top plane is $(1, 1, -3) + \mu(-1, 0, -1)$, and so the vanishing point is $(-4 \times -1/-1, -4 \times 0/-1) = (-4, 0)$. The minor diagonal on the top plane is $(-1, 1, -3) + \mu(1, 0, -1)$ and the vanishing point $(-4 \times 1/-1, -4 \times 0/-1) = (4, 0)$. By similar calculations we find the vanishing points of the major and minor diagonals on the lower face are also $(-4, 0)$ and $(4, 0)$ respectively. The relevant edges are extended to their vanishing points in figure 11.3b. Note that all the lines mentioned lie in the two parallel planes (the top and bottom faces of the cube) and so the vanishing points should be collinear: they are, because $(-4, 0)$, $(0, 0)$ and $(4, 0)$ all lie on the x-axis. By a similar calculation we would find that the vanishing points of the diagonals of the side faces lie on a vertical line through the origin.

Exercise 11.1
Draw a perspective view of a tetrahedron with vertices $(1, 1, -5)$, $(1, -1, -3)$, $(-1, 1, -3)$ and $(-1, -1, -5)$. Find the vanishing points (inside the cone of vision) of lines which join pairs of mid-points of edges of the tetrahedron.

Programming the Perspective Transformation

The procedure for drawing a perspective view of a three-dimensional scene is the same as that for an orthographic projection outlined at the end of chapter 8, in all respects other than the calculation of the co-ordinates of the projected vertices. Unlike the orthographic, in the perspective projection the co-ordinates on the view plane cannot be identified with the OBSERVED x and y co-ordinates of the point. Instead, we need to store the perspective transformation so the ith vertex with OBSERVED co-ordinates vector3 value obs[i] is projected to vector2 pro[i]. The values in array pro are given by

    pro[i].x := —obs[i].x * ppd/obs[i].z;
    pro[i].y := —obs[i].y * ppd/obs[i].z;

for i = 1, 2 ..., nov provided obs[i].z < 0, and these values are subsequently identified with points in the graphics frame for use by a display routine.

As with the orthographic projection, the pro array is calculated in routine project (listing 11.1) and declared globally (listing 7.2) as

    {VAR} pro : vertex2array;

So all our previous display routines that are not specifically orthographic can be called using co-ordinates produced by this new project, and a perspective version of most of our three-dimensional diagrams can be drawn with the simple expedient of replacing the orthographic project with that from listing 11.1.

The Choice of Perspective Plane

The only value required for the perspective transformation which we have not yet discussed is that of ppd, the distance of the perspective plane from the eye. We can see from figure 11.1 that different values of ppd produce pictures of different sizes — which one do we choose? Is there a correct value?

Consider the practical situation. The observer is sitting in front of the viewport of a graphics device and the perspective view plane is identified with the plane of that viewport. Normally the observer is sitting at a distance which is about three times the width of the viewport from the device. In the scale of our mapping from the real-world to the graphics area of pixels, this is a distance 3 * horiz. If we choose ppd less than this value we get a wide angle effect, while if ppd is greater we get the foreshortened effect of a telephoto image. Perspective pictures are independent of the screen size, only the ratio of ppd to horiz matters, not the absolute value of horiz. Therefore, for perspective pictures, horiz may be set to the constant value 1.0. ppd is declared in the global database in listing 7.2.

Clipping

Theoretically, objects may be positioned throughout space, even behind the eye. The formulae derived to represent the perspective projection deal only with points within the *pyramid of vision*. An attempt to apply the formulae to points outside this area, especially those lying behind the eye, gives nonsensical results. The scene must, therefore, be clipped so that all vertices lie within the pyramid of vision before the projection may be applied. The solution to such problems will be discussed in chapter 14, but for the moment we shall assume that the clipping has been done (or is unnecessary) and that all vertices are inside the pyramid of vision. Of course if all z values are strictly negative we can use two-dimensional clipping on the projected scene!

Example 11.3
The cube of example 7.2 placed in its SETUP position can be drawn in perspective (drawit: listing 8.3) using the project of listing 11.1. Figure 11.4 shows the cube viewed from (10, 20, 30) looking back towards the ABSOLUTE origin with direction (−10, −20, −30). Remember to ensure at this stage that your views keep *all* of the scene in front of the eye.

Listing 11.1

```
VAR
    ppd : real ;

PROCEDURE project ;
{ Perspective projection of OBSERVED vertices }
VAR i : integer ;
BEGIN
    ppd := 3.0*horiz ;
    FOR i := 1 TO ntv
    DO IF obs[i].z < 0
       THEN BEGIN
                pro[i].x := -obs[i].x*ppd/obs[i].z ;
                pro[i].y := -obs[i].y*ppd/obs[i].z
            END
END ; { of project }
```

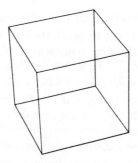

Figure 11.4

STEREOSCOPIC VIEWS

Perspective views are all very well but unfortunately (or fortunately!) we have two eyes. Each eye should have its own perspective view, which will differ slightly from that of the other eye. This is the means by which we appreciate the three-dimensional quality of our world. We use this concept to produce a stereoscopic view of space on a colour graphics display, creating a perspective view for each eye. This leads to a problem. We cannot simply draw two such projections because the left eye will see not only the view created for it, but also that made for the right eye, and vice versa. To stop this confusion we must ensure that each eye sees its own view, but only its view. There are a number of different ways of achieving this: using a *stereoscope* or special polarised glasses synchronised with the appearance of two separate pictures on a screen. We describe the least expensive method, a pair of *stereoscopic spectacles*: two transparent plastic sheets, one red for the left eye and one cyan (or, alternatively, blue or green) for the right eye. In this way the left eye cannot see red lines because they appear the same colour as the white background, both colours having the same red component, but cyan lines appear black, having no red component. Conversely, the right eye cannot see cyan lines, but red lines look black. So we must make two line drawings of a scene: one in cyan for the left eye, and one in red for the right eye. The brain will merge the two black images into one and the cyan and red background into white, to give a three-dimensional effect.

So we devise a method of producing the stereoscopic projection of a general point $p \equiv (x, y, z)$ – that is, two points $p_l \equiv (x_l, y_l)$ for the left eye and $p_r \equiv (x_r, y_r)$ for the right eye – in the WINDOW co-ordinate system on the perspective view plane (see figure 11.5). We sensibly choose the same view plane for both eyes. We will assume that the OBSERVER origin is between the eyes, with the axes otherwise defined in the same way as the previous OBSERVER system, the straight-ahead ray being parallel to the z-axis. The eyes have co-ordinates $(-e, 0, 0)$, left, and $(e, 0, 0)$, right: in listing 11.2, e is given by variable eyedist, which is usually approximately $0.15 *$ horiz. Again the perspective view plane is a distance d (variable ppd) from the origin. In order to find p_r we translate the co-ordinate origin to $(e, 0, 0)$, the right eye, so that p becomes $(x - e, y, z)$ and the perspective transform of this point for the right eye is $(-(x - e) \times d/z, -y \times d/z, -d)$, which, relative to the OBSERVER axes, is $(-(x - e) \times d/z + e, -y \times d/z, -d)$. Similarly the left eye transformation produces $p_1 \equiv (-(x + e) \times d/z - e, -y \times d/z, -d)$. These points have WINDOW co-ordinates $(-(x - e) \times d/z + e, -y \times d/z)$ and $(-(x + e) \times d/z - e, -y \times d/z)$ respectively.

The program to produce a stereoscopic view of a scene is very similar to the perspective program, except that the project routine (listing 11.2) is called twice to create two separate sets of pro values, one for the left eye and the other for the right, and will call wireframe (listing 8.3) for each in turn. The first picture is drawn in red (logical colour 1) on a white background (logical colour 7), and the second picture in cyan (logical colour 6) with the AND line type. This will ensure that whenever a pixel is crossed by lines from both left and right views it will be set to black (logical 0); if this were not the case the lines in the red figure would appear to have holes. If you wish to use a black background, then plotting with the OR line type is required.

For stereoscopic displays it is best to make the view plane cut the object being viewed – that is, make $\sqrt{(eye.x^2 + eye.y^2 + eye.z^2)} = ppd$ (= 3 * horiz). Therefore in the case of stereoscopic views we cannot keep horiz and vert fixed, since for the best projections horiz (and hence vert) depends on eye.

Example 11.4
Draw Plate VI, a stereoscopic view of a cube of example 7.2. horiz is set to 16 and the observer is at $(10, 20, 30)$ looking in direction $(-10, -20, -30)$.

Listing 11.2

```
VAR
    ppd,eyedist : real ;

PROCEDURE project(eyedist : real) ;
{ Stereoscopic projection of vertices }
VAR i: integer ;
BEGIN
{ Find perspective projection for eye position '(eyedist,0,0)' }
    FOR i := 1 TO ntv
    DO IF obs[i].z < 0
        THEN BEGIN
                pro[i].x := -(obs[i].x-eyedist)*ppd/obs[i].z+eyedist ;
                pro[i].y := -obs[i].y*ppd/obs[i].z
            END
END ; { of project }

PROCEDURE drawit ;
```

```
{ Constructs stereoscopic projection }
BEGIN
{ Set vertex counts }
    ntv := nov ; ntf := nof ;
{ Set eye positions }
    ppd := 3.0*horiz ; eyedist := 0.15*horiz ;
{ Consider two eyes (2*eyedist units apart) }
{ First draw red on white background : right eye }
    setype(0) ; setcol(1) ; project(eyedist) ; wireframe ;
{ Then change to left eye and draw XOR with cyan }
    eyedist := -eyedist ;
    setype(3) ; setcol(6) ; project(eyedist) ; wireframe
END ; { of drawit }
```

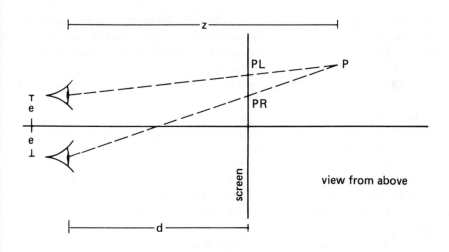

Figure 11.5

Exercise 11.2

Draw stereoscopic views of some of the objects drawn previously in orthographic and perspective projections, including the bodies of revolution and extruded polygons.

Exercise 11.3

Produce stereoscopic hidden line pictures of convex bodies. Now you must not colour in the facets, just draw the visible edges of the object, once in cyan for the left eye, and once in red for the right eye. You will have to change the facetfill routine in listing 10.4 so that it only draws the edges of visible facets and not the facets themselves.

12 A More General Hidden Line Algorithm

Not all users of computer graphics use colour. In fact there are major application areas in architecture and Computer Aided Design with a marked preference for the monochrome line-drawing *blue print* type output. In this chapter we discuss a general hidden line algorithm which, using line-drawing routines only, can produce architectural designs, machine-parts etc., with any line in the scene, which is blocked from view by the bulk of other objects, being suppressed.

Here we consider such an algorithm for use with the **drawit** routine of listing 10.1 and the perspective projection. This algorithm is not truly general, there is a restriction! *No pair of convex polygonal facets in the scene intersect other than at a common polygonal edge!* As usual objects are defined in their ACTUAL position and then the co-ordinates calculated relative to the OBSERVER co-ordinate system. The x, y, z co-ordinates are stored as the **obs** array; the perspective projection onto the WINDOW co-ordinate system is stored in array **pro**.

In order to produce a picture of a given scene with the hidden lines suppressed, each line on the object (an edge of a polygonal facet) must be compared with every facet in the scene. Of course parts of a line may be visible and parts invisible (behind a facet). We will suppose that a typical line in the OBSERVER system is Γ_3 and it joins two points (x'_1, y'_1, z'_1) and (x'_2, y'_2, z'_2). Thus a general point on this line is given by

$$(1 - \phi)(x'_1, y'_1, z'_1) + \phi(x'_2, y'_2, z'_2)$$

Suppose that these two points are projected by perspective onto the two points (x_1, y_1) and (x_2, y_2) in the WINDOW system on the perspective plane. Thus line Γ_3 is projected into the line Γ_2 in this plane, and a general point on the line is

$$(1 - \lambda)(x_1, y_1) + \lambda(x_2, y_2)$$

Note that the point $(1 - \phi)(x'_1, y'_1, z'_1) + \phi(x'_2, y'_2, z'_2)$ does not transform into the point $(1 - \phi)(x_1, y_1) + \phi(x_2, y_2)$: that is, ϕ is not necessarily equal to λ.

We let a typical n-sided facet Ω_3 be projected into a polygonal area Ω_2 on the perspective plane, and we assume that the vertices on this projected facet are

$$\nabla = \{(\bar{x}_i, \bar{y}_i) \mid i = 1, \ldots, n\}$$

Thus the ith edge in Ω_2 has a general point

$$(1 - \mu_i)\,(\overline{x}_i, \overline{y}_i) + \mu_i(\overline{x}_{i+1}, \overline{y}_{i+1}) \text{ where } 0 \leqslant \mu_i \leqslant 1$$

Again the addition of subscripts is modulo n.

In a wire frame perspective picture, every line Γ_2 would be drawn clipped in the viewport; in order to avoid problems with perspective projection we still assume that every object in the scene lies in front of the eye — three-dimensional clipping will be described in chapter 14. Here we assume that objects are solid and hence, if a facet Ω_3 lies between the eye and Γ_3 then part, and perhaps all, of Γ_2 will be hidden. Most facets do not interfere with the view of any one line, and so we sift out some of the more easily recognisable possibilities. We must be careful with the amount of sifting. It is very easy to overdo it and make the overall run time of the algorithm larger than the time with no sifting at all.

(a) We will assume that the facets have been set up with an anti-clockwise orientation. Hence any facet which is projected into a clockwise orientation, and any related superficial facet, can be ignored for the comparison with lines, which, remember, are implicit in the facet data.

(b) Each line will occur in the facet data as a pair of vertex indices v1 and v2. There will be at least one occurrence of a non-superficial line defined from v1 towards v2, with v1 $<$ v2, and so we can ignore non-superficial lines with v1 $>$ v2 provided that all objects in our scene are closed; this order restriction must be relaxed (implying double the processing) if you insist on non-closed objects (see chapter 8).

(c) All lines in a facet which is superficial to an invisible facet can be ignored. We cannot ignore a line v1 to v2 (v1 $<$ v2) on an invisible non-superficial facet, since this may be an edge of a visible facet from v2 to v1 which would be ignored by (b) above.

(d) If Γ_3 lies in facet Ω_3, then Γ_3 is on the surface of the facet and any view of the line cannot be obscured by that facet.

Exercise 12.1

(e) You can program the following sifting method (and three-dimensional clipping: see chapter 14) into listing 12.1. If Ω_2 is not intersected by Γ_2, then Ω_3 can have no effect on the view of the line Γ_3. There are three elementary possibilities given

(1) the vertices ∇ all lie on the same side of Γ_2
(2) ∇ and (x_2, y_2) lie on opposite sides of a line through (x_1, y_1) perpendicular to Γ_2
(3) ∇ and (x_1, y_1) lie on opposite sides of a line through (x_2, y_2) perpendicular to Γ_2.

You may check them individually

(1) $f(x,y) = (y - y_1)\,(x_2 - x_1) - (x - x_1)\,(y_2 - y_1)$ is the analytic representation of Γ_2. If $f(\overline{x}_i, \overline{y}_i)$ has the same sign for all vertices $(\overline{x}_i, \overline{y}_i)$ belonging to

∇, then all the vertices of Ω_2 lie on the same side of Γ_2 and there is no intersection between Γ_2 and Ω_2.

(2) $g(x,y) = (y - y_1)(y_2 - y_1) + (x - x_1)(x_2 - x_1)$ is the analytic representation of the line through (x_1, y_1) perpendicular to Γ_2. If the sign of $g(x_2, y_2)$ is not equal to the sign of $g(\overline{x}_i, \overline{y}_i)$ for all $(\overline{x}_i, \overline{y}_i)$ belonging to ∇, then Γ_2 does not intersect Ω_2.

(3) $h(x, y) = (y - y_2)(y_2 - y_1) + (x - x_2)(x_2 - x_1)$ is the analytic representation of the line through (x_2, y_2) perpendicular to Γ_2. In a manner similar to (2), a facet is ignored if the sign of $h(x_1, y_1)$ is not equal to the sign of $h(\overline{x}_i, \overline{y}_i)$ for all $(\overline{x}_i, \overline{y}_i)$.

You may add these sifting methods to listing 12.1 at the point specified. Any line that passes these first hurdles has to be considered in detail.

We assume that Γ_2 cuts the extended i^{th} edge of Ω_2 at the point

$$(1 - \lambda_i)(\overline{x}_i, \overline{y}_i) + \lambda_i (\overline{x}_{i+1}, \overline{y}_{i+1})$$

If $\lambda_i < 0$ or $\lambda_i > 1$, the Γ_2 intersects the ith edge at a point outside the polygonal area Ω_2; if $0 \leqslant \lambda_i \leqslant 1$ then Γ_2 crosses the area Ω_2 at a point on the ith edge. Since the perspective projection of a convex facet is a convex polygon on the perspective plane, then the number of crossing points is either zero (and hence there is no intersection and the facet can be ignored) or two. In the latter case we find the two crossing points on the line Γ_2 given by the values μ_{min} and μ_{max}. These values must be ordered so that they lie on the line segment between (x_1, y_1) and (x_2, y_2) with $0 \leqslant \mu_{min} < \mu_{max} \leqslant 1$ — that is, the points of intersection are $(1 - \mu_{min})(x_1, y_1) + \mu_{min}(x_2, y_2)$ and $(1 - \mu_{max})(x_1, y_1) + \mu_{max}(x_2, y_2)$.

It is now necessary to discover whether the subsegment of Γ_2 between these two points is visible or not. This is checked by finding the mid-point of the segment $(x_{mid}, y_{mid}) = (1 - \mu_{mid})(x_1, y_1) + \mu_{mid}(x_2, y_2)$, where $\mu_{mid} = (\mu_{min} + \mu_{max})/2$. We then find the unique point $(\tilde{x}, \tilde{y}, \tilde{z})$ on Γ_3 that has (x_{mid}, y_{mid}) as its perspective projection. The line segment is hidden if and only if $(\tilde{x}, \tilde{y}, \tilde{z})$ and the eye lie on opposite sides of the infinite plane containing Ω_3. The equation of the plane containing a facet is found by the method of example 6.7 in the routine **normal** (listing 12.2), and its analytic representation can be used to check the above requirement. Note that $-\tilde{x} \times \mathsf{ppd}/\tilde{z} = x_{mid}$ and $-\tilde{y} \times \mathsf{ppd}/\tilde{z} = y_{mid}$, and also $(\tilde{x}, \tilde{y}, \tilde{z})$ lies on the line Γ_3, and so for some value ϕ

$$\tilde{x} = (1 - \phi) x_1' + \phi x_2' \ , \quad \tilde{y} = (1 - \phi) y_1' + \phi y_2' \ , \quad \tilde{z} = (1 - \phi) z_1' + \phi z_2'$$

Hence

$$x_{mid} = \frac{-(x_1' + \phi(x_2' - x_1')) \times \mathsf{ppd}}{z_1' + \phi(z_2' - z_1')} \quad \text{and}$$

$$y_{mid} = \frac{-(y_1' + \phi(y_2' - y_1')) \times \mathsf{ppd}}{z_1' + \phi(z_2' - z_1')}$$

that is

$$\phi = \frac{x_{\text{mid}} \times z_1' + x_1' \times \text{ppd}}{-(x_2' - x_1') \times \text{ppd} - x_{\text{mid}} \times (z_2' - z_1')}$$

$$= \frac{y_{\text{mid}} \times z_1' + y_1' \times \text{ppd}}{-(y_2' - y_1') \times \text{ppd} - y_{\text{mid}} \times (z_2' - z_1')}$$

This enables us to calculate ϕ, and hence $(\tilde{x}, \tilde{y}, \tilde{z})$, which in turn is used to find whether the subsegment of Γ_2 is visible or not.

This algorithm may be more easily understood by referring to figure 12.1.

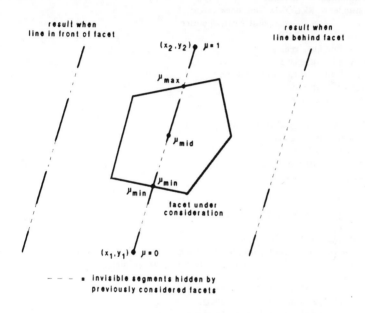

Figure 12.1

Remember that at present we assume that every object is in front of the eye. The hidden line algorithm discussed in this chapter is implemented as procedure **hidden** of listing 12.1 called from **drawit** of listing 10.1. The method is to compare the jth line of the ith facet with the kth facet ($1 <= i, k <= \text{nof}$) in procedure **comparelinewithfacet**. As the algorithm progresses the line will be split into a set of visible segments, the pair of μ values of the end points for each segment is stored in a linear list named **list**. Initially the list will hold the complete line (one cell in the list holding μ values 0 and 1). Whenever a new hidden segment is discovered, specified by μ_{min} and μ_{max} (variables **umin** and **umax**), the list is adjusted in routine **adjustsegmentlist**. On leaving **comparelinewithfacet** the list is either empty and the line is totally invisible, or the list holds the μ

values of the visible segments which are drawn individually in routine **drawsegmentlist**.

Listing 12.1

```
PROCEDURE hidden ;
{ Hidden line algorithm to take the 2-D perspective picture of 3-D }
{ space and cut the line segments in the picture into visible and }
{ invisible parts, and then draw the visible parts. It is assumed }
{ that all vertices are in front of the eye and all facets lie }
{ within the graphics window! }
TYPE listpointer = ^listnode ;
     listnode = RECORD front,back : real ;
                       pointer : listpointer
                END ;
VAR djc,epsilon,f,b : real ;
    i,j,k,v1,v2 : integer ;
    fbegin,fend,index1,index2 : integer ;
    vj1,vj2,dj : vector2 ;
    list : listpointer ;

PROCEDURE drawsegmentlist(vj1,vj2 : vector2 ) ;
{ Draw visible line segments }
VAR mu1,mu2 : real ;
    ptr,oldptr : listpointer ;
    vp1,vp2 : vector2 ;
BEGIN
  ptr := list ;
  WHILE ptr < > NIL
  DO BEGIN
{ Segment joins 'vp1' to 'vp2' }
          mu1 := ptr^.front ; mu2 := ptr^.back ;
          oldptr := ptr ; ptr := ptr^.pointer ; dispose(oldptr) ;
          vp1.x := (1-mu1)*vj1.x+mu1*vj2.x ;
          vp1.y := (1-mu1)*vj1.y+mu1*vj2.y ;
          vp2.x := (1-mu2)*vj1.x+mu2*vj2.x ;
          vp2.y := (1-mu2)*vj1.y+mu2*vj2.y ;
          IF (abs(vp1.x-vp2.x) > epsilon) OR (abs(vp1.y-vp2.y) > epsilon)
          THEN BEGIN
                  moveto(vp1) ; lineto(vp2)
               END
      END
END ; { of drawsegmentlist }

PROCEDURE adjustsegmentlist(mumin,mumax : real ) ;
{ Compare 'mu' values of each visible segment stored in 'list' }
{ with 'mumin' and 'mumax' of newly obscured segment and adjust list }
VAR newlist,ptr,newptr,oldptr : listpointer ;
    mu1,mu2 : real ;
BEGIN
  newlist := NIL ; ptr := list ;
  REPEAT
      mu1 := ptr^.front ; mu2 := ptr^.back ;
      IF (mu2 > mumin) AND (mu1 < mumax)
```

```
THEN BEGIN
          IF (mu1 < mumin)
          THEN BEGIN
                    new(newptr) ;
                    newptr^.front := mu1 ;
                    newptr^.back := mumin ;
                    newptr^.pointer := newlist ;
                    newlist := newptr
                END ;
          IF (mumax < mu2)
          THEN BEGIN
                    new(newptr) ;
                    newptr^.front := mumax ;
                    newptr^.back := mu2 ;
                    newptr^.pointer := newlist ;
                    newlist := newptr
                END
          END
     ELSE BEGIN
                    new(newptr) ;
                    newptr^.front := mu1 ;
                    newptr^.back := mu2 ;
                    newptr^.pointer := newlist ;
                    newlist := newptr
              END ;
     oldptr := ptr ;
     ptr := ptr^.pointer ; dispose(oldptr)
  UNTIL (ptr=NIL) ;
  list := newlist
END ; { of adjustsegmentlist }
PROCEDURE comparelinewithfacet(k : integer) ;
VAR kbegin,kend,l,lv1,lv2 : integer ;
    f1,f2,denom,disc,lambda,mu,mumid,mumin,mumax,nk : real ;
    d,dl,vmid : vector2 ;
    n,vhat : vector3 ;
BEGIN
{ Does line lie in facet 'k'. Compare with each line in facet 'k' }
  kbegin := facfront[k]+1 ; kend := facfront[k]+size[k] ;
{ Line 'l', facet 'k' joins vertices 'lv1' and 'lv2'. Direction 'dl' }
{ If line 'j' is the same as line 'l', consider next line 'j' }
  lv1 := faclist[kend] ;
  FOR l := kbegin TO kend
  DO BEGIN
          lv2 := faclist[l] ;
          IF (abs(dj.x*pro[lv1].y-dj.y*pro[lv1].x-djc) < epsilon)
              AND (abs(dj.x*pro[lv2].y-dj.y*pro[lv2].x-djc) < epsilon)
          THEN EXIT ;
          lv1 := lv2
       END ;
{ Now find if facet 'k' intersects the line }
     mumax := 0.0 ; mumin := 1.0 ;
{ Intersect edge 'l' of facet 'k' with chosen line }
     FOR l := kbegin TO kend
     DO BEGIN
          lv2 := faclist[l] ;
```

```
                    dl.x := pro[lv2].x-pro[lv1].x ;
                    dl.y := pro[lv2].y-pro[lv1].y ;
{ Lines 'j' and 'l' are parallel if 'disc' is zero }
                    disc := dl.x*dj.y-dj.x*dl.y ;
                    IF abs(disc) > epsilon
                    THEN BEGIN
{ Direction from 'vj1' to vertex 'lv1' is 'd' }
                         d.x := pro[lv1].x-vj1.x ;
                         d.y := pro[lv1].y-vj1.y ;
{ 'lambda' is intersection value on edge 'l' with line 'j' }
                         lambda := (dj.x*d.y-dj.y*d.x)/disc ;
{ 'lambda' must be between zero and one }
                         IF (lambda > -epsilon) AND (lambda < 1.0+epsilon)
                         THEN BEGIN
{ Equivalent intersection 'mu' value on line 'j' }
                              mu := (dl.x*d.y-dl.y*d.x)/disc ;
{ Update maximum and minimum 'mu' values }
                                   IF mumax<mu THEN mumax := mu ;
                                   IF mumin>mu THEN mumin := mu
                              END
                         END ;
                    lv1 := lv2
                    END ;
{ Ensure two distinct 'mu' values lying between zero and one }
          IF mumax > 1.0 THEN mumax := 1.0 ;
          IF mumin < 0.0 THEN mumin := 0.0 ;
          IF (mumax-mumin) < epsilon
          THEN EXIT ;
{ 'mumid' is 'mu' value of the mid point 'vmid' between them }
          mumid := (mumax+mumin)*0.5 ;
          vmid.x := (1-mumid)*vj1.x+mumid*vj2.x ;
          vmid.y := (1-mumid)*vj1.y+mumid*vj2.y ;
{ 'vhat' projects into 'vmid' }
          denom := -ppd*(obs[index2].x-obs[index1].x)
                        -vmid.x*(obs[index2].z-obs[index1].z) ;
          IF abs(denom) < epsilon
          THEN BEGIN
                    denom := -ppd*(obs[index2].y-obs[index1].y)
                             -vmid.y*(obs[index2].z-obs[index1].z) ;
                    mu := (vmid.y*obs[index1].z+ppd*obs[index1].y)/denom
               END
          ELSE mu := (vmid.x*obs[index1].z+ppd*obs[index1].x)/denom ;
          vhat.z := obs[index1].z+mu*(obs[index2].z-obs[index1].z) ;
          vhat.x := -vmid.x*vhat.z/ppd ;
          vhat.y := -vmid.y*vhat.z/ppd ;
{ Find normal to facet 'k' }
          normal(k,n,nk,obs) ;
{ Compare functional values of 'vhat' and 'eye' }
          f1 := n.x*vhat.x+n.y*vhat.y+n.z*vhat.z-nk ;
          f2 := -nk ;
          IF abs(f1) < epsilon THEN EXIT ;
          IF abs(sign(f1)-sign(f2)) <= 1 THEN EXIT ;
{ Section of line 'j' is obscured by facet 'k' }
          adjustsegmentlist(mumin,mumax)
END ; { of comparelinewithfacet }
```

```
BEGIN
{ 'epsilon' is the value that is assumed to be zero. This is }
{ sensitive to the word length of your computer, and to the }
{ 'horiz' value; so you may have to find your own 'epsilon' value.}
{ Setting 'horiz=1' for perspective gives our original 'epsilon' }
        epsilon := 0.000001*horiz ;
{ Take the lines from each clipped facet 'i'. Consider the line }
{ from vertex 'index1' to 'index2', where 'index1 < index2' if non-superficial }
{ face. Ignore lines on facets superficial to an invisible facet }
{ Routine only works in scenes where all objects are closed }
    FOR i := 1 TO nof
    DO BEGIN writeln(' facet ',i) ;
        IF (super[i] = 0) OR ((super[i] < >0) AND (orient(super[i],pro) = 1))
        THEN BEGIN
                    fbegin := facfront[i] +1 ;
                    fend := facfront[i] +size[i] ;
                    index1 := faclist[fend] ;
                    FOR j := fbegin TO fend
                    DO BEGIN
                            index2 := faclist[j] ;
                            IF (index1 < index2) OR (super[i] < > 0)
                            THEN BEGIN
{ 'vj1' and 'vj2' are the end points of the j'th projected line of i'th facet }
{ in 2-D space ; direction vector 'dj'. The line is 'y*dj.x=x*dj.y+djc' }
                                    vj1.x := pro[index1].x ; vj1.y := pro[index1].y ;
                                    vj2.x := pro[index2].x ; vj2.y := pro[index2].y ;
                                    dj.x := vj2.x-vj1.x ; dj.y := vj2.y-vj1.y ;
                                    djc := dj.x*vj1.y-dj.y*vj1.x ;
{ Initial line segment is the complete line }
{ (Exercise : 3-D CLIP here, to return clipped line in list). }
                                    new(list) ; list^.pointer := NIL ;
                                    list^.front := 0.0 ; list^.back := 1.0 ;
{ Compare line with every clipped visible facet 'k' }
{ Do not compare line with any superficial facet 'k' }
{ Check if facet 'i' is superficial to facet 'k' }
{ Exit loop if line totally obscured }
                                    k := 0 ;
                                    REPEAT
                                        k := k+1 ;
                                        IF (super[k] =0) AND (i< >k) AND (super[i] < >k)
{ Check if clipped facet 'k' is invisible }
                                        THEN IF(orient(k,pro) = 1)
                                                THEN comparelinewithfacet(k)
                                    UNTIL (k=nof) OR (list=NIL) ;
{ Draw line if part is visible }
                                    IF list < > NIL
                                    THEN drawsegmentlist(vj1,vj2)
                            END ;
{prepare next line 'j' }
                            index1 := index2
                    END
                END
        END
END ; { of hidden }
```

Listing 12.2

```
PROCEDURE normal(face:integer ; VAR n : vector3 ; VAR k : real ;
                 v : vertex3array) ;
{ To find the plane 'X*n.x+Y*n.y+Z*n.z=k' for facet 'face' }
VAR index1,index2,index3,fbegin : integer ;
    d1,d2 : vector3 ;
BEGIN
{ 'index1', 'index2' and 'index3' are first three vertices on 'face' }
    fbegin := facfront[face]+1 ; index1 := faclist[fbegin] ;
    index2 := faclist[fbegin+1] ; index3 := faclist[fbegin+2] ;
{ 'd1' and 'd2' are 3-D directions of the first two lines in 'face' }
    d1.x := v[index2].x-v[index1].x ;
    d1.y := v[index2].y-v[index1].y ;
    d1.z := v[index2].z-v[index1].z ;
    d2.x := v[index3].x-v[index2].x ;
    d2.y := v[index3].y-v[index2].y ;
    d2.z := v[index3].z-v[index2].z ;
{ Facet lies in plane ' n.v = k '}
    n.x := d1.y*d2.z-d2.y*d1.z ;
    n.y := d1.z*d2.x-d2.z*d1.x ;
    n.z := d1.x*d2.y-d2.x*d1.y ;
    k := n.x*v[index1].x+n.y*v[index1].y+n.z*v[index1].z
END ; { of normal }
```

Exercise 12.2

We are assuming that all lines on the object will be drawn on the screen, and no account is taken of two-dimensional clipping or for vertices being behind the eye. The first oversight is a simple one to correct. When the jth line of the ith facet is projected then it must be clipped to the window, and the μ values (if any) of the clipped line are stored as the original list values. Blanking can also be allowed for at this stage. Implement these ideas in listing 12.1. After reading chapter 14 return to the program and allow for three-dimensional clipping where objects can be behind as well as in front of the eye.

Example 12.1

Figure 12.2 shows two cubes defined in listing 7.7, drawn in perspective with the hidden lines removed. Note that if you wished to turn the cubes into two dice (example 10.4) then the database would not have space for all the vertices! You would have to expand it to cope with 2×342 vertices; however, you could reduce the facet space since you only need 2×27 facets.

Exercise 12.3

Draw figure 12.3, a crystallographic example (after Hauy, see Phillips (1960)), which shows how a rhombic dodecahedron can be approximated by a specially ordered stacking of cubes.

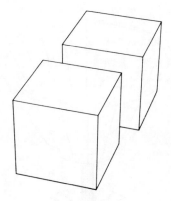

Figure 12.2

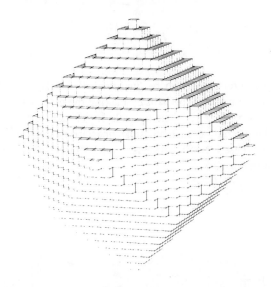

Figure 12.3

Exercise 12.4
Use the body of revolution methods of chapter 9 to draw a goblet with the hidden lines removed: figure 12.4.

Exercise 12.5
In some scenes you will find some abutting facets that are co-planar, as with the hollow cube of example 9.4. The lines of intersection of these co-planar facets would be drawn as visible when the hidden line algorithm is used. Ideally we

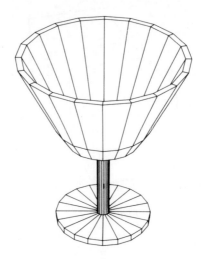

Figure 12.4

would wish these intersections to be 'invisible'. If we flag the edges of a facet that are meant to be invisible, perhaps by making the index (in the facet description) of the vertex at the end of the invisible edge negative, then the hidden line algorithm can be altered so such invisible lines are never considered, and thus never drawn. Use these ideas to produce complex architectural pictures such as the one given in figure 12.5.

Figure 12.5

Exercise 12.6

Write a general hidden line algorithm, without the restriction mentioned at the beginning of this chapter. You will have to pre-process the description for the scene in order to break down the data into extra facets, and introduce more invisible lines, so that your new scene definition is of a form acceptable to the routine written for exercise 12.5.

Exercise 12.7
Produce general hidden line algorithms for the orthographic and stereoscopic projections.

13 A More General Hidden Surface Algorithm

By now you should be aware that there are many different types of hidden line and/or surface algorithm (Sutherland *et al.*, 1974). One variety involves a rectangular array representing the totality of pixels on the screen. We imagine rays of light entering the eye through each of the pixels on the screen. These rays naturally pass through objects in our scene and we can note the co-ordinates of these points of intersection. The array will hold the 'z co-ordinate' (initially minus infinity) of the nearest point of intersection. So we build up a picture by adding new objects, finding where the rays cut the object, and changing the array values (and the pixel colour on the screen) whenever the latest point of intersection is nearer the eye than the corresponding value stored in the array. This technique is very useful if we wish to shade-in areas in subtly differing tones of a given colour (chapter 15). It does, however, have enormous storage requirements and needs a very powerful computer. In this chapter we give another type of general algorithm more suitable for use with small computer systems and raster-scan display devices, which works on the 'back-to-front' principle mentioned earlier.

We assume that a three-dimensional scene is set up in the manner described in chapter 7, and that the hidden surface algorithm is to be initiated in the **drawit** routine which is called from the **scene** routine. We will assume that the perspective projection is being used: as an exercise, equivalent routines can be written for the orthographic projection. We assume that all objects are closed. They need not be convex but each must be closed and its surface composed of *convex* facets which are stored in anti-clockwise orientation. Thus it is impossible to see the underside of any facet — that is, when projected onto the view plane we only see facets which maintain their anti-clockwise orientation. Strictly speaking, this means that we cannot draw planar objects. If these are required for a particular scene then we avoid the problem by storing each facet of a planar object twice — once clockwise and once anti-clockwise — so whatever the position of the eye, on perspective projection we will see one and only one occurrence of the facet. This restriction was imposed to speed up the hidden surface algorithm.

In order to produce a hidden surface picture of a scene stored in terms of right-handed OBSERVED co-ordinates, each facet in the scene must be compared with every other facet (superficial facets excepted) in order to discover

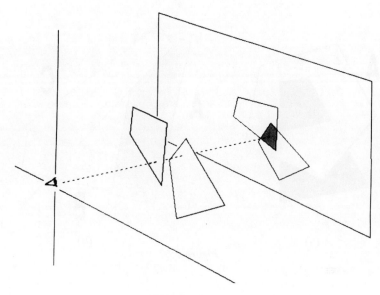

Figure 13.1

whether their projections overlap on the view plane. If this occurs, then one of the facets obscures all or part of the other from view (see figure 13.1).

Because of the above restrictions we need only compare the visible facets — that is, those which when projected keep their anti-clockwise orientation. If they do overlap we then need to find which facet lies in front and which behind. Once this information is compiled we can work from the back of the scene to the front to get a correct hidden surface picture. We do have other limitations: we assume that it is impossible for a facet to be simultaneously in front of and behind another facet; that is, facets do not intersect one another other than at their edges, and we cannot have situations where facet A is in front of ($>$) facet B $>$ facet C $>$ facet A etc., see figure 13.2.

Exercise 13.1
The program can be made completely general if you write a routine which pre-processes the data and divides up each problem facet into new subfacets that do not violate restrictions of the above type.

Our algorithm for discovering whether two facets (m and n) from our data-base do overlap when projected onto the view plane is given in routine **overlap** in listing 13.1. It is a variation of the two-dimensional **overlap** routine of listing 5.8. The method finds the intersection of the projected facets (if any) and identifies the facet nearer the eye (**front**) and that further away (**back**). This information for all comparisons of pairs of facets in the scene enables us to set up a network as described in chapter 2. The complete network is constructed in

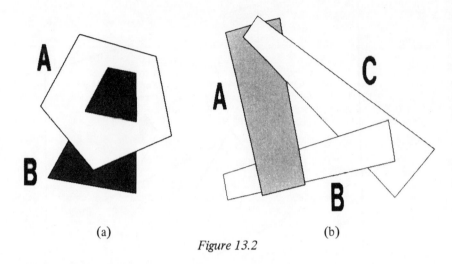

(a)   (b)

Figure 13.2

routine **network** which uses **overlap** to discover if facet **m** is in front of facet **n**, in which case an edge is added to the network leading from node **n** to node **m**. We introduce a new **hidden** routine which executes a topological sort on this network to output the facets in back-to-front order, calling **seefacet** to draw each, along with associated superficial facets. We use the same **drawit** routine as given in listing 10.1 to initiate the hidden surface algorithm.

The **overlap** routine uses the inside/outside technique of chapter 5. We place the x and y co-ordinates of the projected vertices of facet **m** in **vector2array** **f[1, 1..size[m]]**. We then take one projected line from facet **n** and cut off all parts of the facet **m** that lie on the negative side of the line: the resulting polygon is placed in arrays **f[2, 1..numv]**, where **numv** is the number of vertices in the polygon of intersection. We then take the next line and compare it with these values and store the resulting polygon in **f[1, ..]** etc. After all the lines from facet **m** have been used then we are left with the polygon common to both projected facets. If at any time this polygon becomes empty we know that the projected facets do not overlap and so we exit the procedure setting **front = 0**.

If the facets do overlap then we take a line from the eye to intersect a point inside the common polygon on the view plane and find the intersections of this line with facets m and n: the point we choose is the median of the first three points on the polygon. Comparing the z co-ordinates of the respective intersections enables us to discover which of m and n is in **front** and which is at **back**. The co-ordinates of the vertices of the area of overlap are returned in the array **v2d**. The **overlap** routine has more parameters than are strictly needed at this stage, allowing for use with different co-ordinate systems. These will be needed for use by shadow, transparency and reflection routines in chapter 16.

Listing 13.1

```
PROCEDURE overlap(m1,n1 : integer ; VAR front,back,numv : integer ;
                  VAR v2d : vector2array ; p : vertex2array ;
                  v3d : vertex3array ; orientation : integer) ;
{ Finds area of intersection between the window projections of facets }
{ 'm1' and 'n1'. The 3-D co-ordinate system is given by array 'v3d', }
{ while projected co-ordinates are stored in 'p'. The 'nv' vertices }
{ of the intersection area are returned in arrays 'v2d' }
VAR musto : ARRAY[1..2] OF real ;
    i,j,l,m,n,sizem,sizen,l1,l2,index1,index2,insect : integer ;
    f : ARRAY[1..2,1..vectorarraysize] OF vector2 ;
    k,ca,cb,cc,fv1,absfv1,fv2,absfv2,denom,mu : real ;
    e1,e2,v1,v2 : vector2 ;
    mid,norm,vi : vector3 ;
BEGIN
{ 'm' and 'n' are the indices of the facets representing 'm1' and 'n1' }
   m := nfac[m1] ;n := nfac[n1] ;
{ Copy facet 'm' to first storage arrays }
   l1 := 1 ; sizem := size[m] ;
{ If plane 'm1' is degenerate return }
   FOR i := 1 TO sizem
   DO f[l1,i] := p[faclist[facfront[m]+i]] ;
{ The first storage array 'f[l1,1..sizem]' now contains vertices of the }
{ feasible polygon. Slice feasible polygon with each edge of facet 'n'. }
{ Slicing edge has endpoints 'e1' and 'e2' with analytic function }
{              ' ca.y + cb.x + cc = 0 ' .              }
   sizen := size[n] ; e1 := p[faclist[facfront[n]+sizen]] ;
   FOR i := 1 TO sizen
   DO BEGIN
        e2 := p[faclist[facfront[n]+i]] ;
        ca := e2.x-e1.x ; cb := e1.y-e2.y ;
        cc := -ca*e1.y-cb*e1.x ;
{ Slice the feasible polygon edge by edge : 'v1' to 'v2'. 'k1' and 'k2' }
{ indicate whether the first and second points respectively lie on the }
{ slicing edge, on its positive side or on its negative side. }
        v1 := f[l1,sizem] ; fv1 := ca*v1.y+cb*v1.x+cc ;
        absfv1 := abs(fv1) ;
        IF absfv1 < epsilon
        THEN index1 := 0
        ELSE index1 := sign(fv1)*orientation ;
{ Initialise second storage array. }
        numv := 0 ; l2 := 3-l1 ;
        FOR j := 1 TO sizem
        DO BEGIN
             v2 := f[l1,j] ; fv2 := ca*v2.y+cb*v2.x+cc ;
             absfv2 := abs(fv2) ;
             IF absfv2 < epsilon
             THEN index2 := 0
             ELSE index2 := sign(fv2)*orientation ;
{ If 'v1' is not on negative side of slicing edge then include it }
{ in new storage array 'f[l2,...]' }
             IF index1 >= 0
```

```
            THEN BEGIN
                    numv := numv+1 ; f[l2,numv] := v1
            END ;

{ If 'v1' and 'v2' lie on opposite sides of slicing edge then }
{ include the intersection with the edge }
            IF (index1 < >0) AND (index1 < >index2) AND (index2 < >0)
            THEN BEGIN
                    denom := absfv1+absfv2 ; numv := numv+1 ;
                    f[l2,numv].x := (absfv2*v1.x+absfv1*v2.x)/denom ;
                    f[l2,numv].y := (absfv2*v1.y+absfv1*v2.y)/denom
            END ;
{ Second point on current edge becomes first point on next edge }
            fv1 := fv2 ; v1 := v2 ;
            index1 := index2 ; absfv1 := absfv2 ;
        END ;
{ If second array holds fewer than 3 vertices then no overlap exists }
    IF (numv < 3)
    THEN BEGIN front := 0 ; EXIT
        END ;
{ Feasible polygon now becomes that stored in second storage array }
{ Refer 'l1' to this polygon and slice with next edge of facet 'n' }
        sizem := numv ; l1 := l2 ; e1 := e2
    END ;
{ Reach here if non-empty overlap found. Find point within area of overlap }
    mid.x := (f[l1,1].x+f[l1,2].x+f[l1,3].x)/3 ;
    mid.y := (f[l1,1].y+f[l1,2].y+f[l1,3].y)/3 ;
{ Find corresponding points on facets in 3-D }
    mid.z := -ppd ; l := m1 ;
    FOR i := 1 TO 2
    DO BEGIN
        normal(l,norm,k,v3d) ;
        ilpl(zero,mid,norm,vi,k,mu,insect) ;
        musto[i] := mu ; l := n1
    END ;
{ Determine which lies in 'front' }
    IF musto[1] > musto[2]
    THEN BEGIN
            front := n1 ; back := m1
        END
    ELSE BEGIN
            front := m1 ; back := n1
        END ;
{ Copy area of overlap to arrays for exit }
    FOR i := 1 TO numv
    DO BEGIN
        v2d[i] := f[l1,i]
    END
END ; { of overlap }


PROCEDURE hidden ;
{ Executes topological sort on hidden surface network }
TYPE stackpointer = ^stacknode ;
     stacknode = RECORD info : integer ;
                        ptr : stackpointer
                 END ;
```

```
        pointarray = ARRAY[1..maxf] OF stackpointer ;
VAR i,k,numbervisible : integer ;
    nob {,rnob for reflections }: facetarray ;
    list {,rlist for reflections } : pointarray ;
    networkstack : stackpointer ;

PROCEDURE stackpush(VAR stack : stackpointer ; stackvalue : integer) ;
{ Routine to 'push' the integer 'stackvalue' onto the 'stack' }
VAR p : stackpointer ;
BEGIN
{ create new node for 'stack' }
    new(p) ; p^.info := stackvalue ;
    p^.ptr := stack ; stack := p
END ; { of stackpush }

PROCEDURE stackpop(VAR stack : stackpointer ; VAR stackvalue : integer) ;
{ Routine to 'pop' the 'stackvalue' from the 'stack' }
VAR p : stackpointer ;
BEGIN
    IF stack = NIL
    THEN writeln(' Stack is empty')
    ELSE BEGIN
            p := stack ; stackvalue := stack^.info ;
{ Delete front element of 'stack', and dispose }
            stack := stack^.ptr ; dispose(p)
        END
END ; { of stackpop }


PROCEDURE network(VAR numvis : integer ; VAR nob : facetarray ;
                  VAR list : pointarray ; v : vertex3array ;
                  p : vertex2array ; orientation : integer ) ;
{ Constructs network of information on hidden surface ordering }
VAR back,front,i,j,n : integer ;
    w : vector2array ;
BEGIN
{ Initialise number of visible facets }
    numvis := 0 ;
{ Check orientation of each facet, incrementing 'numvis' by one for }
{ each visible one (using 'orientation'). }
    FOR i := 1 TO nof
    DO IF orient(i,p) = orientation
        THEN BEGIN
                nob[i] := 0 ; list[i] := NIL ;
                IF super[i]=0 THEN numvis := numvis+1
            END
        ELSE nob[i] := -1 ;
{ Compare each pair of visible non-superficial facets }
    FOR i := 1 TO nof-1
    DO BEGIN
        writeln(' Considering facet ',i) ;
        IF (nob[i] <> -1) AND (super[i]=0)
        THEN FOR j := i+1 TO nof
                DO IF (nob[j] <> -1) AND (super[j]=0)
                    THEN BEGIN
                            overlap(i,j,front,back,n,w,p,v,orientation) ;
```

```
{ If overlap exists then 'front' obscures 'back' }
                    IF front < > 0
                    THEN BEGIN
                            nob[front] := nob[front]+1 ;
                            stackpush(list[back],front)
                         END
                END
        END
END ; { of network }

PROCEDURE unstack(face : integer ; VAR nob : facetarray ;
                  VAR list : pointarray ; VAR stack : stackpointer) ;
{ Adjusts network structure after 'face' has been drawn}
VAR nf : integer ;
BEGIN
    WHILE list[face] < > NIL
    DO BEGIN
            stackpop(list[face],nf) ;
            nob[nf] := nob[nf]-1 ;
            IF nob[nf]=0
            THEN stackpush(stack,nf)
        END
END ; { of unstack }


{ Declare PROCEDURE 'reflekt' (listing 16.6) here for mirror reflections }

BEGIN
{ Set up the network data structure }
    network(numbervisible,nob,list,obs,pro,1) ;
{ Initialise STACK and PUSH on all back facets }
        networkstack := NIL ;
        FOR I := 1 TO nof
        DO IF (nob[i]=0) AND (super[i]=0)
           THEN stackpush(networkstack,i) ;
{ pop 'numbervisible' facets off stack in turn.}
{ Draw each and adjust data structure }
        FOR I := 1 TO numbervisible
        DO BEGIN
                stackpop(networkstack,k) ;
                IF k=0 THEN EXIT ;
                seefacet(k) ;
{ Add following line when using 'hidden' to draw mirror reflections }
{           IF (tr[colour[k]]<0.0) THEN reflekt(k) ;                    }
                unstack(k,nob,list,networkstack)
            END
END ; { of hidden }
```

The next step is to work out how to use this information to produce the network needed for the final picture. This is achieved by network in listing 13.1. The method is to compare each visible facet with every other (using overlap) and to produce a network of information about the relative positions of the facets (in front or behind). For each visible and non-superficial facet (i say), the idea is to set up a linked list list[i] containing the indices of all facets that lie in front of it, and the array nob[i] will contain the number of facets that facet i obscures. Array **nob** is also used initially to denote if the facet is clockwise and hence invisible (nob[i] = −1), or anti-clockwise and visible (nob[i] = 0). No invisible facet need be included in any comparison. The routine **network** returns the number of visible facets **numbervisible**, together with all of the network edge information. Once again, the co-ordinate arrays are passed as parameters to enable the routine to be used with different co-ordinate systems. We use this network in routine **hidden** to produce a picture. The routine creates a stack onto which the index of any facet that does not obscure any other (that is, whose **nob** value is zero) is pushed. Then one at a time these facets are popped off the stack and drawn on the viewport followed by all the facets that are superficial to it (using the **super** array). Once the facet is drawn, we go down the network linked list for that facet (referred to by **list**) and decrement the **nob** counts for each facet in the list. If the **nob** count for any facet becomes zero then the index of the facet is pushed onto the stack (routine **unstack**). Eventually the stack is emptied and we have the correct partial order to give the true back-to-front hidden surface view. Each facet is drawn in the viewport using a routine **seefacet**, which also displays all associated superficial facets. At this stage it will simply use the polygon drawing routine via a call to **facetfill** (listing 10.4); later it will become more complex.

The linked lists (one for each facet) and the stack are implemented using Pascal pointers, as described in chapter 2. Because of our restriction that facets cannot simultaneously be in front of and behind one another, the stack can only become empty when all the facets have been displayed. Note that we can turn the hidden surface procedure into a hidden line procedure by having a plain background and drawing each facet in the same (background) colour but with the edges of the facet in a different colour.

Example 13.1
We can now draw a hidden surface, perspective view of the cube in figure 10.1 still using the general-purpose **drawit** routine of listing 10.1 but now using the **hidden** of listing 13.1 rather than one given in chapter 10. Placing the data for two cubes (example 8.2) in the database, we can draw figure 13.3 with this routine, impossible with the restricted hidden surface routine of chapter 10.

Exercise 13.2
Construct hidden surface views of scenes composed of cubes, tetrahedra, pyramids, octahedra and icosahedra. See Coxeter (1973) for the information needed to write construction routines for an octahedron, icosahedron, rhombic dodecahedron etc.

Exercise 13.3
Experiment with this routine using the objects generated in chapter 9. For example, create a scene composed of two objects defined in that chapter: a hollow cube containing a star-shaped object as shown in figure 13.4.

Figure 13.3

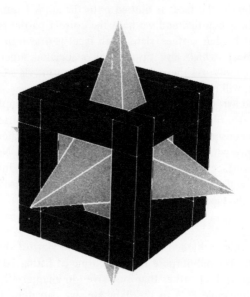

Figure 13.4

Figures such as the camera in Plate I can be drawn and so we are now in a position to consider methods for making our three-dimensional scenes more realistic. We first need to introduce three-dimensional clipping, before introducing such ideas as shading, shadows, reflections etc. Note, however, that all of these ideas are introduced in the context of our overall strategy for scene construction. You will see that the introduction of shadows etc. into scenes that have already been defined and drawn will not require a major rewrite of the previous programs, so that the generation of shadows etc. will be initiated by simple extensions to drawit and perhaps extended alternative facetfill routines. With the exception of some database entries, most other routines, scene, network etc., will remain unchanged and the method of linking the display of complex models ultimately to the primitive routines of chapter 1 is still via the draw_a_picture call to scene.

14 Three-dimensional Clipping

In chapter 5 we considered the clipping of lines and facets in two-dimensional space, determining which parts lay within a rectangular window with dimensions horiz x vert. These methods are also sufficient for dealing with orthographic projections of three-dimensional scenes since the whole of space can be projected onto the view plane and clipped in two dimensions. Dealing with perspective projections is rather more complex. Once again we assume that we have a view plane some distance from the eye along the negative z-axis of the right-handed OBSERVER system. A rectangular (horiz x vert) window on this plane is to be identified with the graphics viewport. In previous chapters we have assumed that the eye is positioned in such a way that each vertex has a strictly negative OBSERVED z co-ordinate. This ensures that every vertex can be projected onto the view plane by a standard perspective projection as defined in chapter 11, whence two-dimensional clipping ascertains which parts of the image lie totally within the window. Suppose, however, that we wish to depict a scene as viewed from a position within the model, such as a point lying in a landscape with a large ground plane. Clearly, parts of the model will lie behind the eye and consequently cannot be projected onto the view plane. Such problems cannot be resolved by two-dimensional clipping and so extended methods must be developed. *Three-dimensional clipping* must determine which parts of a line or facet can be projected onto the window *before* the projection occurs. The perspective projection and subsequent hidden line or surface elimination must be executed upon the clipped scene and hence the information generated by the clipping process must be incorporated into the data structure.

There are consequently two problems that need to be solved. Firstly, we must determine which part, if any, of a line or facet lies in the volume of space projected onto the window, and secondly we must incorporate this information into the data structure representing the scene.

We shall consider only the algorithm for clipping facets for area-fill displays; the application to line drawing is set as an exercise at the end of the chapter. The routines required for clipping are entirely self-contained and are incorporated into the program by a simple extension of the **drawit** routine (listing 14.2).

The Pyramid of Vision

The volume of three-dimensional space which is projected onto the window is a rectangular pyramid of infinite length. This pyramid, which we call the *pyramid of vision*, has its apex at the eye position (the origin of the OBSERVER co-ordinate system) and four infinite edges, each passing through one vertex of the window on the view plane. It is thus bounded by four planes (*clipping planes*), each of which contains the OBSERVER origin and one edge of the rectangular window.

We number the clipping planes as shown in figure 14.1, from 1 to 4 starting from the top plane and moving round clockwise as viewed from the eye position. A point, (x, y, z), lying within the pyramid of vision is projected, by perspective projection, onto the point $(-x \times d/z, -y \times d/z)$ in the window (d is the perpendicular distance from the eye to the view plane).

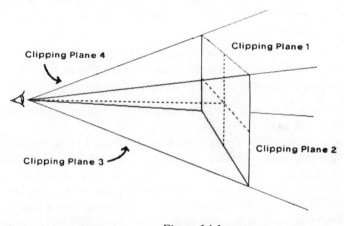

Figure 14.1

Each clipping plane divides space into two halves. The half-space containing the pyramid of vision is said to be the *visible side* of the plane. The four clipping planes must be represented in such a way that we may easily determine whether a point lies on their visible side or not. Consider first clipping plane 1. This plane passes through the top horizontal edge of the view plane window and is therefore perpendicular to the y/z plane. The x orthographic projection of this plane is shown in figure 14.2.

If a point (x, y, z) lies in this plane we must have, by similar triangles

$$\frac{y}{-z} = \frac{\text{vert}}{2d} = \tan \theta_v \text{ (say) so } y = -\tan \theta_v \times z$$

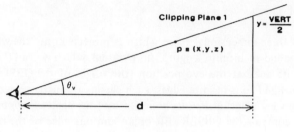

Figure 14.2

and hence for any point lying below the plane, on the visible side

$$y < -\tan\theta_v \times z$$

and for any point above the plane

$$y > -\tan\theta_v \times z$$

Clearly this extends directly to the other three clipping planes. Plane number 3 is defined as above with the angle $-\theta_v$ which has tangent $-\tan\theta_v$ and hence we may derive parameters

On the plane: $y = \tan\theta_v \times z$
Above the plane (on the visible side): $y > \tan\theta_v \times z$
Below the plane (not on the visible side): $y < \tan\theta_v \times z$

and the two vertical clipping planes, 2 and 4, may be treated likewise, using the angle θ_h which has tangent horiz/$2d$.

For a point to lie within the pyramid of vision it must be on the visible side of all four clipping planes. If the z co-ordinate of a point is greater than 0 then it is behind the eye and so cannot be on the visible side of all four clipping planes: if it lies on the visible side of one clipping plane, then it must be on the invisible side of the opposite clipping plane. The routine locate (listing 14.1) determines whether each vertex of a facet lies on the visible side of a given clipping plane and stored the results in the integerarray inside. inside[i] is set to 1 if vertex i lies on the visible side of the clipping plane, 0 if it lies in the plane and -1 if on the other side. The index of vertex i is stored in the array location kfacet[I, i]. The meaning of this array will be explained in due course but for the moment we just note its declaration in the global database:

{VAR} kfacet : ARRAY[1..2, 1..vectorarraysize] of integer;

Any clipping routine in three dimensions must involve the calculation of the point of intersection of a given line with a clipping plane. This problem has already been solved in chapter 6, given two points on the line and the standard vector form for the plane. We must, therefore, determine the vector equations for the clipping planes. Recall that the vector equation of a plane is of the form $n \cdot v = k$ for any point v on the plane, where n is the normal vector to the plane and $k = n \cdot a$ for any fixed point a lying in the plane. Since all four clipping planes pass through the origin we may take $k = n \cdot O = 0$ for all n, so each plane has the form $n \cdot v = 0$. All that remains, therefore, is to determine the normal vector, n, to each.

Once more we shall consider the top clipping plane first and the results derived from this enable us to find the normals to the other three planes.

Since the top clipping plane is perpendicular to the y/z plane, its normal is parallel to the y/z plane and so has zero x co-ordinate. The line of intersection of the clipping plane with the y/z plane has direction $(0, \tan \theta_v, -1)$ and so the normal vector is perpendicular to this line: $(0, -1, -\tan \theta_v)$. (The sense of the normal vector is not important in this instance.)

Accordingly, the normals to the other three planes are

> Clipping plane 2: $(-1, 0, -\tan \theta_h)$
> Clipping plane 3: $(0, -1, \tan \theta_v)$
> Clipping plane 4: $(-1, 0, \tan \theta_h)$

Exercise 14.1

If desired, it is a relatively simple task to further constrain the visible part of space by adding a front and/or back clipping plane. These planes will both be perpendicular to the z-axis (which consequently forms the normal to each) and have constant z-coordinate z_f and z_b respectively, say. A point is thus on the visible side of the front clipping plane if $z < z_f$ and on the visible side of the back clipping plane if $z > z_b$. The normal to both planes is, as mentioned above, the direction $(n_x, n_y, n_z) \equiv (0, 0, 1)$ and the equations have k values $n_z \times z_f$ ($= z_f$) and $n_z \times z_b$ ($= z_b$) for front and back planes respectively. In our programs we do not use a front or back clipping plane but it is a useful exercise to incorporate them into the routines, calling them clipping planes 5 and 6.

Polygon Clipping in Three Dimensions

We may now tackle the clipping of a convex polygon in three dimensions in a manner exactly analogous to the polygon clip routine for two dimensions described in chapter 5. The facet is sliced in turn by each of the clipping planes, whether four or six, and the resulting polygon either degenerates into a polygon with fewer than three vertices, in which case it lies entirely outside the pyramid of vision, or, having been sliced by all clipping planes, it represents the visible portion of the facet, notwithstanding the other facets in the scene.

The information produced by the clipping process must be incorporated into the data structure representing the scene. At the end of the clipping of a facet there are three possible outcomes

(i) The facet remains unchanged since it lay entirely within the pyramid of vision.

(ii) The facet degenerates on clipping and is therefore not visible since it lay entirely outside the pyramid of vision.

(iii) We are left with a new facet consisting of that part of the original facet which lay inside the pyramid of vision.

Information regarding clipped facets must not corrupt the original data. Recall that the original model has nov vertices and nof facets. The total numbers of vertices and facets, inclusive of any which may be created during the processing of the model, are stored as ntv and ntf respectively. The OBSERVED co-ordinates of the vertices are stored in the obs array, and pointers to these arrays are stored in the database as the array faclist through which the facets are defined by the arrays start and size. These are the facets of the original model prior to clipping. Each facet also has an associated pointer nfac. We may use this pointer to refer to a new facet created by the clipping process which is stored at the end of the faclist array in the database. Initially nfac[i] is set to i for each facet i, thus referring to the polygon defined in the original model.)

Suppose we are clipping facet i. If case (i) above occurs we have no problem — the data structure remains unchanged. If case (ii) occurs then the facet must not be drawn and hence need not be considered in the hidden surface elimination algorithm. We indicate this fact by setting nfac[i] to zero. In subsequent processes we use this fact to indicate that facet i lay entirely outside the pyramid of vision — it need neither be drawn nor considered in the hidden surface algorithm but we shall find later, when dealing with shadows, that it cannot be ignored entirely! Note that in setting nfac[i] to zero we do not affect in any way the information in the database which defines facet i. Pointers to its vertices are still stored in the faclist array and are accessible via start[i] and size[i], and in order to restore the structure to its original form we need only reset nfac[i] to equal i.

Now consider case (iii). Suppose that facet i lies partially inside the pyramid of vision. A new facet is created which represents that part of facet i within the pyramid. We store the information concerning this new facet in the next free portions of the relevant arrays of the database, updating ntv and ntf. nfac[i] is referred to this new facet which is then used instead of facet i in both hidden surface elimination and in the final drawing of the object. We must take some care in doing this however, primarily ensuring that the information describing the original, unclipped, model is not destroyed, and also we must try to be as undemanding as possible on extra storage space. It would be easy simply to create a brand new set of vertices for the clipped facet and place these *en bloc* at the end of the obs array in the database, but this could necessitate raising the value of maxv. In many cases, however, only one vertex of the original is clipped out, resulting in only two new vertices being created. We must, therefore, strive to use as much of the original information as possible.

The first requirement is that vertex co-ordinates are not simply copied into new arrays as they are in the two-dimensional clipping routine, but instead we use an array of pointers to the co-ordinate values in the **obs** array. We therefore introduce a two-dimensional storage array **kfacet** which shall be used in exactly the same manner as the previously used **f** array (listing 13.1), except that they contain integer indices of vertices rather than raw co-ordinates. We use two variables, **l1** and **l2**, to distinguish the two portions of the **kfacet** array. Initially **l1** is set to 1 and **l2** to 2.

At the start of the process of clipping facet i, the content of the **faclist** array from **faclist[start[i]** + **1]** to **faclist[start[i]** + **size[i]**] are copied to **kfacet[l1,1..ksize]**, the variable **ksize** being set to equal **size[i]**. The polygon described by the **kfacet** array is therefore facet i. A new variable **nnv** is also introduced at this stage to record the total number of vertices in the model prior to the clipping of facet i. Its value is therefore set to **ntv**.

The facet is clipped by each of the four clipping planes in turn. The polygon defined by **kfacet[l1,1..ksize]** is clipped and indices of the vertices of the resulting polygon are stored as **kfacet[l2,1..n]**. Any new vertices created by the clipping are appended to the **obs** array and **ntv** incremented accordingly. The values of **l1** and **l2** are then swapped **ksize** set to equal **n**, and the process is repeated with the next clipping plane.

At the end of the clipping process we have an array of pointers referring to the vertices of a new facet which may contain a subset of the original vertices together with some new vertices. Once again a number of different cases may arise, each corresponding to one of the three cases outlined above. Firstly, the number of vertices in the reduced polygon may become less than three, indicating that the facet lay completely outside the pyramid of vision. In this case the clipping process may stop — a real gain, particularly if not all of the clipping planes have been used. **nfac[i]** is set to 0 and any new vertices which may have been created can be ignored (by setting **ntv** back to **nnv**) and subsequently overwritten. If this does not happen and no new vertices are created (**ntv** = **nnv**) then the original facet lay completely within the pyramid of vision and no changes need be made to the data structure. The interesting situation, case (iii) above, arises when the final polygon contains at least one new vertex. The new facet must be copied into the database arrays and be referred to by **nfac[i]**. It is by no means certain, however, that all of the new vertices created during the clipping process will be included in the final polygon — many may themselves be clipped out later. We therefore introduce a form of garbage collector into the routine for filtering out those vertices which have been created but not ultimately used (see listing 14.1).

A facet is clipped by the routine **clip** in listing 14.1 which is called for each facet of the scene in turn (including superficial facets) by the routine **clipscene**. The three different cases which may arise from the clipping routine are denoted by a flag **clipindex** which is returned from **clip** with value 1, 2 or 3 corresponding to cases (i), (ii) and (iii) respectively. **clip** creates a new facet, if necessary, and stores it as facet **ntf**. The management of the **nfac** pointers is then carried out by the calling routine **clipscene**.

Listing 14.1

```
VAR
   kfacet : ARRAY[1..2,1..vectorarraysize] OF integer ;
   ksize : integer ;
   inside : integerarray ;

PROCEDURE locate(l,flag : integer ; tth : real ; o : vertex3array );
{ 'flag' (1 or 2) indicates x or y co-ordinates }
{ 'tth' is the tangent of relevant angle }
{ For each vertex 'j', 'inside[j]' is returned as follows: }
{      'inside[j] = 1' if 'j' lies on the visible side of clipping plane   }
{      'inside[j] = -1' if 'j' lies on the invisible side                  }
{      'inside[j] = 0' if 'j' lies in the plane                            }
VAR stth,abstth,coord : real ;
    i,j : integer ;
BEGIN
   stth := sign(tth) ; abstth := abs(tth) ;
   FOR i := 1 TO ksize
   DO BEGIN
         inside[i] := 0 ; j := kfacet[l,i] ;
         IF flag = 1
         THEN coord := o[j].x
         ELSE coord := o[j].y ;
         IF coord*stth < -abstth*o[j].z THEN inside[i] :=  1 ;
         IF coord*stth > -abstth*o[j].z THEN inside[i] := -1
      END
END ; { of locate}

PROCEDURE clip(k : integer ; VAR clipindex : integer) ;
{ Clips facet 'k' }
VAR i,j,n,l1,l2,f,s,nnv,inter,insect,kfi : integer ;
    np : integerarray ;
    base,dir,ipt,norm : vector3 ;
    rval : real ;
BEGIN
{ 'nnv' is total number of vertices prior to clipping facet 'k'}
   nnv := ntv ;
{ Copy pointers to facet vertices into first section of 'kfacet' array }
   ksize := size[k] ; l1 := 1 ;
   FOR i := 1 TO ksize
   DO kfacet[l1,i] := faclist[facfront[k]+i] ;
{ Loop through clipping planes 1 to 4 }
   FOR i := 1 TO 4
   DO BEGIN
         n := 0 ;
{ Find 'norm'al vector of clipping plane and 'in' value of each vertex }
         norm.x := -((i-1) MOD 2) ; norm.y := -(i MOD 2) ;
         IF abs(norm.x) < epsilon
         THEN BEGIN
{ Horizontal clipping plane }
                 norm.z := vert*(i-2)/(2*ppd) ;
                 locate(l1,2,-norm.z,obs)
              END
```

```
                  ELSE BEGIN
        { Vertical clipping plane }
                          norm.z := horiz*(i-3)/(2*ppd) ;
                          locate(l1,1,-norm.z,obs)
                      END ;
            l2 := 3-l1 ; f := ksize ;
    { Slice facet defined by 'kfacet' array with clipping plane 'i' }
    { Consider facet edge joining vertices 'f'(first) and 's'(second) }
              FOR j := 1 TO ksize
              DO BEGIN
                    s := j ;
    { If vertex 'f' is 'inside' then include in new facet }
                  IF inside[f] > =0
                  THEN BEGIN
                              n := n+1 ; kfacet[l2,n] := kfacet[l1,f]
                          END ;
    { If vertices 'f' and 's' are on opposite sides of the plane then }
    { find the intersection of the edge with the plane and include. }
                  IF inside[f]*inside[s] = -1
                  THEN BEGIN
                              base := obs[kfacet[l1,f]] ;
                              dir.x := obs[kfacet[l1,s]].x-base.x ;
                              dir.y := obs[kfacet[l1,s]].y-base.y ;
                              dir.z := obs[kfacet[l1,s]].z-base.z ;
                              ilpl(base,dir,norm,ipt,0.0,rval,insect) ;
                              ntv := ntv+1 ; obs[ntv] := ipt ;
                              n := n+1 ; kfacet[l2,n] := ntv
                          END ;
                    f := s
                  END ;
    { If new facet empty the stop }
            IF n <= 2
            THEN BEGIN
                      clipindex := 2 ; ntv := nnv ; EXIT
                  END
            ELSE BEGIN
                      ksize := n ; l1 := l2
                  END
          END ;
    { Reach here if non-empty facet remains. If new vertices have been }
    { created then sort them and store new facet }
      IF ntv > nnv
      THEN BEGIN
                clipindex := 3 ;
                FOR i := 1 TO ksize
                DO np[i] := i ;
                n := nnv ; ntf := ntf+1 ; facfront[ntf] := last ;
                size[ntf] := ksize ;
    { Storage of vertices with garbage collection: }
    { Sort contents of 'kfacet' array into increasing order }
                FOR i := 1 TO ksize
                DO BEGIN
                      IF i < ksize
                      THEN FOR j := i+1 TO ksize
                            DO IF kfacet[l1,np[i]] > kfacet[l1,np[j]]
```

```
THEN BEGIN
        inter := np[i] ; np[i] := np[j] ;
        np[j] := inter
    END ;

{ If vertex is new (i.e. 'index > nnv') then place in next available }
{ location, else refer to old location }
                kfi := kfacet[l1,np[i]] ;
                IF kfi > nnv
                THEN BEGIN
                        n := n+1 ; obs[n] := obs[kfi] ;
                        faclist[facfront[ntf] + np[i]] := n
                    END
                ELSE faclist[facfront[ntf] + np[i]] := kfi
            END ;
        ntv := n ; last := last + size[ntf]
    END
  ELSE  clipindex := 1
{ If no new vertices created then no clipping was needed }
END ; { of clip }

PROCEDURE clipscene ;
VAR i,clipindex : integer ;
BEGIN
    ppd := 3.0*horiz ;
    FOR i := 1 TO nof
    DO BEGIN
        clip(i,clipindex) ;
        IF clipindex = 3
        THEN nfac[i] := ntf
        ELSE IF clipindex = 2
                THEN nfac[i] := 0
    END
END ; { of clipscene }
```

The routine facetfill (listing 10.4) now draws clipped facets rather than the whole facet.

The State of the Data Structure

Let us take an overview of the data structure as it stands after the three-dimensional clipping. The vertex counts nov and ntv refer respectively to the number of vertices in the original model and the total number of vertices inclusive of all those created by clipping. Thus nov ≤ ntv throughout. Equivalent definitions apply to the facet counts nof and ntf. The pointers in the nfac array refer to the polygon representing the visible portion of a given facet of the model. nfac[i] is no longer necessarily equal to i for every facet i.

The drawit Routine

We mentioned that the clipping routine must be called before any perspective projection onto the view plane can occur and so we insert the call in the new drawit routine (listing 14.2) immediately before the call to the perspective project (listing 11.1).

Listing 14.2

```
PROCEDURE drawit ;
BEGIN
{ Set vertex counts }
    ntv := nov ; ntf := nof ;
    clipscene ; project ; hidden
END ; { of drawit }
```

Example 14.1
Figure 14.3a shows a table-top scene viewed from a distance and not needing clipping. Figure 14.3b shows a close-up clipped view.

Figure 14.3(a)

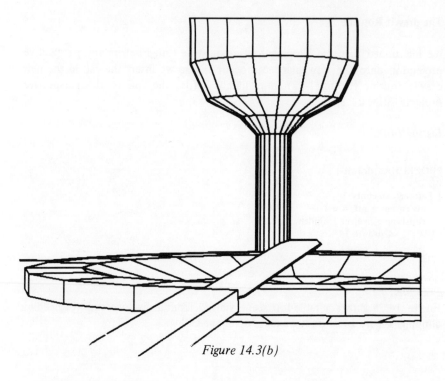

Figure 14.3(b)

Exercise 14.2
Use this method to produce *hidden line* close-up views of three-dimensional models. The only major difference between line drawings and surface drawings is that edges of the clipped polygon may appear as lines on the edge of the viewport. These lines must be suppressed in the corresponding line-drawing **seefacet** routine.

15 Shading

In chapter 10 we introduced the routine **facetfill** to produce the viewport representation of a facet. Up to now this routine has consisted of a simple area-fill using a logical colour prescribed in the data construction routines. We can do much more than this! The realism of the images we produce is greatly enhanced by the use of *shading*. We take advantage of the colour display of the graphics device to model the different appearances of surfaces depending on the light striking them. Plates III, XIII and IX show pictures produced using the shading techniques introduced in this chapter.

Vision is a perception of light reflected onto the retinas of our eyes. Different materials reflect light in different ways, enabling us to distinguish between them, but all that we actually *see* is light. The purpose of a *shading model* is to calculate precisely what light is reflected to the eye from each visible point in a scene and use this information, by selecting a suitable display style for the corresponding pixel, to create realistic images of the scene. Thus there are two distinct problems to consider. Firstly, a mathematical model must be developed to provide the information needed about the light reflected from points in a scene, and secondly, this information must be interpreted for application to new facet display routines.

(Note that a shading model is *not* a hidden surface algorithm. Some other method must still be employed to determine which are the visible points of a scene. Of course, we do not need to consider every visible point individually — there are an infinite number — we simply deal with the finite number of pixels on the graphics viewport. The problem can also be considerably simplified by assuming that the intensity of light reflected from each point on a given facet is the same, but more of this later.)

We shall first turn our attention to a mathematical model for reflected light. This problem is somewhat different from all those which we have considered so far in this book. In previous chapters, we have dealt with purely geometrical concepts: points, lines, planes etc. Light is not a static geometrical object, it is energy. We can, nevertheless, develop a geometrical model for the transmission and reflection of light.

We assume that light consists of an infinite number of closely packed *rays* or *beams* which we may represent as vectors. There are two models which may be used for a light source (see figure 15.1). The *point source* model assumes that all rays emanate from a single point and may take any direction from this point.

This idea corresponds to the properties of a single light bulb or, on a larger scale, the sun. Paradoxically, the sun may also be considered to fall into the second category — *parallel beam illumination* — which models the illumination produced by a point light source 'infinitely' far from the object being illuminated or, alternatively, by a distributed light source. This model assumes that all rays have a common direction.

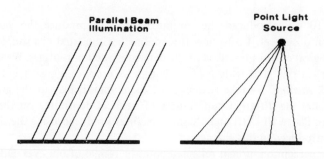

Figure 15.1

Either a parallel beam or a point light source may be represented by a single vector specified in relation to the OBSERVER co-ordinate system. (We shall work with the OBSERVER system throughout this chapter.) The position of a point source is specified by a vector *s* while the direction of the beams in the parallel beam model is specified by a vector *−l*. (Note *minus*! We adopt this notation because in most cases we use the vector in the opposite direction: that is, *l*). In order to calculate the light reflected from a point *p* on a surface we work with the normal to the surface at *p*, which we call *n*, together with a direction vector from *p* to the light source. For the parallel beam model finding this direction is easy — it is the vector *l* for every point *p*. For the point source model the required vector is *s* − *p*, which, for consistency, we shall also call *l*. For calculations involving specular reflection (see later) we also need to know the eye position which is, of course, the origin of the OBSERVER co-ordinate system.

In our programs we assume that a point source of light is used. The ACTUAL position of the point source is input in routine **insource** (listing 15.1) as the co-ordinate triple, the **vector3** point v, with respect to the ABSOLUTE system. The OBSERVED co-ordinates of this **vector3** point, **src**, are calculated and declared in the database:

    {VAR} src : vector3;

Listing 15.1

```
VAR
   src : vector3 ;

PROCEDURE insource ;
{ Reads in position of light source }
VAR v : vector3 ;
BEGIN
   writeln(' Type in the ACTUAL position of the light source') ;
   readln(v.x,v.y,v.z) ;
   { Convert to OBSERVED co-ordinates }
   transform(v,Q,src)
END ; { of insource }
```

Quantifying Light – Intensity and Colour

Rays of light may vary in brightness or intensity. Ultimately, we wish to calculate
the intensity of the light which is reflected to the eye from a point in a three-
dimensional scene and to interpret this information for display on a graphics
device. In order to do this we must be able to map the measure of intensity onto
the set of colours or shades available for display. The range of colours on any
graphics device is finite – there is a limit on brightness. We must therefore impose
a maximum value on intensity so we measure the intensity of light using a real
value between 0 (representing darkness) and 1 (representing 'maximum' brightness).

White light consists of a wide spectrum of waves of varying wavelength, each
corresponding to light of a different colour, ranging from red light at one end of
the spectrum of visible wavelengths to violet at the other. In our somewhat
simplistic conception of this idea we assume that light consists of three components – red, green and blue. We shall quantify light in terms of the intensities
of each of these three components. We call these three intensity values I_{red},
I_{green} and I_{blue} and each takes a *real* value between 0 and 1. In white light these
components are present in equal measure; a value of 1 for I_{red}, 0 for I_{green} and
0 for I_{blue} implies bright red light, whereas 0 for I_{blue} and 0.5 for both I_{red} and
I_{green} implies a more subdued yellow light.

The *colour* of the light is determined by the triple $(I_{red}, I_{green}, I_{blue})$. A
colour $(\lambda \times I_{red}, \lambda \times I_{green}, \lambda \times I_{blue})$ for some $\lambda, 0 \leq \lambda \leq 1$, is said to be a *shade*
of $(I_{red}, I_{green}, I_{blue})$ with *intensity* λ.

The Colour of a Surface

All materials have properties relating the intensity of light which they reflect to that of the light striking them (*incident light*). We call these properties the *reflective coefficients* of the material. We divide the properties into three components corresponding to the red, green and blue components of the light. The values of the R_{red}, R_{green} and R_{blue} coefficients represent respectively the proportion of the incident red, green and blue light which is reflected, each taking a value between 0 and 1. A value of 1 for R_{red} implies that all incident red light is reflected, while values of 0 or 0.5 imply respectively that none or half of the incident red light is reflected.

The *absolute colour* of a material is determined by the relative magnitudes of the R_{red}, R_{green} and R_{blue} coefficients. For a white material all three are equal to 1, for a black material all are 0, while any material with equal R_{red}, R_{green} and R_{blue} values between 0 and 1 is a shade of grey. A large R_{red} coefficient combined with small R_{green} and R_{blue} gives a reddish colour and so on.

The *apparent colour* of a point on a surface is the colour of the light reflected to the eye from the point. This is obviously dependent on the light shining on the surface as well as on the absolute colour and other properties of the surface (for example, transparency, gloss — see later), but in the simple case of a dull (matt), opaque surface illuminated by white light, the apparent colour is always a shade of the absolute colour.

Reflection of Light

There are two distinct ways in which light is reflected from a surface.

All surfaces exhibit *diffuse reflection*. Reflected light is scattered by the surface uniformly in all directions, so the intensity of light reflected to the eye is independent of the position from which the surface is viewed. Furthermore, the apparent colour of the surface is dependent on both the colour of the surface and the colour of the incident light. We shall discuss the precise relationship later.

Glossy surfaces also exhibit *specular reflection*, the effect which produces the *highlights* observed in Plate VIII. A perfect reflector (such as a mirror) reflects an incident ray along a single direction (*r* in figure 15.2). (It is this property which enables us to see perfectly clear images in mirrors.) This type of reflection is called specular reflection — light is not absorbed, it simply bounces off the surface so the colour of specularly reflected light is not dependent on the reflective coefficients of the surface. On slightly imperfect reflectors, some light is also reflected along directions deviating very slightly from *r*, the intensity falling off sharply with increasing deviation. Highlights of the same colour as the incident light are observed when this light is reflected directly to the eye.

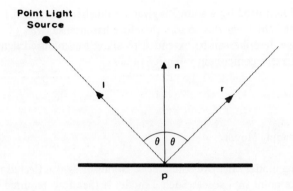

Figure 15.2

Specular reflection is governed by two parameters which we call *m* and *s*. The parameter *m* is a measure of the *gloss* of the surface material and refers to the sharpness of fall-off in intensity of reflection along directions deviating from *r*. It takes an integer value between 0 and about 15. A high value suggests a very glossy surface which exhibits bright, concentrated highlights and hence a sharp fall-off in intensity around the direction *r*. Lower values give less glossy surfaces with highlights more distributed. The parameter *s* may be thought of as the reflective coefficient of the material for specular reflection and we call this the *shine* of the material. The value of *s* varies between 0 and 1. Shiny materials such as metals have high *s* values, close to 1, while dull materials such as paper have low values. Those parts of a glossy surface which are not part of a highlight exhibit only diffuse reflection.

Not all light is reflected straight to the eye, of course. Diffuse reflection, for instance, scatters light uniformly in all directions. This results in a low level of *ambient light* illuminating any scene. This is background light reflected equally in all directions from the ground, walls and any other exposed surfaces. We assume that ambient light illuminates all surfaces of the model equally and ensures that those surfaces which are not exposed to a genuine light source do not appear perfectly black. The colour of ambient light is, of course, dependent on the reflective coefficients of the surfaces from which it has been reflected.

In order to simplify the calculations required in the shading model, we shall assume that all incident light (both source and ambient) is white light, thereby consisting of equal measures of red, green and blue components. When we talk about 'white' light having intensity *I*, (a *real* number), this means that the intensity of each colour component is *I* and so the colour may be described by the triple (I, I, I). The intensity of ambient light is given a value between 0 and 1, which we call I_a. This value is usually fairly low – about 0.3 is best. The maximum intensity of light which may illuminate a scene is 1. This includes both ambient light and light emanating directly from a source. The intensity of the contribution of incident light from a source is therefore limited to $(1 - I_a)$. The intensity of light emitted by a source is given a value between 0 and 1, called I_s, and the incident light from this source therefore has intensity $I_s \times (1 - I_a)$. The models which we describe can be extended to allow for coloured light sources, having three different component intensity values.

Developing a Shading Model

The ideal shading model calculates the precise colour of light reflected to the eye from any visible point in a scene. Such a model is therefore required to return the intensities of the red, green and blue components of this colour for any given point. This we call a *colour shading model*.

Not all graphics devices have sufficient colour capability to display this information, however, so we also consider a simplified model, called an *intensity shading model*, which simply returns the intensity (a real value, λ, between 0 and 1) of light reflected from a given point on a surface in the scene. The apparent colour of the surface at that point is then assumed to be a shade of the surface's absolute colour with intensity λ. This model therefore assumes that all surfaces of the scene are matt and opaque, exhibiting only diffuse reflection.

The shading models use a set of parameters which we call *material properties*. These are the properties which govern the way in which materials reflect light, the reflective coefficients, gloss, shine etc. For an intensity shading model we use just one value, R say, which represents a general reflective coefficient between 0 and 1. A colour shading model may use all of the parameters which we have described.

(1) Ambient light

We begin by modelling the reflection of ambient light which illuminates all surfaces equally, including those facing away from the genuine light source. Rays of ambient light strike a surface from all directions and are reflected uniformly in all directions. The intensity of light reflected to the eye (I_{amb} in the intensity shading model) is therefore independent of all but the intensity of the ambient light and the reflective coefficient of the surface with respect to this light

$$I_{amb} = R \times I_a$$

where I_a is the intensity of incident ambient light and R is the single-valued reflective coefficient of the surface for ambient light. (In theory, the reflective coefficients for ambient light and incident light from a source may be different but we always assume that they are equal.)

In order to produce a colour shading model for the reflection of ambient light, the above equation must be applied three times using the respective reflective coefficients for the three colour components. We use the values R_{red}, R_{green} and R_{blue}

$$I_{amb(red)} = R_{red} \times I_a$$
$$I_{amb(green)} = R_{green} \times I_a$$
$$I_{amb(blue)} = R_{blue} \times I_a$$

(2) Diffuse reflection – Lambert's Cosine Law

Diffuse reflection may be modelled using Lambert's Cosine Law. This relates the intensity of light striking a point on a surface to the cosine of the angle θ between the normal to the surface at that point and the vector from the point to the light source. The intensity of light, I_{diff}, reflected to the eye by diffuse reflection from this point is dependent on the intensity of light striking the point and the reflective coefficient of the surface

$$I_{diff} = R \times (I_s \times (1 - I_a) \times \cos \theta)$$

where I_s is the intensity of the light emitted by the source. The angle θ is called the *angle of incidence* of the light on the surface. Now the normal to the surface is n and the rays of light have direction l, so the angle θ may be calculated through the scalar product $n \cdot l$ which is equal to $|n| \times |l| \times \cos \theta$. Thus the intensity of diffuse reflection from a surface is given by

$$I_{diff} = \frac{R \times I_s \times (1 - I_a) \times (n \cdot l)}{|n| \times |l|}$$

Naturally, if the angle θ is greater than $90°$ then the surface at p faces away from the source and so no light reaches the surface and consequently none is reflected. Although I_{diff} is calculated by the above formula to be less than 0 in this case, it should be set to 0.

The model for diffuse reflection may be further improved by the inclusion of a distance factor: the intensity of light from a given source falls off with increasing distance from the source. At a point a distance d from a source producing light of intensity I_s, the light has intensity I_s/d^2. Thus, if the point p above is a distance d from a given source then the intensity of light from the source which strikes p is I_s/d^2, and this value may replace I_s in the equation above.

More pleasing effects are often achieved by approximating to this fall-off by using $I_s/(d + C)$ for some constant C, as the I_s/d^2 value gives too harsh a fall-off in intensity. Experiment with the value of C to achieve satisfactory results.

The complete intensity shading model is given by the sum of the values I_{amb} and I_{diff}. This gives a real value lying between 0 and 1.

Once again, colour may be introduced into these models by using the equation three times, once for each of the colour components red, green and blue

$$I_{diff(red)} = \frac{R_{red} \times I_s \times (1 - I_a) \times (n \cdot l)}{|n| \times |l|}$$

$$I_{\text{diff(green)}} = \frac{R_{\text{green}} \times I_s \times (1 - I_a) \times (n \cdot l)}{|n| \times |l|}$$

$$I_{\text{diff(blue)}} = \frac{R_{\text{blue}} \times I_s \times (1 - I_a) \times (n \cdot l)}{|n| \times |l|}$$

Exercise 15.1

We can create a type of fog model by taking into account the distance of the point p from the eye (= $|p|$). As this distance increases, so too does the 'fogginess' of the image. We simulate this by defining a light grey colour for fog and, instead of displaying the apparent colour of the reflecting surface at p, we display a weighted average of this apparent colour and the fog colour, increasing the weighting of the fog colour $|p|$ increases. Experiment with this idea. (See Plate XVIII.)

(3) Specular reflection

Specular reflection, as mentioned previously, is exhibited by glossy surfaces. A model for specular reflection, developed by Bui-Tuong Phong (1975), approximates the intensity of specular reflection at a point by $\cos^m \alpha$ where α is the angle between the direction of perfect reflection of light from the point and the vector from that point to the eye (see figure 15.2), and m is the gloss of the surface material. The intensity of light specularly reflected from a surface is also dependent on a function of the angle of incidence of the light, θ. This function, $F(\theta)$ say, may be thought of as the reflective coefficient of the surface with respect to specular reflection, but this coefficient is not constant: incident light striking a surface obliquely (high θ) is reflected to a greater extent than that striking more directly. In general, we approximate $F(\theta)$ by the constant value s, the shine of the surface material. An equation for the intensity of specularly reflected light (I_{spec}), derived from Phong's model, is given by

$$I_{\text{spec}} = I_s \times F(\theta) \times \cos^m \alpha \quad \text{or, alternatively} \quad I_{\text{spec}} = I_s \times s \times \cos^m \alpha$$

Specular reflection of light is independent of the absolute colour of the reflecting surface. Consequently, for white incident light, the intensity of each colour component in the specularly reflected light is given by I_{spec}, calculated as above.

If r is the direction in which light is reflected from the surface and $-p$ is the vector from p to the eye, then the value $\cos \alpha$ is given by

$$\cos \alpha = \frac{r \cdot (-p)}{|r| \times |p|}$$

We may take advantage of elementary laws of physics and trigonometry to simplify this calculation, which enables us to calculate $\cos \alpha$ without first calculating r. The angle of reflection is defined to be the angle between the surface normal at a point p and the direction of reflection r for a perfectly reflecting surface. This angle of reflection is equal in magnitude and opposite in sense to the angle of incidence and consequently

$\dfrac{r}{|r|} + \dfrac{l}{|l|}$ is a vector parallel to n

Now suppose the angle between l and r is ψ, then the angle between l and n is $\psi/2$. Let us further suppose that the angle between l and $-p$ is σ, then $\alpha = \psi - \sigma$ and so $\alpha/2 = (\psi/2 - \sigma/2)$ (see figure 15.3). Thus, if the vector q is given by

$$q = \dfrac{-p}{|p|} + \dfrac{l}{|l|}$$

then $\alpha/2$ is the angle between q and n and so

$$\cos(\alpha/2) = \dfrac{n \cdot q}{|n| \times |q|}$$

We know that $\cos\alpha = \cos^2(\alpha/2) - \sin^2(\alpha/2) = 2 \times \cos^2(\alpha/2) - 1$ and hence we may calculate $\cos\alpha$.

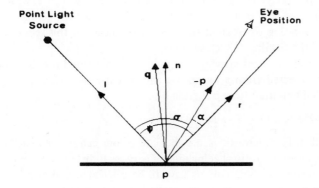

Figure 15.3

Specular reflection can only be used with a colour shading model since the apparent colour of a point near, but not at, a highlight is not simply a shade of either the absolute colour of the surface or the colour of the light, but rather a mixture of the two colours.

It should be pointed out that Bui-Tuong Phong's model does not strictly simulate the specular reflection of light, but simply produces an effect of similar appearance.

Each colour component in the complete colour shading model is calculated by summing the corresponding components of the contributions from reflected ambient light, diffuse reflection and specular reflection. If any colour component exceeds 1 then it is set to 1.

(4) Shadows
If a point is obscured from exposure to a single light source, then the point is said to be *in shadow*. The light emitted from the point is restricted to reflected ambient light, in the absence of other light sources.

(5) Multiple light sources
Any of the shading models detailed above may be extended to deal with illumination from more than one light source simply by taking the average of the contributions from each. The contribution from each light source is calculated as if it were the only source, taking into account the same level of ambient light in each calculation.

(6) Transparent surfaces
For a transparent surface, the apparent colour is also determined by a contribution from light arriving from behind the surface. The extent of this contribution is measured by the transparency coefficient T, which again takes a value between 0 and 1. A perfectly transparent surface is indicated by $T = 1$ while a fully opaque surface has $T = 0$. In chapter 16 we shall examine the geometrical problems of incorporating transparent surfaces into a scene: in this section we shall consider only the shading of such surfaces.

If the intensity of light arriving at a point p from behind is I_b and the intensity of light reflected from p by diffuse and specular reflection is I_p, then the intensity of light emitted from p is given by

$$I_{tran} = T \times I_b + (1 - T) \times I_p$$

Only if all surfaces have the same absolute colour can transparency be taken into account in an intensity shading model, because if different absolute colours occur then 'mixes' of these colours have to be calculated and displayed. For a colour shading model, transparency coefficients may be separated into three components, relating to the proportions of red, green and blue light let through. These components may differ in the same way as may the reflective coefficients of a material: a red filter, for instance, will let through all red light which strikes it, but is perfectly opaque with respect to blue or green light. The three transparency coefficients are, in fact, directly related to the reflective coefficients so instead of specifying three transparency coefficients for a surface, we specify one general value, T, and use the three values $T \times R_{red}$, $T \times R_{green}$ and $T \times R_{blue}$ in the colour equations

$$I_{tran(red)}   = T \times R_{red} \times I_{p(red)} + (1 - T \times R_{red}) \times I_{b(red)}$$
$$I_{tran(green)} = T \times R_{green} \times I_{p(green)} + (1 - T \times R_{green}) \times I_{b(green)}$$
$$I_{tran(blue)} = T \times R_{blue} \times I_{p(blue)} + (1 - T \times R_{blue}) \times I_{b(blue)}$$

Exercise 15.2
Extend the formulae throughout this section so that they deal with a coloured light source.

Incorporating Shading into the Programs

We now turn our attention to the display of information derived from shading models. You do not have to use very expensive colour devices with vast ranges of available colours in order to produce shaded pictures. Provided that you temper your aims according to the capabilities of the display, then satisfactory results can almost always be obtained.

In this section we shall discuss the application of shading techniques to the polygon mesh models which we have used thus far in the parts of this book dealing with three dimensions. Nevertheless, it should be understood that the techniques may be applied equally well to the analytic models described in chapter 17.

The new **drawit** routine (listing 15.2) which co-ordinates the creation of shaded images contains two additional calls — to a routine **colourtable** (listing 15.6) which initialises the set of shades or display styles which are used for the shading, and to the routine **insource** given in listing 15.1. We assume that there are originally **numshade** shades for each of **numcol** colours. The major changes occur at a much lower level in the structured sequence of subroutines, in the facet display routines **seefacet** and **facetfill**.

Listing 15.2

```
VAR
    numcol,numshade : integer ;

PROCEDURE drawit ;
BEGIN
{ Set vertex and facet counts }
    ntv := nov ; ntf := nof ; ppd := 3*horiz ; materialin ;
{ prepare and draw scene }
    colourtable ; clipscene ; project ; insource ; hidden
END ; { of drawit }
```

We mentioned at the beginning of this chapter that the implementation of a shading model can be simplified by assuming that the apparent colour of points on a facet is constant over the facet. For the first two methods outlined below we *must* use this approach since the apparent colour is not displayed explicitly by each pixel, rather it is suggested by the densities of various colours over the whole facet.

Recall that the shading models all calculate a measure of the light reflected to the eye from a single point on a surface. For constant shading over a facet, such as was used for Plate II (a constant shaded version of the camera of Plate I), however, a slightly different approach must be adopted. Obviously, the normal vector *n* is the same for any *p* on the facet but, if a point light source is used, the vector *l* will vary across the facet and so an average value must be taken. What we do is to average the x, y and z co-ordinates of the vertices of the facet and use the median thus calculated as p, thus determining an average value for I. Every point on the facet is then assumed to reflect light of the same colour and intensity as that reflected at p. For convex polygons the median always lies within the polygon. The median of a facet is calculated by a call to the routine midpoint given in listing 15.3.

Listing 15.3

```
PROCEDURE midpoint(face : integer ; VAR midpt : vector3) ;
VAR i,j : integer ;
BEGIN
{ Finds the mid-point of facet 'face' in OBSERVED co-ordinates }
    midpt.x := 0.0 ; midpt.y := 0.0 ; midpt.z := 0.0 ;
    FOR i := 1 TO size[face]
    DO BEGIN
            j := faclist[facfront[face]+i] ;
            midpt.x := midpt.x+obs[j].x ;
            midpt.y := midpt.y+obs[j].y ;
            midpt.z := midpt.z+obs[j].z
       END ;
    midpt.x := midpt.x/size[face] ;
    midpt.y := midpt.y/size[face] ;
    midpt.z := midpt.z/size[face]
END ; { of midpoint }
```

The implementation of the shading models requires that the material properties of the various surfaces be represented in the programs. We use the concept of *material* in the same way as we have used colour in preceding chapters — an integer value, colour[i], is associated with each facet i and this integer now refers to a particular material, and a corresponding set of material properties, rather than to a logical colour and these must be declared in the global database. For intensity shading models this declaration consists of an array representing the single-valued reflective coefficient and three arrays defining the components of the absolute colours of the materials

{VAR}r,rm,gm,bm : ARRAY [1..maxmaterl] OF real;

The value of maxmaterl is set by a CONST declaration — we use 10. For later colour shading models we require the three reflective coefficients, the gloss and shine parameters and the transparency coefficient, and we have the declarations

{VAR}rm,gm,bm,sm,tr : ARRAY [1..maxmaterl] OF real;
mm : ARRAY [1..maxmaterl] OF integer;

The material properties must be set up through the scene routine. As an example we give a materialin routine (listing 15.4) which reads the values in from a file named 'materl.dat'. Remember that rm, gm, bm, sm and tr would take real values between 0 and 1 while mm is an integer varying between 1 and about 15.

Listing 15.4

```
CONST
    maxmaterl = 10 ;

VAR { for intensity shading model }
    r,rm,gm,bm : ARRAY[1..maxmaterl] OF real ;
{ for colour shading model replace above declaration with :- }
{   rm,gm,bm,sm,tr : ARRAY[1..maxmaterl] OF real ;              }
{   mm : ARRAY[1..maxmaterl] OF integer ;                       }
    numat : integer ;

PROCEDURE materialin ;
{ Routine to input an ACTUAL scene }
VAR front,i,j : integer ;
BEGIN
{ Read number of materials }
    assign(indata,'materl.dat') ; reset(indata) ;
    read(indata,numat) ;
{ Read in the material properties for intensity shading model }
    FOR i := 1 TO numat
    DO read(indata,r[i],rm[i],gm[i],bm[i]) ;
{ For colour shading model replace above statement with :- }
{   DO read(indata,rm[i],gm[i],bm[i],sm[i],mm[i],tr[i]) ;   }
    close(indata)
END ; { of materialin }
```

We now outline various methods for the interpretation of intensity information ranging from a simple sampling method to a full implementation of a colour model.

(1) Random sampling

This method may be used when a very limited number of colours or shades is available; it uses an intensity shading model (implemented in the routine intensityshade in listing 15.5).

Listing 15.5

```
PROCEDURE intensityshade(p,norm : vector3 ; index : integer ;
                         VAR lambda : real ) ;
{ Intensity shading model : returns intensity 'lambda' }
{ vector 'p' is the point from which light is reflected }
{ vector 'norm' is the surface normal at that point }
{ surface material 'index' }
```

```
VAR ptosrc : vector3 ;
    ambient,cosval,dotprod,modnormal,modptosrc : real ;
BEGIN
{ Calculate direction from vector 'p' to source }
    ptosrc.x := src.x-p.x ;
    ptosrc.y := src.y-p.y ;
    ptosrc.z := src.z-p.z ;
{ Calculate the angle between the surface normal and this direction }
    dotprod := dot3(norm,ptosrc) ;
    modnormal := sqrt(sqr(norm.x)+sqr(norm.y)+sqr(norm.z)) ;
    modptosrc := sqrt(sqr(ptosrc.x)+sqr(ptosrc.y)+sqr(ptosrc.z)) ;
    cosval := dotprod/(modnormal*modptosrc) ;
    IF cosval < 0 THEN cosval := 0 ;
{ Set 'ambient' light level to 0.3 }
    ambient := 0.3 ;
{ 'lambda' is the intensity returned }
    lambda := r[index]*((1-ambient)*cosval+ambient)
END ; { of intensityshade }
```

The facetfill routine (listing 15.7) displays a facet not by using a simple area-fill in a colour indicated by the colour array, but instead by using the intensity value as a measure of the probability that any pixel within that area should be displayed in a given shade of the chosen logical colour. Suppose we have 3 shades (numshade = 3) of each of the numcol colours, graded from dark (index 1) to light (index 3), set up in a colour look-up table by a routine which we call colourtable. If you have a graphics device that can specify colours by their RGB values (see later) then you can use the routine given in listing 15.8, otherwise you must write your own routine to create this table. For reasons explained later, we suppose the table has indices 2, ... 3 * numcol + 1. If the intensity of light reflected from a surface is low, then there is a greater probability of a pixel ɔn the surface being a darker shade and correspondingly smaller probabilities for the middle and lighter shades. A high intensity, close to 1, implies a large probability that a given pixel in the relevant area will be set to the lighter shade. The shade for display is chosen by a routine randomcolour (listing 15.6) using a random function based on the intensity of reflected light. The seefacet and facetfill routines which implement the random sampling method are also given in this listing. Note that seefacet determines the intensity of light reflected from a facet, through a call to intensityshade, and then calls facetfill which displays the facet, pixel by pixel, using shades randomly selected by randomcolour.

Listing 15.6

```
PROCEDURE randomcolour(col : integer ; lambda : real) ;
{ Assuming numshade=3 select logical colour between 2*3*col and 4+3*col }
{ the colour table having been set up by routine 'colourtable' }
BEGIN
    IF lambda < 0.15
    THEN setcol(2+3*col)
```

```
        ELSE IF lambda >0.95
             THEN setcol(4+3*col)
             ELSE IF lambda < 0.55
                     THEN IF (random*0.4+0.15) < lambda
                         THEN setcol(3+3*col)
                         ELSE setcol(2+3*col)
                     ELSE IF (random*0.4+0.55) < lambda
                         THEN setcol(4+3*col)
                         ELSE setcol(3+3*col)
END ; { of randomcolour }

FUNCTION max(i,j : integer) : integer ;
BEGIN
   IF i>j THEN max := i ELSE max := j
END ; { of max }

FUNCTION min(i,j : integer) : integer ;
BEGIN
   IF i<j THEN min := i ELSE min := j
END ; { of min }

PROCEDURE facetfill(face : integer ; lambda : real) ;
{ Displays facet 'face' in a 'shade' with intensity lambda }
VAR i,index,ix,iy,j,next,pixval : integer ;
    xmax,xmin,ymax,ymin : integer ;
    pixpol : pixelarray ;
    pix : pixelvector ;
    bottom,top,factor : real ;
BEGIN
   j := nfac[face] ;
{ Find the pixel co-ordinates of the vertices }
   FOR i := 1 TO size[j]
   DO BEGIN
          pixpol[i].x := fx(pro[faclist[facfront[j]+i]].x) ;
          pixpol[i].y := fy(pro[faclist[facfront[j]+i]].y)
       END ;
{ Fill facet by a scan line approach }
   ymax := pixpol[1].y ; ymin := ymax ;
   FOR i := 2 TO size[j]
   DO BEGIN
          IF pixpol[i].y > ymax THEN ymax := pixpol[i].y ;
          IF pixpol[i].y < ymin THEN ymin := pixpol[i].y
       END ;
   IF ymax >= nypix THEN ymax := nypix-1 ;
   IF ymin <0 THEN ymin := 0 ;
   FOR iy := ymin TO ymax
   DO BEGIN
          xmin := nxpix ; xmax := -1 ; index := size[j] ;
          FOR next := 1 TO size[j]
          DO BEGIN
                 IF (max(pixpol[index].y,pixpol[next].y) >= iy) AND
                    (min(pixpol[index].y,pixpol[next].y) <= iy) AND
                    (pixpol[index].y <> pixpol[next].y)
                 THEN BEGIN
                             top := pixpol[next].x-pixpol[index].x ;
```

```
                    bottom := pixpol[next].y-pixpol[index].y ;
                    factor := (iy-pixpol[index].y)*top/bottom ;
                    pixval := pixpol[index].x+round(factor) ;
                    IF pixval < xmin THEN xmin := pixval ;
                    IF pixval > xmax THEN xmax := pixval
                    END ;
                index := next
            END ;
        IF xmax > = nxpix THEN xmax := nxpix-1 ;
        IF xmin <0 THEN xmin := 0 ;
        IF xmin < = xmax
        THEN FOR ix := xmin TO xmax
            DO BEGIN
                    pix.x := ix ; pix.y := iy ;
                    randomcolour(colour[face],lambda) ;
                    setpix(pix)
                END
        END
END ; { of facetfill }


PROCEDURE seefacet(face : integer) ;
{ 'seefacet' routine for Random Sampling shading }
VAR lambda,dummy : real ;
    midpt,norm : vector3 ;
    newface,pt : integer ;
BEGIN
{ Find the mid-point and normal of facet 'face' }
    midpoint(face,midpt) ; normal(face,norm,dummy,obs) ;
{ Find the intensity of reflected light }
    intensityshade(midpt,norm,colour[face],lambda) ;
{ Display the facet }
    facetfill(face,lambda) ;
{ Repeat for each superficial facet on facet 'face' }
    pt := firstsup[face] ;
    WHILE pt>0
    DO BEGIN
            newface := permheap[pt].info ; pt := permheap[pt].pointer ;
            midpoint(newface,midpt) ; normal(face,norm,dummy,obs) ;
            intensityshade(midpt,norm,colour[face],lambda) ;
            facetfill(face,lambda)
        END
END ; { of seefacet }
```

Listing 15.7

```
PROCEDURE facetfill(face : integer ; lambda : real) ;
VAR i,j,pattern : integer ;
    poly : vector2array ;
BEGIN
{ Set display style to 'pattern' corresponding    }
{ to intensity 'lambda' and given colour of face }
    findlogicalcolour(colour[face],lambda,pattern) ;
    patternset(pattern) ; j := nfac[face] ;
```

```
{ Copy vertex co-ordinates to 'poly' array }
   FOR i := 1 TO size[j]
   DO BEGIN
           poly[i].x := pro[faclist[facfront[j] + i]].x ;
           poly[i].y := pro[faclist[facfront[j] + i]].y
           END ;
{ Display facet }
   polyfill(size[j],poly)
END ; { of facetfill }
```

Example 15.1
Figure 15.4 shows a sphere displayed using the random sampling method of
shading using three colours, black (1), medium grey (2) and white (3).

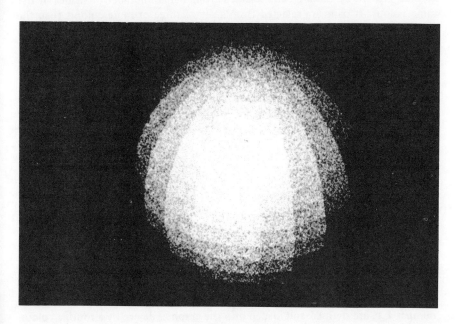

Figure 15.4

(2) Pixel patterns

A more formal application of the above idea may be adopted if the device being
used provides for a patterned area-fill. In this method pixels are not considered
individually, but in small square blocks of, perhaps, 2 × 2 or 3 × 3 pixels which
we call *pixel patterns*. The larger the blocks used, the greater is the number of
shades that may be obtained but, in turn, resolution is sacrificed.

Pixel patterns may involve a simple combination of black and white or a
variety of combinations of shades of the same colour in sets of two, three or
more.

There are five elementary 2 × 2 pixel patterns

B	B
B	B

F	B
B	B

F	B
B	F

F	F
B	F

F	F
F	F

where B = background colour and F = foreground colour. Each of the remaining possible combinations gives the same shade as one of these five (there are $2^4 = 16$ combinations all together).

If we use B = black and F = white then we have at our disposal five graded shades ranging from black through three shades of grey to white. More shades may be created by mixing pairs selected from a small number of shades of the same colour. If pairs are selected from a set of three or more colours then the sorting of the shades into order of intensity is not automatic. You will have to sort them into a suitable order yourself. You will discover that some shades do not fit into the order at all and have to be discarded. Nevertheless, with a little effort you can usually create a satisfactory set.

Typically, storage is provided for a number of patterns which may be accessed by integer indices ranging from 2 up to a maximum number, **numpat + 1**, say. These patterns are defined in terms of a *unit block* of ($h \times v$) pixels, say. Each pixel within this unit block is given a binary value, 0 or 1. A value of 0 implies that the pixel is displayed in background colour and a value of 1 implies foreground colour. The precise form of this definition varies from device to device. An area is pattern-filled using pattern I by repeating the unit block of pattern I throughout the area.

Exercise 15.3

We assume that **numpat(= numcol ∗ numshade)** patterns, with indices 2,3, . . . , **numpat + 1**, are defined and loaded into the graphics device by a routine **colourtable**, this time defined by the user. This peculiar numbering is used to make the setup of patterns equivalent to that of the structure of the colour table we use in listing 15.8. Each pattern must represent a shade of a given colour, where the ith shade of the jth colour will be pattern **1 + i + (j − 1) ∗ numshade**. Within each of the **numcol** consecutive sets of **numshade** patterns, the pattern with the smaller indices will represent the darker shades of colour, while those with the higher indices will represent the lighter shades. The user must also write a routine **patternset** which sets the pattern display style for the graphics device, so that the choice of patterns is a meaningful representation of shades of the **numcol** colours. The **facetfill** routine of listing 15.7 will fill in the indicated polygonal area with the chosen **pattern** found by **findlogicalcolour** of the listing 15.8. Of course you must ensure that the **polyfill** routine has been re-written to pattern-fill. The display will be co-ordinated by the **seefacet** routine of listing 15.7 for the intensity shading model. Note how the real intensity value returned from **intensityshade** is used by selecting the correct pattern for display.

Example 15.2
Figure 15.5 shows an object displayed using 2 × 2 pixel patterns derived from five different shades of red.

Figure 15.5

(3) The RGB colour model

Although some graphics devices have relatively few colours, hence the need for the random sampling and pattern fill, many devices allow for very flexible definition of colours through the specification of red, green and blue components. On some of these, an effectively infinite range may be available as each component can be specified by a real number between 0 and 1. More typically the components are defined by three 8-bit integers (between 0 and 255) which, nevertheless, gives us a choice from some 16 million possible colours. Only a subset of these colours may be displayed at one time and these are stored in the colour look-up table. We assume that this table stores the definitions of 256 actual colours in terms of their red, green and blue component values. Each entry in the colour look-up table (that is, each logical colour) has an integer index, between 0 and 255. The colour of light reflected from a point is calculated, and a suitable colour from the colour look-up table is selected for display. This method requires careful attention to the storage of and access to colours in the colour look-up table.

The colour look-up table is the only interface between the three-dimensional calculations and the image display. The display can be meaningless if the table is not properly set up. We use two routines for manipulating the colour look-up table. The table is initialised by a routine colourtable which is called by the new drawit routine given in listing 15.2. Having ascertained the colour needed for display, we need to find (or define) the corresponding entry in the colour look-up table. This is essentially a sorting and searching problem, solved by a routine findlogicalcolour.

There are two ways in which we can tackle the problem, giving us two pairs of colourtable and findlogicalcolour routines. The first method is to pre-define the entries in the colour look-up table in such a way that we know exactly where to find a suitable colour through a simple calculation, without the need for a time-consuming search. Use of this method restricts us to an intensity shading model (intensityshade in listing 15.5). Suppose that a scene contains numcol different absolute colours and we want to choose between numshade shades of each ranging from zero intensity up to unit intensity. The logical colours are divided into numcol equal sized blocks (of numshade entries), each block representing a series of shades of a given absolute colour. The index of the absolute colour of the surface to be displayed indicates which block of logical colours we should consider and we use the real intensity value returned by intensityshade to determine the position in this block of the logical colour corresponding to that intensity. The initial construction of the colour look-up table is executed by the routine colourtable given in listing 15.8, and the logical colour to be used for display is found by the accompanying routine findlogicalcolour. The facet is then filled by facetfill (listing 15.8) with the correct shade.

Listing 15.8

```
PROCEDURE findlogicalcolour(abscol : integer ; intensity : real ;
                            VAR logcol : integer ) ;
{ Routine to find the logical colour, 'logcol', corresponding to }
{ a shade of absolute colour 'abscol' with given 'intensity' }
BEGIN
    logcol := 2 + (abscol-1)*numshade + trunc(0.9999*intensity*numshade)
END ; { of findlogicalcolour }

PROCEDURE colourtable ;
{ Initialises colour look-up table. }
{ Creates 'numshade' shades of 'numcol' colours }
VAR i,j,n : integer ;
    shade : real ;
BEGIN
    writeln(' Type in number of colours and number of shades') ;
    readln(numcol,numshade) ;
{ leave logical colours 0 and 1 set to default values }
    n := 1 ;
{ Initialise all list pointers }
```

```
        FOR i := 1 TO numcol
        DO FOR j := 1 TO numshade
           DO BEGIN
                    shade := (j-1)/(numshade-1) ; n := n+1 ;
                    rgblog(n,shade*rm[i],shade*gm[i],shade*bm[i])
                  END
    END ; { of colourtable }


    PROCEDURE facetfill(face : integer ; lambda : real) ;
    { Displays facet 'face' in a 'shade' with intensity 'lambda' }
    VAR i,j,index : integer ;
        poly : vector2array ;
    BEGIN
        findlogicalcolour(colour[face],lambda,index) ;
        setcol(index) ; j := nfac[face] ;
    { Find the pixel co-ordinates of the vertices }
        FOR i := 1 TO size[j]
        DO BEGIN
                poly[i].x := pro[faclist[facfront[j]+i]].x ;
                poly[i].y := pro[faclist[facfront[j]+i]].y
              END ;
        polyfill(size[j],poly)
    END ; { of facetfill }
```

This method substantially restricts the number of possible colour shades, and so in order to make full use of our colour shading model, a second method is used in which the entries of the colour look-up table must be defined as and when required. Three values between 0 and 1, representing the red, green and blue components of the apparent colour of a point or surface, are returned by the colour shading model implemented in routine **cshade** (listing 15.9).

Listing 15.9

```
PROCEDURE cshade(p,norm : vector3 ; ic : integer ;
                          VAR red,green,blue : real ) ;
{ Colour shading model }
VAR ptosrc,q : vector3 ;
    ambient,cosa,cosaover2,cosval,dotprod,specular : real ;
    modnormal,modp,modptosrc,modq : real ;
BEGIN
{ Calculate direction from vector 'p' to source }
    ptosrc.x := src.x-p.x ;
    ptosrc.y := src.y-p.y ;
    ptosrc.z := src.z-p.z ;
{ Calculate the angle between the surface normal and this direction }
    dotprod := dot3(norm,ptosrc) ;
    modnormal := sqrt(sqr(norm.x)+sqr(norm.y)+sqr(norm.z)) ;
    modptosrc := sqrt(sqr(ptosrc.x)+sqr(ptosrc.y)+sqr(ptosrc.z)) ;
    cosval := dotprod/(modnormal*modptosrc) ;
    IF cosval < 0 THEN cosval := 0 ;
{ Set ambient light level to 0.3 }
```

```
   ambient := 0.3 ;
{ Calculate the diffuse reflection colour components }
   red := rm[ic]*((1-ambient)*cosval+ambient) ;
   green := gm[ic]*((1-ambient)*cosval+ambient) ;
   blue := bm[ic]*((1-ambient)*cosval+ambient) ;
{ Calculate the vector 'q' }
   modp := sqrt(sqr(p.x)+sqr(p.y)+sqr(p.z)) ;
   q.x := -p.x/modp+ptosrc.x/modptosrc ;
   q.y := -p.y/modp+ptosrc.y/modptosrc ;
   q.z := -p.z/modp+ptosrc.z/modptosrc ;
   modq := sqrt(sqr(q.x)+sqr(q.y)+sqr(q.z)) ;
{ Calculate the specular reflection contribution }
   cosaover2 := dot3(q,norm)/(modnormal*modq) ;
   cosa := 2*sqr(cosaover2)-1 ;
   IF cosa < 0.0001
   THEN specular := 0.0
   ELSE specular := sm[ic]*exp(ln(cosa)*mm[ic]) ;
{ Calculate the components of the reflected light }
   red := red+specular ;
   IF red > 1 THEN red := 1 ;
   green := green+specular ;
   IF green > 1 THEN green := 1 ;
   blue := blue+specular ;
   IF blue > 1 THEN blue := 1
END ; { of cshade }
```

Given the three colour components of a colour required for display, a search through the existing entries in the colour look-up table is executed to find if a 'sufficiently similar' colour has been stored. If such a colour is found, then this is used for display. If no 'sufficiently similar' colour has been stored then a new actual colour is created, stored as the next available logical colour, and this is used for display. Problems arise in determining what is 'sufficiently similar' and in optimising the search methods used.

The definition of 'sufficiently similar' depends on two things: the number of shades of a colour required and the size of the colour look-up table. If we are too strict then we may find that the available number of logical colours is not large enough. If we are not strict enough then the accuracy of the image is undermined. About 25 different shades of a given colour are sufficient for most images. Therefore we consider an existing actual colour to be sufficiently similar to a newly calculated colour if each of the calculated R, G and B components are within 0.04 of the respective existing components. A larger number of different shades may be displayed by decreasing this value, but care must be taken not to exceed the available number of logical colours. Note that the information in the colour look-up table must be stored in the program as well as in the display device memory for the implementation of this method.

The question of search method is very important. If an image is shaded pixel by pixel then the colour look-up table is accessed many thousands of times and any slight delay in the search will result in a greatly increased processing time for the whole image. What we do is identify a subset of the entries in the colour look-up table which have to be considered in a search, and we sort these entries, in order of increasing red component, so that the search through this subset is as efficient as possible. We implement this method using a number of linked lists within the colour look-up table, one list associated with each absolute colour. A pointer is associated with each entry in the colour look-up table, referring to the next item in the list which contains that entry. The first item in each list is referred to by the array element licol[i] for each absolute colour i. The entries in the colour look-up table, and the associated linear lists, are declared in the global database (listing 15.10):

```
{VAR}  licol : ARRAY[1..10] OF integer;
       iptr : ARRAY[1..256] OF integer;
       r,g,b;ARRAY[1..256] OF real;
       newcolour : integer;
```

where newcolour is the next free entry and iptr[i] refers to the next entry in the linear list containing logical colour $i - 1$.

When the apparent colour of a point on a surface is calculated, the list of logical colours associated with the absolute colour of the surface is scanned until one of three cases occurs

(i) a sufficiently similar colour is found: this colour is used for display
(ii) a colour with greater red component is found: the new colour is inserted into the list *before* the colour with greater red component and the new colour is used for display
(iii) the end of the list is reached: the new colour is added to the end of the list and used for display.

The colour look-up table is initialised by the new routine colourtable, and the table is updated and a suitable logical colour found by the new routine findlogicalcolour, both given in listing 15.10.

Of course, if your graphics device has 'infinite' colours there is no need for a colour table, you can identify each facet or pixel with its own unique shade.

Listing 15.10
```
VAR
    licol : ARRAY[1..10] OF integer ;
    iptr : ARRAY[1..256] OF integer ;
    r,g,b : ARRAY[1..256] OF real ;
    newcolour : integer ;

PROCEDURE colourtable ;
{ Initialises colour look-up table. Leave first two colours assigned
{ to default values - first new colour is the third in table }
VAR i : integer ;
BEGIN
    newcolour := 3 ;
```

```
{ Initialise all list pointers }
   FOR i := 1 TO 10  DO licol[i] := 0 ;
   FOR i := 1 TO 256 DO iptr[i] := 0
END ; { of colourtable }

PROCEDURE findlogicalcolour(red,green,blue : real ; i : integer ;
                           VAR colour : integer) ;
{ Find logical colour corresponding to 'red', 'green', 'blue' components }
CONST limit = 0.04 ;
VAR j,jptr : integer ;
    continue : boolean ;
BEGIN
{ 'j' and 'jptr' refer to logical colour list for absolute colour 'i' }
   j := licol[i] ; jptr := -1 ; continue := (j < >0) ;
   WHILE continue
   DO BEGIN
         IF (abs(red-r[j]) < limit) AND
            (abs(green-g[j]) < limit) AND (abs(blue-b[j]) < limit)
         THEN BEGIN          { Corresponding colour found }
                  colour := j-1 ; EXIT
              END
         ELSE
            IF (red > r[j])
            THEN jptr := j ;
{ Check next item in the list; leave if red value too large }
            IF (red > r[j]-limit)
            THEN BEGIN
                     j := iptr[j] ; continue := (j < >0)
                 END
            ELSE continue := false
      END ;
{ Existing list doesn't contain suitable logical colour: add new colour }
   IF (jptr > 0)
   THEN BEGIN
            iptr[newcolour] := iptr[jptr] ; iptr[jptr] := newcolour
        END
   ELSE BEGIN
            iptr[newcolour] := licol[i] ; licol[i] := newcolour
        END ;
   r[newcolour] := red ; g[newcolour] := green ; b[newcolour] := blue ;
   rgblog(newcolour-1,red,green,blue) ;
{ Return index of this this new colour : }
{ list item 'newcolour' is }
{ logical colour 'newcolour-1' }
   colour := newcolour-1 ; newcolour := newcolour+1
END ; { of findlogicalcolour }
```

The seefacet and facetfill routines used in conjunction with an RGB colour shading model may take one of a number of forms.

(3.1) Constant shading

The simplest and quickest method of displaying a facet is by *constant shading*, see Plate II. We assume that the shade is constant across any facet and once the logical colour referring to the required shade has been determined the surface is displayed on the viewport using a simple area-fill. The **seefacet** and **facetfill** routines used for constant shading are given in listing 15.11. Plate IV shows a picture of an Infinite Periodic Minimal Surface (a structure used in crystallography) produced using these routines.

Listing 15.11

```
PROCEDURE facetfill(face,index : integer) ;
{ Displays facet 'face' in a 'shade' with given 'index' }
VAR i,j : integer ;
    poly : vector2array ;
BEGIN
  setcol(index) ; j := nfac[face] ;
{ Find the pixel co-ordinates of the vertices }
  FOR i := 1 TO size[j]
  DO BEGIN
      poly[i].x := pro[faclist[facfront[j]+i]].x ;
      poly[i].y := pro[faclist[facfront[j]+i]].y
    END ;
  polyfill(size[j],poly)
END ; { of facetfill }


PROCEDURE seefacet(face : integer) ;
{ 'seefacet' routine for constant shading }
VAR dummy,red,green,blue : real ;
    midpt,normv : vector3 ;
    index,newface,pt : integer ;
BEGIN
{ Find the mid-point and normal of facet 'face' }
  midpoint(face,midpt) ; normal(face,normv,dummy,obs) ;
{ Find apparent colour of facet 'face' }
  cshade(midpt,normv,colour[face],red,green,blue) ;
  findlogicalcolour(red,green,blue,colour[face],index) ;
{ Display the facet }
  facetfill(face,index) ;
{ Repeat for each superficial facet on facet 'face' }
  pt := firstsup[face] ;
  WHILE pt>0
  DO BEGIN
      newface := permheap[pt].info ; pt := permheap[pt].pointer ;
      cshade(midpt,normv,colour[newface],red,green,blue) ;
      findlogicalcolour(red,green,blue,colour[newface],index) ;
      facetfill(newface,index) ;
    END
END ; { of seefacet }
```

Although sufficient for scenes made up entirely of matt, planar surfaces, this method has a number of disadvantages. The results obtained on models representing curved or glossy surfaces are somewhat unsatisfactory – the polygons making up the approximation to a curved surface are clearly distinguishable and the highlights produced are unconvincing since they are constrained to be made up only of entire facets. Increasing the number of facets helps to some extent but we may produce far more convincing images of approximated curved surfaces by using interpolation methods.

(3.2) Gouraud shading

Gouraud's method of *intensity interpolation shading* (Gouraud, 1971) goes a long way towards solving the problems. A surface is displayed by individually shading the pixels of its image and thus smoothing out the intensity discontinuities. This is generally referred to as *smooth shading*. The intensity of light reflected at each vertex of a facet is determined and the intensity at each internal point may then be calculated by interpolation between these values. The trick is in calculating the intensity at the vertices. Suppose we have a number of facets approximating to a curved surface. Each vertex lies in the real curved surface and is contained in the boundaries of a number of the approximating facets. The *vertex normal* array vna may be found by averaging the *surface normals* of the facets containing the vertex in their boundaries. This is implemented in the routine setnormal given in listing 15.12, which should be called by a new observe routine which calculates the ACTUAL normal vectors. The OBSERVED co-ordinates of these vectors, array vno, are subsequently calculated in the new observe routine, also in listing 15.12. The *vertex intensity* (or, alternatively, the apparent colour at the vertex) may be calculated using one of the previously discussed shading models. The intensity or colour at each point within the facet may then be determined, using a *scan-line* approach, by interpolation between the vertex intensities as shown in figure 15.6. The intensity at point A is found by interpolating between those at points 1 and 2, the intensity at B is found by interpolating between 3 and 4, and finally the intensity at C is found by inter-polating between A and B.

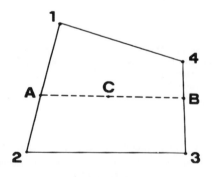

Figure 15.6

Gouraud shading is implemented using the **seefacet** and **facetfill** routines in listing 15.12. The full implementation requires a small addition to one other routine. Each vertex of the scene has associated with it a vertex normal. What about the vertices created by clipping? Since a projected facet is displayed by interpolating between the intensities at its vertices, we need to know the intensities at these new 'clipping plane' vertices. This necessitates a new calculation in the clipping routine **clip** given in listing 14.2. When a new vertex is created by calculating the point of intersection between a facet edge and a clipping plane, its vertex normal is also calculated and stored by interpolating between those at the end-points of the facet edge. This can be executed using the **mu** value found by the intersection calculation. We leave this modification as an exercise.

Listing 15.12

```
VAR
     vna,vno : vertex3array ;

PROCEDURE setnormal ;
{ Routine to calculate ACTUAL vertex normals }
VAR i,j,k : integer ;
     norm : vector3 ;
     dummy : real ;
BEGIN
{ Initialise vertex normals }
   FOR i := 1 TO nov
   DO BEGIN
          vna[i].x := 0 ; vna[i].y := 0 ; vna[i].z := 0
          END ;
{ Calculate vertex normals by looping through facets and including the }
{ facet normal in the calculation of normal at each vertex on the facet }
   FOR i := 1 TO nof
   DO BEGIN
          normal(i,norm,dummy,act) ;
          FOR j := 1 TO size[i]
          DO BEGIN
                 k := faclist[facfront[i]+j] ;
                 vna[k].x := vna[k].x+norm.x ;
                 vna[k].y := vna[k].y+norm.y ;
                 vna[k].z := vna[k].z+norm.z
                 END
          END
END ; { of setnormal }

PROCEDURE observe ;
VAR i : integer ;
BEGIN
   setnormal ;
   FOR i := 1 TO nov
   DO BEGIN
```

```
        transform(act[i],Q,obs[i]) ;
        vno[i].x := Q[1,1]*vna[i].x+Q[1,2]*vna[i].y+Q[1,3]*vna[i].z ;
        vno[i].y := Q[2,1]*vna[i].x+Q[2,2]*vna[i].y+Q[2,3]*vna[i].z ;
        vno[i].z := Q[3,1]*vna[i].x+Q[3,2]*vna[i].y+Q[3,3]*vna[i].z
      END
END ; { of observe }


PROCEDURE facetfill(face : integer ; red,green,blue : realarray) ;
{ Fills facet using a scan line approach }
VAR i,j,jsize,ix,iy,newv,oldv,xmax,xmin,ymax,ymin,col : integer ;
    poly : pixelarray ;
    pix : pixelvector ;
    mu : real ;
    redval,greenval,blueval,redstep,greenstep,bluestep : real ;
    redmax,greenmax,bluemax,redmin,greenmin,bluemin : real ;
BEGIN
  j := nfac[face] ;
{ Find the pixel co-ordinates of the vertices }
  FOR i := 1 TO size[j]
  DO BEGIN
        poly[i].x := fx(pro[faclist[facfront[j]+i]].x) ;
        poly[i].y := fy(pro[faclist[facfront[j]+i]].y)
      END ;
{ Find minimum and maximum y values }
  ymax := poly[1].y ; ymin := poly[1].y ;
  FOR i := 2 TO size[j]
  DO BEGIN
        IF poly[i].y > ymax THEN ymax := poly[i].y ;
        IF poly[i].y < ymin THEN ymin := poly[i].y
      END ;
{ For each y, find maximum and minimum x values and }
{ the corresponding interpolated colour values }
  FOR iy := ymin TO ymax
  DO BEGIN
        pix.y := iy ;
        xmin := nxpix ; xmax := -1 ; oldv := size[j] ;
        FOR newv := 1 TO size[j]
        DO BEGIN
            IF (max(poly[oldv].y,poly[newv].y) >= iy ) AND
               (min(poly[oldv].y,poly[newv].y) <= iy ) AND
               (poly[oldv].y <> poly[newv].y)
            THEN BEGIN
                mu := (iy-poly[oldv].y)/(poly[newv].y-poly[oldv].y) ;
                ix := trunc((1-mu)*poly[oldv].x+mu*poly[newv].x+0.5) ;
                redval := (1-mu)*red[oldv]+mu*red[newv] ;
                greenval := (1-mu)*green[oldv]+mu*green[newv] ;
                blueval := (1-mu)*blue[oldv]+mu*blue[newv] ;
                IF ix < xmin
                THEN BEGIN
                        xmin := ix ; redmin := redval ;
                        greenmin := greenval ;
                        bluemin := blueval
                      END ;
                IF ix > xmax
```

```
                    THEN BEGIN
                            xmax := ix ; redmax := redval ;
                            greenmax := greenval ;
                            bluemax := blueval
                          END
                 END ;
              oldv := newv
           END ;
{ Set colour component increments }
        IF xmin < xmax
        THEN BEGIN
                redstep := (redmax-redmin)/(xmax-xmin) ;
                greenstep := (greenmax-greenmin)/(xmax-xmin) ;
                bluestep := (bluemax-bluemin)/(xmax-xmin)
              END
        ELSE BEGIN
                redstep := 0 ; greenstep := 0 ; bluestep := 0
              END ;
{ For each pixel on scan-line, find colour and display }
        redval := redmin ; greenval := greenmin ; blueval := bluemin ;
        FOR ix := xmin TO xmax
        DO BEGIN
                findlogicalcolour(redval,greenval,blueval,colour[face],col) ;
                setcol(col) ; pix.x := ix ; setpix(pix) ;
                redval := redval+redstep ;
                greenval := greenval+greenstep ;
                blueval := blueval+bluestep
              END
        END
END ; { of facetfill }

PROCEDURE seefacet(face : integer) ;
{ 'seefacet' routine for Gouraud shading }
VAR red,green,blue : realarray ;
    facenorm,norm,p : vector3 ;
    i,j,index,newface : integer ;
    dummy : real ;
BEGIN
{ Calculate surface normal to facet 'face' }
    normal(face,facenorm,dummy,obs) ;
{ Calculate shade at each vertex using vertex normals }
    FOR i := 1 TO size[face]
    DO BEGIN
            j := faclist[facfront[face]+i] ;
            IF (abs(vno[j].x) > epsilon) OR (abs(vno[j].y) > epsilon)
                    OR (abs(vno[j].z) > epsilon )
            THEN norm := vno[j]
            ELSE norm := facenorm ;
            p := obs[j] ;
            cshade(p,norm,colour[face],red[i],green[i],blue[i])
          END ;
{ Display facet, interpolating between these shades }
        facetfill(face,red,green,blue) ;
{ Repeat for each superficial facet }
        index := firstsup[face] ;
```

```
WHILE index > 0
DO BEGIN
      newface := permheap[index].info ;
      index := permheap[index].pointer ;
      FOR i := 1 TO size[newface]
      DO BEGIN
            j := faclist[facfront[newface]+i] ;
            IF (abs(vno[j].x) > epsilon) OR (abs(vno[j].y) > epsilon)
                    OR (abs(vno[j].z) > epsilon )
            THEN norm := vno[j]
            ELSE norm := facenorm ;
            p := obs[j] ;
            cshade(p,norm,colour[newface],red[i],green[i],blue[i])
      END ;
{ Display facet, interpolating between these shades }
            facetfill(newface,red,green,blue)
      END
END ; { of seefacet }
```

Plate VII shows a goblet displayed using Gouraud shading. Some problems remain with Gouraud shading, mainly involving facets which face almost directly towards the light source. In figure 15.7, for example, points A and B both have the same intensity and so interpolating between them results in a constant intensity across the surface, making it appear flat. Problems also occur with the depiction of highlights produced by specular reflection.

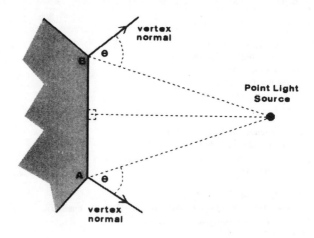

Figure 15.7

(3.3) Phong interpolation

These problems are eliminated by using Phong's *normal vector interpolation shading* (Phong, 1975). This method involves the calculation of the normal vector at each point on a surface by interpolating between the normals at the vertices, and thence calculating the shade by applying a shading model at that point. This method produces considerably more accurate and pleasing results but is accordingly more time-consuming in implementation. The **seefacet** and **facetfill** routines needed for normal interpolation shading are given in listing 15.13.

Listing 15.13

```
PROCEDURE facetfill(face : integer) ;
{ Fills facet using a scan line approach }
VAR i,j,index,inter,ix,iy,newv,oldv,xmax,xmin,ymax,ymin,col : integer ;
    mu,constant,red,green,blue : real ;
    vint,vmin,vmax,facenorm,p,step,windpt,zero : vector3 ;
    poly : pixelarray ;
    pix : pixelvector ;
    normv : vertex3array ;
BEGIN
    j := nfac[face] ;
{ Find surface normal to 'face' }
    normal(face,facenorm,constant,obs) ;
{ Find the pixel co-ordinates of the vertices }
    FOR i := 1 TO size[j]
    DO BEGIN
          index := faclist[facfront[j]+i] ;
          poly[i].x := fx(pro[index].x) ;
          poly[i].y := fy(pro[index].y) ;
          normv[i] := vno[index]
        END ;
{ Find minimum and maximum y values }
    ymax := poly[1].y ; ymin := poly[1].y ;
    FOR i := 2 TO size[j]
    DO BEGIN
          IF poly[i].y > ymax THEN ymax := poly[i].y ;
          IF poly[i].y < ymin THEN ymin := poly[i].y
        END ;
{ For each scan line find maximum and minimum x values and }
{ the corresponding normal vectors }
    FOR iy := ymin TO ymax
    DO BEGIN
          pix.y := iy ;
          xmin := nxpix ; xmax := -1 ; oldv := size[j] ;
          FOR newv := 1 TO size[j]
          DO BEGIN
                IF (max(poly[oldv].y,poly[newv].y) >= iy ) AND
                   (min(poly[oldv].y,poly[newv].y) <= iy ) AND
                   (poly[oldv].y <> poly[newv].y)
                THEN BEGIN
                      mu := (iy-poly[oldv].y)/(poly[newv].y-poly[oldv].y) ;
                      ix := trunc((1-mu)*poly[oldv].x+mu*poly[newv].x+0.5) ;
                      vint.x := (1-mu)*normv[oldv].x+mu*normv[newv].x ;
                      vint.y := (1-mu)*normv[oldv].y+mu*normv[newv].y ;
                      vint.z := (1-mu)*normv[oldv].z+mu*normv[newv].z ;
```

```
                    IF ix < xmin
                    THEN BEGIN
                            xmin := ix ; vmin := vint
                            END ;
                    IF ix > xmax
                    THEN BEGIN
                            xmax := ix ; vmax := vint
                            END
                END ;
            oldv := newv
        END ;
{ Set colour component increments }
        IF xmin < xmax
        THEN BEGIN
                step.x := (vmax.x-vmin.x)/(xmax-xmin) ;

                step.y := (vmax.y-vmin.y)/(xmax-xmin) ;
                step.z := (vmax.z-vmin.z)/(xmax-xmin)
                END
        ELSE BEGIN
                step.x := 0 ; step.y := 0 ; step.z := 0
                END ;
{ For each pixel on scan-line, find colour and display }
        vint.x := vmin.x ; vint.y := vmin.y ; vint.z := vmin.z ;
        FOR ix := xmin TO xmax
        DO BEGIN
{ Find WINDOW co-ordinates of point }
                windpt.x := ix/xyscale-horiz*0.5 ;
                windpt.y := iy/xyscale-vert*0.5 ;
                windpt.z := -ppd ;
                zero.x := 0 ; zero.y := 0 ; zero.z := 0 ;
                ilpl(zero,windpt,facenorm,p,constant,mu,inter) ;
                cshade(p,vint,colour[face],red,green,blue) ;
                findlogicalcolour(red,green,blue,colour[face],col) ;
                setcol(col) ; pix.x := ix ; setpix(pix) ;
                vint.x := vint.x+step.x ;
                vint.y := vint.y+step.y ;
                vint.z := vint.z+step.z
                END
        END
END ; { of facetfill }


PROCEDURE seefacet(face : integer) ;
{ 'seefacet' routine for Phong normal interpolation shading }
VAR index,newface : integer ;
BEGIN
{ Call 'facetfill' to display facet 'face' }
    facetfill(face) ;
{ Repeat for each superficial facet }
    index := firstsup[face] ;
    WHILE index > 0
    DO BEGIN
            newface := permheap[index].info ;
            index := permheap[index].pointer ;
            facetfill(newface)
            END
END ; { of seefacet }
```

The camera in Plate III was displayed using Phong's normal interpolation shading on the model used to produce Plates I and II. Also see Plate VIII of a Phong shaded chess piece.

Exercise 15.4

We can use shading models to simulate *texture* on a surface. The simplest method of simulating texture is provided by *random variation*. The shade of a pixel is calculated using one of the shading models detailed above. This shade is then altered slightly by a random function and the pixel displayed in this altered shade. This gives an appearance of roughness to the surface.

A more formalised method of texturing is achieved by distorting the normal vector using some *texture function*, see Plate IX. Instead of assuming that the normal to a facet is constant across the facet, we use the texture function to vary the normal from pixel to pixel, giving each pixel a different shade and thereby introducing a textured appearance (Blinn and Newell, 1976; Blinn, 1978). Experiment with these ideas.

Various Methods of Colour Definition

Although the RGB method of colour definition is the one most easily applied to a shading model, it is by no means the only method and is probably not the most easily understood since it does not correspond to our intuitive classification of colours. Other methods attempt to adhere more closely to these intuitions.

The HLS method (Ostwald, 1931), which is used by Tektronix, defines a colour in terms of its Hue, Lightness and Saturation. The RGB model is commonly represented as a unit cube in three-dimensional space, the three mutually perpendicular axes corresponding to red, green and blue (see figure 15.8). Each point within this cube (with co-ordinates (R, G, B)) defines a colour. The HLS model, on the other hand, is represented by two right hexagonal pyramids joined at their bases (figure 15.9). The lightness (L) is measured along the axis of the pyramid, ranging from white ($L = 1$) at the apex of one pyramid, to black ($L = 0$) at the apex of the other. The hue (H) is an angle between 0° and 360° measured around the L-axis in an anticlockwise direction as viewed from the point $L = 1$. On the Tektronix system, $H = 0°$ corresponds to blue, $H = 60°$ to magenta, followed by red, yellow, green and cyan at 60° intervals. The saturation of a colour (or a point) is the distance of the point from the L-axis. $S = 1$ gives the pure colour and $S = 0$ gives the grey value on the axis. Full intensity colours occur at $L = 0.5, S = 1$.

Another method, which is similar to the HLS method, is the HSV method (Smith, 1978). This model is represented by a single right hexagonal pyramid (figure 15.10). The Hue value (H) is measured as an angle around the axis exactly as with the HLS model. Value (V) is measured along the axis of the cone and ranges from black at the apex ($V = 0$) to white at the point where the axis intersects the hexagonal base ($V = 1$). The saturation (S) corresponds exactly to saturation in the HLS model. S is the distance of a point (representing a colour) from the axis of the cone. $S = 0$ represents a grey colour on the axis of the cone

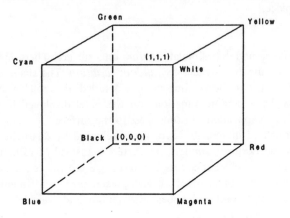

Figure 15.8

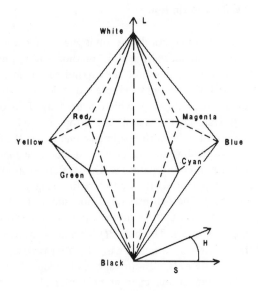

Figure 15.9

whereas $S = 1$ gives the pure colour. Full intensity colours occur at $V = 1, S = 1$.

Neither the lightness in the HLS model, nor the value in the HSV model corresponds to intensity. Our colour shading model *must* use the RGB model. However, you can define the colour of a surface in terms of either HLS or HSV and convert the colour to its RGB equivalent before calculating any shades. The routines **hlsrgb** and **hsvrgb** given in listing 15.14 may be used to convert HLS and HSV respectively to RGB.

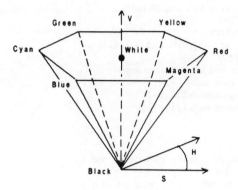

Figure 15.10

Listing 15.14

```
PROCEDURE hlsrgb( h,l,s : real ; VAR r,g,b) ;
{ Converts 'h','l','s' colour to 'r','g','b' using function 'comparison' }
{ RANGES :-  'h': 0 to 360,  'l','s','r','g','b' : 0 to 1 }
VAR v1,v2 : real ;

        FUNCTION comparison(h,v1,v2 : real ) ;
        VAR hue : real ;
        BEGIN
           IF h > 360
           THEN hue := h-360
           ELSE IF h < 0
                   THEN hue := h+360
                   ELSE hue := h ;
           IF hue < 60
           THEN comparison := (v2-v1)*hue/60+v1
           ELSE IF hue < 180
                   THEN comparison := v2
                   ELSE IF hue < 240
                           THEN comparison := (v2-v1)*(240-hue)/60+v1
                           ELSE comparison := v1
        END ; { of comparison }

BEGIN
{ Zero saturation means grey }
   IF(s < epsilon)
   THEN BEGIN
           r := 1 ; g := 1 ; b := 1
           END ;
```

```pascal
    ELSE BEGIN
{ Calculate parameters 'v1' and 'v2' }
        IF(l < 0.5)
        THEN BEGIN
                v1 := l-l*s ; v2 := l+l*s
             END
        ELSE BEGIN
                v1 := l-(1-l)*s ; v2 := l+(1-l)*s
             END ;
{ Use 'v1' and 'v2' to find colour components }
        r := comparison(h,v1,v2) ;
        g := comparison(h-120,v1,v2) ;
        b := comparison(h+120,v1,v2)
        END
END ; { of hlsrgb }


PROCEDURE hsvrgb(h,s,v : real ; VAR r,g,b : real ) ;
{ Converts 'h','s','v' colour to 'r','g','b' }
{ RANGES :-   'h': 0 to 360,   's','v','r','g','b' : 0 to 1 }
VAR hue,r,x,y,z : real ;
    i : integer ;

        PROCEDURE set(VAR r,g,b : real ; x,y,z : real) ;
        { Sets 'r','g','b' to equal 'x','y','z' respectively }
        BEGIN
            r := x ; g := y ; b := z
        END ; { of set }

BEGIN
{ Zero saturation means grey }
    IF (s < epsilon)
    THEN BEGIN
            r := v ; g := v ; b := v
         END ;
    ELSE BEGIN
{ Place HUE in range [0,6) }
            IF hue > (360-epsilon)
            THEN hue := 0
            ELSE hue := h/60 ;
{ 'i' is integer part of 'hue', 'r' is fractional part }
            i := trunc(hue) ; r := hue-i ;
{ Calculate parameters 'x','y' and 'z' }
            x := v*(1-s) ; y := v*(1-s*r) ; z := v*(1-s*(1-r)) ;
{ Find colour components }
            CASE i OF
            0 : set(r,g,b,v,z,x) ;
            1 : set(r,g,b,y,v,x) ;
            2 : set(r,g,b,x,v,z) ;
            3 : set(r,g,b,x,y,v) ;
            4 : set(r,g,b,z,x,v) ;
            5 : set(r,g,b,v,x,y)
            ENDCASE
         END
END ; { of hsvrgb }
```

There are many other colour models: a comprehensive study is given by Foley and Van Dam (1981).

A vast amount of work has been done in recent years on the development of shading models in computer graphics and much has been written on the subject (Blinn, 1977; Whitted, 1980). Images of remarkable realism can be achieved and you will find it very rewarding to delve deeper into this field. We must move on, however. In the next chapter we shall consider the incorporation of such concepts as shadows, reflections and transparent surfaces into our polygon mesh model.

16 Shadows, Transparent Surfaces and Reflections

A facet which obscures all or part of another facet from exposure to a light source is said to *cast a shadow* onto this other facet. A shadow cast by a convex polygonal facet, J, onto another convex polygonal facet, I, is also a convex polygon which may be considered to lie on the surface of facet I. We call this polygon a *shadow polygon* . The amount of light reflected from a point in shadow was discussed in chapter 15: in this chapter we turn our attention to the finding and displaying of shadow polygons. We shall describe an algorithm which may be used to achieve this aim. This algorithm is merely an example to show how the problem can be tackled. There are many alternative solutions (Crow, 1977). The criterion for finding shadows is very similar to that for finding hidden surfaces and most hidden surface algorithms can be adapted accordingly. The method which we describe here is based on the general hidden surface algorithm of chapter 13.

There are two main problems to solve

(i) incorporating shadow polygons into the data structure
(ii) finding the vertices of the shadow polygons.

The solution to the first problem is considerably simplified if we use a single light source. Initially we shall assume this to be the case and we shall discuss the extension to multiple light sources later.

Representing Shadow Polygons – Superficial Facets

Superficial facets were introduced in chapter 9 for the representation of surface detail polygons. The concept fits exactly our requirement for the storage of shadow polygons. A superficial facet lies on the surface of a larger facet which we call its *host facet*. It need not be considered in hidden surface elimination since in all cases it is displayed only if its host facet is displayed.

The shadow polygons are stored in exactly the same way as the ordinary facets of a scene and may thus be referred to by simple integer indices which we store in the dynamic heap (chapter 13). We introduce a new item into the global database

    {VAR} lsh : facetarray;

lsh[i] is an integer which points to the starting location of a linear list contained in the **heap** array which holds the indices of all facets which represent shadows on facet i of the scene.

Initially all shadow lists are empty and so lsh[i] is set to 0 for each i. Now suppose we find that facet j casts a shadow onto facet i and that this shadow is a polygon with nsv vertices. The OBSERVED co-ordinates of these vertices are appended, in order, to the **obs** array and the indices of these vertices are stored in the **faclist** array as faclist[last + 1] . . . faclist[last + nsv]. ntf is incremented by 1, start[ntf] is set to last, size[ntf] to nsv, and last is reset to last + nsv. Finally the value ntf is pushed onto the list lsh[i]. See listing 16.1.

In order to find the complete set of shadow polygons, we must compare the facets of a scene in pairs to determine whether either casts a shadow onto the other, hence the similarity to a hidden surface algorithm. We shall examine the details of this comparison later, but first let us consider the question of precisely which pairs need be compared. We may discard some comparisons immediately for one of four reasons

(i) Both facets lie entirely outside the pyramid of vision or both facets are oriented clockwise when projected onto the view plane. In either case we can see neither facet and so there is no need to find the shadows since they are not going to be displayed anyway. It is important to note, however, that a facet which we cannot see can still cast a shadow onto a facet which we can see. Therefore, if either facet of a pair may be seen then the pair must be considered.

(ii) Both facets are superficial facets. It is important that we find the shadows cast by an ordinary facet onto a superficial facet since these will, in general, be of a different colour from those cast onto the host facet. However, we need not consider shadows cast *by* a superficial facet since these will only be parts of those cast by the larger host facet.

(iii) One of the facets is superficial to the other: the facets are coplanar and hence no shadow is cast.

(iv) One of the two facets faces away from the light source. If a facet faces away from the light source then it can neither cast a shadow nor have a shadow cast upon it. No such facet need be considered.

Each of these cases is checked for in the routine **shadow** (listing 16.1) before a pair of facets is compared. This routine creates and stores information about shadows cast and calls two routines, **prepare** and **compare**, which will be described later in the chapter (listing 16.3). **prepare** creates a new co-ordinate system which facilitates the calculation of shadows and **compare** compares two facets, i and j, returning the OBSERVED co-ordinates of the vertices of the shadow cast (if any) together with the integers **front** and **back** indicating that facet **front** casts a shadow onto facet **back**. If front = 0 then no shadow is cast.

Listing 16.1

```
VAR
    prol : vertex2array ;
    lsh : facetarray ;
    vl : vertex3array ;

PROCEDURE shadow ;
{ Calculates and stores all shadow polygons }
VAR back,front,i,j,k,nsv : integer ;
        shadpol : vector3array ;
        normindex : ARRAY[1..maxf] OF integer ;
BEGIN
{ Set up co-ordinate system for shadow calculation }
    prepare ;
{ Determine orientation of facets }
    FOR i := 1 TO nof
    DO BEGIN
            IF orient(i,pro) = 1
            THEN normindex[i] := 0      { Facet 'i' faces towards eye }
            ELSE normindex[i] := -1 ; { Facet 'i' faces away from eye }
            IF orient(i,prol) = 1
            THEN lsh[i] := 0      { Facet 'i' faces towards light }
            ELSE lsh[i] := -1    { Facet 'i' faces away from light }
        END ;
{ Compare pairs of facets : 'i' and 'j' }
    FOR i := 1 TO nof-1
{ If facet 'i' faces away from light source then don't use it }
    DO IF lsh[i] = 0
            THEN FOR j := i+1 TO nof
{ If facet 'j' faces away from light source then don't use it }
{ If both facets 'i' and 'j' are superficial then don't compare }
{ If neither facet 'i' nor 'j' can be seen then don't compare }
{ If one facet is superficial to the other then don't compare }
                DO IF (lsh[j] = 0)
                        AND (normindex[i]+normindex[j] < > -2)
                        AND ((super[i] = 0) OR (super[j] = 0))
                        AND (super[i] < > j) AND (super[j] < > i)
                    THEN BEGIN
                            compare(i,j,front,back,nsv,shadpol) ;
{ No shadow if 'front' facet superficial or 'back' facet cannot be seen }
                        IF (front < > 0)
                            AND (super[front] = 0)
                            AND (normindex[back] = 0)
                        THEN BEGIN
{ Create new facet representing shadow polygon }
                                ntf := ntf+1 ; size[ntf] := nsv ;
                                facfront[ntf] := last ;
                                FOR k := 1 TO nsv
                                DO BEGIN
                                        ntv := ntv+1 ;
                                        obs[ntv] := shadpol[k] ;
                                        faclist[last+k] := ntv
                                    END ;
```

```
                        last := last+nsv ;
{ Push the new facet onto the list of shadows ('lsh') facet back }
                        push(lsh[back],ntf)
                  END
            END
END ; { of shadow }
```

Displaying shadow polygons

With the data structure constructed in the manner described above, the display
of shadows is a relatively trivial matter. There are essentially three problems to
consider — deciding when to draw a shadow, setting the colour and calculating
the viewport co-ordinates of the vertices of the polygon to be plotted.

The first two are easy. When a host facet has been displayed we immediately
scan the linear list of indices of shadow polygons and draw them in the logical
colour returned by a shading model considering only ambient light on the
material of the host facet. The third problem requires a little more consideration.
The polygon may have to be clipped before it can be displayed, since it may lie
partly or entirely outside the pyramid of vision. The routine clip (listing 14.2)
is therefore invoked, returning a value clipindex which describes the clipping
done. If clipindex = 1, then no clipping was necessary and the projections of the
vertices of the shadow polygon are calculated and the polygon displayed. If
clipindex = 2 then the shadow polygon lies totally outside the pyramid of vision
and so should not be displayed. If clipindex = 3 then clipping has occurred and a
new facet with index ntf has been created. This new facet is displayed and then
discarded from the database by setting ntv, ntf and last to their previous values.

When all of the shadow polygons on a main facet have been displayed, we
move onto the superficial facets on that main facet. Each is displayed in turn
followed by the shadows lying on it.

This process is programmed in the routine displayshadows (listing 16.2)
which is called from the alternative routine seefacet (also given in listing 16.2).

Listing 16.2

```
PROCEDURE displayshadows(face : integer ) ;
{ Displays shadows on given 'face' }
VAR redval,greenval,blueval,ambient : real ;
    clipindex,col,i,index,newface,nlast,nnf,nnv,starti : integer ;
BEGIN
{ Set colour to that given by reflected ambient light }
    ambient := 0.3 ;
    redval := rm[colour[face]]*ambient ;
    greenval := gm[colour[face]]*ambient ;
    blueval := bm[colour[face]]*ambient ;
    findlogicalcolour(redval,greenval,blueval,colour[face],col) ;
{ Scan list of shadows, drawing each in turn }
    index := lsh[face] ;
    WHILE index > 0
```

```
     DO BEGIN
          newface := heap[index].info ; index := heap[index].pointer ;
          nnv := ntv ; nnf := ntf ; nlast := last ;
          clip(newface,clipindex) ;
          IF clipindex < >2
          THEN BEGIN
                    IF clipindex = 1
                    THEN nfac[newface] := newface
                    ELSE nfac[newface] := ntf ;
{ Calculate projections of vertices }
                    FOR i := 1 TO size[nfac[newface]]
                    DO BEGIN
                         starti := faclist[facfront[nfac[newface]]+i] ;
                         pro[starti].x := -obs[starti].x*ppd/obs[starti].z ;
                         pro[starti].y := -obs[starti].y*ppd/obs[starti].z
                    END ;
{ Draw shadow }
                    facetfill(newface,col) ;
                    nfac[newface] := newface ;
                    ntv := nnv ; ntf := nnf ; last := nlast
               END
          END
END ; { of displayshadows }

PROCEDURE seefacet(face : integer) ;
{ 'seefacet' routine for constant shading display with shadows }
VAR dummy,red,green,blue : real ;
     midpt,normv : vector3 ;
     index,newface,pt : integer ;
BEGIN
{ Find the mid-point and normal of facet'face' }
     midpoint(face,midpt) ; normal(face,normv,dummy,obs) ;
{ Find apparent colour of facet 'face' }
     cshade(midpt,normv,colour[face],red,green,blue) ;
     findlogicalcolour(red,green,blue,colour[face],index) ;
{ Display the facet }
     facetfill(face,index) ;
     displayshadows(face) ;
{ Repeat for each superficial facet on facet 'face' }
     pt := firstsup[face] ;
     WHILE pt>0
     DO BEGIN
          newface := permheap[pt].info ; pt := permheap[pt].pointer ;
          cshade(midpt,normv,colour[newface],red,green,blue) ;
          findlogicalcolour(red,green,blue,colour[newface],index) ;
          facetfill(newface,index) ; displayshadows(newface) ;
     END
END ; { of seefacet }
```

Finding the shadow polygons

All that remains is to find the vertices of a shadow cast by one facet onto
another.

A shadow polygon is a projection of one facet onto another (figure 16.1).

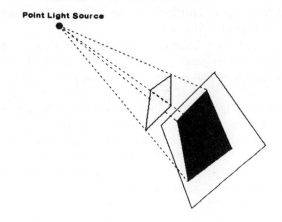

Figure 16.1

We may make use of the properties of linear projections to enable us to use the **overlap** routine (listing 13.1) to find shadow polygons.

Recall that a projection is described by a set of *lines of projection.* (For an orthographic projection, these lines are parallel; for a perspective projection they emanate from a single point.) The projection of a vertex onto a plane is the point of intersection between the plane and the line of projection passing through the vertex (if such a point exists). The projection of a facet onto a plane is the polygon in the plane whose vertices are the projections of the vertices of the facet. In this instance, the lines of projection are the light rays.

Our aim is to find out which, if either, of two facets, I or J, casts a shadow onto the other and to calculate the co-ordinates of the vertices of the shadow if it exists. If we have a projection plane onto which both facets may be projected, the area of overlap of the two projected facets is the projection of the shadow polygon. (If the overlap is empty then no shadow is cast.) The shadow is cast by the facet nearer the light source onto that further away: information which may also be gleaned from the **overlap** routine. We may determine the three-dimensional co-ordinates of the vertices of the shadow polygon by calculating the intersections between the light rays passing through the projections of these vertices and the plane containing the host facet. This is the general strategy: how do we implement it?

The first question is which plane do we choose for the projection? We only compare facets a pair at a time so, in theory, for any given pair, we can choose any plane onto which all of the vertices of both facets may be projected, and then choose a different plane for each pair. This method would be excessively time-consuming, requiring many transformations for each comparison. It is preferable to use the same plane for the projection of each pair of facets and we could then calculate and store the projected co-ordinates of all vertices before beginning the process of comparisons. Can we find a suitable plane? This depends on the choice of type of light source.

If we use parallel beam illumination then we have a parallel projection since all lines of projection are parallel. In this case we may choose any plane perpendicular to the direction of the light rays and this gives us an orthographic projection.

If we use a point light source then all lines of projection emanate from a single point — a perspective projection. In this case the choice of plane is not so easy and enforces a restriction upon the positioning of the light source. Given a point in the centre of the scene, we define a direction vector, d, from the light source to this point. We define a new right-handed co-ordinate system, called the LIGHT co-ordinate system, with the origin at the light source and the negative z-axis along the direction d. The co-ordinates of each vertex relative to this system are calculated. We call these co-ordinates *light-related co-ordinates*. The restriction which we impose is that the light source is positioned in such a way that every vertex has a strictly negative light-related z co-ordinate, in which case any projection plane perpendicular to the negative z-axis of the LIGHT system may be used.

The transformation to a co-ordinate system with the eye at the origin and the negative z-axis along a prescribed direction was described in chapter 8 (routines findQ, look3 and observe). The situation described above is exactly analogous. We find the LIGHT co-ordinate system using a transformation of the OBSERVER system. (If we use a parallel beam illumination then there is no particular point which may be identified in analogy to the eye so we choose an arbitrary point, the existing origin of the OBSERVER system — the choice of this point does not affect the shadows found. The negative z-axis takes the direction of the light beams, l). From now on we shall assume the use of a point light source. The matrix, S, representing the transformation from OBSERVER co-ordinate system to LIGHT co-ordinate system, is calculated in the routine lightsystem in listing 16.3. This calculation is very similar to that in findQ in listing 8.1. The routine also calculates the inverse matrix, S^{-1} (SI in the listing), for a reason that will become clear later. The matrices S and SI are declared globally

{VAR} S,SI : matrix4×4;

along with the light-related co-ordinates of all vertices

{VAR} vl : vertex3array;

The vertices are projected onto the projection plane perpendicular to the negative z-axis of the LIGHT system and the x and y light-related co-ordinates of the points are declared

{VAR} prol : vertex2array;

These projected co-ordinates are all of the form $(x, y, -d)$ where d is the perpendicular distance of the projection plane from the light source. The value of d does not affect the shadows found and so we arbitrarily use the value **ppd** (the perspective plane distance, defined in chapter 11). The light-related co-ordinates of all vertices are found in the routine **prepare** (listing 16.3).

With the co-ordinates of all vertices of a scene stored in this form we may proceed with the comparisons. Given the indices of two facets i and j we must find the area of overlap between the projections of these facets. We may use the **overlap** routine (listing 13.1) to provide this information. Recall that a call to this routine returns the following information

> front,
> back: if no area of overlap exists then **front** is returned as 0, otherwise **front** and **back** contain the indices of the facets nearer to the origin and further from the origin respectively
> shp: a **vector2array** area containing the projected x and y co-ordinates of the vertices of the area of overlap relative to the co-ordinate system implied by the parameters, in this case the LIGHT system

This information is all we need. If **front** is returned as 0 then no action need be taken. Otherwise a shadow polygon has been found, representing a shadow cast by facet **front** onto facet **back**. We must calculate the OBSERVED co-ordinates of the vertices of this polygon for return to the **shadow** routine. All we have at the moment are the projected light-related co-ordinates of the vertices. We may find the three-dimensional light-related co-ordinates by calculating the intersections of the light rays passing through these projected vertices with the plane containing facet **back**. The vector representation of this plane may be found using the routine **normal** in listing 12.2 and the point of intersection found by **ilpl** listing 6.2. The light ray passing through a point with light-related co-ordinates (x, y, z) is given by the line $(0, 0, 0) + \mu(x, y, z)$ since the light source is at the origin.

The OBSERVED co-ordinates of the vertices may then be found by applying the transformation represented by S^{-1} to the light-related co-ordinates. The transformation from projected light-related co-ordinates to OBSERVED co-ordinates is achieved by the routine **restore** in listing 16.3.

Listing 16.3

```
VAR
    S,SI : matrix4x4 ;

PROCEDURE lightsystem ;
{ Sets up light co-ordinate system }
VAR E,F,G,H,V,W : matrix4x4 ;
    alpha,beta,gamma,dist,xmax,ymax,zmax,xmin,ymin,zmin : real ;
```

```
      i : integer ;
      direct : vector3 ;
BEGIN
{ Find the centre point of the scene }
   xmax := -99999.9 ; ymax := -99999.9 ; zmax := -99999.9 ;
   xmin :=  99999.9 ; ymin :=  99999.9 ; zmin :=  99999.9 ;
   FOR i := 1 TO nov
   DO BEGIN
           IF obs[i].x > xmax THEN xmax := obs[i].x ;
           IF obs[i].x < xmin THEN xmin := obs[i].x ;
           IF obs[i].y > ymax THEN ymax := obs[i].y ;
           IF obs[i].y < ymin THEN ymin := obs[i].y ;
           IF obs[i].z > zmax THEN zmax := obs[i].z ;
           IF obs[i].z < zmin THEN zmin := obs[i].z
        END ;
   direct.x := (xmax+xmin)/2-src.x ;
   direct.y := (ymax+ymin)/2-src.y ;
   direct.z := (zmax+zmin)/2-src.z ;
{ Calculate translation matrix 'F' }
   tran3(src.x,src.y,src.z,F) ;
{ Calculate rotation matrix 'G' }
   alpha := angle(-direct.x,-direct.y) ; rot3(3,alpha,G) ;
{ Calculate rotation matrix 'H' }
   dist := sqrt(sqr(direct.x)+sqr(direct.y)) ;
   beta := angle(-direct.z,dist) ; rot3(2,beta,H) ;
{ Calculate rotation matrix 'V' }
   dist := sqrt(sqr(dist)+sqr(direct.z)) ;
   gamma := angle(-direct.x*dist,direct.y*direct.z) ; rot3(3,-gamma,V) ;
{ Combine the transformations to find 'S' }
   mult3(G,F,W) ; mult3(H,W,E) ; mult3(V,E,S) ;
{ Reverse the process to find the inverse of 'S (SI)' }
   tran3(-src.x,-src.y,-src.z,F) ;
   rot3(3,-alpha,G) ; rot3(2,-beta,H) ; rot3(3,gamma,V) ;
   mult3(H,V,W) ; mult3(G,W,E) ; mult3(F,E,SI)
END ; { of lightsystem }


PROCEDURE prepare ;
{ Finds light-related co-ordinates of each vertex }
VAR i : integer ;
BEGIN
   lightsystem ;
   FOR i := 1 TO ntv
   DO BEGIN
           transform(obs[i],S,vl[i]) ;
           prol[i].x := (-vl[i].x*ppd)/vl[i].z ;
           prol[i].y := (-vl[i].y*ppd)/vl[i].z
        END
END ; { of prepare }

PROCEDURE restore(face,nsh : integer ; VAR shadpol : vector3array) ;
{ Finds OBSERVED co-ords of vertices from projected light-related co-ords }
VAR i,l : integer ;
     dummy,val : real ;
     normv,vectori : vector3 ;
BEGIN
```

```
        normal(face,normv,val,vl) ;
        FOR i := 1 TO nsh
        DO BEGIN
                shadpol[i].z := -ppd ;
                ilpl(zero,shadpol[i],normv,vectori,val,dummy,l) ;
                transform(vectori,SI,shadpol[i])
            END
END ; { of restore }


PROCEDURE compare(i,j : integer ; VAR front,back,nsh : integer ;
                                 VAR shadpol : vector3array ) ;
{ Compares facets 'i' and 'j', finding shadow cast by one on other }
VAR k,stofaci,stofacj : integer ;
    shp : vector2array ;
BEGIN
{ Adjust 'nfac' values so that unclipped shadow is found }
    stofaci := nfac[i] ; stofacj := nfac[j] ;
    nfac[i] := i ; nfac[j] := j ;
{ Call 'overlap' to find the projection of the shadow }
    overlap(i,j,front,back,nsh,shp,prol,vl,l) ;
{ Reset 'nfac' values }
    nfac[i] := stofaci ; nfac[j] := stofacj ;
{ If 'front' is 0 then no shadow is cast }
{ Otherwise find OBSERVED co-ordinates of shadow's vertices }
    IF front < > 0
    THEN BEGIN
            FOR k := 1 TO nsh
            DO BEGIN shadpol[k].x := shp[k].x ;
                     shadpol[k].y := shp[k].y
                END ;
            restore(back,nsh,shadpol)
        END
END ; { of compare }
```

The **drawit** *routine*

Shadows may be calculated and stored by a single call to **shadow**. We incorporate this call into the new **drawit** routine (listing 16.4).

Listing 16.4

```
PROCEDURE drawit ;
BEGIN
{ Set vertex and facet counts }
    ntv := nov ; ntf := nof ; ppd := 3*horiz ; materialin ;
{ prepare and draw scene }
    colourtable ; clipscene ; project ; insource ; shadow ; hidden
END ; { of drawit }
```

Example 16.1

Plate X shows the scene of deck-chairs displaying using shadows.

Exercise 16.1

Rewrite the routines given so far in this chapter for use with parallel beam illumination instead of a point light source.

Exercise 16.2

Note that the ACTUAL positions of shadow polygons are totally independent of the eye position. If multiple views of a scene are required, with fixed light source, we may store shadow polygons in such a way that we need not recalculate them for each new view. Rewrite the routines to store shadows in this way. You must store the ACTUAL co-ordinates of the vertices instead of the OBSERVED co-ordinates, and hence you must transform the ACTUAL co-ordinates to OB-SERVED co-ordinates in the **displayshadows** routine before calculating the pro-jected co-ordinates. Furthermore, you cannot eliminate comparisons so freely in the **shadow** routine — you must find the shadows cast onto a facet regardless of whether it can be seen in any particular view. Finally, the indices of shadow polygons must be stored on the permanent heap rather than the dynamic heap, as the latter is emptied before each view.

Exercise 16.3

The algorithm which we describe deals with a single light source. It can be ex-tended to cope with multiple light sources. The shadow polygons generated by each light source must be calculated and stored. With each such polygon an integer must be associated, indicating which light source does not illuminate the polygon, together with a colour calculated from the illumination by all of the other light sources.

When the time comes to draw a facet the following process must be followed

(i) Draw the facet.

(ii) Draw the shadow polygons generated by light source 1.

(iii) Draw the shadow polygons generated by light source 2, storing the inter-sections with each of those generated by light source 1.

(iv) Draw the areas of intersection which have been stored (shadow polygons generated by light sources (1 and 2)) in a colour determined by illumination by all light sources except 1 and 2.

(v) Draw the shadow polygons generated by light source 3, storing the areas of intersection with each of those generated by light sources 1, 2 and (1 and 2) respectively.

(vi) Draw the shadow polygons generated by light sources (1 and 3), then (2 and 3), then (1, 2 and 3).

The process must be limited by a maximum number of light sources. The implementation of this process is a major programming exercise (see project 19 in chapter 18).

Transparent Surfaces

It was mentioned in chapter 15 that many hidden surface algorithms can be adapted to allow for the inclusion of transparent surfaces in the data for a scene. This is by no means a trivial exercise. For a full simulation, taking into account specular reflection, refraction etc., a ray-tracing approach (mentioned in chapter 10) must be adopted (Kay and Greenberg, 1979; Whitted, 1980). Nevertheless, if we accept certain limitations, we can deal with transparent surfaces in the polygon mesh model using the topological ordering algorithm of chapter 13. In the algorithm described here, we impose some restrictions — we do not allow for the inclusion of shadows, nor do we allow for the possibility of rays passing through more than one transparent surface (so if there are several transparent facets in a scene, they must all be in the same plane, or else viewing positions must be chosen carefully). The algorithm can be extended to take these possibilities into account, however, and we shall discuss such extensions at the end of the explanation.

Having imposed the above restrictions, we may adapt the hidden surface algorithm with only minimal changes to existing routines (**hidden** and **unstack**: listing 13.1). Recall that we use the routine **overlap** (listing 13.1) to find the area of intersection between the projections of two facets and we deduce that the corresponding three-dimensional area on the front facet obscures the corresponding area on the back facet. Suppose, however, that the front facet is transparent. Instead of the overlapped part of the back facet being obscured, it is visible in an apparent colour influenced by the colour and extent of transparency of the front facet. (Note that a transparent surface is visible from either side and so each must be stored twice in the database unless one side is always totally obscured by non-transparent surfaces.)

We implement this idea in the following manner

(i) Use the routine **network** to construct the network structure as before.

(ii) Before commencing the drawing of a scene, all of the transparent surfaces are displayed. This ensures that all of the parts of these facets which 'obscure' no other facet will be visible in the completed image.

(iii) The **hidden** routine proceeds as before, first **push**ing all those facets which obscure no other (**nob**[i] = 0) onto a stack.

(iv) One value is **pop**ped from the stack, giving the index, **k** say, of the next facet to be displayed. If facet **k** is transparent (**tr**[k] > 0) then it is not displayed, otherwise it is.

(v) The list (**list**[k]) of facets obscuring **k** is then scanned as before, and each corresponding **nob** value is reduced by 1 and a facet **push**ed onto the stack if its **nob** value becomes zero. If an obscuring facet is transparent then the area of overlap between this facet and facet **k** is calculated and displayed in a colour found by mixing the apparent colour of facet **k** with that of the transparent facet, in the manner described in chapter 15. (Our restrictions ensure that this cannot occur if facet **k** is transparent.)

(vi) The steps (iv) and (v) are repeated and the process continues until the stack becomes empty.

The new **hidden** and **unstack** routines and the declaration of array **tr** are given in listing 16.5.

Listing 16.5

```
VAR
    tr : ARRAY[1..maxmaterl] OF real ;


PROCEDURE hidden ;
{ Hidden surface algorithm for transparent surfaces }

TYPE stackpointer = ^stacknode ;
     stacknode = RECORD info : integer ;
                        ptr : stackpointer
                 END ;
     pointarray = ARRAY[1..maxf] OF stackpointer ;

VAR i,k,numbervisible : integer ;
    nob : facetarray ;
    list : pointarray ;
    stack,networkstack : stackpointer ;
    face,nvis : integer ;

( routines from listing 13.1 }
{ PROCEDURE stackpush(VAR stack : stackpointer ; stackvalue : integer) ; }
{ PROCEDURE stackpop(VAR stack : stackpointer ; VAR stackvalue : integer) ; }
{ PROCEDURE network(VAR numvis : integer ; VAR nob : facetarray ;
                         VAR list : pointarray ; v : vertex3array ;
                         p : vertex2array ; orientation : integer ) ; }

PROCEDURE unstack(face : integer ; VAR nob : facetarray ;
                      VAR list : pointarray ; VAR stack : stackpointer) ;
VAR poly : vector2array ;
    red1,green1,blue1,red2,green2,blue2 : real ;
    tranval,redtran,greentran,bluetran,dummy : real ;
    mid,normv : vector3 ;
    nf,front,back,n,col : integer ;
BEGIN
{ Calculate apparent colour of facet 'face' : redval, greenval, blueval }
    normal(face,normv,dummy,obs) ; midpoint(face,mid) ;
    cshade(mid,normv,colour[face],red1,green1,blue1) ;
{ Scan list of facets obscuring 'face' }
    WHILE (list[face] <> NIL)
    DO BEGIN
          stackpop(list[face],nf) ; nob[nf] := nob[nf]-1 ;
          IF nob[nf] = 0 THEN stackpush(stack,nf) ;
{ If obscuring facet is transparent then find overlap with 'face' and draw }
          IF (tr[colour[nf]] > 0)
          THEN BEGIN
                  overlap(face,nf,front,back,n,poly,pro,obs,1) ;
                  normal(nf,normv,dummy,obs) ; midpoint(face,mid) ;
                  cshade(mid,normv,colour[nf],red2,green2,blue2) ;
```

```
                  tranval := tr[colour[nf]] ;
                  redtran := (1-tranval)*red1+tranval*red2 ;
                  greentran := (1-tranval)*green1+tranval*green2 ;
                  bluetran := (1-tranval)*blue1+tranval*blue2 ;
                  findlogicalcolour(redtran,greentran,bluetran,colour[nf],col) ;
                  setcol(col) ; polyfill(n,poly)
            END
      END
END ; { of unstack }
BEGIN
   network(nvis,nob,list,obs,pro,1) ; stack := NIL ;
   FOR i := 1 TO nof
   DO BEGIN
         IF (tr[colour[i]] > 0) THEN seefacet(i) ;
         IF (nob[i] = 0) THEN stackpush(stack,i)
      END ;
   FOR i := 1 TO nvis
   DO BEGIN
         stackpop(stack,face) ;
         IF face=0 THEN EXIT ;
         IF (tr[colour[face]] < = epsilon) THEN seefacet(face) ;
         unstack(face,nob,list,stack)
      END
END ; { of hidden }
```

Example 16.2

Plate XI shows a scene viewed through two coloured transparent facets.

Exercise 16.4

If transparent surfaces overlap in a view then the calculations are not quite so simple. When the area of overlap between a transparent facet and the facet k is calculated and displayed, it must also be stored as a facet superficial to k. If another transparent facet is encountered in the list of those obscuring k, then the overlap of this facet with k must be calculated, displayed and stored, along with the overlap with the previously created superficial facets. Furthermore, if the projections of two transparent facets overlap in an area onto which no other facet is projected, then a mixture of the facet colours and the background colour must be displayed. Implement a hidden surface algorithm which allows for overlapping transparent facets. Note that the order in which you store the areas of overlap is important — the part of a facet seen through i transparent facets cannot be displayed until those parts viewed through j $(0 \leqslant j < i)$ transparent facets have been displayed. The method of tackling this problem bears many similarities to the solution of the problem of shadows cast by multiple light sources (exercise 16.3).

Exercise 16.5

The inclusion of shadows in the view of a scene containing transparent surfaces poses three problems

(i) Dealing with shadows cast by transparent surfaces.

(ii) Dealing with shadows cast onto transparent surfaces.

(iii) Dealing with shadows on other facets which are visible through a transparent surface.

The first of these problems proves difficult only in determining the colour of the shadow, the other two provide many more difficulties. Think about these problems. The implementation of an algorithm which allows for both shadows and multiple transparent surfaces is a large exercise (see project 19 in chapter 18) and is more easily tackled using a ray-tracing approach.

Reflections

Suppose one facet in a scene is a mirror. We should be able to see the reflection of the scene in this *mirror*. We can use some of the techniques which we have already introduced to produce an image of such a reflection.

We call the plane containing the mirror facet the *mirror plane*. In chapter 6 we described the calculation of the reflection of a point in a plane. If we calculate the reflection of each vertex of the scene in the mirror plane, we have the *physical reflection* of the scene. (Note that here we are creating a new set of points with co-ordinates specified in relation to the *same* co-ordinate system — the OBSERVER system.) The facet definitions still hold (with indices now referring to the corresponding vertices in the new set of points) except that where the vertices were listed in anti-clockwise orientation around a facet in the true model, the orientation is clockwise in the reflected model (figure 16.2).

How can we relate this physical reflection with the reflection observed in the mirror? Imagine that the mirror facet is a window surrounded by an infinite plane. The reflection in the mirror is precisely the part of the physical reflection which can be seen through (and beyond) this window. Those parts of the physical reflection which lie in front of the mirror cannot be seen in the reflection since in the real scene they lie behind the mirror. The problem thus reduces to projecting the reflected scene onto the view plane and drawing only those parts which intersect with the projection of the mirror and lie behind the mirror in reflected space — a problem once again solved by the **overlap** routine (listing 13.1). There is a major drawback to any algorithm for finding reflections of scenes. If you sit in front of a mirror with another mirror behind you, what do you see? You see a reflection of yourself in the mirror in front of you, but you also see a reflection of the mirror behind you, in which you see a reflection of your back and of the mirror in front of you, in which you see a reflection of the mirror behind you and so on! The process is infinite and there is no way round this. We must either insist that a scene contains no mirrors which may reflect each other, or else we simply ignore infinite reflections of mirrors, allowing for only a limited number of *levels of reflection*. We shall impose a limit of one level

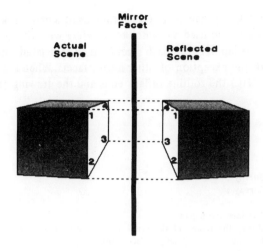

Figure 16.2

of reflection, so when reflected in another mirror, a mirror facet is considered as an ordinary, non-reflecting facet.

There remain two questions. Firstly, at what stage do we draw the reflection and secondly, how do we apply the hidden surface algorithm to the reflected scene? The reflection is seen as if it were superficial to the mirror facet. We therefore draw it immediately after drawing the mirror facet, in a colour generated by mixing the facet colour and the mirror colour. We modify the hidden routine of listing 13.1 to call a new routine reflekt (listing 16.6) with parameter k if facet k is a mirror facet. This routine calculates and draws the reflection of the scene in facet k. We need some method of indicating that a facet is a mirror. We use the transparency coefficient stored in the array tr. No mirror may be transparent, so this value is redundant (always zero). Therefore we indicate that a facet in material i is a mirror by setting facet tr[i] to -1.0.

The routine reflekt is of the same form as the routine hidden (listing 13.2). The reflected co-ordinates of each vertex reflect and the projections proref thereof are declared globally:

```
{VAR} reflect : vertex3array;
      proref : vertex2array;
```

The routine network is called with the reflected co-ordinate arrays as parameters to set up a network of information about which facets obscure others in the view of the reflected scene. Two new arrays, rlist[1..maxf] and rnob-[1..maxf] are used to store the information about the network. These arrays correspond to the arrays list and nob and are used to avoid interference with the hidden surface network relating to the general view (see listing 13.1).

The new network is sorted exactly as before, using a new stack referred to by the integer stack2 (again used so as not to interfere with the general ordering) and the area of overlap between each facet (and all associated superficial facets) is displayed, with the exception of other mirror facets. When the stack becomes empty (stack2 = NIL) the routine reflekt ends and the drawing of the real scene continues.

Listing 16.6

```
VAR
    reflect : vertex3array ;
    proref : vertex2array ;

PROCEDURE reflekt(face : integer) ;
{ Calculates and draws the image of the scene as seen reflected in 'face' }
VAR col,nv,mvis,i,intersection,front,back,newface : integer ;
    red1,red2,green1,green2,blue1,blue2 : real ;
    val,mu,redval,greenval,blueval : real ;
    mid,normv,oddvector : vector3 ;
    poly : vector2array ;
    stack2 : stackpointer ;
    rnob : facetarray ;
    rlist : pointarray ;
BEGIN
{ Initialise the stack of facets to be drawn }
    stack2 := NIL ;
{ Calculate the normal to 'face' and reflection of each vertex }
    normal(face,normv,val,obs) ; midpoint(face,mid) ;
    cshade(mid,normv,colour[face],red1,green1,blue1) ;
    FOR i := 1 TO ntv
    DO BEGIN
            ilpl(obs[i],normv,normv,oddvector,val,mu,intersection) ;
            reflect[i].x := obs[i].x+2*mu*normv.x ;
            reflect[i].y := obs[i].y+2*mu*normv.y ;
            reflect[i].z := obs[i].z+2*mu*normv.z ;
{ Project the reflected vertices onto the perspective viewing screen }
            proref[i].x := -reflect[i].x*ppd/reflect[i].z ;
            proref[i].y := -reflect[i].y*ppd/reflect[i].z
        END ;
{ Call 'network' to create a topological order of facets to be drawn }
    network(mvis,rnob,rlist,reflect,proref,-1) ;
{ Draw facets in topological order }
    FOR i := 1 TO nof
    DO IF rnob[i] = 0 THEN stackpush(stack2,i) ;
{ 'mvis' is the number of facets visible in the 'mirror' }
    FOR i := 1 TO mvis
    DO BEGIN
            stackpop(stack2,newface) ;
            IF newface = 0 THEN EXIT ;
            IF face < > newface
            THEN BEGIN
{ Find 'overlap' with mirror and draw }
                    overlap(face,newface,front,back,nv,poly,proref,reflect,-1) ;
```

```
          IF front = face
          THEN BEGIN
                    normal(newface,normv,val,obs) ;
                    midpoint(newface,mid) ;
                    cshade(mid,normv,colour[newface],red2,green2,blue2) ;
                    redval := (red1+red2)/2 ;
                    greenval := (green1+green2)/2 ;
                    blueval := (blue1+blue2)/2 ;
          findlogicalcolour(redval,greenval,blueval,colour[newface],col) ;
                    setcol(col) ; polyfill(nv,poly)
               END
          END ;
     unstack(newface,rnob,rlist,stack2)
     END
END ; { of reflekt }
```

Example 16.3
Plate XII shows a hollow cube reflected in three mutually perpendicular walls.

Exercise 16.6
Extend the algorithm so that the reflections of shadows may be displayed.

Exercise 16.7
We have allowed for only one level of reflection. The maximum level could, of course, take any value. Extend the algorithm to allow for, say, three levels. (You must either introduce some form of recursion, or else write a new routine for each level of reflection.)

Exercise 16.8
All of the listings given in this chapter use the constant shading approach, assuming that the intensity of reflected light is constant across a facet. Rewrite the routines for use in Gouraud's and Phong's interpolation models and produce scenes such as that shown in Plate VIII.

As you can see, the inclusion of such concepts as transparent surfaces, mirrors and shadows in polygon-based hidden surface routines necessitates excessive numbers of comparisons and very careful manipulation of data. We have reached the limit of such algorithms. For more realistic images, with almost unlimited scope for simulating the many aspects of illumination, we must turn to analytic modelling and the techniques of ray-tracing (chapter 10) and the quad-tree and oct-tree algorithms which we describe in chapter 17.

17 Analytic Representation of Three-dimensional Space

In this chapter we shall discuss an exciting recent development in the representation of objects in three-dimensional space. We take a totally different approach to the definition of a scene: instead of approximating surfaces with a polygonal mesh, we define them as combinations of *primitive objects*. Each primitive object is mathematically defined in terms of an analytic function: we have already introduced this idea in the analytic representation of surfaces in chapter 6. This approach allows a very simple definition of many scenes, but the ease of definition has to be paid for with a large increase in processing overheads, although not necessarily in program complexity. To illustrate these ideas we look at two implementations. The first, the *quad-tree* (Sidhu and Boute, 1972; Tanimoto, 1977; Hunter and Steiglitz, 1979; Woodwark, 1984), will be used to draw simple *molecular models* composed of a grouping of spheres of arbitrary radius and position. A program, using listings 1.1, 1.3, 3.3, 7.1 and 8.1 linked to the **draw_a_picture** routine of listing 17.1 is used to illustrate it. Also required are **dot3** (listing 6.1), **insource** (listing 15.1), **findlogicalcolour** and **colourtable** (listing 15.10), and **cshade** (listing 15.9). Secondly there is the *oct-tree* method (Clark, 1976; Meagher, 1982): we do not give a program but outline the method and also describe the construction of a binary tree defining a scene as the union, intersection and complement of various primitives. (Such a description can also be used with ray-tracing and the quad-tree method.)

The Quad-tree Algorithm

The polygonal mesh method uses the basic philosophy of using polygonal facets to approximate a surface, and projecting that approximation ultimately onto the viewport where a picture is drawn. The opposite approach of accurately representing the surface should imply that an infinite number of surface points need be considered. The philosophy behind the analytic methods is to do just this, knowing that drawing a picture on a graphics viewport infers only a finite number of pixels, hence introducing a way to avoid a potentially infinite process.

Here we introduce a quad-tree approach to an orthographic view of a scene composed of a list of objects stored in OBSERVED position. Although we restrict ourselves to spheres (the simplest of all three-dimensional objects), the method is valid for many other types of primitive objects, provided the relevant routines have been written.

We start by considering a square of 2^N by 2^N pixels on the viewport. (At a general stage we have a *pixel square* of 2^n by 2^n pixels: $0 \leqslant n \leqslant N$.) This can be considered as a real square on the orthographic view plane; the proper scaling between the two has been created by the **start** routine (listing 1.3). We imagine that the view plane square is extruded in front of and behind the plane to form an infinitely long square-sectioned prism or *rod*. The boundary of this rod is in fact formed by the orthographic projection lines through every point on the real square. Obviously any object in the three-dimensional scene that does not intersect this solid rod can have no effect on the colouring of any pixel in the corresponding pixel square.

Given a pixel square, we start with the *old list* of objects that may possibly intersect the corresponding rod and check each possible intersection. Initially, when $n = N$, the list will contain all the objects in the scene. If there is no intersection for a given object then that object is deleted from the list; if there is an intersection or if there is any doubt (as a result of the use of approximations to speed up the processing), then the object is added to the *new list*. The pixel square can be divided up into four smaller pixel squares, each 2^{n-1} by 2^{n-1} pixels. We then equate the old list with the new list and repeat the above process with all four new squares. If at any time the list becomes empty then no object can affect the given pixel square and so the pixels should be left in the background colour. Since the scene is not empty then this process of dividing pixel squares into quarters can apparently go on indefinitely, except for the fact that once n becomes zero we are dealing with a single pixel and the process must terminate.

Only one of the remaining objects in the list which corresponds to a given pixel can be used to colour in that pixel. Finding which object is easy, we simply take the line of projection through the centre of the pixel and find the object in the list with largest z co-ordinate on that line. Then we can use the shading techniques of chapter 15 in routine **cshade** to colour in the pixel. Listing 17.1 assumes point source illumination model. Note that there is no need to clip the scene before display, clipping is implicit in the quad-tree process.

Example 17.1

We implement this idea in listing 17.1 on a list of spheres. Rather than use rods with square cross-section, we introduce cylindrical rods that contain the square-sectioned rods: instead of the rod being formed by extruding a pixel square 2^n by 2^n pixels in the viewport, we extrude the circle of radius $2^n/\sqrt{2}$ which passes through the four corners of the pixel square. We do this to make calculations easier; note any object outside the cylindrical rod must be outside the square-sectioned rod, however there may be objects that lie outside the square-sectioned rod but which intersect the cylindrical rod. This may mean that objects which ultimately have no effect may be added to new lists, but this is a small price to pay for the ease of calculation. These irrelevant objects will finally be deleted when considering the intersection of the line of projection through the pixel.

Note how the multiple lists are stored in the listore (list store) array. Because the above process is implicitly recursive we have to use a stack to store pixel squares and their associated list pointers for future processing. topofstack points to the topmost elements of the stack. Each element in the stack is a RECORD of four fields, pix, the pixel coordinates of the bottom left-hand corner of the square identified by the stack entry, edge the edge length of that square. left and right are pointers into the integer array listore holding the list of spheres relevant to this square. Note how the process has built-in garbage collection! We assume that the viewport is 1024 by 768 pixels, and so initially we divide it into twelve individual 256 by 256 pixel squares (2^8 by 2^8), and initiate the quad-tree algorithm for each: this implies that we do not need more than 36 elements in the stack (why?). Plate XIII shows a smooth shaded orthographic projection of a molecular model composed of spheres defined by the data read by listing 17.1.

Listing 17.1

```
PROGRAM main_program(input,output,indata,outdata) ;

CONST
    sizeofpixelarray = 32 ; epsilon = 0.000001 ;
    pi=3.1415926535 ;

TYPE
    pixelvector = RECORD x,y : integer END ;
    pixelarray  = ARRAY[1..sizeofpixelarray] of pixelvector ;
    vector2 = RECORD x,y : real END ;
    vector3 = RECORD x,y,z : real END ;
    matrix4x4 = ARRAY[1..4,1..4] OF real ;

VAR
    currcol,nxpix,nypix : integer ;
    indata,outdata : text ;
    horiz,vert,xyscale : real ;
    nov,newcolour : integer ;
    eye,direct,src : vector3 ;
    Q : matrix4x4 ;
    rm,gm,bm,sm : ARRAY[1..10] OF real ;
    mm : ARRAY[1..10] OF integer ;
    licol : ARRAY[1..10] OF integer ;
    iptr : ARRAY[1..256] OF integer ;
    r,g,b : ARRAY[1..256] OF real ;
    act,obs : ARRAY[1..500] OF vector3 ;

{ Routines from Listing 1.1 and other routines including

PROCEDURE start(horiz : real) ;
```

```
FUNCTION angle(x,y : real) : real ;
PROCEDURE tran3(tx,ty,tz : real ; VAR A : matrix4x4 ) ;
PROCEDURE rot3(m : integer ; theta :real ; VAR A : matrix4x4 ) ;
PROCEDURE mult3(A,B : matrix4x4 ; VAR C : matrix4x4 ) ;
PROCEDURE transform(v : vector3 ; A : matrix4x4 ; VAR w : vector3) ;
PROCEDURE findQ ;
PROCEDURE look3 ;
FUNCTION dot3(p1,p2 : vector3) : real ;
PROCEDURE insource ;
PROCEDURE cshade(p : vector3 ; VAR norm : vector3 ; ic : integer ;
                          VAR red,green,blue : real ) ;
PROCEDURE colourtable ;
PROCEDURE findlogicalcolour(red,green,blue : real ; i : integer ;
                          VAR colour : integer) ;
                                                      }

PROCEDURE draw_a_picture ;  { spherical ball model }
CONST maxspheres = 100 ; maxlist = 2000 ;
TYPE stackvalue = RECORD   pix : pixelvector ;
                             edge,left,right : integer
               END ;
     stackptr   = ^stacknode ;
     stacknode  = RECORD info : stackvalue ; next : stackptr END ;

VAR i,ix,iy,nball,numats : integer ;
    screenpixel : pixelvector ;
    topofstack : stackptr ;
    midpt : vector3 ;
    ballrad : ARRAY[1..maxspheres] OF real ;
    material : ARRAY[1..maxspheres] OF integer ;
    listore  : ARRAY[1..maxlist] OF integer ;

PROCEDURE push(pixel : pixelvector ; e,l,r : integer ) ;
VAR p : stackptr ;
BEGIN
   new(p) ;
   p^.info.pix := pixel ; p^.info.edge := e ;
   p^.info.left := l ; p^.info.right := r ;
   p^.next := topofstack ; topofstack := p
END ; { of push }

PROCEDURE pop(VAR pixel : pixelvector ; VAR e,l,r : integer ) ;
VAR p : stackptr ;
BEGIN
   pixel := topofstack^.info.pix ; e := topofstack^.info.edge ;
   l := topofstack^.info.left ; r := topofstack^.info.right ;
   p := topofstack ; topofstack := topofstack^.next ;
   dispose(p)
END ;  { of pop }

PROCEDURE ballsin ;
VAR i : integer ;
BEGIN
{ Read in BALL data. There are 'nball' balls }
   assign(indata,'spheres.dat') ; reset(indata) ;
```

```
        readln(indata,nball) ;
        IF nball > maxspheres
        THEN
            writeln(' Exceeding maximum number of spheres' )
        ELSE
            colourtable ; { prepare colour table }
{ i'th ball has actual centre 'act[i]' and radius 'ballrad[i]' }
{ and is composed of 'material[i] }
            FOR i := 1 TO nball
            DO readln(indata,act[i].x,act[i].y,act[i].z,ballrad[i],material[i]) ;
{ Read in data on 'numats' materials }
            readln(indata,numats) ;
            FOR i := 1 TO numats
            DO readln(indata,rm[i],gm[i],bm[i],sm[i],mm[i])
END ; { of ballsin }

PROCEDURE pixball(pixel : pixelvector ; newl,newr: integer) ;
{ find unique ball used to colour given 'pixel' }
VAR i,lsi,maxball,colour : integer ;
    d,distsq,zz : real ;
    red,green,blue : real ;
    normal : vector3 ;
BEGIN
{ Find which ball is relevant to current pixel }
{ Go through list store and find ball ('maxball') closest to observer }
    midpt.z := -10000.0 ; maxball := 0 ;
    FOR i := newl TO newr
    DO BEGIN
            lsi := listore[i] ;
            distsq := sqr(ballrad[lsi])-sqr(midpt.x-obs[lsi].x)
                                    -sqr(midpt.y-obs[lsi].y) ;
            IF distsq >= 0.0
            THEN BEGIN
                    zz := obs[lsi].z+sqrt(distsq) ;
                    IF zz > midpt.z
                    THEN BEGIN
                            midpt.z := zz ; maxball := lsi
                        END
                END
        END ;
    IF maxball <> 0
    THEN BEGIN
{ Find vector 'normal' to surface of chosen ball }
{ at a point which is projected onto (xmid,ymid) }
            normal.x := midpt.x-obs[maxball].x ;
            normal.y := midpt.y-obs[maxball].y ;
            d := sqr(ballrad[maxball])-sqr(normal.x)-sqr(normal.y) ;
            IF d < 0.0
            THEN normal.z := 0.0
            ELSE normal.z := sqrt(d) ;
{ Shade the 'pixel' with colour of ball 'maxball' }
            cshade(midpt,normal,material[maxball],red,green,blue) ;
            findlogicalcolour(red,green,blue,material[maxball],colour) ;
            setcol(colour) ; setpix(pixel)
        END
END ; { of pixball }
```

```
PROCEDURE quadsplit(pixel : pixelvector ; edge,newl,newr : integer) ;
VAR newpixel : pixelvector ;
    halfedge : integer ;
BEGIN
{ split given pixel square into four Quarters }
{ (also pixel squares, but with sides halved) }
        IF edge = 1
        THEN
{ If we are at pixel level then colour in pixel, and consider }
{ next pixel square on the stack }
            pixball(pixel,newl,newr)
        ELSE
{ Not at pixel level. Break pixel squares in 4 quarters and add }
{ to stack. Then take next pixel square off stack and continue }
        BEGIN
            IF newr > 4996
            THEN BEGIN
                    writeln(' listore is full') ; EXIT
                END ;
            halfedge := edge DIV 2 ;
            FOR i := 1 TO 4
            DO BEGIN
                    newpixel.x := pixel.x + ((i-1) DIV 2)*halfedge ;
                    newpixel.y := pixel.y + (i MOD 2)*halfedge ;
                    push(newpixel,halfedge,newl,newr)
                END
        END
END ; { of  quadsplit }

PROCEDURE quadtree ;
{ The QUAD-TREE ALGORITHM }
VAR edge,l,newl,r,newr,lsi : integer ;
    half,dist,rodrad : real ;
    pixel : pixelvector ;
BEGIN
{ Pop pixel-square info off stack : process it, stop if stack empty }
    WHILE topofstack < > NIL
    DO BEGIN
{ Pixel square has edge size info.e = 'edge', and bottom left corner }
{ 'info.pixel'.  A circle containing the square of pixels is extended }
{ backwards to form a rod. Go through 'listore' using present }
{ pixel square and see which balls are relevant to current rod }
{ listore[i] where info.left < = i < = info.right holds this information }
            pop(pixel,edge,l,r) ;
{ Real centre of pixel square is 'midpt', circle of radius 'rodrad' }
{ totally contains pixel square. 'rodrad' thus radius of current rod }
{ 'half' is half the edge size of the current real cube }
            half := 0.5*edge/xyscale ; rodrad := half*sqrt(2.0) ;
            midpt.x := (pixel.x-512)/xyscale + half ;
            midpt.y := (pixel.y-384)/xyscale + half ;
{ Create a new list of balls relevant to present pixel square and }
{ store in 'listore' between indices 'newl' and 'newr' }
            newr := r ; newl := newr+1 ;
            FOR i := l TO r
            DO BEGIN
{ Distance between centre of ball (a circle in 2D) and centre of pixel square }
```

```
{ (in real units) must be less than the combined radii of circle and rod }
{ 'lsi' is sphere index of i'th element of 'listore'}
                lsi := listore[i] ;
                dist := sqrt(sqr(obs[lsi].x-midpt.x)+sqr(obs[lsi].y-midpt.y)) ;
{ If ball 'lsi' still under consideration then add to 'listore' }
                IF dist < = ballrad[lsi]+rodrad
                THEN BEGIN
                        newr := newr+1 ; listore[newr] := lsi
                    END
            END ;
{ If new 'listore' not empty enter quad-split routine, pop stack and continue }
            IF newl < = newr
            THEN quadsplit(pixel,edge,newl,newr)
        END
END ; { of quadtree }
BEGIN
    look3 ; insource ;
{ Read in data on spheres in ACTUAL position }
    ballsin ;
{ Put spheres in observed position, vertex act[i] go to vertex obs[i] }
    FOR i := 1 TO nball
    DO transform(act[i],Q,obs[i]) ;
{ Viewport assumed to be 1024 by 768 pixels. Divide it into }
{ 12 256-square pixel blocks and push them onto stack }
    topofstack := NIL ;
    FOR i := 1 TO nball
    DO listore[i] := i ;
    FOR ix := 0 TO 3
    DO FOR iy := 0 TO 2
        DO BEGIN
                screenpixel.x := ix*256 ; screenpixel.y := iy*256 ;
                push(screenpixel,256,1,nball)
            END ;
{ Initiate QUAD-TREE process }
    quadtree
END ; { of draw_a_picture }

BEGIN   { main PROGRAM block }
{ Prepare graphics device }
    writeln(' Type in horizontal size of window') ;
    readln(horiz) ; start(horiz) ;
{ Draw a picture using a PROCEDURE 'draw_a_picture' }
    draw_a_picture ;
    finish
END. { of 'main' PROGRAM }
```

Exercise 17.1

Incorporate the parallel beam shading model into this program. Extend the colouring process to allow for multiple light sources.

Exercise 17.2

If each pixel is considered to be composed of 2^M by 2^M sub-pixels then the quad-tree process may be continued to the sub-pixel as opposed to the pixel level. Should you then combine the colours chosen for each sub-pixel you will achieve a simple *anti-aliasing* method for the colouring of that pixel. Implement this.

Exercise 17.3

Incorporate shadows in the program. It is a simple matter to discover if a pixel is in shadow; just find the three-dimensional surface point equivalent to the pixel and draw a line from that point to the light source. If this line intersects any other object then the pixel will be in shadow, and you colour it accordingly.

Exercise 17.4

Use these ideas in an extended program, including finite cylinders in the model, which draws orthographic projections of a 'ball and spoke' molecular model which is smooth shaded and exhibiting specular reflection, such as that shown in Plate XIV.

Exercise 17.5

Use the perspective projection instead of orthographic. Now instead of a cylindrical rod, you will have a circular cone with apex at the observer position.

The Oct-tree Algorithm

The representation of objects

We now consider the orthographic projection of more complicated scenes, composed of objects chosen from a small set of object categories: most oct-tree programs allow for sphere, half-space, infinite cylinder, cone, torus and helix types, but the list can be extended by the user if special shapes are required. For each category there will be a primitive object defined in a SETUP position, usually around the origin. It will have a well-defined analytic form, allowing us to identify its *inside, outside* and *surface*, and this will be presented as a subroutine in the program. For example, we can consider the primitive sphere with unit radius centred at the origin or the primitive half-space defined by that half of space with positive y co-ordinates — that is, bounded by the x/z plane through the origin with normal $(0, 1, 0)$. That is, the sense of the normal direction points into the half-space.

To place an object in ACTUAL position it is necessary to transform the primitive object from SETUP to ACTUAL position using a matrix P. All information about an ACTUAL object will be combined together in a *record*, which must contain

(1) an identification of the object category

       sphere, half-space, cylinder etc.

(2) the SETUP-to-ACTUAL matrix P and also the inverse P^{-1}, and
(3) colour, texture information etc.

All the ACTUAL objects in a scene can be listed in an array of records, individual objects being identified by their index in the array.

The *complement* of an ACTUAL object (all of space except that object) is also allowed. If an object has array index n, then the complement is indicated by $-n$.

For example, if object number 2 is a sphere of radius 2 centred at $(6, 2, 0)$, the record for this object would contain

$$P = \begin{pmatrix} 2 & 0 & 0 & 6 \\ 0 & 2 & 0 & 2 \\ 0 & 0 & 2 & 0 \\ 0 & 0 & 0 & 1 \end{pmatrix} \text{ and } P^{-1} = \begin{pmatrix} 0.5 & 0 & 0 & -3 \\ 0 & 0.5 & 0 & -1 \\ 0 & 0 & 0.5 & 0 \\ 0 & 0 & 0 & 1 \end{pmatrix}$$

along with the category identifier (sphere), colour and other material properties information. The complement of object 2 is thus identified with index -2.

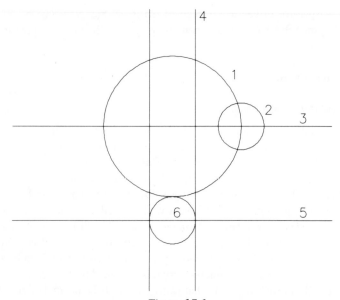

Figure 17.1

Representing a Scene with a Binary Tree

We will discuss the use of binary trees for representing a combination of primitive three-dimensional objects by referring to figure 17.1 and Plate XV. Figure 17.1 is a line drawing identifying the various objects in the scene and how they inter-relate and Plate XV is a proper oct-tree orthographic view of the scene which consists of a hemisphere (sphere 1 intersected with half-space 3) with a spherical hole (object 2) cut out, a finite cylinder (infinite cylinder 4 bounded by half-spaces −3 and 5) and finally sphere 6. Note how object 3 is used twice in the definition of the final scene!

The tree, will have two types of node, the first holding a spatial operation (union '∇' which we identify with the logical operator OR, or intersection 'Δ' which we identify with logical operator AND) and two edges, and the second type, a leaf, holding an object index or its complement ('−' which we identify with logical operator NOT). We can think of such a binary tree as an operator (from the root node) combining the two subtrees indicated by the two edges leaving the root. Since a subtree is also a tree, we have a recursive definition that leads ultimately to the leaf-subtrees that consist solely of the ACTUAL objects in the construction of a scene. We can therefore write out a tree in *infix* notation as

(subtree) operator (subtree)

Thus in our example, the hemisphere with the hole on its edge is constructed first from the intersection of sphere 1 with the complement of sphere 2

$$(1) \Delta (-2)$$

and then the resulting subtree intersected with the half-space 3

$$((1) \Delta (-2)) \Delta (3) \tag{17.1}$$

The finite cylinder with the spherical base is found by intersecting the infinite cylinder 4 with the complement (note) of half-space 3 and with half-space 5, before adding in sphere 6

$$(((-3) \Delta (4)) \Delta (5)) \nabla (6) \tag{17.2}$$

Note it does not matter that part of sphere 6 lies inside the finite cylinder − that is, we do not have to slice off the top half of sphere 6 before unioning it with the finite cylinder. The two parts (expressions 17.1 and 17.2) are then unioned together to give the final tree that describes the scene. The infix notation for this tree is thus

$$(((1) \Delta (-2)) \Delta (3)) \nabla ((((-3) \Delta (4)) \Delta (5)) \nabla (6))$$

There need not be a unique way of setting up a tree for any given scene; in particular note that no spatial meaning is implied in the left/right ordering of the subtrees for any given node.

The Binary Tree Reduction

The oct-tree approach to the display of a three-dimensional scene assumes that the viewport is considered as a square block of 2^N by 2^N (say) pixels, each pixel with unit side. Note a square viewport! Each pixel is considered to be the display on the viewport of the square which is the orthographic projection of a small cube (a *voxel* or volume pixel) in space onto the view plane. What we do in the oct-tree method for displaying a three-dimensional surface is to approximate to that surface by covering it with voxels, and to project these voxels into pixels on the viewport. Routine start (listing 1.3) is used to evaluate the scale relating voxels to pixels.

Extruding this image of a viewport composed of 2^N by 2^N pixels into three dimensions, we can think of the viewport as the projection of a cube of 2^N by 2^N by 2^N voxels with sides parallel to OBSERVER co-ordinate axes. Nothing outside this cube will be drawn, so there is no need for explicit clipping, since clipping is implied by the oct-tree algorithm. At a general stage in the process we will be using other cubic blocks of say 2^n by 2^n by 2^n voxels ($0 \leqslant n \leqslant N$). By transforming the vertices of this real cube, first by Q^{-1} (the inverse of the ACTUAL to OBSERVED matrix Q) and then by P^{-1}, it is possible to transform the cube relative to the SETUP position of a given primitive object. We then *evaluate* the analytic form of the primitive object to discover if the transformed cube lies inside, outside or crosses the surface of the primitive SETUP object. That is to see if the untransformed cube intersects the OBSERVED position of the ACTUAL object. These three outcomes correspond to the three logical values TRUE, FALSE and UNSURE respectively. As our explanation of the algorithm progresses you will note that the oct-tree method does not actually consider solid objects. Basically we are in the process of finding every single voxel which intersects a surface in the scene: we do not care about cubes of voxels lying totally inside or totally outside the objects in the scene.

We start with the 2^N by 2^N by 2^N cube of voxels and use this information to *reduce* the tree. At a general stage in the process we assume that we are working with a cube in three-dimensional space of 2^n by 2^n by 2^n voxels and a given tree. We then take each of the objects remaining in the tree and, with their corresponding functions, discover if the cube is inside, outside or crosses the surface of that object (TRUE, FALSE, UNSURE) and use the results to reduce the tree according to the following Boolean rules (compare Δ, ∇ and $-$ with AND, OR and NOT)

(1) replace the index of each object totally containing the transformed cube by TRUE
(2) replace the index of each object containing no part of the transformed cube by FALSE
(3) leave alone the indices about which we are UNSURE
(4) ($-$TRUE) becomes (FALSE)
(5) ($-$FALSE) becomes (TRUE)
(6) (TRUE) Δ (subtree) or (subtree) Δ (TRUE) become (subtree)
(7) (TRUE) ∇ (subtree) or (subtree) ∇ (TRUE) become (TRUE)
(8) (FALSE) ∇ (subtree) or (subtree) ∇ (FALSE) become (subtree)
(9) (FALSE) Δ (subtree) or (subtree) Δ (FALSE) become (FALSE).

Suppose in our example we evaluate the six objects for a given cube and get values UNSURE, FALSE, FALSE, UNSURE, TRUE and UNSURE respectively, and we reduce the tree

$$(((1) \triangle (-2)) \triangle (3)) \triangledown ((((-3) \triangle (4)) \triangle (5)) \triangledown (6))$$
$$= (((1) \triangle (-FALSE)) \triangle (FALSE)) \triangledown ((((-FALSE) \triangle (4)) \triangle (TRUE)) \triangledown (6))$$
$$= (((1) \triangle (TRUE)) \triangle (FALSE)) \triangledown ((((-FALSE) \triangle (4)) \triangle (TRUE)) \triangledown (6))$$
$$= ((1) \triangle (FALSE)) \triangledown ((((-FALSE) \triangle (4)) \triangle (TRUE)) \triangledown (6))$$
$$= (FALSE) \triangledown ((((-FALSE) \triangle (4)) \triangle (TRUE)) \triangledown (6))$$
$$= (((-FALSE) \triangle (4)) \triangle (TRUE)) \triangledown (6)$$
$$= (((TRUE) \triangle (4)) \triangle (TRUE)) \triangledown (6)$$
$$= ((4) \triangle (TRUE)) \triangledown (6)$$
$$= (4) \triangledown (6)$$

and the tree cannot be reduced further: so as far as this cube is concerned only objects 4 and 6 and their union are relevant, and the other objects can be ignored. Note that although we were UNSURE of object 1, it is still deleted from the tree.

The Oct-tree Display

After the binary tree has been reduced we are left with either an *empty tree* of the form (TRUE) or (FALSE) or a non-empty tree which contains no occurrence of TRUE or FALSE. A tree is empty when neither that particular cube, nor any of its 2^n by 2^n by 2^n constituent voxels, intersect the surface of the remaining combination of objects defined by the binary tree. This means that these voxels will have no influence on the colour of their corresponding viewport pixels and so no further processing of this cube need be done. If the tree is non-empty then there is an intersection. Provided $n > 0$, we break the cube into eight cubes (whence oct-tree), each 2^{n-1} by 2^{n-1} by 2^{n-1} voxels, and repeat the process on the reduced tree, ensuring that the cubes nearest the observer along the line of projection (that is, with larger OBSERVED z co-ordinates) are processed before those furthest away. Eventually we reach the level of individual voxels ($n = 0$), and we have discovered a voxel that intersects the surface of an object in the scene. The pixel corresponding to this voxel *may* then be coloured on the viewport. The colour depends on which object, remaining in the tree, is nearest the observer, and of course on the particular shading model used. The nearest object is found by intersecting the line of projection through the corresponding pixel with each remaining object in turn. Not every one of the 2^N by 2^N by 2^N voxels in our original cube is considered. The process can be made more efficient by noting that when a 2^n by 2^n square of pixels on the viewport has already been coloured in, then there is no need to consider any cube of voxels that lie behind this square. This is the reason we insisted on a particular order when breaking a cube of voxels into eight.

It may also be more efficient, in the massive amount of calculation required by this algorithm, to use a sphere which totally includes the cube of voxels rather than the cube itself. The radius of this sphere will be the scaled equivalent of 2^{n-1} x $\sqrt{3}$ times the pixel size. This may mean that certain objects will be left in the tree when they should have been deleted, but the gain from a simplified calculation more than compensates.

The picture of a more complex scene drawn using this process is shown in Plate XVI.

Exercise 17.6
Implement the orthographic oct-tree method using just spheres, cylinders and half-spaces. Shadows can be introduced in a manner similar to the quad-tree method.

Exercise 17.7
Each voxel can be considered as 2^M by 2^M by 2^M sub-voxels. If you implement the oct-tree process down to the sub-voxel level, and hence create equivalent sub-pixels, you can again combine the colours of the sub-pixels to introduce a simple anti-aliasing method.

Exercise 17.8
Use the perspective projection instead of the orthographic projection. Now instead of a cube of voxels in space, you will have slices of a pyramidal cone with apex at the observer.

What Next?

If you have reached this point in our book and you have understood all the methods, then you will now be ready to experiment with the research level problems of computer graphics. Problems of animation, texture, display techniques (polygonal mesh *versus* ray-tracing *versus* oct-tree), refraction and reflection, multiple light sources, more realistic shadows taking diffraction into account (that is, with umbra and penumbra), adding patches to polygonal mesh models (Bezier, 1974; Gordon and Riesenfeld, 1974), using bicubic curves etc. We can recommend you move on to the books of Newman and Sproull (1973) and Foley and Van Dam (1981) for excellent surveys of these problems, and we wish you much enjoyment in your future study of computer graphics.

18 Projects

Project 1

Produce a program package that can draw Data Diagrams. It must include listings for the construction of Bar-Charts and Histograms, Pie-Charts, and both Discrete and Continuous graphs. An example of a discrete graph is given in figure 18.1. Note you must be able to add text to your diagrams, and also have a facility for drawing labelled axes as well as the option of drawing in various graphics modes (XOR etc.). See Angell (1985) for an implementation of data diagrams on the IBM Personal Computer.

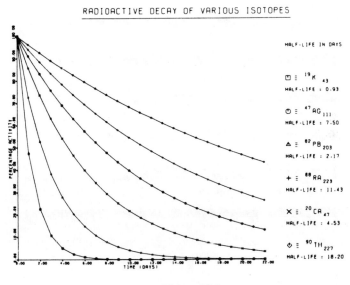

Figure 18.1

Project 2

Create a database that can be used to draw various orthographic views of the Globe. It is best to store the vertex and facet information in its Mercator projection, and then project this onto a sphere. Use two colours, blue for the sea and green for the land (you could also use white for the ice-caps). Only areas on the visible hemisphere need be drawn. If you are using a raster screen then write a new primitive function which returns the colour of any specified pixel. Once the globe is drawn, the centre of the pixel position on the screen implies a unique three-dimensional point on the globe. Use the colour of each pixel and the normal to the globe at the corresponding point to smooth-shade the globe, assuming one (or even multiple) light sources. See Plate XVII.

Project 3

Construct a program that draws musical notation — bar lines, staves, quavers, rests etc. Incorporate it in another program that composes(?) music: figure 18.2 shows the result of one such program.

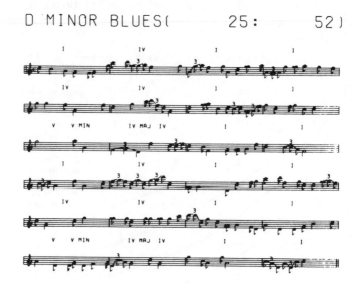

Figure 18.2

Project 4

Experiment with optical illusions and 'impossible figures'. You can get ideas from the many books on the subject, we recommend Tolansky (1964), to produce diagrams such as figure 18.3.

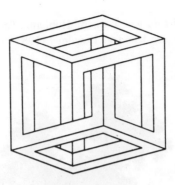

Figure 18.3

Project 5

Construct a wide range of moiré patterns, sometimes called net-curtain patterns. These are created by drawing a large number of lines and curves; the variety and density of the small areas caused by the intersections are perceived as a cloudy effect. See figure 18.4, formed by the intersection of four sets of concentric circles. The density of lines must be carefully chosen: if there are too many lines then we see a solid mass; if there are too few then a moiré pattern is not discernible.

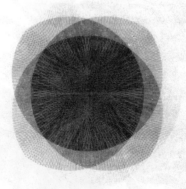

Figure 18.4

Project 6

Read Mandelbrot's book on *Fractals* (Mandelbrot, 1977), and produce two-dimensional pictures such as figure 18.5. Also use these methods to create three-dimensional surfaces. From the work of Hubbard, Peitgen and Richter create Julia patterns such as figure 18.6 (see Dewdney (1985)).

Figure 18.5

Figure 18.6

Project 7

Write a program that can draw a hemispherical 'wooden' bowl, similar to the one shown in figure 18.7. The bowl has a flat rim and base and hemispherical sides. It is carved from a tree composed of a number of co-axial cylinders: the surfaces of the cylinders (the tree rings) form the pattern on the rim, base and side of the bowl; that is, they are the curves of intersection of the base and rim planes and side hemisphere with the cylinders. You can imagine the bowl to be part of a unit sphere, and the parameters which uniquely define a bowl are the radii of the cylinders, the centre of the hemisphere, the normal to the base and rim planes, and the fractions which define the base and inner and outer rim. *Hint* — for ease of calculation place the axis of the cylinders along the z-axis and centre the sphere on the y-axis.

Alternatively, you could attempt to solve this problem using the quad-tree or oct-tree methods.

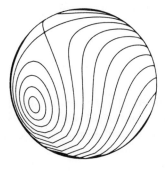

Figure 18.7

Project 8

As scenes get more sophisticated then the methods we describe for setting up the database become inefficient. If a single type of complex object is used repeatedly then it may be preferable to store the SETUP data for that object just once, and define the scene as a list of matrices and pointers — each pointer indicating the SETUP data for a given object, and each matrix being the SETUP to ACTUAL matrix which places it in position. Such a reduced description of a three-dimensional scene obviously necessitates a rewrite of many of the routines given in this book!

Project 9

All the three-dimensional programs in this book are written using the assumption that all facets are convex. Any concave facets must be split into convex facets by the programmer before the SETUP stage. Automate the process which inputs possibly concave polygonal facets and then changes each non-convex polygon into a series of convex polygons (Chazelle and Incerpi, 1984; Fournier and Montuno, 1984) and places them directly into our database.

Project 10

Construct a variety of two-dimensional mazes (rectangular or circular) on an interactive graphics console. Incorporate a facility that enables users to find their way through the maze, using a mouse as an indicator. Also program the 'best path' through each maze. Use the three-dimensional techniques from this book to give three-dimensional views inside the maze. The very special structure of mazes should allow you to write your own efficient back-to-front hidden surface elimination algorithm.

Project 11

Figure 18.8a shows the facets of a cube unfolded and laid out flat. Figure 18.8b shows the cube partially reconstructed. Write a movie that follows the complete reconstruction of the cube. Use other more complex regular figures — such as a pentagonal dodecahedron — instead of a cube.

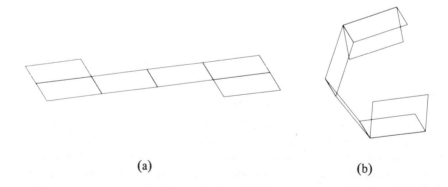

(a)   (b)

Figure 18.8

Project 12

Write programs to produce 10–20-second advertisements; any product will do as the subject of the film. If computer time is a problem, then produce single frames from the advertisement. Mix together the two-dimensional and three-dimensional techniques of this book, and use any special facilities available on your graphics device.

Project 13

Write a program that draws tessellated lattice patterns, such as the popular Islamic design shown in figure 18.9. It should take a line and/or polygon sequence, together with the lattice information, and generate a design clipped inside a given rectangle. The symmetry of such patterns can be classified into 17 *space groups* (Dana, 1948; Phillips, 1960; Donnay and Donnay, 1969; Whittaker, 1981) which are given the symbols pg, mm etc. Your program should use this standard crystallographic notation to indicate the symmetry group. Crystallography is a fount of good ideas for drawing unusual patterns.

Figure 18.9

Project 14

Experiment with 'ball and spoke' chemical models. Use the line-drawing techniques of chapter 12 to draw stereoscopic pictures. Expand the quad-tree program of chapter 17 to draw pictures such as Plate XIV. In this case you must include an analytic primitive for the cylinder as well as for the sphere. Include specular reflections, and even multiple light sources and shadows.

Project 15

Suppose you are given two co-planar convex polygons with a non-trivial inter-section, defined by the two vector sequences $\{p_1, p_2, \ldots, p_m = p_1\}$ and $\{q_1, q_2, \ldots, q_n = q_1\}$. Using the 'inside and outside methods' of chapter 3 find the new body, not necessarily convex, defined by $\{r_1, r_2, \ldots, r_k = r_1\}$, which is the union of the two original polygons.

Figure 18.10 shows a slice through an 'interpenetrant cubic onion' — that is, an object that is composed of a series of concentric non-intersecting surfaces (or 'skins'), each skin being similar to figure 9.3. The complete slice is the combination of slices through individual surfaces; each single slice is the union of the slices through the two cubes that form the skin. Thus the above technique can be used. Note that the two polygons formed from each skin may not intersect, and in certain cases one or both of the polygons may even be empty.

This is another example from crystallography: it shows the idealised X-ray topograph of the perfect twinned crystal of Fluorite.

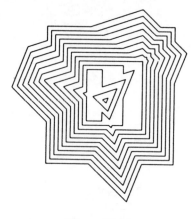

Figure 18.10

Project 16

A convex polyhedron can be considered as the body of intersection of a number of half-spaces, where each half-space is defined by an infinite plane. Given such a set of planes (assuming that the origin is inside the corresponding half-space), then the polyhedron can be calculated using the 'inside and outside' methods of chapter 6. If you start with a very large tetrahedron and successively cut away any part of the remaining polyhedron that lies outside the half-space, you will eventually be left with the required polyhedron. See Plate V.

Project 17

Extend the three-dimensional polyhedral description of objects into the fourth dimension (Sommerville, 1929; Manning, 1956; Coxeter, 1973; Rucker, 1977; Abbot, 1978; Banchoff, 1978). Each vertex will be given by a vector of four numbers and so requires a five by five matrix for transformations. Each four-dimensional polyhedron will have three-dimensional polyhedra for facets. Each polyhedron will itself be bounded by two-dimensional facets, which are themselves bounded by lines, which are finally defined by pairs of vertices. The simplest orthographic projection of a four-dimensional point is where we ignore two of the co-ordinates (as opposed to one, z, in three dimensions). There are many more complex projections! What are translation, scale and rotation in the fourth dimension? See the four-dimensional hypercube in figure 18.11.

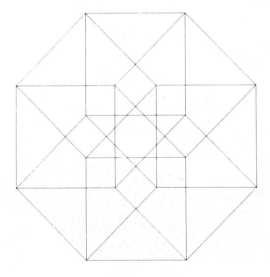

Figure 18.11

Project 18

Incorporate our polygonal mesh programs in a CAD/CAM package. All communication with the program must be interactive, including any object definition.

Project 19

Experiment with the advanced ideas mentioned in chapter 16. Extend the shadow algorithm to deal with illumination from multiple light sources (see exercise 16.3) and include transparent surfaces (see exercise 16.5).

Project 20

Write a program which is a line-drawing version of the mathematical surface construction shown in chapter 9. Now you have to use a 'front-to-back' method: the opposite of the painter's algorithm. You must superimpose a grid on the figure as we did in the colour version, and then find the front edge of the figure and set it as a linear list of line segments. This list will be the variable top boundary of the picture. Then going back through the lines in the grid, find which grid lines cross the top boundary lines in this list, which are below, and which are above. Depending on each case you must adjust the boundary linear list of line segments – ignoring the 'invisible line segments', while adding the visible segments and deleting lines from the boundary list that are no longer on the new top boundary. See figure 18.12.

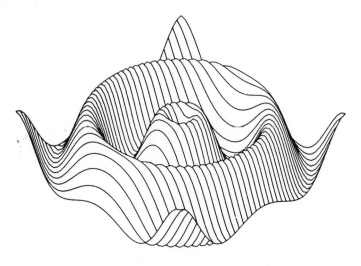

Figure 18.12

Project 21

Study the Bezier Surface (Bezier, 1974) and B-Spline Surface (Gordon and Riesenfeld, 1974) methods for constructing a polygonal mesh for three-dimensional solid objects, given only a small number of reference points. Implement the B-spline technique in conjunction with our three-dimensional display programs.

Project 22

Provided that there are no topological problems relating objects in a scene (that is, A over B over C over A not allowed), then it is possible to construct a network of facets so that any two facets A and B are connected by an edge, A to B, if and only if there is some observation point from which both facets are visible and A is behind B. If one such point is found, then it is impossible to find another observation point which inverts the connection (Tomlinson, 1982). The network of ALL the facets in the scene (not just those visible from a given observation point) can be topologically ordered. Drawing only those facets visible from any given observation point in this order furnishes a hidden surface algorithm, provided objects do not move relative to one another after the network has been constructed. Extend our hidden surface algorithm to include this idea.

Project 23

A general project which runs throughout this book is to cannibalise the given programs to make them more efficient, both in time and storage requirements. This will involve rewriting the code for certain algorithms. One obvious example is to use 3 by 4 matrices for three-dimensional transformations, since the bottom rows of the 4 by 4 matrices we use are always (0   0   0   1). There are many other places where we placed clarity of explanation before efficiency of code.

Appendix

In chapter 1 we described nine primitive routines needed to interface all the programs from this book with a general graphics device. In this appendix we will give examples of these routines for specific commercial devices and packages.

GINO-P

This very popular graphics package was designed specifically for line drawing and so we implement only the routines needed for wire diagrams and hidden line displays in the listing A.1.

Listing A.1

```
{     ******************************
      *  Graphics Primitives for    *
      *          GINO-P             *
      *  NOTE : Line drawing only   *
      ******************************  }

{ GINO calls are all in CAPITALs }

PROCEDURE finish ;
{ Flush buffers. }
BEGIN
   DEVEND
END ; { of finish }

PROCEDURE erase ;
{ Move to next frame or clear screen. }
BEGIN
   PICCLE
END ; { of erase }

PROCEDURE setpix(pixel : pixelvector) ;
```

```
BEGIN
   DOT(pixel.x,pixel.y)
END ; { of setpix }

PROCEDURE movepix(pixel : pixelvector) ;
BEGIN
   MOVTO2(pixel.x,pixel.y)
END ; { of movepix }

PROCEDURE linepix(pixel : pixelvector) ;
BEGIN
   LINTO2(pixel.x,pixel.y)
END ; { of linepix }

PROCEDURE prepit ;
{ Assume dimensions of graphics frame is 184 mms by 140 mms.    }
{ Set up viewport dimensions - define pixel to be .1 mm squared }
BEGIN
   nxpix := 1840 ; nypix := 1400 ;
{ Prepare graphics and baud rate, and clear frame. }
   DEVBEG ; DEVSPE(2400) ; UNITS(0.1) ; erase
END ; { of prepit }
```

G.K.S.

The Graphical Kernel System allows the use of both vector and raster modes. Our primitives can be implemented as listing A.2.

Listing A.2

```
{    *****************************
     *   Graphics Primitives for   *
     *          G.K.S              *
     *     (use local bindings)    *
     *****************************        }

{ GKS calls are all in CAPITALs }
{ You must use correct bindings for following GKS statements. }

VAR image : ARRAY[1,1] OF integer ;
    lastpixel : pixelvector ;

PROCEDURE finish ;
BEGIN
   DEACTIVATE WORKSTATION(1) ;
   CLOSE WORKSTATION(1) ; CLOSE GKS
END ; { of finish }

PROCEDURE setcol(col : integer) ;
BEGIN
{ Select logical colour 'col' }
   SET POLYLINE INDEX(col) ;
```

```
      SET FILL AREA INDEX(col) ;
      image[1,1] := col
END ; { of setcol }

PROCEDURE erase ;
BEGIN
{ Clear graphics screen. }
   CLEAR WORKSTATION(1,ALWAYS)
END ; { of erase }

PROCEDURE setpix(pixel : pixelvector) ;
BEGIN
{ Set pixel with co-ordinates pixel to current colour. }
   CELL ARRAY(pixel.x,pixel.y,1,1,image)
END ; { of setpix }

PROCEDURE movepix(pixel : pixelvector) ;
BEGIN
{ Store current position in lastpixel }
   lastpixel := pixel
END ; { of movepix }

PROCEDURE linepix(pixel : pixelvector) ;
VAR x,y : ARRAY[1..2] OF real ;
BEGIN
{ Draw line to position pixel }
   x[1] := lastpixel.x ; y[1] := lastpixel.y ;
   x[2] := pixel.x ; y[2] := pixel.y ;
   POLYLINE(2,x,y)
END ; { of linepix }

PROCEDURE polypix(n : integer ; poly : pixelarray ) ;
VAR i : integer ;
    x,y : realarray ;
BEGIN
{ Fills polygonal area with n vertices poly[1],...,poly[n] }
   FOR i := 1 TO n
   DO BEGIN
         x[i] := poly[i].x ; y[i] := poly[i].y
      END ;
   FILL AREA(n,x,y)
END ; { of polypix }

PROCEDURE rgblog(i : integer ; red,green,blue : real ) ;
BEGIN
{ Sets logical colour i in colour look-up table to (red,green,blue) }
   SET COLOUR REPRESENTATION(1,i,red,green,blue) ;
   SET POLYLINE REPRESENTATION(1,i,1,1,i) ;
   SET FILL AREA REPRESENTATION(1,i,SOLID,1,i)
END ; { of rgblog }

PROCEDURE prepit ;
VAR j,r,g,b : integer ;
BEGIN
{ Set up viewport dimensions, assume sqaure 512 by 512. }
```

```
   nxpix := 512 ; nypix := 512 ;
   OPEN GKS ;
{ Raster Device implied by '8'. }
   OPEN WORKSTATION(1,6,8) ;
   SET WORKSTATION WINDOW(1,0.0,512.0,0.0,512.0) ;
   SET WORKSTATION VIEWPORT(1,0.0,1.0,0.0,1.0) ;
   SELECT NORMALISATION TRANSFORMATION(1) ;
   ACTIVATE WORKSTATION(1) ;
{ Set up default colour table. }
   j := 0 ;
   FOR b := 0 TO 1
   DO FOR g := 0 TO 1
      DO FOR r := 0 TO 1
         DO BEGIN
                  rgblog(j,r,g,b) ; j := j + 1
            END ;
{ Set up default foreground colour. }
   setcol(7)
END ; { of prepit }
```

A Microfilm Package: Dimfilm

This approach (see listing A.3) can be used for line drawings and the pixel-based analytic programs, but because it is a photographic process the painter's algorithm may not be used! It is possible to implement this algorithm by creating your own bit map array and using the graphics commands to alter the values in this array. When the plotting is finished you can use the finish routine to dump the bit-map onto microfilm, pixel by pixel! We set this as an exercise.

Listing A.3

```
{     ****************************
      *   Graphics Primitives for   *
      *          DIMFILM          *
      *      microfilm system     *
      ****************************               }

{ DIMFILM calls in CAPITALs }

VAR rtab,gtab,btab : ARRAY[1..256] OF real ;

PROCEDURE finish ;
{ Call DIMFILM routine to flush buffer. }
BEGIN
   DIMEND
END ; { of finish }

PROCEDURE setcol(col : integer) ;
BEGIN
   RGB(rtab[col+1],gtab[col+1],btab[col+1])
END ; { of setcol }
```

```
PROCEDURE erase ;
{ The viewport should not be cleared when using microfilm. }
BEGIN
END ; { of erase }

PROCEDURE setpix(pixel : pixelvector) ;
BEGIN
   POINT(pixel.x,pixel.y)
END { of setpix }

PROCEDURE movepix(pixel : pixelvector) ;
BEGIN
   OFF2(pixel.x,pixel.y)
END ; { of movepix }

PROCEDURE linepix(pixel : pixelvector) ;
BEGIN
   ON2(pixel.x,pixel.y)
END ; { of linepix }

PROCEDURE polypix(n : integer ; poly : pixelarray ) ;
{ see LISTING 5.6 , if no area fill available on microfilm }

PROCEDURE rgblog(i : integer ; red,green,blue : real ) ;
BEGIN
   rtab[i+1] := red ; gtab[i+1] := green ; btab[i+1] := blue
END ; { of rgblog }


PROCEDURE prepit ;
VAR j,r,g,b : integer ;
BEGIN
{ Set up viewport dimension. }
   nxpix := 1024 ; nypix := 768 ;
{ Prepare 35mm camera and define viewport size. }
   D35C ; BOUNDS(0.0,1024.0,0.0,768.0)
{ Set up default colour table. }
   j := 0 ;
   FOR b := 0 TO 1
   DO FOR g := 0 TO 1
      DO FOR r := 0 TO 1
         DO BEGIN
                  rgblog(j,r,g,b) ; j := j+1
               END ;
{ Set up default background and foreground colour. }
   setcol(0) ; erase ; setcol(7)
END ; { of prepit }
```

The Tektronix 4100 Range

This range of machines is very popular although the colour capabilities are limited. We implement our primitives in listing A.4. You must refer to the sections on random sampling and pixel patterns of chapter 15 to make the best use of our routines.

Listing A.4

```
{    ******************************
     *   Graphics Primitives for   *
     *   TEKTRONIX 4100 Series    *
     ******************************                    }

TYPE char2array : ARRAY[1..2] OF char ;
     char5array : ARRAY[1..5] OF char ;
     char8array : ARRAY[1..8] OF char ;

VAR list : char8array ;
    escapecode : char2array ;
    currentcolour : integer ;

procedure host(i : integer ; VAR count : integer ) ;
VAR j : integer ;
BEGIN
{ Create integer parameter for host syntax. }
   j := abs(i) ;
   IF j < 16
   THEN BEGIN
              count := count + 1 ;
              IF i < 0
              THEN list[count] := chr(j + 32)
              ELSE list[count] := chr(j + 48)
        END
   ELSE BEGIN
              list[count + 1] := chr((j DIV 16) + 64)
              IF i < 0
              THEN
                 list[count + 2] := chr((j MOD 16) + 32)
              ELSE
                 list[count + 2] := chr((j MOD 16) + 48) ;
              count := count + 2
        END
END ; { of host }

procedure convertpixel(pixel : pixelvector; VAR ch : char5array ) ;
{ Converts pixel co-ordinates to character array. }
VAR ex1,ex2,hix,hiy,lox,loy : integer ;
BEGIN
   ex2 := pixel.x MOD 4 ;
   lox := (pixel.x DIV 4) MOD 32 ; hix := pixel.x DIV 128 ;
   ex1 := pixel.y MOD 4 ;
   loy := (pixel.y DIV 4) MOD 32 ; hiy := pixel.y DIV 128 ;
   ch[1] := chr(32 + hiy) ; ch[2] := chr(96 + 4*ex1 + ex2) ;
   ch[3] := chr(96 + loy) ; ch[4] := chr(32 + hix) ; ch[5] := chr(64 + lox)
END ; { of convertpixel }

PROCEDURE finish ;
BEGIN
{ Return to TEXT mode. }
   writeln(escapecode,'%!1')
END ; { of finish }
```

```
PROCEDURE setcol(col : integer) ;
{ Select logical colour 'col'. }
VAR count : integer ;
BEGIN
   count := 0 ; host(col,count) ;
   writeln(escapecode,'ML',list[1]) ;
   currentcolour := col
END ; { of setcol }

PROCEDURE erase ;
{ Clear graphics screen. }
VAR c1,c2 : char5array ;
    zero,pix : pixelvector ;
BEGIN
   zero.x:=0 ; zero.y:=0 ; convertpixel(zero,c1) ;
   pix.x:=639 ; pix.y:=479 ; convertpixel(pix,c2) ;
   writeln(escapecode,'RR',c1,c2,'0')
END ; { of erase }

PROCEDURE setpix(pixel : pixelvector) ;
{ Set 'pixel' to current colour. }
BEGIN
   movepix(pixel) ; linepix(pixel)
END ; { of setpix }

PROCEDURE movepix(pixel : pixelvector) ;
{ Move current position to 'pixel'. }
VAR c1 : char5array ;
    largepix : pixelvector ;
BEGIN
   largepix.x := trunc(pixel.x*4095.0/639.0+0.5) ;
   largepix.y := trunc(pixel.y*4095.0/639.0+0.5) ;
   convertpixel(largepix,c1) ;
   writeln(escapecode,'LF',c1)
END ; { of movepix }

PROCEDURE linepix(pixel : pixelvector) ;
{ Draw line to position 'pixel'.}
VAR c1 : char5array ;
    largepix : pixelvector ;
BEGIN
   largepix.x := trunc(pixel.x*4095.0/639.0+0.5) ;
   largepix.y := trunc(pixel.y*4095.0/639.0+0.5) ;
   convertpixel(largepix,c1) ;
   writeln(escapecode,'LG',c1)
END ; { of linepix }

PROCEDURE polypix(n : integer ; poly : pixelarray ) ;
{ Fill polygonal area. }
VAR c1 : char5array ;
    count,i : integer ;
    largepix : pixelvector ;
BEGIN
   movepix(poly[1]) ; count := 0 ;
   host(-currentcolour,count) ;
```

```
        writeln(escapecode,'MP',list[1]) ;
        largepix.x := trunc(poly[1].x*4095.0/639.0+0.5) ;
        largepix.y := trunc(poly[1].y*4095.0/639.0+0.5) ;
        convertpixel(largepix,c1) ;
        writeln(escapecode,'LP',c1,'0') ;
        FOR i := 2 TO n
        DO linepix(poly[i]) ;
        writeln(escapecode,'LE')
END ; { of polypix }


PROCEDURE rgblog(i : integer ; red,green,blue : real ) ;
{ Set logical colour I to (red,green,blue). }
VAR count,j,r,g,b : integer ;
BEGIN
    r := trunc(red*100) ; g := trunc(green*100) ; b := trunc(blue*100) ;
    count := 0 ;
{ Create integer array parameters for host syntax. }
    host(i,count) ; host(r,count) ;
    host(g,count) ; host(b,count) ;
    write(escapecode,'TG14') ;
    FOR j := 1 TO count DO write(list[j]) ;
    writeln
END ; { of rgblog }


PROCEDURE prepit ;
VAR c1,c2 : char5array ;
    j,r,g,b : integer ;
    zero,pix : pixelvector ;
BEGIN
{ Define escape character. }
    escapecode[1] := ' ' ; escapecode[2] := chr(27) ;
{ Set up viewport dimensions. }
    nxpix := 640 ; nypix := 480 ;
{ Send device into graphics mode. }
    writeln(escapecode,'%I0') ;
    writeln(escapecode,'RU1;6') ;
    writeln(escapecode,'LL3') ;
{ Set up viewport size. }
    zero.x:=0 ; zero.y:=0 ; convertpixel(zero,c1) ;
    pix.x:=639 ; pix.y:=479 ; convertpixel(pix,c2) ;
    writeln(escapecode,'RS',c1,c2) ;
{ Set colour mode to RGB. }
    writeln(escapecode,'TM111') ;
{ Set up default background and foreground colours }
    j := 0 ;
    FOR b := 0 TO 1
    DO FOR g := 0 TO 1
        DO FOR r := 0 TO 1
            DO BEGIN
                    rgblog(j,r,g,b) ; j := j+1
                END ;
{ Set up default background and foreground colour. }
    setcol(0) ; erase ; setcol(7)
END ; { of prepit }
```

A Full-colour Raster Display

For full implementation of routines given in this book a raster display with at least 256 colours is needed. Listing A.5 gives the primitives for a typical device of this type.

Listing A.5

```
{      *****************************
       *  Graphics Primitives for   *
       *         a typical          *
       *    Raster Scan Device      *
       *****************************                    }
PROCEDURE finish ;
{ This routine is redundant.
BEGIN
END ; { of finish }

PROCEDURE setcol(col : integer) ;
{ Select logical colour 'col'. }
BEGIN
{ Assume typical command SEC = 'SEt Colour'.}
   writeln(' #SEC ',col:3)
END ; { setcol }

PROCEDURE erase ;
{ Clear graphics screen. }
BEGIN
{ Assume typical command ERA = 'ERAse Screen. }
   writeln(' #ERA')
END ; { of erase }

PROCEDURE setpix(pixel : pixelvector) ;
{ Set pixel with co-ordinates 'pixel' to current colour. }
BEGIN
{ Assume typical command WPX = 'Write PiXel'. }
   writeln(' #WPX ',pixel.x:4,',',pixel.y:4)
END ; { of setpix }

PROCEDURE movepix(pixel : pixelvector) ;
{ Move current position to 'pixel'. }
BEGIN
{ Assume typical command MOV = 'MOVe current position'. }
   writeln(' #MOV ',pixel.x:4,',',pixel.y:4)
END ; { of movepix }

PROCEDURE linepix(pixel : pixelvector) ;
{ Draw line to position 'pixel'.}
BEGIN
{ Assume typical command LIN = 'LINe to'. }
   writeln(' #LIN ',pixel.x:4,',',pixel.y:4)
END ; { of linepix }
```

```
PROCEDURE polypix(n : integer ; poly : pixelarray ) ;
{ Fills polygonal area with n vertices poly[1],...,poly[n]. }
VAR i : integer ;
BEGIN
{ Assume typical command POL = 'POLygon fill'. }
    write(' #POL ',n:3);
    FOR i := 1 TO n
    DO write(',',poly[i].x:4,',',poly[i].y:4) ;
    writeln
END ; { of polypix }


PROCEDURE rgblog(i : integer ; red,green,blue : real ) ;
{ Sets logical colour i in colour look-up table to (red,green,blue).}
VAR r,g,b : integer ;
BEGIN
    r := trunc(red*255) ; g := trunc(green*255) ; b := trunc(blue*255) ;
{ Assume typical command SCT = 'Set Colour Table'. }
    writeln(' #SCT ',i:3,',',r:3,',',g:3,',',b:3)
END ; { of linepix }


PROCEDURE prepit ;
BEGIN
{ Set up viewport dimensions. }
    nxpix := 768 ; nypix := 576 ;
{ Send device into graphics mode, assume escape character is '#' }
    writeln(' #GRA') ;
{ Set up default background and foreground colours. }
    setcol(0) ; erase ; setcol(7)
END ; { of prepit }
```

Bibliography and References

Abbot, E. A. (1978). *Flatland*. Basil Blackwell, Oxford

Aho, A. V., Hopcroft, J. E. and Ullman, J. D. (1983). *Data Structures and Algorithms*. Addison-Wesley, Reading, Massachusetts

Angell, I. O. (1985). *Advanced Graphics on the IBM Personal Computer*. Macmillan, London

Appel, A. (1968). *Some Techniques for Shading Machine-Renderings of Solids*. SJCC 1968, Thompson Books, Washington, D.C., pp. 37–45

Banchoff, T. (1978). 'Computer Animation and the Geometry of Surfaces in 3 and 4 D.' *Proc. International Congress of Mathematicians. Helsinki*

Bezier, P. (1974). 'Mathematical and practical possibilities of UNISURF.' In Barnhill, R. E. and Riesenfeld, R. F. (eds), *Computer Aided Geometric Design*. Academic Press, New York

Blinn, J. F. (1977). 'Models of light reflection for computer synthesized pictures.' SIGGRAPH '77 Proc., published as *Computer Graphics*, 11(2), Summer, pp. 192–198

Blinn, J. F. (1978). 'Simulation of wrinkled surfaces.' SIGGRAPH '78 Proc., published as *Computer Graphics*, 12(3), August, pp. 286–292

Blinn, J. F. and Newell, M. E. (1976). 'Texture and reflection in computer generated images.' *Communications of the ACM*, 19(10), October, pp. 542–547

Chazelle, B. and Incerpi, J. (1984). 'Triangulation and shape complexity.' *ACM Transactions on Graphics*, 3(2), April, pp. 135–152

Clark, J. (1976). 'Hierarchical geometric models for visible surface algorithms.' *Communications of the ACM*, 19(10), October

Cohn, P. M. (1961). *Solid Geometry*. Routledge and Kegan Paul, London

Coxeter, H. S. M. (1973). *Regular Polytopes*. Dover Publications, New York

Crow, F. (1977). 'Shadow algorithms for computer graphics.' SIGGRAPH '77 Proc., published as *Computer Graphics*, 11(2), Summer, pp. 242–247

Dana, E. S. (1948). *A Textbook on Mineralogy*. Wiley, New York

Davenport, H. (1952). *The Higher Arithmetic*. Hutchinson, London

Dewdney, A. K. (1985). 'Computer Recreations.' *Scientific American*, August, pp. 8–14

Donnay and Donnay (1969). *International Tables for X-Ray Crystallography*. Kynoch Press, Birmingham

Finkbeiner, D. T. (1978). *Introduction to Matrices and Linear Transformations.* W. H. Freeman, San Francisco

Foley, J. D. and Van Dam, A. (1981). *Fundamentals of Interactive Computer Graphics.* Addison-Wesley, Reading, Massachusetts

Fournier, A. and Montuno, D. Y. (1984). 'Triangulating simple polygons and equivalent problems.' *ACM Transactions on Graphics,* 3(2), April, pp. 135-152

Gardner, M. (1978). *Mathematical Carnival.* Pelican, London, Chapter 18, pp. 240-254

Gordon, W. J. and Riesenfeld, R. F. (1974). 'B-Spline curves and surfaces.' In Barnhill, R. E. and Riesefeld, R. F. (eds), *Computer Aided Geometric Design.* Academic Press, New York

Gouraud, H. (1971). 'Continuous shading of curved surfaces.' *IEEE Transactions on Computers,* C-20(6), June, pp. 623-628

Heath, T. L. (1956). *The Thirteen Books of Euclid's Elements.* Dover Reprints, New York

Hopgood, F. R. A., Duce, D. A., Gallop, J. R. and Sutcliffe, D. C. (1983). *Introduction to the Graphical Kernel System (G.K.S.).* Academic Press, London

Horowitz, E. and Sahni, S. (1976). *Fundamentals of Data Structures.* Pitman, London

Hunter, G. M. and Steiglitz, K. (1979). 'Operations on images using quad-trees.' *IEEE Transactions Pattern Anal. Machine Intell.,* PAMI-1(2), April, pp. 145-153

Kay, D. and Greenberg, D. (1979). 'Transparency for computer synthesized images.' SIGGRAPH '79 Proc., published as *Computer Graphics,* 13(2), August, pp. 158-164

Knuth, D. (1973). *The Art of Computer Programming.* Addison-Wesley, London

Mandelbrot, B. B. (1977). *Fractals.* W. H. Freeman, San Francisco

Manning, H. P. (1956). *Geometry of Four Dimensions.* Dover Publications, New York

Mathematical Applications Group, Inc. (1968). '3-D simulated graphics.' *Datamation,* February

McCrae, W. H. (1953). *Analytical Geometry of Three Dimensions.* Oliver and Boyd, London

Meagher, D. (1982). 'Geometric modelling using Octree encoding', *Computing Graphics and Image Processing,* No. 19, pp. 129-147

Newman, W. M. and Sproull, R. F. (1973). *Principles of Interactive Computer Graphics.* McGraw-Hill, London

Ostwald, W. (1931). *Colour Science.* Winsor and Winsor, London

Phillips, F. C. (1960). *An Introduction to Crystallography.* Longmans, London

Phong, Bui-Tuong, (1975). 'Illumination for computer generated pictures.' *Communications of the ACM,* 18(6), June, pp. 311-317

Rucker, R. V. B. (1977). *Geometry, Relativity and the Fourth Dimension.* Dover Publications, New York

Sidhu, G. S. and Boute, R. T. (1972). 'Property encoding: applications in binary picture encoding and boundary following.' *IEEE Transactions on Computers*, C-21(11), November

Smith, A. R. (1978). 'Color gamut transform pairs.' *Computer Graphics*, 12(3), August, pp. 12-19

Sommerville, D. M. Y. (1929). *An Introduction to the Geometry of N Dimensions*. Dover Publications, New York

Stroud, K. A. (1982). *Engineering Mathematics*. Macmillan, London

Sutherland, I. E., Sproull, R. F. and Schumacker, R. A. (1974). 'A characterization of ten hidden-surface algorithms.' *Computing Surveys*, 6(1), March, pp. 1-55

Tanimoto, L. (1977). 'A pyramid model for binary picture complexity.' *Proc. IEEE Computer Society Conference on Pattern Recognition and Image Processing, June 1977*

Tolansky, S. (1964). *Optical Illusions*. Pergamon, New York

Tomlinson, D. J. (1982). 'An aid to hidden surface removal in real time CGI systems.' *The Computer Journal*, 25(4), pp. 429-441

Whittaker, E. J. W. (1981). *Crystallography*. Pergamon, Oxford

Whitted, T. (1980). 'An improved illumination model for shaded display.' *Communications of the ACM*, 23(6), June, pp. 343-349

Wilson, J. R. and Addyman, A. M. (1982). *A Practical Introduction to Pascal — with BS6192*, 2nd edn. Macmillan, London

Woodwark, J. R. (1984). 'Compressed quad-trees.' *The Computer Journal*, 27(3), pp. 193-288

Index

Index of Database CONSTants, TYPEs and VARiables

Index of PROCEDURE Listings